A TALK IN THE WOODS

Voices Along the Appalachian Trail

CARY SEGALL

BACK BURNER BOOKS
MADISON, WISCONSIN

Back Burner Books
Madison, WI 53704
www.BackBurnerBooks.com
info@backburnerbooks.net

Maps by Haley Schulz (haleyum.com)
Edited by Terry Shelton
Cover photo by Kevin Revolinski
All photos are by Cary Segall or contributed photos (*c.p.*),
unless otherwise noted

Cover design by Back Burner Books

Library of Congress Control Number: 2023924608
ISBN: 978-1-7363341-1-9 (Paperback)
ISBN: 978-1-7363341-5-7 (ebook)

First Edition, July 2024

APPALACHIAN TRAIL
BACKPACKERS PRAISE
A TALK IN THE WOODS

"Cary does what few other Appalachian Trail writers do: He relates his journey through the people he encounters on the trail...rather than enumerating his 5-million steps. His straightforward prose brings to light both the adventure of long-distance hiking and the people who make it such a compelling journey. ...you can drop in on almost any page to experience the richness of the other lives that make the trail what it is today."
— Cosmo Catalano Jr., a longtime AT volunteer, has hiked 600 miles of the trail

"What distinguishes this book from the many others written about the Appalachian Trail is Cary's genuine interest in hikers' stories. ...while we come to know Cary, we learn even more about the trail and the people who love it... This book is a much-needed addition to AT lore."
— Joanna "Seeker" Ezinga, thru-hiked the AT

"Cary has written a must-read book for anyone interested in the Appalachian Trail...a wonderful account of hikers and their stories and makes you feel as if you're sitting around the campfire listening to them."
— Andy "Captain Blue" Niekamp, section-hiked the entire AT five times

"Cary's interactions with people really make the book stand out from most other hiking books I've read. I kept smiling as I read it....I felt like I was right on the trail."
— Maury "Deacon" Hall, section-hiked the entire AT

"...full of potential tips related to the Appalachian Trail and insights that would help any novice or potential hiker looking to tackle a hiking adventure. ...this is a human-interest book with wonderful tales of the microcosm that is the AT hiking community....valuable insights for those contemplating their own AT adventure or just seeking entertainment."
— Pete "NoBigDeal" Smith, thru-hiked the AT

"Cary has accurately captured what life is like when hiking the Appalachian Trail through the stories he sought from the individuals who hike it...a page-turner...You won't want the story to end."
— Jeffrey "Baby Steps" Johnson, section-hiked the entire AT

"...a testament to human-interest journalism... it restores a sense of shared humanity to a topic that is normally rather deceptively solitary, and to a trail that is probably one of the most social in the world."
— Angela "Walkie" Shirley, thru-hiked the AT

Read more at BackBurnerBooks.com

For my son, Craig, who's hiked many miles with me on trails throughout the United States and Canada, and my mother, Shirley, who was still walking paths in national parks with me at the age of 84.

APPALACHIAN TRAIL
KATAHDIN
100- MILE WILDERNESS
ME
VT
WHITE MOUNTAINS
NH
NY
MA
CT
PA
NJ
MD
SHENANDOAH NATIONAL PARK
WV
VA
GREAT SMOKY MOUNTAINS NATIONAL PARK
TN
NC
SPRINGER MOUNTAIN
SC
GA
AT
N
W
E
S

Foreword

There is no way back...
My eyes are blind
In that direction...
There is only the road
Ahead...!
Don West – Appalachian poet

I GUESS THIS STARTED SOMEWHERE, SOMETIME, SOMEHOW. Maybe a spark? By design? By mistake? By fire? By ice? Land and water contained in an orb moving through the universe. The land shifted sideways, sometimes in opposing directions, creating mountains over the eons. The land broke apart and moved within the orb with water filling the spaces between. Rain carved the topography. A cellular life form appeared in the ocean, then moved back and forth between land and water, then just lived on the land.

The slitherers became crawlers and then the crawlers finally stood up on two appendages and they constantly moved through the landscape in search of sustenance so they could physically survive in all seasons, as the orb moved around the big light. After securing ways of staying in one place, some of these sedentarians developed a curiosity to revisit their past nomadic lifestyles and to find out what was around the next horizon.

Money finally entered the scene, along with the dichotomy of work and leisure which became competing forces. Now was it people controlling profits or profits controlling people?

A rising middle class had disposable income and some free time to wander and explore. Explorations by foot and boat came to be; wagons and carts pulled by an easily controlled, lower-level species carried things for the ever increasing comfort levels of these adventurers.

There were pilgrimages and walkabouts and quests and crusades for self-discovery or enlightenment, personal growth through overcoming challenges, or obtaining power by oppression through conquests. The machines came and with them a gradual dehumanization that is increasing in pace. Things with cold metal and chemicals strangle or suffocate human feelings and thoughts.

Simple and clear has become complex and ambiguous, causing a few of us to wonder "Which side are we on?" or to question "What is freedom?" and "Am I free?"

Fear is the antithesis to freedom and we have evolved to become afraid of our water and our blood and our breath, and to questioning our minds and bodies bringing us back to our start eons ago with land (i.e. bodies) and water (i.e. blood).

And now a recent addition to this mix of the distant past. A footpath. A slender lifeline of freedom and simplicity; of adventure and challenge; of self-discovery; of nomadic community; and possibly a key to help people navigate a dehumanizing world and to still retain and sustain the freedom inherent in living entities.

The trail is a gift given to us by thousands of volunteers over 87 years. These people who work much more by the heart than by the hour deserve the credit for this diamond in the rough—not the government nor the corporations—non-profit or for-profit.

The trail would be much different, though, if people didn't walk it—for a day, a week, a month or for a lifetime.

Enter a curious, caring, competent newspaper reporter who unselfishly gave up his original goal of a thru-hike because he became fascinated by the people he encountered on the trail and he wanted to take the time and effort to share their stories with you, the reader.

What you have in your hands is a sterling representation of life on the Appalachian Trail from 2014 to 2018. These stories of loners and lovers; givers and takers; winners and losers are captivating. They remind me of Edgar Lee Masters' *Spoon River Anthology.* They are easy to read and shine with their authenticity. This piece of literature could easily be made into a play with an ensemble playing multiple parts.

Cary Segall has done a remarkable job in covering the human side of this pilgrimage route – the hard work and generosity of the trail maintainers that make it all possible; the hostel owners along the way; the shuttlers; the people who feel a purpose offering "trail magic" to the pilgrims.

And the pilgrims themselves—nomads escaping their pasts and hoping for healthier futures; wanderers strengthening their existing relationships or enjoying making new ones; scouts venturing out to find the safest way forward for themselves in the ever increasing hostile environment of the "real world"; ramblers seeking natural beauty in the wildflowers, the vistas, the streams and lakes, and the kaleidoscopic colors of the sunrises and sunsets.

All these stories are here and they beg the reader to identify with some of these travelers on the way to becoming. Who resonates with you—your dream and aspirations?

And finally, what is the purpose of this green line through the ancient Appalachians? Weren't we made to wander and discover on our own two feet? Do these natural ramparts formed by fire and ice give us temporary mortals meaning? Or, through our stories do we give the mountains meaning?

Thank you Cary Segall for giving us an opportunity to contemplate what might be the answers to these questions.

4/30/24
Warren Doyle, Ph.D.
Founder/Director
Appalachian Folk School, Mountain City, Tennessee

Warren hiked the entire Appalachian Trail a record 18 times from 1972 to 2018. He teaches people how to successfully hike long distances on the trail during five-day courses at his Appalachian Trail Institute, which he runs out of the Appalachian Folk School at his home, 12 miles south of Damascus, Virginia, in northeastern Tennessee. Warren also leads long-distance hikes on the trail in which participants cover the distance with day hikes and van support. He used to lead similar hikes in which participants thru-hiked the entire trail.

Introduction

WHEN I MET LISA "MAMA BEAR" MURRAY, she was 46 and had backpacked 621 miles of the Appalachian Trail with her 4-year-old twins, Tess "Little Butt" and Cole "Strong Man," who were 3 when they started the trail on Springer Mountain in northern Georgia, celebrated their fourth birthday along the trail in North Carolina and were headed 398 more miles to Harpers Ferry in West Virginia. I hiked with Mama Bear and the twins, who were known as the Cubs on the trail, for a day and a half in Virginia and was amazed to watch the exuberant children easily and happily handle the rooty, rocky, often arduous trail.

Tom "Grey Eagle" Young was 75 and still backpacking after 1,998 miles when I met him in Maine, despite his having dealt with an ulcer, sciatica, shin splints, falls that injured his arm and put a gash in his head, and a lightning strike that knocked him off the trail and left him crying and terrified. He said he was determined to finish his nearly 2,200-mile thru-hike from Springer to Katahdin, a mammoth mountain in northern Maine, because of his age and because he had a wife of 52 years who wasn't happy he started and would never let him do it again.

Trail legend Warren Doyle was 65, had completed the AT a record 17 times, nine with thru-hikes and eight with section hikes, and was working on completing it an eighteenth time with section hikes when I met him in Vermont. He was leading a group of 12 that he'd trained to thru-hike on a strict schedule with just daypacks, while he carried their extra clothes and equipment in a van, the ninth time he'd led such a group. Three of the hikers told me they would never have hiked the trail without Warren's help and inspiration. When I asked him why he kept hiking the same trail, he responded rhetorically: "Why do people go to church?"

Mama Bear, Little Butt, Strong Man and Grey Eagle, who had taken trail names, like nearly all AT backpackers, and Warren were among hundreds of interesting, sometimes fascinating, people I wrote about after meeting and interviewing them while I hiked the entire trail in sections from 2014 to 2018. In addition to hikers, I wrote about hostel owners who house hikers, restaurant owners who feed them, trail angels who help them, shuttle drivers who take them from place to place, ridge runners who patrol the trail, volunteers who maintain it and others with connections to hikers and the AT.

When I started the trail, though, I hadn't planned to write about it, despite having written and edited stories for a living for 21 years at the Wisconsin State Journal, a daily newspaper in my hometown of Madison. That's because there had been many memoirs written about Appalachian Trail hikes, many of which I'd read, and I didn't think I'd have much to add. But, I'm a reporter at heart, and after discovering in just a few days that there are lots of great stories on the AT, I wanted to write them.

I discovered my first great story on Springer Mountain, during my first morning on the trail, when I met Maury "Deacon" Hall, who was 68 and whose backpack's base weight, without food or water, was an extraordinarily light 11 pounds, about half the weight of mine, which weighed 20 and was lighter than the packs of most other hikers, including some packs that weighed as much as 60 pounds and even more. Two of those hikers with 60-pound packs had stopped on the 8.8-mile, 1,902-foot climb to the Springer summit and the start of the AT to lighten their load by burning some of their clothes in a bonfire that I saw as I climbed the mountain.

Deacon was the most meticulous backpacker I'd met in 43 years of backpacking and he told me how he kept his pack so extremely light, and how while at home he prepared and planned his meals for the trail, where he would pick up food packages he'd mailed, how many miles he'd hike each day and where he'd stay each night. He planned to section hike the trail over four years.

After talking with Deacon and others during my first few days of backpacking, I decided to tell the tale of the trail by writing the stories of the people I met and adding a little about me and my hike to tie the stories together. I spoke with nearly everyone I met to learn a little about them, and then, if I thought I wanted to write about someone, I'd say I was a reporter writing a book about the trail and ask if I could interview and write about them. Nearly everyone said yes and was happy to answer my questions.

Then, I'd occasionally take a day off hiking in a town near the trail and use a computer in a library, hostel or motel to write stories that I emailed to friends, relatives and people I met on the trail who said they'd like to read them. I wrote the stories in the present tense and all of the facts are accurate as of the time I wrote about.

Interviewing people soon became my favorite part of the hike because I learned lots about the people I spoke with and they gave me much to ponder as I backpacked through woods and up and down mountains day after day after day. I'd think about what I'd learned about the people and how I wanted to write their stories.

But I knew that spending time doing interviews and taking days off to write would make it harder to finish my planned thru-hike, which is defined by the Appalachian Trail Conservancy, the organization that manages the trail for the National Park Service, as hiking the entire trail within 12 months, from south to north, from north to south or any which way in a variety of sections.

The vast majority of thru-hikers, though, start on Springer in March or April and take about six months to finish the trail by hiking through 14 states to Katahdin. They aim to summit Katahdin, which means "the greatest mountain" and was named by the Penobscot Indians, by mid-October because it's around then that the mountain is closed for climbing until December.

I had less time than nearly all of the northbound thru-hikers because I didn't start until May 21. I'd waited until then because I'd run the 20-mile Syttende Mai race in mid-May from the Capitol Square in Madison to the small city of Stoughton for 36 years straight, and I didn't want to break my streak in 2014.

That meant I had only about five months to make a traditional thru-hike and would have to average about 15 miles a day, including days off. But I was in great shape from running since I ran cross country in high school and, even though I was 64, I was still running 50 to 70 miles a week. I thought I'd be able to finish in time, even if I did do interviews and stop occasionally to write.

However, the more interviews I did, and the more I stopped, I realized that my goal of a thru-hike in five months was in jeopardy. So, after hiking 965.6 miles and reaching Front Royal, Virginia, at the north end of

Shenandoah National Park, on July 30, I wrote my last stories from the trail. I decided that I'd keep interviewing people, but I'd make more time to hike by writing the stories when I got home. I was still under the gun, but interviewing people and writing their stories had become more important to me than a thru-hike and I knew that, if I failed, I could most likely return in 2015, interview more people, tell more stories and finish the trail.

By Labor Day, I'd hiked 1,444.8 miles through nine states and had reached a train stop along the trail for a commuter train to New York City. I had 740.5 miles to go and knew I might not finish in time to climb Katahdin. But more importantly, I was one of the last northbound thru-hikers, if not the last, and I was running out of people to talk with. So, knowing that I could easily return by train to the spot I left, I took the train to New York and flew home.

I returned in 2015, but was stopped by illness. A bruised knee from a fall slowed me in 2016. Bad weather kept me from reaching the Katahdin summit in 2017 and I finally finished in 2018 with hundreds of great stories to tell.

In addition to writing about Mama Bear and her twins, I've written about many other parents backpacking with their children, such as Polly "SunButter" Sullivan, who was 36 and section hiking with Isabella "Butterfly," 12; Elijah "Mountain Dude," 14; Gabriel "Trash Panda," 15, and their dogs Mountain Mutt and Gooch when I met the family in Maine during their third year on the trail. SunButter said that they were including the AT in their attempt to hike the 5,400-mile-long Eastern Continental Trail from Key West, Florida, to Belle Isle, just off the coasts of Labrador and Newfoundland, and had already hiked nearly 1,000 miles in Florida and about 800 miles of the AT . "It is one thing to talk about your dreams and another to take action," SunButter told me. "I don't fear failure, only regret."

When I met Jeffrey "Baby Steps" Johnson, who was 55, and his son, Chris, who was 24, in North Carolina in 2014, they were nearly finished with the trail they had started hiking together in 1997, when Chris was 8. Baby Steps said the hike had been a wonderful experience and that he had a great relationship with his son: "It's really a strong bond and the hike is one of the best things we've done."

When I met thru-hikers Kathy "Splash" Koning, then 56, and her son, Dan "Smoke" Koning, then 26, in Vermont, Splash told me that thru-hiking the AT had been her longtime dream and that she had jumped at the chance to do it with her son when he decided to thru-hike. When her employer wouldn't give her six months off her job as a clinical social worker to backpack the trail, she quit a job she loved and was happy with her decision after four months on the trail: "I love living outdoors. I love the simplicity of it. Every day you get up and head to Katahdin. I think it's cool to have a dream, set a goal, and go for it."

Most thru-hikers were in their 20s and Grey Eagle and Deacon were the oldest backpackers I met. But I met several others in their 60s, including Lynne "Marmie" Beeson, who was 62 and had backpacked the entire trail over the previous two years. When I met her in North Carolina, she was backpacking the first 500 miles again. When I asked why she was hiking the same section of trail she'd hiked two years before, she said: "This trail gets in your blood. It's a very social trail."

The trail had gotten in the blood of many hikers, like Marmie and Warren, and I interviewed and wrote about others who loved the trail and had hiked it multiple times, such as Andy "Captain Blue" Niekamp, who was 53 and backpacking the entire AT in sections for the fourth time in 26 years when I met him in eastern Pennsylvania. He told me he hiked the trail over and over and over again because it's "like an old friend who doesn't change very much" and was his "personal fountain of youth."

Marcia "Tumbler" Terry, who was 43, and Winston "Ratman" Terry, who was 49, were thru-hiking the AT for the third time and were southbound when I met them in Massachusetts. They'd hiked northbound the first time when they were dating and the second time on their honeymoon. "This trail turned my life around," said Ratman, adding that he'd dedicated his life to the Lord because of all the kindnesses they received. "He answered many, many prayers," said Tumbler.

But most people who plan to thru-hike quit for various reasons, such as being out of shape, bored, sick, injured, or, in the case of Molly "Stick Ninja" Carlson, who was 27, and Catharine "Pixel" Kosinski, who was 23, when I met them in Tennessee, simply tired of the trail. I met the couple shortly after they quit their planned thru-hike and they told me they just weren't enjoying it anymore. "I'm tired of walking. I'm tired of nature," said

Stick Ninja, who also said she missed cable TV and air conditioning. "I want to drive places, so it takes 30 minutes, instead of three days," said Pixel."

Topi "Finn" Ruohisto, who was 27 when I met him in Vermont, told me he got sick of the trail in Virginia and called his thru-hike since then "one thousand miles of nothingness." But he was still determined to finish. "I have my pride," he said, "and I told Facebook friends and work friends I'm going to do it."

Others, such as Ellie "Grace Note," Hamilton, who was 65 when I met her in Maine in 2017, quit a thru-hike, but return to the trail intent on completing it. Grace Note said she made it from Georgia to Maryland in 2009 before leaving the trail because she'd lost too much weight. Since then, she'd hiked trail sections and hoped to finish not long after I met her, although she found Maine and New Hampshire very difficult. "I'm enjoying part of it, but there are times that I feel like throwing in the towel," she said. "It's much, much harder than I expected it would be."

Some hikers hit the trail after surviving illnesses that could have killed them, such as Phil "Right Click" Valentine, who was 55 and a recovering alcoholic and drug addict, and had beaten stage 4 cancer of the tongue. When I met him in New York, he told me that God had called him to thru-hike the trail. "I want to leave a legacy," he said, "that people in recovery from alcohol and other addiction, people in recovery from cancer, we do survive and we go on to do extraordinary things."

Tom "Cardioman" Wells, who was 53 when I met him in Tennessee, decided to thru-hike two years after surviving a heart attack caused by a blocked artery called the widow maker and a year after his wife died of cancer. He quit his job, sold his house and headed to Springer. "I think for me, I just want to do whatever I can with the time I have," he said. "I can't put things off."

Other hikers overcame serious disabilities to hike, such as Tony "Mississippi" Lang, who was 48 and thru-hiking with an artificial hip and titanium rod in his thigh after his hip was shattered by a bullet in Afghanistan, and a knee repaired with a plate and 20 screws after a dirt-bike crash. He had decided to try hiking the Georgia section of the trail and when that worked out, he just kept going. When I met him in New Hampshire, he was headed to Katahdin. "It's amazing what walking can do," he said. "It's healed me."

Some hikers met on the trail, started hiking together, and later married, such as thru-hikers Rich "Shark" Edwards and Laura "Thimble" Edwards, who were expecting a baby boy and living with their 21-month-old daughter in a house along the trail when I met them. They got to live in the house, which was owned by the National Park Service, in exchange for caring for a nearby AT shelter, next to a Pennsylvania highway, and keeping an eye on two nearby viewpoints on the trail. "When we got off the trail, we wanted to do something linked to the trail," Thimble said. "We like the trail culture and want our daughter exposed to it."

Many hikers, like Thimble and Shark, had tried to find a way to stay connected to the trail after finishing it. Some bought hostels that serve AT hikers and others, like Jeff Taussig, started one.

Jeff, who had hiked the entire trail in sections and was 63 when I met him, lived most of the year with his wife, Regina, in Richfield, Ohio. But he spent summers a couple miles outside of Manchester Center, Vermont, where the couple bought two homes and a barn. They worked with a contractor to turn the larger house into a hostel and the smaller one into a place for Jeff to live during the hiking season. Then, they opened the Green Mountain House Hiker Hostel for AT hikers. Jeff, who didn't have a trail name, said running the place was a lot of work and that he struggled to break even, but that he enjoyed it, nevertheless: "The hiking community is a friendly bunch and the hikers come from such diverse backgrounds. They have great stories to tell. It's a lot of fun."

Paul "Ole Man" Renaud, who was 66 when I met him and his wife, Jaime "NaviGator" Renaud, who was 55, stayed in the Appalachian Trail Lodge, the closest hostel to Katahdin, in Millinocket, Maine, after Ole Man finished his section hike and learned it had been for sale for 10 years. Two days later, they agreed to buy the place and the nearby Appalachian Trail Cafe. Since then, they've fixed up the hostel and cafe, started shuttling hikers and opened a gear shop to help outfit southbound thru-hikers who start arriving in late May. The couple said they loved the work and the hikers, who came from across the globe. They also loved the off-season, when they saw the rest of the world. They took everything they needed in their carry-on bags and stayed in hostels.

Other hikers, such as Victoria "Bluegrass" Jofery, had stayed in touch with the trail by getting a ridge-runner job to patrol a trail section during the busy season. Bluegrass, who was 25 and had a degree in psychology when I met her in Maine, had thru-hiked the trail and then returned to her job working with developmentally delayed children. But, she said, "I realized I just wanted to be back on the trail. I wanted to be back outside." So, she became a ridge runner and said she answered questions about the trail, gave group lectures, did basic trail maintenance and provided local community outreach. "I love it," she said. "I've never done something more meaningful. I've never loved a job so much."

Others, like thru-hiker John "Web Breaker" Hedrick, had stayed in touch with the trail by becoming active in one of the 31 clubs primarily responsible for maintaining it and keeping it open. When I met Web Breaker, he was 72, president of the Potomac Appalachian Trail Club, and was cutting vegetation back from one of two sections of trail he was maintaining in Virginia. He said he volunteered four hours a day at what was almost a full-time job. "Without volunteer support, you wouldn't have an Appalachian Trail," Web Breaker said. "Parts would be closed within two years. To me, trail magic is good maintenance."

Backpackers certainly appreciate good trail maintenance, but the vast majority of hikers consider trail magic the free food, water, soda, beer, lodging, campsites and rides that folks like Norman Anderson gave hikers.

Norman was 91 when he picked me up near the trail in his 2003 Buick Le Sabre Custom and gave me a free 4.5-mile ride to his hometown of Waynesboro, Virginia, as he'd done countless times for hikers for 40 years. Norman told me he and a friend founded the program in which many area residents gave hikers a ride from the trail to town and back. Norman said he'd kept giving hikers rides "because it's one of the civic things I do and I meet a lot of interesting people."

In the morning, Carol Sloan, who was 69, gave me a ride back to the trail, and said she'd been giving hikers rides for 11 years. She said she often gave rides from mid-May to the end of June, when most thru-hikers are in the area, sometimes many times a day. "It's easy. I can pick you up and return in twenty minutes," she said. "It's interesting. People who hike the trail are not the people you expect to hike the trail. I've picked up a woman with a nine-year-old kid and a dog."

When I met trail angels Rick Combs, who was 60, and his friend, Kate, who was 61, they were grilling chicken for sandwiches and also offered AT backpackers cold cuts, chips, carrots, fruit salad, strawberries, oranges, cookies and muffins on a table under a canopy at an AT trailhead in New Hampshire. They said they'd driven about 120 miles from their Massachusetts hometown because they were "looking for more remote locations where people need stuff." The pair said they'd been trying to climb all of the 48 peaks over 4,000 feet in New Hampshire and decided to help thru-hikers after meeting many of them on the trail. "We've spent more money and had less fun doing other things," said Kate, who was helping care for her 6-month-old granddaughter, Layla Jean, the result of a romance that began when her daughter, Jocelyn Baldor, who was 33, met fellow backpacker Lucas Fykes, who was 32, on the AT. The couple, who hiked together from North Carolina to Massachusetts, were also at the trailhead and said they got engaged when they were hiking again in North Carolina and Lucas proposed at the spot where they'd met.

After I arrived at her house near the trail in Massachusetts, iconic trail angel Marilyn "Cookie Lady" Wiley gave me three oatmeal chocolate chip cookies, which is what she gave each hiker who stopped. She told me that she'd been giving cookies to backpackers for about 25 years and that she baked them in batches of 150, then froze them, and had handed out 1,800 by early August. She and her husband, Roy Wiley, who was 84, also let hikers camp for free in their yard. Cookie Lady, who was working part time as a dietician, even though she was two days shy of 80, told me she figured the hikers "need the oatmeal." Most of the time, I enjoy it," she said. "I like knowing about the hikers. Why they're doing the trail."

I like knowing about the hikers, too, and about nearly everyone else I met and interviewed while backpacking the AT, and I've enjoyed writing about them and preserving their stories, as my way of giving back to the trail. I hope you enjoy them.

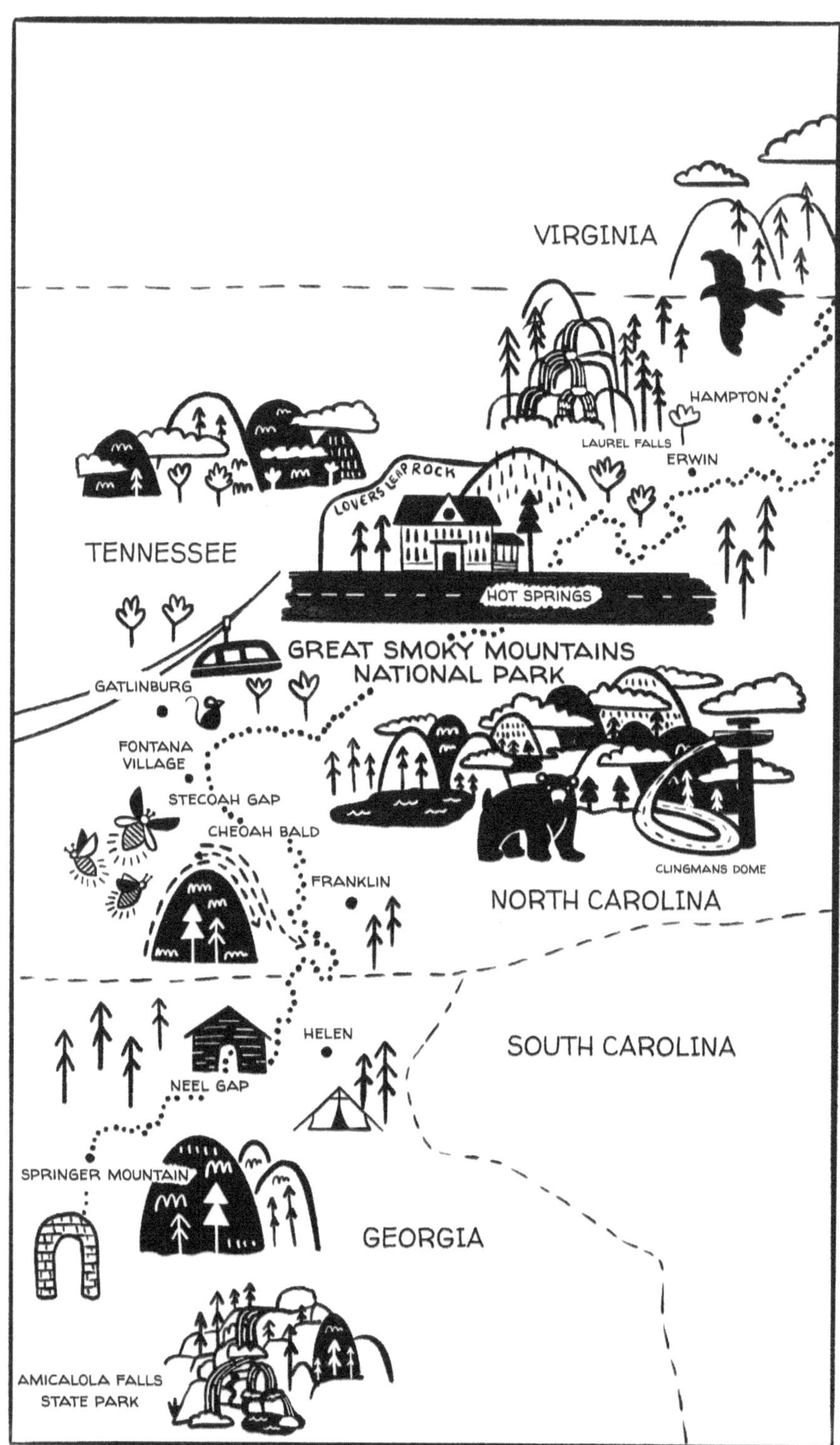

VIRGINIA
HAMPTON
LAUREL FALLS
ERWIN
LOVERS LEAP ROCK
TENNESSEE
HOT SPRINGS
GREAT SMOKY MOUNTAINS NATIONAL PARK
GATLINBURG
FONTANA VILLAGE
STECOAH GAP
CHEOAH BALD
FRANKLIN
CLINGMANS DOME
NORTH CAROLINA
HELEN
SOUTH CAROLINA
NEEL GAP
SPRINGER MOUNTAIN
GEORGIA
AMICALOLA FALLS STATE PARK

1

THE SUN IS JUST RISING WHEN I step off the Amtrak train in Gainesville, Georgia, heading to Amicalola Falls State Park and the Appalachian Trail approach trail, about 40 miles away.

I plan to walk to the edge of town and hitchhike to the park, just like the hitching I often did in Wisconsin and across the country when I was in my late teens and early 20s. I've got a sign with the park's name on it and I figure that a friendly local will see my sign and backpack, figure that I'm heading to the trail, and pick me up.

When I stop at a nearby convenience store to ask for directions, a guy outside asks if I'm going to the trail. When I say yes, he asks if I want a ride.

"How much?" I ask. "Ninety dollars," he says. "I think I'll hitch," I say. "How much are you willing to pay?" he asks, reminding me of the ticket dealers who often sell me tickets to University of Wisconsin football and basketball games on game day. "I may look old," I say, "but I still think like I did when I was in my twenties, so I'm going to try hitching."

I also want to see a little of Gainesville, a city of about 35,000 known as the "Poultry Capital of the World" because it has lots of chicken processing plants. And I need to buy some food for breakfast, and for lunch on the trail. So, I start backpacking a few miles to the outskirts of town and stop at a Subway to get a vegetarian sub and three chocolate chip cookies. I also stop at a Publix grocery store and buy an apple fritter, a bag of tortilla chips, the *Gainesville Times* newspaper and what I figure will be my last *New York Times* for quite a while.

After reaching the edge of town, I hold up my Amicalola Falls State Park sign and wait for the ride I think will come fairly soon. One woman does stop soon, but not to give me a ride. She sticks her hand out the window with a wad of bills. I thank her for her kindness, but say I don't need money, just a ride to the park. After she drives away, I think I should have surprised her and given her some money, instead, just for being so nice.

Cary at the start of the AT approach trail

After about 15 minutes, a fellow stops and takes me a few miles to a convenience store/pizza place/gas station, where he says it'll probably be easier to get a ride. He's wrong. So, after about 45 minutes of standing in the increasingly warm sun, I offer a guy getting gas $50 for a ride to the park.

He says his name is Billy and asks where the park is. When I tell him, he says it'll cost him $20 in gas just to get there and back in his vintage Oldsmobile. "I'll buy you the gas, too," I say, and it's a deal.

"Do you have a gun?" Billy asks, as we drive away. "No," I say. "I don't go anywhere without a gun," he says, and shows me where he'd been shot by burglars in his home.

Billy says he grew up in Wilmington, North Carolina, then the home of basketball great Michael Jordan, but never played against Jordan. He did, though, play small forward at Lamar University in Beaumont, Texas, and got a tryout with the Atlanta Hawks. He says he should have played professionally in Europe after he was cut, but his then wife didn't want to go.

When we get to the park, Billy says he's glad to learn about it and is going to return with his girlfriend. I thank him and he drops me off at the visitor center, where I meet a couple who thru-hiked the trail together in 2004, when she was 40 and he was 50, and were visiting some of their favorite trail spots on the 10th anniversary of their adventure. They wish me luck, as does another woman who had hiked the Pacific Crest Trail, which stretches 2,653 miles from Mexico to Canada through the mountains of California, Oregon and Washington. I hope to backpack that, too.

I enter the visitor center to look around and then register on the thru-hiker log that the park sends to the Appalachian Trail Conservancy (ATC), which is headquartered just off the trail in Harpers Ferry, West Virginia, 1,019 trail miles from here, not counting the 8.8-mile approach trail that starts just outside the center. I'm the 1,348th hiker to register this year.

I also list my pack weight, as did the other hikers, after weighing it on the scale outside. Its base weight, without food and water, is 20 pounds, on the low end. With food, it weighs 31. I see one pack on the list with a base weight of 8 and another of 11. I ask the center staffer how the hikers managed to get their pack weights that low.

"They're most likely getting support from people who meet them at trailheads and might be spending nights in a van," he says.

I tell him that 40 years ago my former girlfriend, and a guy I'd introduced her to, made elaborate plans to thru-hike. They were hiking the approach trail when she decided it was too hard for her and returned to the park. I thought that was very strange then, but he says it's not uncommon and that some backpackers even quit on the 604 steps to the top of the spectacular, cascading, 729-foot-high Amicalola Falls, named from the Cherokee words that mean tumbling waters.

I know from ATC statistics that about half of the backpackers who leave Springer make it to Harpers Ferry and that about half of those make it 1,166.3 more miles to the top of Katahdin. In 2013, 2,250 northbound hikers registered, 1,130 made it to Harpers Ferry and 589 reported finishing the trail. I hope to be one of the 25 percent who finish and I'm happy and excited as I start hiking.

I think I'll be able to make it to Katahdin, after finding the approach trail quite easy, and arrive at the top in time to take pictures of the Cohutta

Mountains to the west in the setting sun, and of a rock with a bronze plaque and a white blaze marking the start of the AT. The plaque, placed by the Georgia Appalachian Trail Club, has the figure of a backpacker next to the words "A Footpath for Those who seek Fellowship with the Wilderness." There's another register here.

Then, I hike 0.2 mile more to the first of 245 shelters along the trail and meet the sole occupant, Monica, 22, who has just graduated from the University of Missouri and also hopes to hike to Maine.

Monica's lying in her sleeping bag on the wood floor of the three-sided shelter that sleeps 12, and reading with the fading light from the side that's open. She says she'd flown to Atlanta and taken a commuter train to the northernmost stop. That's where Survivor Dave Levy, who shuttles hikers from Atlanta to the trail, and elsewhere, picked her up.

He took her about 80 miles to Big Stamp Gap, which is on a remote U.S. Forest Service road that intersects the trail a mile north of the Springer summit. If she had gone to the state park, instead, the drive would have been about 65 miles.

Monica had then hiked to the start of the trail and returned to the shelter.

I'm familiar with the gap because I drove there with my son, Craig, to see Springer for the first time and meet thru-hikers during his spring break, when he was a high school junior in 1999. We had camped at the state park the night before. On the drive down the mountain, I realized we were almost out of gas, and then mainly coasted until I saw some people at a cabin. I told them our predicament and they gave us enough gas to reach a nearby town,

Several other hikers have set up tents near the shelter, partly for privacy, partly for the softer surface, and partly to avoid the mice that infest many shelters. I've decided not to bring a tent and to rely on shelters, often spaced about seven or eight miles apart. I've saved weight, but have given up the flexibility of being able to camp at any suitable site along the trail, unless I'm sure it isn't going to rain and I can sleep without a tent and not get soaked.

I'd been influenced by the memoir of a thru-hiker who'd told his brother, who had hiked the trial without a tent, that he was going to take one because it would only weigh three or four pounds. His brother's response was: "How much do they weigh when they're wet?"

I put my sleeping pads and bag on the shelter floor, Monica and I talk for a while, and then I walk downhill to a nearby stream for water. Nearly all backpackers treat their water to try to avoid water-borne illnesses, especially the serious intestinal problems caused by Giardia.

Some use a filter, including a rather heavy pump, some use chemicals, and some use ultraviolet light from a SteriPEN. I already own a pump and a SteriPEN, which needs batteries; but I've opted for a new-to-me Sawyer MINI water filter, which seems simple to use and weighs just two ounces.

The filter is screwed onto a 16-ounce semi-hard plastic bag, after the bag is filled with water. Then, the water is squeezed through the filter into a water bottle or just drunk straight from the filter. The bag was easy to fill from the faucet in my kitchen, but isn't so easy to fill from the stream. However, I eventually get enough for the night and return to the shelter.

Then I enjoy atypical backpacking food: Brunkow cheese curds, and Stella's multi-grain bread and spicy cheese bread from last Saturday's Dane County Farmers' Market around the Capitol Square in Madison, figuring that I'm willing to carry the extra weight for a while to enjoy the delicious taste of home.

I've been kind of cavalier about my food supply, unlike many hikers who carefully plan their meals in advance and send boxes of dehydrated and/or freeze-dried food to hostels, post offices, and motels along the way.

I've also been influenced by the memoir of a backpacker who decided she didn't like cooking and then saved weight by mailing her stove and pot home. I brought no stove or pot, and just brought the bread and cheese, along with Clif Bars, PowerBars, and bags of almonds, raisins, prunes and dried blueberries. I plan to resupply and eat in restaurants in the many towns near and on the trail.

By the time I finish eating, it's nearly dark and I still have to hang my food bag 10 feet off the ground on cables nearby to keep it away from bears. A sign on the Springer summit warns hikers not to camp there because of bear activity, and to camp near the shelter, instead.

But I can't figure out how to use the cables in the twilight. I return to the shelter to ask Monica and she says, "Just pull on the cables." I try, but that doesn't work and Monica isn't inclined to get out of her cozy sleeping bag to help me.

So, I hang the bag the way I've done when I've backpacked in grizzly country out West. I get my 50 feet of cord, tie one end to a rock and throw it over the cable; then I untie the rock, tie on my bag, pull the bag up with the other end of the cord, and tie the cord to a tree.

I return to the shelter, crawl into my bag and am nearly asleep when a mouse scampers across my head. I yell at the mouse, but I know that will unlikely deter it, or what I assume are plenty of others; so, I put the bag over my head and fall asleep.

My sleep is fitful; not because of the mice, but because of the light, three-quarter-length, self-inflating Therm-a-Rest pad that I bought for Craig in 1989, when he was 7 and we drove to Glacier National Park for his first backpacking trip. I'd put the pad on my old, thin, light, three-quarter-length, foam RidgeRest pad, and the pair don't provide much cushioning on the hard floor.

So, I get up as soon as the sky starts to lighten and the birds begin to sing. Monica is still sleeping, so I carry my stuff to a picnic table outside and start packing up.

2

Maury Hall is most likely the most meticulous backpacker on the Appalachian Trail, or on any trail, for that matter, and that's why his backpack's base weight is an extraordinarily light 11 pounds.

Hall crawls out of his tent near the Springer shelter, as I'm packing to leave, and introduces himself by his trail name of Deacon. Most AT hikers either give themselves a trail name, or take one suggested by others. Deacon, 68, of Port Clinton, Ohio, has picked a name that reflects his role in his Catholic church.

Deacon says he was an electrical engineer working on headlights and taillights at Ford in 2009, when he decided he wanted to pursue his childhood dream of backpacking the Appalachian Trail.

He says the dream began in 1956 when he was an 11-year-old Boy Scout and his scoutmaster "mesmerized us boys" in describing the AT. "I thought that was pretty amazing," he says, "and I'm going to do that trail someday."

Deacon says his house in Mansfield, Ohio, was next to a deep woods and he "spent hours exploring this world, where the dream took root." But regular life got in the way: "As life goes, education, work, family and financial responsibility through the years prevented me from pursuing that dream."

In 2009, though, with his three children grown and the support of his wife, Yvonne, he wrote the Appalachian Trail Conservancy for information and started reading online journals of AT hikers to learn how best to backpack the trail, especially how to pack light. "My hobby was doing research," he says.

I didn't, on the other hand, even know there were such journals. I'd read many books about AT hikes, but none of those hikers packed exceptionally light and none used the equipment Deacon is using, probably because it didn't exist or wasn't common when they wrote the books.

I have, though, known to pack light since I was 21 and biked from my hometown of Green Bay, Wisconsin, to Los Angeles with my friend Joe Brunette. It didn't take long before we realized we'd packed way too much and mailed many pounds of stuff home, and since then I've packed light on many bike and backpacking trips.

Deacon, who had never backpacked, started buying very light equipment and then retired in May 2012 before hiking the rugged northern 166.5 miles of the 272-mile Long Trail, which stretches the length of Vermont through the Green Mountains from Canada to Massachusetts. The southern 105.5 miles are easier and coincide with the AT. In 2013, he backpacked the entire Long Trail and figured he was ready to live his dream.

He plans to hike the entire trail in four years, so that he doesn't leave Yvonne alone for too long, and this year plans to take 34 days to backpack about 468 miles and finish in Damascus, Virginia.

Like Monica, he flew into Atlanta and took the commuter train to the northernmost stop. But he got a ride from a driver with the Hiker Hostel, which is 21 miles east of the state park, about three miles outside the small city of Dahlonega. For $80, he got the ride, a night at the hostel, breakfast and another ride to the park or Springer trailhead. He chose the park and was the guy who listed the 11-pound pack. I knew about the hostel's deal, which also applied to a ride from Gainesville, but the guidebook said it was only good until April 20, and I wanted to go straight to the park, anyway.

Deacon says his LightHeart Gear Solong 6 tent cost $700 and weighs an extremely light 27 ounces. It's made from a strong, extra-light, extra-pricey waterproof fabric called Cuben Fiber, which is composed of a sheet of polyethylene laminated between two sheets of polyester. His Zpacks Exo backpack is made from the same material and weighs only 21.9 ounces, and he's using a Zpacks 23.5-ounce down quilt good to 20 degrees, instead of a sleeping bag.

I'd never heard of either company, or of Cuben Fiber or quilts, and had thought I'd been doing OK by relying on REI for my equipment, including a 29-ounce down sleeping bag, also good to 20 degrees, that I'd bought in 2001 for a cross-country bike trip with Craig, and an internal-frame Osprey

Exos 58 backpack that weighs 38 ounces, less than half of the external-frame pack that I'd been using.

Deacon made his dinners at home with recipes he learned from a guy named Babelfish5 on the Hungry Hammock Hanger website. Then he dehydrated them in an Excalibur-9 shelf dehydrator and put them in quart Ziplock bags that he shipped in boxes with the rest of his food to places he planned to stay along the trail, such as hostels.

He says he used Excel spreadsheets to thoroughly plan everything about his hike, including how many calories and how much protein, fat and carbohydrates he'll need each day, what he'll eat, how far he'll hike each day, and where he'll spend each night. He carries 1.83 pounds of food per day for full days on the trail, and less when he can eat in a store, hostel or restaurant.

I, on the other hand, figure I'll eat what I feel like eating when I'm hungry, hike until I feel like stopping, spend the night wherever it seems right, and buy food when I can get it.

When it's time for supper, Deacon uses a 0.1-ounce Gram Cracker stove to hold a 0.5-ounce Esbit fuel cube inside a 1.35-ounce Caldera Cone to boil two cups of water in eight minutes in an aluminum Foster's beer can that weighs 1.1 ounces and holds 25.4 ounces. He pours the water into the Ziplock bag and, voila, dinner is served.

After dinner, he brushes his teeth with half a toothbrush and no toothpaste because his dentist said it isn't necessary. Instead of nail clippers, he uses an emery board and instead of a case for his glasses, he uses a teensy bit lighter bubble wrap.

Deacon's using the same Sawyer water filter that I'm using, but, instead of the semi-hard plastic bag that came with the filter and is hard to fill, he's using Evernew collapsible plastic water bottles that also screw onto the filter. They're bigger and more pliable, and much easier to fill than the Sawyer bag. They're also lighter than the regular hard plastic water bottles that I'm carrying.

Deacon has plenty of water and plans to dump most of it because water weighs 8.34 pounds per gallon and there are plenty of springs and streams along the section of trail we're about to hike. So, he gives me some and I fill my two pint water bottles, for now, although I plan to usually carry no water, unless I learn that there's little where I'm hiking.

The springs are marked, along with many other trail features, such as distances, elevations, shelters, hostels and towns, in "The A.T. Guide," which we're both using. It's produced and updated annually by David Miller, whose trail name is "AWOL" because he quit his IT job to do a thru-hike in 2003. Miller's also written a memoir called *AWOL on the Appalachian Trail*, which I've read. He's the guy whose brother hiked the trail without a tent.

Deacon's plans call for him to take three days to reach Neel Gap, which is 31.7 miles and eight mountains away, and his first resupply point. He plans to spend tonight at Hawk Mountain Shelter, which is at the top of the first mountain we'll need to climb and 7.9 miles away, and his second night at Gooch Mountain Shelter, 7.7 miles and three more mountains away.

But I immediately upset his detailed plans when I point out that the climbs don't look too tough and we can easily make it to Gooch Mountain Shelter tonight and Neel Gap tomorrow. He agrees and we plan to meet at the shelter tonight.

But first Deacon shows me how to use bear cables, which is simple enough that I feel foolish for not figuring it out myself. But it was nearly dark and I'm no engineer and not mechanically inclined. He says that I have to detach the cable from the tree it's clipped to before pulling on it, a step that Monica had either forgotten to mention, or assumed I was smart enough to figure out myself.

The loop of cable has hooks on it to hold food bags, and runs over a pulley on a long cable about 10 feet off the ground and stretched between two trees. After the bag is hooked, the cable is pulled and clipped to the tree, and the bag is out of the reach of bears.

Then, we say goodbye to Monica and start hiking. Deacon heads straight to the trail. I stop to use the privy, which is like an outhouse, but on a platform with just three walls and no door. After that, I also head north and quickly reach Big Stamp Gap, where Survivor Dave Levy, who shuttled Monica to the trail yesterday, is dropping off a couple backpackers.

Survivor Dave says he also shuttles hikers in his Ford Expedition to and from other trailheads, including from Neel Gap back to Atlanta. He says about 20 percent of the hikers he shuttles from Atlanta to the trail quit and call him for a ride when they reach Neel Gap, and some call him before that, including approach-trail dropouts.

I don't expect I'll want to soon leave the well-trod trail, which is about a yard wide and easy to follow. It's blazed with two-inch-wide-by-six-inch-tall white rectangles, which are painted mainly on trees and sometimes on rocks and other spots. Shortly before a significant turn or a side trail, there are two blazes, with one above the other, to alert hikers. Side trails, such as those to shelters, views or water sources, are blazed in blue.

From the Springer Mountain shelter, at an altitude of 3,733 feet, I'll be headed down to another forest service road at 2,530 feet, up to the summit of Hawk Mountain at 3,209 feet, down to Horse Gap at 2,681 feet, up to Sassafras Mountain at 3,342 feet, down to Cooper Gap at 2,940 feet, up to Justus Mountain at 3,226 feet, down to Justus Creek at 2,619 feet, and up to Gooch Mountain Shelter at 2,821 feet.

It's a day of ups and downs in the beautiful Chattahoochee National Forest, but I'm always up while hiking through a forest floor blanketed with ferns and spring wildflowers, such as pink and white trilliums, purplish cranesbill and whitish-yellow Solomon's seal. The understory includes lots of rhododendrons, some with purple flowers, but most done blooming, and an occasional flame azalea with beautiful bright orange flowers. They're topped by a diverse hardwood forest that includes oaks, maples, beeches, tulip poplars and sassafras.

I'm using hiking poles, which I'd never used before, but bought after reading about how they make hiking easier, and I'll try to always use them again. They're great for helping me keep my balance while hiking over rocks and streams, and also let me use my arms to provide an extra push, especially when climbing mountains.

In the evening, after 15.6 miles of fairly easy hiking, I reach the side trail to the shelter, which is 0.1 mile away. I start talking with the few hikers there and learn they're out for a few days. Then, I see Deacon lying on the wood floor and he looks up.

"I thought I heard a familiar voice," he says.

He had hiked much faster than me with his much lighter load and had already been there a few hours. We talk a bit and then I get water and settle down to a meal of bread, cheese curds and tortilla chips, while I read yesterday's *New York Times* and *Gainesville Times*. Everyone's surprised by the papers and the chips, which apparently aren't commonly backpacked on the trail.

Then, I hang my food bag on the bear cables and decide to sleep outside the shelter for the comfort of a softer surface and to avoid the mice. I place my tarp, pads and bag on the ground, what AT backpackers call cowboy camping, and then use my headlamp to read for a while before quickly falling asleep.

In the morning, Deacon and I are once again the first ones up at the first light, and I eat a chocolate PowerBar before starting the 15.9-mile hike to Neel Gap, where there's a gear, grocery and gift store, and a hostel. Deacon plans to pick up his first food package there.

The terrain's similar, but I don't have as easy a time hiking it as I did yesterday. After eight miles, I start feeling a little weak and nauseous and realize I feel the same way I've sometimes felt in the late miles of a marathon when I haven't eaten enough during the race. I find a nice bed of leaves to lie on and rest, then eat a lot and feel rejuvenated.

That's good because I'm about to climb 1,581 feet over five miles to the 4,461-foot summit of Blood Mountain, the highest Georgia mountain on the trail. Thunderstorms, common in the mountains in the afternoon, rumble around me, and then over me when I'm about halfway up.

It starts pouring, then hailing, and I miss a turn in the trail in the downpour. I walk about a quarter mile on a side trail before noticing it's blazed in blue. I turn around and by the time I reach the AT, the storm's over. I'm soaked, but my wet tech T-shirt feels good on what's become a tough, rocky climb to the summit. My pack and the contents are a little moist because I hadn't taken time to put on my waterproof pack cover.

When I reach the rocky mountaintop, though, the sun's shining and the views of mountain ridge, after mountain ridge, after mountain ridge in the distance are beautiful. And so are the rhododendrons, which are still blooming because of the cooler temperatures at the higher elevation.

There's an enclosed stone shelter on the mountaintop, but I can't stay because I don't have the bear-resistant canister that's required due to active bears in the area. So, I carefully follow the rather steep, rocky trail down 2.4

miles to the gap at 3,125 feet, and arrive at Mountain Crossings store and hostel around sunset.

I've been looking forward to seeing the place, which Winton Porter, who owned it from 2001 to last fall, has written about in an entertaining book called "Just Passin' Thru," which chronicles his life with his wife and two young daughters and the many characters he dealt with, including his employees, backpackers and hangers-on.

The iconic, attractive stone buildings housing the store, hostel, and home above the hostel were built by the Civilian Conservation Corps, which started construction in 1934 and finished in 1937, the same year the AT was completed. The CCC also built the stone shelter on Blood Mountain.

The buildings, which were used as a dining hall and inn until the mid-1960s, are called Walasi-Y, which was the name of the Cherokee village that was nearby in the 1800s and means "home of the great frog." The AT goes through the covered breezeway connecting the store and hostel and is the only place the trail passes under a roof. The place was going to be torn down in the 1970s, but some locals worked to save it and it became Mountain Crossings in 1983.

Winton became well known for the "shakedowns" that he and his employees provided for hikers who struggled to make it to Neel Gap with heavy, overloaded backpacks and wanted to shed pounds. They helped hikers get rid of unneeded and poor equipment, sold them the proper gear and mailed home what the hikers wanted to keep.

In the book, Winton writes about a hiker from New Orleans who arrived with a pack weighing more than 70 pounds and was so grateful when he left with one weighing 33.5 that he surprised Winton with overnight delivery of crawfish from a seafood restaurant in Louisiana. Winton says the heaviest pack he handled weighed 136 pounds and the hiker carrying it said it weighed 140 when he started the hike. The next heaviest weighed 89.

The entire place is closed, unlike any other hostels I've stayed at, which are open late. The bathrooms are open, though, so I walk through the breezeway and lay my tarp, pads and sleeping bag near a picnic table in the back.

I'm about to eat more bread and cheese curds when two guys invite me to eat with them. They're college students who have set up their tent in a clearing a little way up the trail and have come down to have dinner at another picnic table. They have quite a spread that includes canned peaches, jam in a glass jar, salmon, cheese, tortillas and a bottle of whiskey.

They say that they'd never backpacked, or even camped, before, and weren't sure what to bring on their trip of a few days. So, they brought a lot and they're happy to share. They're living at their Atlanta homes after one spent a school year at Penn and the other a school year at Yale and are interesting to talk with. They say their parents aren't campers and that until recently they hadn't known about the beautiful forested mountains and trail, just a short drive from home. My parents, Shirley and Sol, also weren't campers, but I went camping with my friend Joe after we got our driver's licenses and could take ourselves.

I eat too much and start feeling a little nauseous after lying down to sleep. Then the nausea gets worse, but I feel better after vomiting for the first time since running the Crater Lake Marathon up and down hills at high elevation in Oregon 22 years ago when I was on my annual monthlong summer camping trip with Craig.

In the morning, I'm about to leave when I see Deacon coming out of the hostel. "You should have come in," he says. "The door wasn't locked." I go in and look around at the empty hostel. It's nice, but I'm glad I hadn't slept there because then I probably wouldn't have met and had dinner with the guys from Atlanta.

It's just after dawn, nobody else is around and the store hasn't opened. Deacon has me take a picture of him hiking through the breezeway and then we head to Low Gap Shelter, 11.5 miles and four mountains away.

3

I FOLLOW DEACON ON THE CLIMB out of the gap to the top of Levelland Mountain, where there are great views of the surrounding summits, just as there have been on the top of four of the other nine mountains I've climbed so far.

On the rest, though, the view has been mainly of bushes, trees and other vegetation, the same as it's been on the rest of the trail, as I've hiked through thick forests. That's why the AT is often called "the green tunnel." The trail also has often been lined with rhododendrons that arch over it and make it actually feel like a tunnel. The color must have been spectacular at the lower elevations when the bushes were blooming and full of purple flowers.

There are more people passing through the tunnel today because it's the Friday before Memorial Day, and I hike and talk with a few of them. Joe Kehoe, of Atlanta, is taking his son Ryan, 10, on his first backpacking trip and they're hiking 21.2 miles from Neel Gap to Unicoi Gap. Ryan keeps pointing out the snails on the trail, which I hadn't noticed. Joe shows me a black snake and a garter snake.

Jeff Strunk, who's hiking for about a week, says he's from Illinois. When I ask where in Illinois, he says Peoria, and adds that he usually doesn't say that because hardly anyone he tells has heard of it. I've been there, though, and know that it's known as the epitome of mainstream America and it's often been said that a good way to test a product or production is to see if it "plays in Peoria."

Jeff says he has three weeks of vacation a year and often backpacks. He's backpacked the rugged 93-mile Wonderland Trail around Mount Rainier. Craig and I saw the trail when he was 8 and we backpacked in Mount Rainier National Park, and I've thought of returning to hike it. Jeff has also backpacked the AT in the scenic White Mountains of New Hampshire, where the trail is very steep and very rocky, so he doesn't consider the Southern Appalachians too tough.

Ryan and Joe

"In New Hampshire, they don't believe in switchbacks," he says, referring to the way the trail often swings gradually from side to side to side on climbs to mountaintops. The hike is longer that way, but also easier.

In the Whites, Jeff says, the trail goes nearly straight up and hikers often have to put their poles away and use their hands to climb. But the Whites are about 1,750 miles away, and, if I make it that far, I say, I should be in good enough shape that the steeper climbs won't be a problem.

Jeff and I also talk about footwear. He's wearing boots, like many hikers, while I'm wearing the same New Balance 940 running shoes and Thorlo running socks I wear while running and walking at home.

I'd read many horror stories of hikers getting blister, after blister, after blister because their feet got wet, soft and more vulnerable to blisters from sweating all day in hot, rigid boots. Some hikers pierced the blisters, covered them with duct tape, and kept walking. Some had to leave the trail for days because of the pain and/or to get infected blisters treated.

I'd also read that most hikers don't need the extra ankle support that boots provide, and that wearing a pair of one-pound shoes, rather than four-pound boots, is the energy-saving equivalent of carrying 12 to 18 pounds less in your pack. And, hikers who wear boots usually also carry a pair of more comfortable footwear, which means even more weight. My 940s weigh 14 ounces each and I've had no problems with my ankles, which are strong because, when I'm not backpacking, I run on trails nearly every day.

Jeff hadn't had any problems with boots until talking with me. But in the evening, after he, Deacon, Joe, Ryan and I reach Low Gap Shelter, he shows Deacon and me a big blister he's gotten near a big toe on the bottom of one foot. Deacon tells Jeff he has some extra sticky tape, if Jeff wants to pierce the blister and put tape over his skin. But Jeff decides to stick it out because he has only one day and 9.7 miles of hiking left.

I tell Jeff about Deacon's remarkably low pack weight and then Deacon tells him how he does it. Jeff says it's obvious Deacon's an engineer and then tells us about two overloaded backpackers he met at a shelter on the Springer approach trail, which is where he stayed the night Deacon and I stayed at the Springer shelter.

He says the two men, who are from Columbus, Ohio, and plan to thru-hike, had started with 60-pound packs and were burning some of their clothes in a bonfire to cut their pack weight. I'd seen the men standing around the fire about 100 yards away when I hiked the approach trail and wondered why they had a big fire on a warm day, but hadn't stopped to talk with them because I wanted to hike the 1.5 miles to the summit before sunset. I figure they likely got shakedowns at Mountain Crossings, if they didn't quit before then.

There are many weekenders camped in tents near the shelter, and they're all still in them when I leave, walk the side trail to the AT, and head what I think is north. Quickly, I realize I'm heading the wrong way because the rising sun is on my left. I know many hikers have made the same mistake and gone much farther when the sky was cloudy. Some got the trail name "Wrong Way," while others were named "Wrong Turn." So, I vow to be more careful to remember which way I turn to reach a shelter, and to turn the same way when l return to the trail.

I had told Deacon, who left before me, that I probably wouldn't see him again because I'm going to get a ride from Joe to the small city of Helen to spend the night after we reach the gap. I want to check on some things at home, take a shower and buy some food.

Jeff, Joe and Ryan soon catch me and we hike together, more or less, until we get to the gap and Highway 75. I say goodbye to Jeff, then ride with Joe and Ryan to Helen, about nine miles away. Along the way we see tons of tubers floating down the Chattahoochee River. And, when we get closer to Helen, traffic slows, as a half-mile-long line of cars slowly snakes through town.

I had planned to stay at the Best Western, which, like many motels in towns near the trail, offers hikers a deeply discounted rate. But I didn't know that Helen's a tourist town and that the motels will probably still be crowded because it's the Sunday before Memorial Day.

I ask Joe to drop me at the Best Western, anyway, and before I leave, he says a prayer for me. He composes a nice one on the spot, asking Jesus to grant me a safe and enjoyable trip. I don't have the heart to tell him I'm a nonreligious Jew. I just hope I'll have better luck with Jesus than I did in January, when a pastor said a similar prayer before the First Light Marathon in Mobile, Alabama.

I've run about 80 marathons in 28 states and the Mobile race was only the second one with a prayer at the start. I suffered a hamstring injury at mile 5 and had to drop out, which was my first severe hamstring injury ever, and the first time I had to drop out of a marathon because of an injury during the race. The other marathon with a starting prayer, also to Jesus, was in 2012 in North Carolina, another Bible Belt state. That time, I did OK.

The friendly manager at the Best Western says the place is full and that, regardless, the rooms for which hikers normally pay $50 are going for three times that. She says, though, that the Super 8, a block away, might have rooms. She calls and asks, and says the manager will give me the hiker $50 rate, even though she could easily charge me the going rate of $100.

The Best Western manager also gives me chocolate chip cookies, my favorite kind, and says I can come back and use the computer, which I want to use to check some things because, unlike nearly all hikers, I don't have a cell phone on the trail, or at home, because I don't want to be in constant contact with the world. The manager also tells me that the folks at Betty's Country Store give hikers a free ride to the trail every morning at 11.

People are very nice in crowded, touristy Helen, which looks like a Bavarian Alpine village, complete with good German food. I figure it must have had German settlers, like a couple towns in the Midwest I'd visited that use their German heritage to boost tourism.

I learn, though, that Helen, a city of about 500, has no history of German settlement, and was a just a typical humdrum Appalachian town in northern Georgia in 1968 when some bright city entrepreneurs decided that turning the town into a fake Alpine village would attract tourists. They were right.

I want to see more of Helen, but first I take a shower and change into my town clothes. I've got two short-sleeve tech T-shirts, one for the trail and one for town. They're made from polyester, so they wick moisture from my skin and dry quickly. I've also got two pairs each of socks, underwear and running shorts, and I've got one long-sleeve tech T-shirt and pair of tights for town and trail, a rain jacket and a cap.

Before leaving, I take my trail shirt, shorts, socks and underwear and repeatedly run water over them in the sink until they're soaked and then wring them out until most of the dirt is gone, and then hang them to dry.

Then, I use the Best Western computer for a while before walking a mile, or so, from the western edge of town to the eastern edge, to buy food at Betty's, a rustic grocery store, and ask Dru Shelton, who works at the store owned by her sister, if they really do give hikers free rides to the trail. She says that the tradition was started by her mother after her parents founded the store in 1973, and that she and her sister had continued it.

I say I'll be back at 11, unless I get a ride sooner by hitching. Then I buy more nontraditional trail food: tortilla chips, pastry, a pound of baby carrots, a tomato and bread, along with the *Gainesville Times*. I also buy a few types of scrumptious chocolate cupcakes at Crumbs & All, normally

$3.25, but on sale for a buck, so the employees can sell out and go home, and then I get dinner at a Mexican restaurant.

After eating, I return to the motel and make sandwiches for the trail with peanut butter I get from the backpacker box. The boxes are often placed at motels, hostels and other spots along the trail for hikers to leave unwanted items for other hikers to take. Then, I sleep in a bed for the first time in a week.

After a restful night and a big continental breakfast, I walk back to Betty's and arrive about 9 with plans to hitchhike and then get a ride at 11, if I'm not successful. I buy today's *Gainesville Times* and then find a good place to hitchhike across the street.

There's little traffic on Memorial Day and most of the people who pass me don't seem to be Helen residents, who would likely know that I'm a harmless hiker trying to get back to the trail.

After about half an hour, one of those residents, Lester Roberts, stops. He says he wasn't headed to the trailhead, but had seen me and turned around to give me a ride. Lester knows a lot about my home state of Wisconsin and neighboring Minnesota because he makes one round trip a week from Georgia through Wisconsin to Albert Lea, Minnesota, with aluminum for Larson Manufacturing, which makes storm doors and windows.

Lester drops me at Unicoi Gap and I start the steep climb to Rocky Mountain and then to Tray Mountain, which both provide splendid views. The sky's partly cloudy, with a little rain in the afternoon from thunderstorms.

I'm surprised to see an unopened package of freeze-dried beef stroganoff on a stump next to the trail; then a few miles later see a mesh food bag with several packages of freeze-dried food hanging from a tree limb about six feet over the path. I figure someone must be trying to cut weight by cutting food. But I don't think that leaving it out in the open where bears can get it is a good idea.

Late in the day, I'm only thinking about reaching Deep Gap Shelter, which is 1.1 miles away, when I reach the top of Kelly Knob and see two guys camping.

"Good evening," I say. They laugh, explaining that they'd just told each other that they didn't expect to see anyone else there so late in the day. I ask why they didn't hike the rest of the way to the shelter and they say they were simply too tired to go any farther.

The men, 48 and 52, are both named Anthony and are both from Fayetteville, North Carolina. They say they're trying a short backpacking trip on the AT because a friend had hiked the whole thing and often told stories about it. They just wanted to see it for themselves, and now they've seen enough.

They say they're the guys who left the food, along with five other packages of freeze-dried food that I hadn't seen, and that a hiker or hikers had likely picked up. Their main problem appears to be the weight of their packs. They've each set up a tent big enough for two and each have a stove and fuel.

When they keep calling me "sir," I say, "You're too old to call me sir." They say that in the South, that's what they call everyone.

We say goodbye and then I hike in the fading light down the mountain to the shelter, where there are many people in tents and hammocks, apparently trying to stretch the Memorial Day weekend, and one hiker, Larry "20-Year Plan" Polley, set up to sleep in the shelter.

20-Year-Plan, 50, of suburban Louisville, says he got his trail name because he plans to hike the AT in 100-mile sections over 20 years. He tells me he's met Monica, who told him she's a swimmer and is hiking only about eight miles a day until she gets her "trail legs." He also says he's seen her step over a snake and suggested she use "Snake" as a trail name. She told him she'd think about it.

20-Year-Plan also had talked to the men who dumped the food. "I told them," he says. "your packs are bigger then my first apartment.'"

4

WHEN I LEAVE THE SHELTER JUST BEFORE DAWN, 20-Year-Plan is sleeping and the others are still in their tents or hammocks. I haven't gone far when I hear a crash in the underbrush to my right. I turn and glimpse a black bear running away. It's the first bear I've seen on my hike. Seconds later, I hear another crash and look again, but see nothing. A second bear, I figure.

I'm excited to see a bear, although I've seen black bears and grizzlies during my trips with Craig. I've always been wary of grizzlies, but not of black bears because they generally run from people and rarely attack. In fact, there have been no fatal bear attacks on the trail since it was completed 77 years ago and only 15 in the United States, or about one every five years, in the same time.

The only person killed by a bear near the trail was a 50-year-old Tennessee woman who was hiking on a trail in Great Smoky Mountains National Park, about seven miles from the AT, when she was attacked by a bear and her yearling in May 2000. She's the only person killed by a black bear in a national park and was the first in the Southeast. Since then, a black bear killed a 6-year-old girl in 2006, far from the trail in Cherokee National Forest in southeast Tennessee.

After 3.6 miles, I reach Dick's Creek Gap and Highway 70. There's a van there from the Top of Georgia Hostel, a half mile away, and the driver asks if I want a ride to the place. The new hostel, which was started by thru-hiker Bob "Sir-Packs-Alot" Gabrielsen has a great reputation.

For $20, hikers get a comfortable bed in a clean bunkroom with hot showers; free shuttles three times a day to the city of Hiawasee, 11 miles away; free long-distance calls and computer use; a laundry; the option to buy dinner, along with food and fresh bread to go; and backpacking advice from Sir-Packs-Alot.

Everything sounds great, but it's way, way too early to stop, so I say "thanks," and keep hiking. Just before I enter the woods, I spot two store-bought bottles of water. I ask the van driver if he'd put them there and he says no.

I take one and enjoy my first taste of the "trail magic" that many backpackers, especially the bubble of thru-hikers who start in March and April, look forward to. The magic, often food and soda provided free at road crossings, is supplied by "trail angels" who like to help thru-hikers, and might have hiked all, or some, of the trail themselves.

I'm missing most of the magic by starting in late May, but I'm also missing the crowds and I like having the trail mostly to myself and not having to worry that I won't find space in a shelter or hostel. If I were to try another thru-hike and didn't have a race I wanted to run in mid-May, I'd still start late to avoid the crowds, but I'd begin in late April or early May to see more rhododendrons blooming and have more time to reach Katahdin.

Late in the day, I start the rugged climb to Courthouse Bald and, after six days and 78.5 miles, see a sign on a tree marking the border of Georgia and North Carolina. I cross into my second state and enter the Nantahala National Forest, which I'd seen the first time in 1972 when I was 22 and took my first backpacking trip, and first trip to the Appalachians, with the Hoofers Outing Club at the University of Wisconsin in Madison. A group of us spent about a week backpacking the AT during spring break.

Back then, the trail wasn't nearly as popular as it is today and only 59 people hiked the entire trail from the time it was completed in 1937 through 1969. Myron Avery, who was the first person to complete it, was also the person primarily responsible for making it a reality and he finished it in sections in 1936, while flagging and measuring the route.

Avery dedicated his life to the trail that was proposed in a 1921 article by Benton MacKaye, a forester, conservationist and co-founder of The Wilderness Society. Avery was president of the Appalachian Trail Conference, now called the Appalachian Trail Conservancy, from 1931 to 1952, and, aside from his family and his work as a lawyer, had time for little else. He was on the trail 50 weekends a year until he died in 1952 of a heart attack at age 52.

In 1970, Ed Garvey, an AT activist, did a well-publicized thru-hike at the age of 55 and then wrote the popular book "Appalachian Hiker: Adventure of a Lifetime," which was published in 1971. He was one of 10 people to finish the trail in 1970, and inspired the hiker boom, with 783 more people finishing it in the 1970s, 1,438 in the 1980s, 3,346 in the 1990s and 5,970 from 2000 to 2009.

I thought after my first AT hike that I'd want to backpack the whole trail, but I didn't think it would take 42 years before I'd try. Since then, though, I've backpacked, hiked and run parts of the trail in seven states; but the vast majority of it will be new to me.

I saw Baxter State Park in northern Maine, where the trail ends at Baxter Peak on the top of Katahdin, in 1999 when Craig was 17 and we were headed home in August from a trip to Nova Scotia. We got to the park extra early to get a coveted permit to climb Katahdin and were about halfway up the extremely steep, rocky, 5.2-mile trail to the top when it got very misty and foggy and we decided to turn back.

We were disappointed then, but now I'm glad we didn't make it; so that, if I make it this time, I'll be seeing the summit for the first time. And I'm hoping that Craig, 32, who's an environmental lawyer at the California Air Resources Board in Sacramento and is working to slow global warming, will be there to see it with me.

At the border, I meet a father and son from Georgia who are setting up camp for the night. They tell me that they'd seen a bear on the trail I'd just hiked and that it had watched them and then walked away.

The father asks if I have a trail name. When I say no, he glances at my red "Madison Mini-Marathon" T-shirt, which I got at a half marathon, and suggests "Marathon Man." "Thanks for the suggestion," I say," but I think the name's too common, at least off the trail."

I resume my climb, put the waterproof cover on my pack when it starts raining, and walk quickly the last mile of my 15.4-mile day to Muskrat Creek Shelter. I'm surprised to see familiar-looking water bottles on the table and a familiar guy lying in the shelter. "I don't believe it," says Deacon.

Neither do I, because he kept hiking when I stopped in Helen, and he was hiking faster than me, anyway. So, neither of us had expected to see each other on the trail again. But, without me to push him, he'd reverted to the schedule he'd planned on the spreadsheet at home. That called for the previous night at a campsite just north of Dick's Creek Gap and tonight at Muskrat Creek.

Deacon (c.p.)

The Memorial Day hikers have returned home and we're the only people at the shelter. Near the entrance, backpackers have hung pieces of twine from a rafter, threaded each piece through a can lid or other object and tied it to a stick. Hikers can hang packs and bags from the sticks, and the lids and objects are supposed to keep mice from reaching them.

Deacon tells me that the nearby stream is flowing slowly and that I'll have to scoop water from a pool. I'd learned the scooping method before leaving Madison when I watched a YouTube video by chance. I'd cut the bottom end off of a disposable plastic water bottle and now I use it to collect water for my regular wide-mouth bottle.

I'd learned after my first night at Springer to collect water with the wide-mouth bottle and then pour it into the plastic bag with which I squeeze water through my filter. I squeeze the water into another bottle, or just suck it right from the filter. It's very quick and easy.

After eating, I read the shelter register. There are notebooks at each shelter in which hikers can comment on the weather, their hike or anything else. Most of the comments are mundane, but they're fun to read, nevertheless.

I've been enjoying the comments of an apparently exuberant woman who's about five days ahead of me and seems to write something about the day and/or her hike in just about every register. The messages, in her flowery handwriting, all contain the word "awesome" at least once, and often more than once, reminding me of my exuberant Madison running friend, Jess Mederson, who also liberally uses "awesome" when she talks or writes.

The awesome trail woman signs her notes "Leah (no trail name) NOBO," which stands for northbound. In the Muskrat Creek register, she's ended her note by writing: "Awesomness. Onward and upward," and, for extra emphasis, added a smiley face.

I'm surprised to see a note left on December 6 for Monica, and think it might be meant for the Monica I met at Springer.: "Hey Monica," the note says, "If you read this next spring, congratulations on your 1st state crossing -- from Buck + Stubb SOBO."

I figure that Buck and Stubb, like most southbound thru-hikers, left Katahdin in late May or early June, when it opens for climbing. They were among 334 other hikers who left Katahdin last year on planned thru-hikes, about 15 percent of the 2,250 who left Springer. Ninety-six reported finishing.

5

WHEN JEFFREY "BABY STEPS" JOHNSON took his nearly 8-year-old son on a short backpacking trip on the Appalachian Trail 17 years ago, he had no thoughts of them someday backpacking all of it together.

Baby Steps, 55, a doctor from the Boston suburb of Hingham, says he was just looking for something healthy to do with Chris when he and his wife, Susan, 54, took him on a two-night backpacking trip in the White Mountains in 1997 that included 4.6 miles on the AT. They didn't have to carry much because they ate and slept in bunkhouses, called huts, which are run by the Appalachian Mountain Club.

"It was a nice easy way to break Chris in to walking all day long. When we did that, there was no master plan of doing the whole trail," says Baby Steps, whom I meet a bit after talking with Chris shortly after leaving Muskrat Creek Shelter in the morning.

Chris, 24, who's heading south and has no trail name, says he and his dad started hiking the trail in sections after the hike, when he was a month shy of 8, and will finish at Springer in about 82 miles. He says he's studying for a doctorate in physics at the University of Massachusetts Lowell. We talk a little more and then he says he wants to keep hiking, and that I should talk more with his dad.

As I resume hiking, I think about Lowell, which Craig and I explored one April day in 1997 when he was 15 and had come with me to Boston when I ran the marathon and he ran the first ten miles with me. The day after the race, we took the train to Lowell to see Lowell National Historical Park, which tells the story of the abandoned textile mills in the city, which is known as the cradle of the American Industrial Revolution. We also saw Kerouac Park, a memorial to Jack Kerouac, who grew up in Lowell and wrote *On the Road*, the novel based on the adventures of him and his Beat Generation friends exploring America.

I read the book in high school and it influenced me, as it did many others, and sparked my desire to see the country and have adventures of my own. My parents weren't travelers or hikers like Chris and his dad, and the farthest I'd been from Green Bay by the time I graduated high school was Chicago, about 210 miles south.

But, after graduation, I quickly set out to change that. I bought a plane ticket to Zurich, Switzerland, and hitched and took trains around Europe. I then took six years to get my wildlife ecology degree from the UW because I'd take semesters off to see the United States and Mexico by biking, hitchhiking, flying and driving, sometimes with a driveaway car. I learned in *On the Road* that I could drive cars around the country for companies that charge people to get the cars delivered. Drivers got a tank of gas and 400 miles a day to deliver them.

After about half a mile of hiking and reminiscing, I meet Baby Steps, who says that since their first backpacking trip, he and Chris have hiked more of the trail every year and are now hiking the last 206.8 miles from Newfound Gap to Springer. I tell him that Chris seems to be in a hurry to get there.

"He's always in a hurry," says Baby Steps, adding that they usually hike apart, but meet for lunch and dinner.

He says Susan and their daughter, Holly, 21, were with them when they did another short hike on the AT in 1997, and one in 1998, which is when he started thinking about hiking the entire trail with Chris. In 1999, the two drove to Baxter State Park and climbed Katahdin, which is very steep and difficult, and he had to push Chris up to help him over the huge boulders on the trail.

"We thought that if we could do that, we could do the whole thing," Baby Steps says. "Upon coming home, we made a pact to do the whole trail."

They backpacked for a week or two each summer and twice hiked for about 10 days after Thanksgiving, when Chris had time off from college. Holly climbed Mount Greylock in Massachusetts with them, but, other than that, Holly and Susan didn't join them.

Baby Steps says he named himself because he takes small steps, especially downhill, to ease the stress on his knees, which have arthritis and cartilage issues from his many years of playing sports, including football and baseball at Dartmouth College in Hanover, New Hampshire, where the Appalachian Trail goes right through town.

Baby Steps and Chris (c.p.)

He took his first backpacking trip with an incoming group of freshmen at Dartmouth, played defensive end on the football team, and on the baseball team played catcher, which, he says, was probably the main cause of his knee problems. He says using hiking poles also lessens the impact on his knees.

He says his feet get sore in the first few days of each hike, so he has to break them in every year when he and Chris hit the trail, unlike most other section hikers, who have to break in their legs.

"The term trail legs would be less applicable for me," he says. "I have to get trail feet."

He says Chris doesn't have a trail name because he decided, after reading registers at shelters, that "you don't get a trail name unless someone gives it to you," and nobody has, which is the trail name philosophy I've adopted.

Baby Steps says they started increasing their mileage in 2001 because Chris was nearly 12, and that by the fall of 2008 they had hiked 999 miles during the summer and had finished Maine and New Hampshire, the two toughest states, as well as Vermont, Massachusetts, Connecticut, New York and 111 miles of Pennsylvania.

"We both enjoyed it," he says. "I thought it was going to be a good accomplishment to talk to people about."

In late 2008, they decided to try their first cold-weather hike because Chris had started college and had December off.

"I jumped at the opportunity to get Chris to squeeze in another section of the AT with me," says Baby Steps, "and he agreed."

Baby Steps says that hike resulted in his best tale from the trail. He says that on November 30 Susan and her sister Carol drove him and Chris from Hingham to Swatara Gap in Pennsylvania, where they had ended their southbound hike in July. The drive took six to seven hours and they arrived at the gap on Highway 72 about 3 p.m., with the sun to set at 4:40 on a cloudy day.

The two women headed home and he and Chris headed south, planning to spend the night at Rausch Gap Shelter, 6.1 miles away, but it turned out to be a much, much longer hike for Baby Steps.

He says that within a few minutes Chris was out of sight and that he soon found himself on a trail with white blazes similar to those on the AT, but larger with rounded corners. He quickly realized he was on the wrong trail, which he later learned was a hunting trail, turned around and was soon back on the AT, which was covered with a thin crusted layer of snow. He noticed footprints in the snow that appeared to be from a man's hiking boots and were headed in the opposite direction he was hiking. He figured they were from a hiker earlier in the day.

Baby Steps says he soon crossed a highway, as he expected, as the sun set and a light, steady snow began to fall. The trail had the elevation gain and turn he'd expected and, after what he figured was about six miles, he put his headlamp on and started looking carefully for signs to the shelter, which he knew was just off the trail.

"At what must have been around 7 p.m., I was relieved to arrive at a shelter. But it was empty. No Chris. I called out Chris' name, but there was no answer."

He learned it was the William Penn Shelter when he saw a sign or read the register and figured he'd missed the Rausch Gap Shelter and was at the next shelter southbound, not knowing that the William Penn Shelter was 7.3 miles north of Swatara Gap and that he'd been hiking in the wrong direction since he returned to the AT from the hunting trail.

He also hadn't realized that the footprints he saw were almost certainly from him or Chris and that the highway he'd crossed was the one from where he and Chris had started their hike. So, he turned around and headed what he thought was north to the shelter he thought he'd missed, and was now hiking south, as the light snow continued to fall.

"The snowflakes were now floating straight down steadily, slowly, and a little more heavily, and each flake reflected brightly when my headlamp beam struck them. It was beautiful." he says. "I was significantly slowed, not only by the darkness, but by the need to be looking left, then right, then left again to make sure I didn't miss a turnoff to the correct shelter and to make sure I saw each AT blaze."

He says his headlamp started dimming and he had to change the battery several times overnight. He was lucky, he says, that he had six to eight extra batteries for a hike that stretched on and on and on.

"I started to become somewhat concerned as I was now descending at a significant rate without seeing any sign of a shelter. I had no explanation other than that I must have missed a turnoff to the Rausch Gap Shelter due to the darkness and my inattention. But I had no other choice but to continue heading back, being careful to see everything around me on the way."

Eventually, he reached the highway where he had started, still thinking he had been heading north.

"On the other side of the road I found no AT blazes and certainly I wouldn't want to proceed on what I perceived to be the northbound direction on the AT, which we had already covered the previous summer, albeit in the opposite direction."

He rechecked his map and thought the climb, 90-degree turn at the top of a ridge and view of a town in the valley were what he'd expected, but didn't think to check the name of the first shelter south of the Rausch Gap Shelter. If he had, he would have seen it not only wasn't the William Penn

Shelter, but it was 18 miles south of the Rausch Gap Shelter, and realized his mistake.

Now, though, he wanted to call Chris to tell him what he thought had happened and that he was OK. He says didn't carry a cell phone because he thought they were of little use on the trail and not worth the weight. But Chris had one, so he decided to try to flag down a motorist to ask to use a phone. The little traffic, though, consisted mainly of big, fast-moving trucks in the next hour, or so.

"It was around 3 a.m.," he says, "when I finally got the attention of a car driver who was traveling slowly enough to respond to my waving of my hands over my head, while standing partially in the road."

He explained his predicament to the woman who stopped and she said he could use her phone.

"I think she trusted me to some degree because of the fact I was clearly still a clean-cut hiker, still wearing my backpack, she knew that the AT was nearby and I later learned that she saw the shine of the gold wedding band on my finger."

Then, though, he realized he didn't know Chris' number; so, he called his wife, who had stopped at an inn and was sleeping, to get it. He left a message, but she didn't listen to it before calling the strange number back, and was surprised to hear his voice. He told her the situation and got Chris' number, which he called and got no answer.

After that, Judy, the woman who had stopped and was on her way to work at a chicken processing plant, pointed to where he had left the trail on the north side of the highway and where it continued south a bit down the road, and he realized what had happened: "It suddenly dawned on me that I had somehow got turned around early in my hike." He says he hadn't recognized the William Penn Shelter because he and Chris hadn't stayed there in July. He thanked Judy and then kept heading south.

He says he was relieved when he finally saw a sign saying the Rausch Gap Shelter was ahead and hiked faster "out of concern that it was now opening day of hunting season in Pennsylvania and it would soon be dawn. I made sure to wear my bright orange hat, to lessen the probability that I'd be mistaken for a deer by a trigger-happy hunter on opening day. I could not have been happier when I reached the shelter about 7 a.m. and found Chris asleep."

He told Chris how his expected three-hour hike of about six miles had turned into a hike of about 22 miles and a 16-hour ordeal. Chris told him that he'd waited for about an hour after reaching the shelter before walking back about a mile to look for him. Then, he decided it'd be best to return to the shelter and wait.

"After all, we had already done 999 miles of the AT together since 1997, and, so far, I had not made any disastrous decisions or had any major injuries, so why worry? And he had no cell phone service. We decided to try to sleep for a few hours and then resume our hike."

Meanwhile, Susan had called the Pennsylvania State Police, who told her to call the ATC Mid-Atlantic Regional Office in Boiling Springs, Pennsylvania. She called the office and told the man who answered what had happened. He asked her how old her husband and son were and how long they'd been hiking the AT. After she told him, he said, "Don't worry about them. They'll be fine."

Baby Steps says that they backpacked for seven more days and ended up hiking 118 miles and finishing Pennsylvania. After they returned home, he and Susan called Judy to let her know he and Chris had made it home safely and get her address so they could send her a thank-you gift.

"She told Susan that she had trusted me that night because she saw that I was wearing a wedding ring and that what I told her that night was so strange and outlandish that no one intending to cause her harm would have made that story up."

The next year they also did a summer hike and a hike just after Thanksgiving in which they had to hike through snow drifts for several days, some as high as their knees. By the end of that hike, they'd finished 1,431 miles and were in southern Virginia.

In 2012, Chris graduated college and decided to hike 985 miles of the trail again from the Connecticut-New York border to Damascus, where he met his dad to hike 190 more miles to Hot Springs, North Carolina.

When I ask why Chris hiked much of the trail twice, Baby Steps says: "He just enjoyed backpacking and wanted to get in good shape."

Last summer, they planned to hike 164.1 miles from Hot Springs to Winding Stair Gap, which is where I'm heading tomorrow, but had to quit after 67.1 miles when Chris sprained his ankle badly. Luckily, he was just a mile from Newfound Gap and the highway that runs through the center of Great Smoky Mountains National Park.

Baby Steps hiked to the gap and left his pack, then returned to get Chris' pack, while Chris, using hiking poles for balance, hopped on one foot to the gap. Park volunteers gave them a ride of about 15 miles to a clinic in Gatlinburg, Tennessee, where X-rays found soft tissue swelling, but no fracture. Chris left with a cast boot and crutches and they headed home.

Now, with less than a week of hiking left until he and Chris reach Springer, he's "very happy and gratified that we're about to complete this epic journey, but a little sad that it won't be continuing." He says the hike has been a wonderful experience and that he has a great relationship with his son.

"It's really a strong bond and the hike is one of the best things we've done."

I tell him that my son, Craig, said pretty much the same thing after we'd biked about 3,000 miles together in the summer of 2001 on the TransAmerica Bicycle Trail from Astoria, Oregon, to Carbondale, Illinois, after his freshman year at the University of Chicago. He was about to board the train to Chicago to go back to school, while I was going to bike about 1,200 miles solo the rest of the route to Yorktown, Virginia.

Even though Craig often complained about how hard the biking was, especially the many long, steep mountain climbs, and thought twice of quitting early in the ride in Oregon, once when he could have taken the train home, and another time when he could have taken the bus, he said before boarding the train that it was the best trip he'd ever taken, which I was happy to hear.

I also tell him that he's lucky Chris is still hiking with him and that Craig, 32, usually prefers to hike alone, or with his friends, which I understand, even though I'd like to join him more often, or have him join me. I say that I took Craig on his first backpacking trip when he also was nearly 8.

We took four days to drive to Glacier National Park in northern Montana. I'd planned an easy three-day and two-night trip and thought we'd do day hikes after we finished. But I hadn't told Craig about the black bears and grizzlies in Glacier. He learned about them when he read the warning pamphlet at a park campground after we arrived and said: "I want to go home."

I said: "We don't have to go backpacking. If you don't want to go, we can just do day hikes." He said he wanted to call his mother, my former wife, and, after talking with her, he said he'd think about it. In the morning, he decided to go. As we hiked, he constantly rang his bear bells, even more when we saw a sign warning of grizzly activity on the trails to the south.

I say goodbye to Baby Steps and soon meet two other backpackers trying to hike the entire trail in sections. Mouser, 50, of Dayton, Ohio, and Bear, 53, of Bucks County, Pennsylvania, say that after their current trip they will have completed 1,000 miles, or nearly half the trail, since starting in 2008. They call themselves "framers" because they're still using heavy external frame packs, unlike the vast majority of backpackers, including me, who are using packs with internal frames.

"After not having hiked for 30 years," Bear says, "we were surprised how tough the trail had gotten."

They say it's harder to hike the AT in sections than to thru-hike because they have to make many more trips to the trail, like Chris and Baby Steps, and just as they're getting their trail legs after a few weeks of hiking, they have to return to work. But, Mouser says, "As section hikers we can choose to go down the tough grades."

I stop for the night at Carter Gap Shelter, where I meet Paul "Lone Wolf" Shanahan, 52, of Lopatcong, New Jersey, who's also hiking the entire trail in sections. He started in 2007 and is planning to finish this year. Now, he's hiking about 165 miles from Fontana Dam, North Carolina, to Springer, and in September he plans to hike the last 188.2 miles from outside Stratton, Maine, to Katahdin. I tell him that maybe I'll see him again then.

Meanwhile, I plan to hike about 16 miles to Winding Stair Gap and then hitch 11 miles to Franklin, North Carolina, for food and to spend the night.

In spots along the trail, I stop to take pictures of mounds of beautiful bluets, small four-lobed pale blue flowers with yellow centers, and of large clusters of shelf mushrooms, which have brown centers ringed by bright yellow, on the sides of trees. The woods are full of photogenic mushrooms and I think these are edible chicken of the woods, named because they taste like chicken. But I'm not sure enough to pick some and eat them, and I'd rather leave them so that other hikers can enjoy seeing them, regardless.

I also spot my first wild strawberries, pick one and enjoy the sweet taste. By the time I get to the gap, I'm drenched from about three hours of thunderstorms, but the rain has stopped, the sun is shining, and I feel great.

I get on the shoulder of Highway 64 and start hitchhiking. But, after about ten minutes, I decide to move to what I think is a better spot for cars to see me, and to stop. That's when I luckily see the "FRANKLIN - 11 MILES" sign, and realize I've been hitching in the wrong direction, even though, if I'd checked the guidebook, I'd have seen that Franklin is to the east. So, I almost made a mistake like Baby Step's and learn it's easy to do and that I need to be more careful.

I cross the highway, stick out my thumb and quickly get a ride from Georgeanna Morton. She says that she and Logan Seamon, whom she married May 3, are the new owners of Mountain Crossings store and hostel, which they bought from Winton Porter last fall.

Georgeanna says she and Logan, then her boyfriend, thru-hiked the AT in 2009 after they graduated from Appalachian State University in Boone, North Carolina. After returning home, they weren't sure what do next when Georgeanna happened to attend an outdoor trade show with her dad and ran into Winton. She told him about her and Logan's dilemma and he told her they could work at Mountain Crossings and that he had a place there for them and their dog to live. They took the job and their dilemma was solved.

I tell her that I arrived at Mountain Crossings around sunset to find it closed and then slept on the grass out back. I suggest that she put up a sign for late arrivals that says the hostel is open and hikers should pay in the morning. She says she was just having that sign made.

She also says that many couples break up on the trail and that she and Logan are a happy exception. When I ask if she has any good advice for me, she says: "If you think you want to quit, wait three days until you finally decide."

6

Georgeanna drops me off at Haven's Budget Inn, where the hiker rate is $40 for a room, or $15 for a bed in the Penny Pincher Hiker's Den, a hostel across the street that sleeps four. Pam, the manager, says there's one man in the den and I figure the man is Deacon, who told me he would stay at Haven's.

So, I say, "I'll pinch pennies."

"There's just one key," Pam says, "and the guy staying there has it, so go and knock on the door."

I knock, but nobody answers, so I return to the motel and ask Pam why there's just one key for a hostel with four beds. She shrugs and says Ron Haven, who owns the place, has the others.

Ron is known for helping hikers with discounted rates and for shuttling customers for free in March and April to and from the trail and around town for supplies. But it's not helpful and a lousy way to run a business to leave his manager one hostel key, I think, before sitting down to use the guest computer, while I wait for Ron or the guy staying in the hostel to return.

After about 15 minutes, I cross the street and knock on the hostel door again; this time there's an answer, but the voice isn't Deacon's.

"Who's there?" asks a guy in a voice that appears to be quite apprehensive. Then the door opens, and I recognize Aaron, whom I've talked with briefly on the trail a couple times.

"I'm glad to see you!" he says, adding that he's very leery of the men hanging around outside the single rooms in the same building. They remind me of the homeless men, often alcoholics, who hang out in the library and other spots in Downtown Madison.

I tell Aaron, who's in his late 30s and from rural northwest Wisconsin, that he has nothing to worry about, even though the men do look like drunken derelicts. I ask Aaron if I can buy him dinner, but he says he's already eaten. So I walk a couple blocks to a pizza place. There's a special on the larges, so I buy two vegetarians because hikers have prodigious appetites and I think Aaron might still be hungry.

But, surprisingly to us, we can't even polish off one large, so I put the rest in the fridge for tomorrow, when Aaron's leaving for Atlanta and a flight home after a short backpacking trip.

I'm thinking of heading back to the trail in the morning, but, when I wake up, I decide instead to go to the library and start writing about my hike. I've already got some good stories and think that if I don't start writing now, I might never do so. It'll be my first day of the trek with no hiking, what backpackers call zero days.

But first, I want to see a little more of Franklin, a city of about 4,000 that calls itself the "Gem Capital of the World" because it's in an area known for the mining of gems, such as rubies, sapphires, and garnets. More valuable to me than gems, though, are the big, thick chocolate brownies on special for 99 cents at a downtown bakery. I buy the five on display.

When I leave, I see Deacon, who says he's also staying at Haven's, but had opted for a private room. He says he's going to leave tomorrow, and that we can get a ride back to the trail together. Then I spend much of the day writing at the library and send my first story to friends and relatives. I figure that will get me responses and motivate me to keep interviewing people and keep writing.

In the evening, I walk a few blocks to a place I'd seen the night before when I got the pizza. It's Caffe Rel, a gourmet French restaurant. But if I hadn't checked it out last night when I bought the pizzas, I'd never have known about it because it shares a building with the Hot Spot gas station and convenience store.

And that's not all it shares. After a great dinner, I ask a waitress where the restrooms are. She points to a curtain and tells me they're behind it. I part the curtain and find a glass door leading to the restrooms in the Hot Spot. The men's room has a machine from which both the convenience store and restaurant customers can buy condoms. I bet it's the only gourmet restaurant in the world with such an option.

In the morning, Deacon and I eat an early breakfast at a greasy spoon, and then I return to the hostel to get my pack, and carry, for the first time on any of my backpacking trips, pizza and brownies. The brownies and leftover pizza are heavier than traditional backpacking food, of course, but tastier, too, and, I think, well worth carrying for a delicious lunch and dinner.

Then I meet Deacon at the motel's office, where Kathy Miller, who makes a living shuttling hikers to AT trailheads as far away as Springer, which is about 80 miles by road, picks us up for the ride back to the trail.

Kathy has about 400,000 miles on her 1987 Jeep Cherokee, but she says that she's had no problems with it, other than an occasional flat tire. I find that hard to believe, after asking her a few other questions and having trouble hearing her answers because the Jeep sorely needs a new muffler. But she at least gets us to the trail with no problem, and we're glad of that.

After she drops us off, I sit and take some notes, while Deacon heads up the 10.1-mile climb to Wayah Bald, which will be the highest summit on the trail so far at 5,342 feet.

Many of the mountaintops in the Southern Appalachians are called balds and have great views because they're covered mainly with native grasses and shrubs, such as rhododendrons, instead of the trees that would normally be expected at such elevations. Scientists aren't sure why the grassy balds developed but think it might have been due to grazing. Also, balds with shrubs often have poor drainage and highly acidic soil, which inhibits tree growth.

On the way to the top, I talk with a group of Baptist Auburn University students who have limited backpacking experience and are in the woods mainly to place a plastic bag full of Bibles in several shelters.

We don't talk about religion, but we do talk about Auburn's miraculous victories over Georgia and Alabama during the 2013 football season with last-minute touchdowns on a Hail Mary pass and a 109-yard return of a missed field goal. During those games, at least, Jesus must have been an Auburn fan.

After I reach the bald and enjoy the magnificent views, the sunny sky gets cloudy, it starts raining, and my shoes and socks are dripping wet by the time I hike another 4.8 miles to Cold Spring Shelter.

"You made it!" says Deacon, who's sharing the shelter with a guy hiking sections.

"Do you have a trail name?" I ask the section hiker. "Tom," he says. "Do you have a real name?" I ask. "Tom," he says again. "Funny," I say. "I don't have a trail name, either."

Tom, 40, an IT salesman from Atlanta, has some great bear stories, including one that causes Deacon to rethink his practice of not making the effort to hang his food bag from a tree branch at shelters without bear cables.

Last year, Tom says, he and five or six others were staying inside Low Gap Shelter, where Deacon and I had stayed our fourth night on the trail. The shelter has bear cables, but one guy left his food bag on the table in front of the shelter.

"I said, 'Do you mind hanging your food?'" Tom says. "He said, 'Aww, it's okay.'"

Then, Tom says, everyone fell asleep only to be awakened "by banging and all kinds of commotion."

"We thought a hiker's coming in late. All the headlamps came on and we saw a big bear sitting at the table tearing into the food bag. Everybody started freaking out. Everybody started throwing stuff at it and yelling. It grabbed the food bag and took off into the woods."

We all chuckle and then Deacon hangs his food bag and I grab mine to enjoy the pizza and brownies I had lugged up the mountain. I share some with Tom and Deacon, who had laughed at me for backpacking the heavy food but isn't laughing now.

"The brownies are like fudge," Tom says, "must be 500 calories."

The lingering smell of pizza and brownies apparently appeal to the mice, too, because they keep popping out from under the shelter. Tom keeps shining a light on them and they retreat, but then pop out again.

Finally, he's seen enough, and decides to set up his tent, even though it's still sprinkling. His Zpacks tent, like Deacon's tent, is extra light and extra expensive. It's also made of waterproof Cuben Fiber, so in the morning Tom just brushes off the rainwater before repacking it and it gains little weight. Pricey, but well worth it, I think.

Deacon doesn't feel like going out in the dark and the damp to set up his tent and settles in for the night in the shelter. When a mouse runs across his head, he yells and then covers his head with his quilt, but the mice keep scurrying over his legs. I sit at a table just outside the shelter reading and, by the time I crawl into my bag a few hours later, the mice have appeared to retire, too.

I stay up well after dark reading and writing with my headlamp most nights, while nearly all of the other hikers go to sleep just after sunset. I often wake up a few times during the night, anyway, and I'm always happy to see the sky lighten, and hear the birds begin singing, so that I can pack up and start hiking.

In the morning, I put on my wet socks and wet shoes and start walking under a sprinkling sky. I see for the first time on the trail patches of pink lady's slippers, terrestrial orchids with a pink flower that looks like a slipper, on top of a green stalk that's about a foot high.

After about three hours of hiking, I reach the observation tower at Wesser Bald. By then, the sky has cleared and the panoramic view of the mountains I've climbed, and am yet to climb, is impressive.

While I'm savoring the last of my spicy cheese bread and enjoying the view from the tower, Alex, 21, arrives. He says he was 14 when his father introduced him to backpacking. Last month, his father drove him to Springer after he graduated from Carnegie Mellon University in Pittsburgh, with a master's degree in civil engineering.

Alex says he left Springer on May 24, two days after me; but had taken no zero days, while I've taken one, so we've been hiking about the same pace. We hike together and talk for several miles, and Alex tells me he had hiked with Casey, 23, a Michigan ski instructor, and that he's the guy who had signed in at Amicalola Falls State Park with a pack that had a base weight of eight pounds, three pounds lighter than Deacon's. Alex says Casey, like Deacon, has a Cuben Fiber pack, but had to quit because of a knee injury.

I plan to spend the night at the Nantahala Outdoor Center, a whitewater rafting resort with a restaurant, bar, outing-goods store, and several bunkhouses for rafters and hikers. Alex stops at a shelter a mile before the center, where he plans to take a zero day tomorrow and then stay overnight.

After arriving at the center, I go to the general store and ask reservation clerk Brant Brantley for a bunk. When Brant learns I'm from Madison, he says he knows Jim Alexander there. I ask if he's the Jim Alexander who heads the state Judicial Commission, which investigates errant judges. I know Jim from my time as a reporter covering mainly the Wisconsin Supreme Court and Court of Appeals and federal court.

He says he knows Jim because Brant had helped set up a similar commission in Mississippi and had run it for 30 years before retiring at 56. Now, he's 60 and happily pursuing his love of whitewater paddling on the Nantahala River.

I'm the only person in any of the six-bed bunkhouses on Sunday night and have the clean showers and spacious kitchen all to myself. I eat dinner at the restaurant and fill up some more with nuts from the hiker box and the community orange juice in the fridge. Then, I fall asleep while being serenaded by a chorus of frogs just outside my window.

The frogs are still croaking before dawn when I awake early to begin my climb of 3,300 feet over nearly eight miles to 5,062-foot Cheoah Bald. The pink flower cups of blooming mountain laurel make the miles especially pretty, but I'm too early for either the huckleberries or blueberries (they look much the same), which are plentiful, but still small and green.

I have the trail all to myself, all the way to the top, where the vast view makes the climb well worth it. Just below the bald, I meet a couple who've been hiking part of the 115-mile Bartram Trail, which heads west from the AT. The trail follows part of the much longer route that naturalist William Bartram took from 1773 to 1776 in his exploration of much of what became the U.S. South.

It's late afternoon by the time I finish the 2.4-mile descent to Locust Grove Gap, where the guidebook says there's water at the end of a blue-blazed trail to the west. It's the last water listed until Brown Fork Shelter, 5.5 miles away and my destination for the night. So, I walk about a half mile round trip to get water, then rest in the grass for a bit before hiking up and out of the gap.

After what seems like a mile, I think the trail doesn't seem to have the ups and downs I see in the guidebook profile. I see no white blazes, but also remember no other trails but the AT, and the trail for water, leading out of the gap. And I'm absolutely positive I left the gap heading north.

So, I keep hiking, and keep climbing, even though the trail looks a little familiar in spots. Then, it looks exactly the same when I see the Bartram Trail again. I've climbed Cheoah Bald from both sides now, and I have no idea how I made the mistake, since I was well aware of where I should have left the gap.

Like Baby Steps, I've hiked in the wrong direction, but in my case, thankfully, it's only 2.3 miles and during the day. By the time I retrace my steps, it's getting late, and there's no way I can reach the shelter before dark; so, I make a half-mile round trip to get water again and then start quickly hiking the 1.9 miles to Stecoah Gap and a wayside along Highway 143, where I plan to spend the night. It's nearly dark when I reach the wayside, with two picnic tables and a sign that says, "No Camping."

I'm exhausted, so I ignore the sign. I put my tarp, pads and sleeping bag on the ground and quickly fall asleep. When I awake after a nap, I'm astounded by the lights blanketing the huge hillside across the highway.

Fireflies light up the hill, like cameras flashing throughout the crowd when the headliner first appears at a rock concert. And I have the stunning show all to myself. My mistake has led to a bright payoff.

I've seen something similar once before; it was in 2006 when I was near the shore of the Kickapoo River, a beautiful quiet-water canoeing stream in southwest Wisconsin, with Shari Perlman, my girlfriend then. We'd been amazed, like I am now, and I wish I was seeing them with her again.

Shari and I had a great time for 2 1/2 years traveling and running marathons and other races together. I was always happy to make the 289-mile drive from my Madison home to spend time with her in the Minneapolis suburb of Minnetonka.

But Shari likes cruises and nice hotels, while I like camping and hostels. She tried doing things my way because she also liked me, and we took camping trips to the Southwest and California our first year together. The next year we took a three-week trip to the Canadian Rockies, Yellowstone, the Grand Tetons, and the Badlands. We had lots of fun running trails and hiking, but Shari said she'd much rather be returning to an upscale lodge in Banff or Lake Louise, instead of what I thought were great Canadian national park campgrounds.

At the end of the trip, she said she'd spent her last night in a tent and had seen enough parks and waterfalls. We broke up, but that lasted only a week because we liked everything else about each other.

The next summer, though, I headed west alone to visit Craig, who was a legal intern for Earthjustice, a public-interest environmental law firm, in Bozeman, Montana. Craig and I ran a road race in Bozeman, and then I ran half marathons in Oregon and Montana, before returning to spend a few days with Shari. We broke up again then, but were about to get together a few months later, when she met a guy who liked her, and also liked doing things her way. And he was also willing to start running, so they could run together. Now they're married, and she and I talk and email each other once in a while, as friends.

So, I'm nostalgic and a little sad as I watch the fireflies, alone, this time. But I enjoy the show, anyway. When it ends, I eat a little, drink a little, and fall asleep again.

7

LYNNE "MARMIE" BEESON HIKED the entire Appalachian Trail over the last two years and now she's backpacking the first 500 miles of it again.

Marmie, 62, of Elberton, Georgia, is standing next to a table full of stuff and packing it up when I arrive at Brown Fork Gap Shelter after a steep 2.4-mile climb from the wayside where I'd spent the night.

Marmie's the first woman of my generation I've seen on the trail, so I'm intrigued and want to learn more about her. We talk a bit while she packs, but she's soon ready to leave and I want to get water from a spring near the shelter and eat a little breakfast. So, she says she'll stop for lunch at the next shelter, 6.1 miles away, and wait for me so that we can talk more there.

"There you are," Marmie says, when I arrive. When I ask how long she's been waiting, she says about 70 minutes. I didn't stay at the last shelter for more than half an hour and I hiked quickly after leaving, so I know she's in great shape and a faster hiker than me.

She says that she should have hiked the trail 40 years ago, but still thinks like she did when she was in her 20s, when she took time off from college to travel, including one long bike trip, and got a master's degree in environmental interpretation from Clemson.

"I had always wanted to hike the AT. I should have done it in college," she says. "The next thing you're married. Then you have kids. Then you have to get a real job."

I also think like I did when I was in my 20s and took time off from college to travel, including one long bike trip. And I'd wanted to thru-hike the AT since then, but instead got married, had a child and got a job. And I got my bachelor's degree in wildlife ecology from Wisconsin before doing environmental interpretation for three years as a seasonal ranger-naturalist in Everglades National Park in Florida, Bighorn Canyon National Recreation Area in Montana, and Assateague Island National Seashore, off the coast of Maryland and Virginia. I did things such as lead hikes and bike trips and give tram and campfire talks.

So, in many ways, Marmie reminds me of me.

She says her husband, Jim, gained 30 pounds when she was pregnant with her first child and kept gaining while she had six more. So, he doesn't hike with her and neither do her son, six daughters and eight of her nine grandchildren.

Her children are too busy with their jobs and families to hike, she says. Three of her daughters, she adds, "wouldn't be caught dead in the woods."

But she traveled and hiked all over the country as the head of the federal reservation fee program for national parks, monuments and forests. In fact, she's the first person I've met who seems to have been to as many places in the United States as I've been, and I've taken Craig to all 50 states and nearly all of the national parks and monuments. We talk about some of them.

Marmie says that she hiked the AT in two very long sections in 2012 and 2013. Backpackers call what she did each year a LASH, or long-ass section hike.

She started her hike after shoulder surgery, so Jim shuttled her camping gear through Georgia, North Carolina and Tennessee and met her at trailheads, while she carried a daypack. That's what hikers call slackpacking and some are happy to do it when they get the chance. Others think they're not backpacking the trail if they don't carry their loaded pack the entire way.

Marmie says she doesn't get hung up on labels and thinks it's great if people get out in the woods and hike, no matter how they do it. So, she's really happy that one of her granddaughters, whose trail name is Bandana Belle, likes to backpack and climbed Springer with her to celebrate her 8th birthday.

She says that her trail name is the name she chose for her grandchildren to call her. She took it from Marmee, the name of the unconventional and progressive mother in the novel "Little Women."

We talk more as we hike 5.5 miles to Fontana Village, when we both plan to stop for the night. She says she's going to hike 335 more miles to

Virginia's Grayson Highlands State Park, which is known for its wild ponies, to see the rhododendrons in bloom.

When I ask why she's hiking the same trail she'd hiked two years before, she says: "This trail gets in your blood. It's a very social trail."

Marmie and Jasper (c.p.)

Marmie says there are actually a surprising number of older women on the trail, and many, many more men and women in their 20s who aren't sure what to do with their lives. She says they often get nervous when they get near the finish because they have no idea what they'll do when they're done.

"The closer they get to Katahdin, the more stressed they get because they haven't figured out what to do yet."

I plan on getting a room for $59, the hiker's half-price rate at the fancy Fontana Lodge, while Marmie has mailed stuff to The Hike Inn, about 6 shuttle miles away, where she plans to stay. But The Hike Inn is full, so we both get a short shuttle to the lodge and stay there.

When I see my room, I'm impressed because it's quite cushy. The few times that I stay in a motel it's the cut-rate kind, such as Motel 6, except for road trips when I've taken my mother, who likes nice places, to see national parks.

I'm just getting settled when I'm surprised by the phone ringing. I answer and Deacon invites me to meet him and Marmie on the lodge patio for dinner. He says he met Marmie at the shelter where she was waiting for me, and then saw her in the lodge and learned I was there, too.

We enjoy talking and I'm glad to see pizza on the menu because the pizza I backpacked from Franklin tasted great for a few days, even though it got a bit soggy, and I've decided to make vegetarian pizza one of my backpacking staples. I order two larges, one to eat now and one to pack.

In the morning, Marmie has to wait to get her package delivered from The Hike Inn, while Deacon and I are going to take a shuttle back to the trail. I'm sure she'll catch up with me and I'm looking forward to hiking with her and learning more about her, if I can keep up with her when she catches me, and if she wants to hike with me.

Although I enjoy hiking alone and often prefer it because then I can hike at my own pace and stop when and where I want, I also enjoy companionship, and I think Marmie would be a great companion for a while.

But I say goodbye for now and leave with Deacon. Also on the shuttle are Patrick "Avatar" Vance, 45, of Atlanta, and his son Connor "Tic Tac" Vance, 10. Avatar says they started backpacking the trail together when Tic Tac was 7, just like Baby Steps and Chris, and have hiked nearly 110 miles, so far. This year, they're planning to double that with a hike through Great Smoky Mountains National Park from Fontana Village to Hot Springs.

When I ask Tic Tac what he likes best about backpacking, he says: "Reaching the shelter, so I can relax and stop walking." But he adds: "It's pretty fun to be in the woods when all you have is in your backpack."

Tic Tac, Avatar and Deacon head for the national park, while I stop to see the shelter fondly known as the "Fontana Hilton." It sleeps 20 near the shore of Fontana Lake, which was created when the Tennessee Valley

Authority in the early 1940s built Fontana Dam on the Little Tennessee River to provide electricity to the rural area and to Alcoa to produce aluminum. The TVA provides showers and flush toilets near the shelter for hikers.

Inside the shelter, I meet Chef John Wayne, 42, a character I've been reading about in shelter registers and laughing. I've been gaining ground on him since I started, and I've been hoping to meet him.

He's a big and amiable guy and is wearing a cowboy-type hat over his shoulder-length hair. He's carrying at his side the bayonet his father had in Vietnam and is wearing big, heavy, steel-toed boots he bought for $2 at a Goodwill store.

He's worked as a chef and has become known for his cooking on the trail. He says he's carried as much as 25 pounds of unconventional backpacking food, such as mushrooms, avocados, onions, cream cheese and hard-boiled eggs, and has a watermelon in his backpack now. He also has a ukulele, heavy camera gear and a six or seven pound two-person tent someone gave him to replace the even heavier four-person tent he started with. I tell him I don't even carry a tent and he says he's been thinking of ditching his.

Chef says he's in no hurry and tries to "enjoy the moment" and see everything interesting on and near the trail. So, it's no surprise that I caught him, even though he left Springer 18 days before me.

"I do want to do a thru-hike," he says, "but, realistically I won't make it."

He asks me my trail name and I say I don't have one. He suggests "Trail Runner." I say: "Thanks, but I think that's too common. Then, he suggests "Blaze Runner," a play on the name of the movie "Blade Runner." "That's pretty good," I say. "Maybe, I'll use it."

I leave while Chef is taking pictures of graffiti written on the shelter's walls and then stop for a while at the dam visitor center. By the time I walk across the dam to a remote road to the national park's southern entrance, Chef catches me and we take pictures of each other at the Great Smoky Mountains National Park sign.

Then, we walk together to the trail entrance, and, before we start hiking, Chef takes his tent and leaves it next to a car in the parking lot. He stops to take pictures of butterflies and I say it was nice meeting him and start the long, steep climb into the Smokies.

The park's name comes from the whitish-blue haze that slightly blurs the views and that is caused by natural hydrocarbons emitted by the vegetation interacting with ozone in the atmosphere. The park is the most visited U.S. national park and is world renowned for its remarkable biodiversity.

Forests cover 96 percent of the park, with much of that old growth. The park has 137 tree species and 155 shrub species, while 246 bird species have been seen there. The park also has 81 mammal species, including about 1,500 black bears, or about two per square mile. A sign at the entrance warns hikers that bears are active in the area and shouldn't be approached because they've attacked people.

I've paid $20 online for a thru-hiker permit that lets me spend seven nights in the Smokies, in which 70.5 miles of the AT follow the Tennessee and North Carolina border through the middle of the park. I've climbed about three miles of trail when a hiker heading south warns me of a bear about 50 yards ahead:

"There was a bear on the trail just over the ridge," says AT@70. He adds that he thinks he scared it away.

I enjoy seeing bears, but I've never seen one just in front of me on a trail. So, I decide this might be an ideal time to learn a little about AT@70. He says he had originally planned to thru-hike and wanted to be at Davenport Gap, at the north end of the park, on his 70th birthday on April 29, because his last name is Davenport. So, he started March 18 at Springer, but lasted only three days.

"I wasn't in quite as good a shape as I thought I was," he says. "I just got discouraged with it. I called my wife and said: 'Come and get me.' "

But he hasn't given up backpacking the AT and he's now trying to get 100 miles in before returning to his home in Augusta, Georgia. Before leaving, he tells me he saw the biggest rattlesnake he's ever seen on Rocky Top, a mountain about 14 miles ahead.

AT@70 heads south and I continue north on the alert for the bear. I don't see it, but I see plenty of big, fresh bear droppings on the trail. Hikers have marked the droppings with sticks – partly, I guess, so other hikers won't step in them and partly so they'll know there was a bear around recently. I also see a note held on the trail with rocks left by hikers two days ago warning of a bear on the trail just ahead.

But I've seen no bears by the time I arrive at Mollies Ridge Shelter, my home for the night, after hiking 9.9 miles and climbing 2,724 feet since I entered the park.

The shelter holds 12 and I plan to grab a space early because the park lets backpackers hiking for just a short time in the park reserve most of the spots. Thru-hikers get what's left on a first-come, first-served basis. Hikers are required to sleep in the park's shelters, if there's room, because of the bears. But, if there are more people than the shelter will hold, some thru-hikers will sleep outside of it.

Shortly after I arrive, a young couple show up and I hear them speaking with what sounds like a foreign accent.

"Where are you from?" I ask. "Indiana," the woman answers. Her companion asks me if fires are allowed. I say I'm not sure, but that the rules are on a board on the shelter wall. Then, I hear them speaking in a foreign language.

"What language is that?" I ask. "Pennsylvania Dutch," the woman answers. "We're Amish."

She says her name is Sarah and that she's 22, and that her boyfriend, Myron, is 26. She says that they're thru-hikers and most likely the only Amish on the trail.

"I'd heard about (the AT) a lot," Sarah says. She says they decided to try it "basically to try and find ourselves and get away from everyone."

Sarah says they took the train to Gainesville, as I did, and left from Springer on May 8, two weeks before me. But they had to take several days off to get skin problems diagnosed and treated.

Sarah says she might return to live with the Amish, but Myron says he's more likely to keep seeking adventure. After they finish the hike, he says, "We want to get a sailboat."

By the time we finish talking, Myron has a fire going and they plan to cook on it. But before they can, Chef John Wayne, who has also arrived, places his pot on it. When he realizes the couple are about to cook, he apologizes, but they say to go ahead.

Chef John Wayne

By the time everyone's eaten and it's gotten dark, there are only seven hikers and plenty of room for all. Then we spot headlamps in the distance and four college students out for a few days show up. They're a little nervous because, at dusk, they suddenly saw a bear right next to them, just off the trail. But they settle down and, in a little while, everyone but me is asleep.

I'm also the first one awake, as usual, and I quickly pack up and head deeper into the Smokies.

8

Patrick "Brother Bear" Sellers and Jill "Sunflower" Sellers quit their jobs and sold their house in Wichita, Kansas, so that they could thru-hike the Appalachian Trail.

Brother Bear, 29, and Sunflower, 27, say they're taking a zero day at Derrick Knob Shelter after hiking 12 miles yesterday from the shelter I left this morning. Brother Bear says he was a firefighter and Sunflower was a nurse when they watched a documentary on the trail in November 2012.

"She said, 'Let's do that,'" Brother Bear says. "I told her she was nuts." But he came around and they started planning for the hike. "You always think of things you want to do in life," he says. "We wanted to do it before we had children."

They decided to sell their house first because they don't plan to return to Wichita and don't want to make mortgage payments while hiking. But that took a year, which is why they left Springer May 4, instead of in March, which they would have preferred.

Brother Bear says he got his name because he's a nice guy, quite hairy, and was crawling on a log to get water from a stream when he almost fell in, which reminded Sunflower and another thru-hiker of a bear. Sunflower says her name is short for Sunflower Girl, which is what she calls herself because the Kansas state flower is the wild native sunflower.

Sunflower says that their first evening in the national park they were about 1-1/2 miles south of the shelter in which I spent last night when Brother Bear spotted a bear sitting on the side of a hill near the trail, about 50 yards away, with its back to them. When he blew a whistle, the bear turned to look, but didn't leave. Then, they clicked their hiking poles together several times and the bear ambled up the hill in the direction of the shelter. They clicked their poles, talked loudly and whistled the rest of the way to the shelter. I figure that it was likely the same bear that frightened the college students last night.

They say that earlier in their hike they were climbing a mountain and were startled when they heard lots of squealing and then saw a few chicks run away, while a ruffed grouse hen flapped its wings in the brush. The bird then flew around their heads while screaming and whining before landing, doing a circle and running away in the opposite direction of the chicks to distract them from the babies. Later, they saw other grouse with chicks that did the same thing.

Brother Bear says they hiked very slowly at first. They managed four miles on the first day and on the second Sunflower rolled her ankle when she stepped on a small root, but they still hiked 5.7.

"Our calves were sore for three weeks," he says.

He says, though, that they're determined to continue, unlike the five hikers they've met who had planned to thru-hike, but then decided to quit. One got a job offer, Brother Bear says, and the others got injured or just tired of the trail.

"We would love to make it," he says, "but we're not going to be depressed if we don't make it this year. We'll just return next year."

They might be returning from Alaska, where they're thinking of moving after the hike.

Before speaking with the couple, I drank lots of water from a spring near the shelter because I'd just hiked 12 miles in about six hours without water and I was very thirsty.

When I started hiking this morning, I took no water because the day was cloudy and cool and the guidebook showed a spring after 8.2 miles, just after the 1,320-foot climb to Rocky Top, where AT@70 had seen the huge rattlesnake. Other hikers had commented in the shelter register about the snake, as well as a copperhead in the same area. So, I was cautious on the summit, even though I figured the snakes wouldn't be on the rocks because there was no sun to warm them.

I was right about the snakes and had mixed feelings about not getting to see them, but my feelings weren't mixed about the views from the mountain. They were magnificent. I climbed a little higher to Thunderhead Mountain and then descended to the spring. I was thirsty after the long climb, and was looking forward to a drink.

The spring, though, was dry, which surprised me because the water sources so far have been reliable. I checked the guidebook and saw there was no more water until the shelter. I knew I could make it without water because the weather had stayed cloudy and cool, but I was still relieved when I arrived.

I say goodbye to the Sellers and start hiking the 5.5 miles to Silers Bald Shelter, where I plan to spend the night. On the way, I see a turkey sitting on the trail. When I approach, it rushes away with about a dozen squealing chicks that were sitting beneath it, which I've never seen before. The cloudy day turns rainy and I've got to climb nearly 700 feet to reach the shelter; so I'm a little wet and a little tired when I arrive.

Avatar and Tic Tac are there, along with three teenage boys who are out for a few days of adventure. Later, a father and his daughter, who had just finished college, arrive from the north. He's surprised that I've hiked so far in a day.

Like the previous shelters in the national park, there are no privies, just a shovel and a sign pointing to the "toilet area." In light of the crowded shelters in the Smokies, I figure that it might be hard to dig a hole and unearth only dirt, and, fortunately, I don't need to try.

In the middle of the night, I wake from a dream, in which I was yelling, "You idiot. You idiot." When I hear one of the boys say "What's going on?" I realize I must have been yelling in my sleep, to which I return.

The rain has stopped by morning, but the sky is still cloudy when I'm the first to leave again. I've decided to hike 12.5 miles to Newfound Gap, where Chris and Baby Steps stopped last year after Chris injured his ankle, and Highway 441 runs through the park.

I plan to hitchhike 15 miles to the tourist town of Gatlinburg, where I can buy food and spend Friday and Saturday night, when I figure the shelters will be more crowded with hikers out for the weekend. I also want to watch the Belmont on Saturday to see if California Chrome can win the Triple Crown.

After less than two miles of easy hiking, I reach Double Spring Gap Shelter, where I learn Deacon had spent the previous night, and meet Rick "Gobnu" ("growing old, but not up") DeMars, 62, who's been in the Navy, and Sandy "No Hurry" Demars, 64, who had worked for the Defense

Department. The couple, from Orange Park, Florida, say that they, like Brother Bear and Sunflower, had seen a documentary on the trail.

"Years and years ago I saw a PBS special on the AT and recorded it," Gobnu says. "It fascinated me. It became kind of a thing that someday I wanted to do that. It seemed kind of unreal."

But he says most of the couple's camping has been in RVs and they hadn't planned to sleep on the ground again. Nevertheless, the thought of hiking the trail stayed with them.

"We would talk about it for years, but it was usually after a bottle of wine or six-pack," Gobnu says. "And, by the next morning, we'd sober up."

One of those mornings, though, they decided to actually try it. Gobnu says they each ran about 22 miles a week and biked 100. So, they thought they were ready to tackle a thru-hike and started on April 23 with 50-pound packs. They averaged six miles a day for a few days and then shed about 10 pounds of gear from each pack.

"I thought I was in shape, before I hit the mountains," Gobnu says.

He adds that they took a week off the trail to travel to the town of Erie, Michigan, where South Erie Park was being named for Grace Connolly, No Hurry's 92-year-old mother. Now, he says, they'll be happy if they make it 1,064 miles to Pennsylvania, which is nearly halfway.

"One of the things we realized is to make it all the way in a season, you miss a lot," Gobnu says. "You don't really see the trail. All you see is the people ahead of you. We just decided to enjoy it. There are times we'll get to a vista, put out our tarp, and just enjoy the view."

"We figure we'll come back next year and finish it," says No Hurry, who adds that the first thing they'll do after returning home is take a cruise.

Gobnu says the two really enjoy getting to know the other hikers. "People," he says, "are the best part of the trail."

I agree and set out to meet more of them during the 8.8 miles to Newfound Gap. I meet plenty after climbing more than 1,100 feet to Clingmans Dome, the highest point on the AT at 6,643 feet. There's a road to a parking area near the dome and an observation tower on top; so, there are lots of people taking in the 360-degree view, which isn't great because of low-hanging clouds that part only occasionally to let us see a bit of the valleys below.

While I'm on the tower, the three teens who were in the shelter last night arrive and one tells me I scared him when I yelled during the night. He says he thought there must have been a bear in the shelter. I tell him about my dream and we all laugh about it.

I leave the crowd and resume hiking before stopping to see a remarkable ruffed grouse displaying for a gaggle of hens by puffing up black ruffs around its neck and flaring its tail. Seeing such a sight is another first for me. The hens seem annoyed by my presence, so I leave them to be courted in private.

Then, I stop at a spring to fill my water bottles. I'd lost the cap to one of them with a narrow neck a week ago, and yesterday had seen what I thought were a couple twigs at the bottom. So, I haven't been drinking to the bottom and decide to see if I can flush out the twigs. I fill up the bottle and dump the water out quickly. But what I thought were twigs aren't twigs at all. They're the legs of a drowned mouse. For the last day, I've been drinking dead-mouse flavored water.

When I reach Newfound Gap, I see a large parking lot full of cars and many people who have stopped for a view, or to hike a few steps, or even a few miles, on the Appalachian Trail. So, I figure it shouldn't be too hard to get a ride to Gatlinburg.

I find a good spot, just north of the lot, so that drivers leaving can see me when they stop before the highway, and drivers on the highway have room to pull over and stop. Many drivers leaving the lot look right at me, then drive by; finally, after about 15 minutes, a woman on the highway pulls over to pick me up, and tells me to sit in the front of her car.

"I smell," I warn her. "I smell, too," says Sonya "Rock Slide" Carius, explaining that she's just spent six days backpacking 57.3 miles of the AT in Georgia, and is going to stop to see her 12-year-old son at a scout camp, near Gatlinburg, before heading home to Columbus, Ohio.

Rock Slide, 41, says, she's "been on bits of the trail at different times" and became captivated by its beauty last year in Virginia. She then started reading many books about the AT and "caught the bug." Seeing the views and wildlife, along with "meeting people, most of whom are very cool," are a few of her favorite things about the trail.

She says I'm the first hitchhiker she's ever picked up, but, she figures I'm OK, since I'm a backpacker. We talk about the trail and about backpacking before we leave the Smokies and enter the anti-park of Gatlinburg, which is full of kitschy shops, museums and restaurants that serve the tourists who pack the sidewalks that stretch for about a mile.

Rock Slide drops me at the north end of town and I shop around for a motel room. At one ritzy motel, the young couple checking in do a double take when they see me.

"We just saw you at Newfound Gap," the woman says. "Howdya get here so fast?"

"I got a ride. Why didn't you pick me up?" I ask.

"We don't pick up hitchhikers," she says.

"Hitchhikers in the park are backpackers. They're safe," I say, hoping that maybe I've gotten a ride for the next backpacker they see in the Smokies.

Their motel is pretty pricey at more than $100 for a room, so I keep shopping before the clerk at the Howard Johnson's is nice enough to give me a great hiker deal – a room for two nights, including an all-you-can-eat continental breakfast, for $110. So, I check in and then leave to explore Gatlinburg.

I crave vegetables and ask a parking lot attendant if there's a place in town with a good salad bar. He recommends Shoney's, one of a chain of restaurants, many in the Southeast. I've never eaten at a Shoney's because I avoid chains and look for local places when I travel.

But I do check out this one and find that the attendant is absolutely right. The cheap all-you-can-eat buffet is full of a wide variety of vegetables, salad fixings and desserts for less than $8, or a little more than $11 with the addition of fish and meat.

I don't eat meat, but I often eat fish on Fridays in Wisconsin, where Friday fish dinners in restaurants and taverns are a popular tradition. It's Friday in Gatlinburg, so I decide to enjoy a taste of home and choose the pricier option; then sit down to enjoy my first all-you-can-eat meal of the trip, the top meal option of every thru-hiker, and the first time I really feel the urge to stuff myself, which is often the goal of my fellow backpackers. I eat until I can't eat another bite.

Rock Slide (c.p.)

During dinner, I enjoy another special treat – a daily newspaper. The *Knoxville News Sentinel* has a big front-page color picture of fireflies that looks just like the mass of fireflies on the North Carolina hillside that I marveled at alone. The fireflies in the paper's picture, captioned "LIGHT SHOW SPECTACULAR," were being enjoyed by about a thousand people in the Elkmont area of Great Smoky Mountains National Park.

The story says the beetles are synchronous fireflies, and are the only fireflies in America that can synchronize their greenish-yellow flashing light patterns. It says the show lasts for about two weeks and that the park started limiting spectators after large crowds became unmanageable. The park runs shuttles to the viewing area and last year people from 48 states saw the spectacular lights, which the fireflies flash to attract a mate. I feel pretty special knowing that I had a private showing.

Outside the restaurant, there are no fireflies, but lots of bright, colorful lights and a crowd of tourists unlike those I've seen in the many other tourist towns I've visited across the United States and Canada.

Many are smoking; many are stopping at the shops that offer free samples of moonshine; many are holding hands; many are holding hands with one hand and smoking with the other; many are out-of-shape and everyone's really friendly. Few of them look like the type of folks I see in national parks, so I assume that, unlike most tourists in towns near national parks, most of those in Gatlinburg are there to see Gatlinburg, not to spend much, if any, time in the Smokies.

They remind me of a crowd full of Tea Party members and supporters that I saw in 2011 at a rally with the keynote speaker being Sarah Palin, the Republican candidate for vice president in 2008, on the Capitol grounds in Madison. And my impression of the Gatlinburg crowd makes sense after I learn that Gatlinburg is known as the "Redneck Riviera." The hand-holding makes sense, too, after I also learn that Gatlinburg is known as the "Wedding Capital of the South."

The next morning I fill up again at the motel breakfast before seeing a little more of Gatlinburg and writing a little more about my hike. I stop at an outing-goods store to see if I can find a cap for my water bottle to keep mice out, but have no luck.

There's no grocery store nearby, so I stop at Walgreens to buy a bit more food for the trail. I figure I don't need much because I'm within two days hike of a hostel that sells food, and then another two days from Hot Springs. So, I get just a pound of almonds and a couple extra-large Hershey's chocolate bars with almonds. Then, I watch California Chrome fail in his bid for the Triple Crown and stuff myself at Shoney's again.

I get up early on Sunday, eat a big breakfast and then head back to the trail. I walk through town, and then start hitching back to Newfound Gap, as I walk back to the park. Soon, a van pulls over and James and Rhonda Strickland, of LaFayette, Georgia, offer me a ride to the trail. James, 51, says he'd love to hike the whole trail with his sons, 25 and 21. But he has a pacemaker and he's got to get his health under control first.

The Stricklands stop at the gap and give me a can of soda from their cooler before saying goodbye. I thank them and have hiked just a couple miles when I meet for the first time a volunteer working on the trail.

9

PETE BENTSEN, A RETIRED REGISTERED NURSE, says he's known as "Pete The Trail Maintainer" and that he's been volunteering to maintain a few miles of trail in the Smokies for three years.

Pete, 67, who lives in Oak Ridge, Tennessee, about 80 miles from Newfound Gap, says he usually spends about 10 hours a day, two days a week from April through November, working on the Appalachian Trail and two more 10- hour days each week working on the Cumberland Trail in eastern Tennessee.

Pete's the first volunteer trail maintainer I've met, but I expect to meet many more because the trail is maintained mainly by volunteers from 31 hiking clubs. About 6,000 volunteers work on the trail and many of them, like Pete, are each responsible for a mile, or two, or three.

Pete says he's clearing debris from water bars, which steer water from the trail during rain and keep it from eroding. He also clears vegetation from the 3.1 miles of trail he maintains and builds rock steps "carefully by hand," as well as teaches others how to build them. He pries rocks from the trail for the steps and also uses rocks nearby.

He says he has to be careful picking rocks because he can't use those with moss that might be home to rare scorpion spiders. Then he shows me what's left of a huge tree that was toppled by a hurricane in November 2012. He had to cut all of the branches between the tree trunk and trail by hand to make a tunnel for hikers to walk through until April, the only month when chain saws can be used in the park.

Pete is passionate about his goal "to keep the trail open so folks can hike, so people can get out and exercise."

But he says his time as a volunteer is nothing compared to that of Dick Katelle, 68, a volunteer who's spent 51 years working on a mile of trail between Pete's two sections of trail in the Smokies, and got an award for the first 50 years last year.

Pete The Trail Maintainer

While I'm talking with Pete, a backpacker stops briefly to talk with us, and then heads north with me. Scott, 36, says that he turned down a chance to move into management from his bartending job in southeast Florida because he's had his heart set on thru-hiking the trail since high school.

He says he worked into May, though, to make more money for the hike and left Springer on May 18. He plans to hike to Damascus, where his dad is going to pick him up for a family vacation, and then drive him to Katahdin, so that he can climb it and then hike south to Damascus and finish the trail.

Scott, 36, is the first thru-hiker I've met who's doing what's called a flip-flop hike, which 53 people reported completing in 2013. He's a photographer and is carrying eight pounds of camera equipment in his 40-pound pack, 20 pounds lighter than the 60 he started with. We hike together a mile, or so, to the short side trail to Charlies Bunion, a rock outcropping with what's supposed to be a great view.

Just then, a thru-hiker who'd been hiking with Scott stops briefly, and I tell him about the view. He says he's "on a roll" and keeps hiking, while Scott and I hike west to the outcropping and a view that's especially beautiful because the sun is shining and there's no haze.

Scott leaves, while I linger to enjoy the view. I figure I'll talk to him more later at the shelter. There are only a few day hikers on the rock, even though it's only four miles from the gap. But that doesn't surprise me because I've hiked and run many miles in national parks and monuments and have seen few people more than a mile from the road.

After I return to the AT, I haven't hiked far when I meet two more people working on trail maintenance. They're Michael Collins, 26, of Brevard, North Carolina, and Katie Oliver, 19, of Bahama, North Carolina.

Michael says they're working for the Smokies Wilderness Elite Appalachian Trail crew, one of six Appalachian Trail Conservancy crews with a paid staff and volunteers. The SWEAT crew concentrates on trail maintenance, while the other five focus on trail relocation and rehabilitation, as well as bridge and shelter construction.

The volunteers get free food and shelter, and learn about trail construction and maintenance. Michael, the assistant crew leader, says he really enjoys his paid job from May through August, and then spends much of the rest of the year traveling.

"I'm doing this because I love being outdoors working for the ATC in the Smokies and I believe in working for what you care about. I believe in the wilderness."

Katie, a college student studying exercise physiology, says she's volunteering for four weeks because the trail is important to her. "I enjoy backpacking, and it's nice hard work to give back to the trail."

The work sounds like something I'd like to volunteer to do someday, but, for now, I let Michael and Katie go back to work and I keep hiking. The trail through this part of the Smokies follows the top of a mountain ridge and there are many great views of Tennessee to the west and of North Carolina to the east, so I really enjoy the sunny day.

There's still plenty of light when I reach Tri-Corner Knob Shelter after 15.4 miles and about eight hours. That's a pretty good pace, considering all of the time I stopped to enjoy the views and talk to the volunteers. And I'm not at all tired. So, I figure a couple days of stuffing myself in Gatlinburg really paid off, and I plan to do the same in trail towns from now on.

There are several guys at the shelter, but I don't see Scott, who must have stopped at the shelter 5.2 miles back. I've got plenty of light, so I decide to do the stretches I do after running, and start chatting with Jeff Forman, 51, a doctor from Suffolk, Virginia. Jeff says he and his son, David, 16, take weekend trips on the trail and try to hike a longer section each year. This year, they're backpacking through the park.

Jeff says he started backpacking in 2010 after David became a Boy Scout and, when asked what he'd like to do as a Scout, said he wanted to go backpacking. So, the troop started doing weekend backpacking trips on the AT and Jeff helped lead them. After David said he'd like to take a longer trip, Jeff helped lead the Scouts in 2011 when they hiked about 100 miles of the AT through Shenandoah National Park in Virginia. He says his wife, Tricia, 54, and daughter, Maria, 21, have no interest in backpacking or camping of any kind.

Jeff tells me about a funny incident last night at Icewater Spring Shelter, three miles north of Newfound Gap, when Chef John Wayne tried to light a fire. I tell him I'd met Chef and hoped I might see him again because he's quite a character, but he apparently stopped at the same shelter Scott's probably at tonight.

Jeff says that there were about eight people at the shelter last night and that many of them had tried, but failed, to start a fire because the wood was too wet. Then a West Point junior, who had a red bottle of gasoline for his stove, asked Chef if he wanted to use some of it to start a fire.

He said, "Yea, sure, give me the gasoline."

Then, Jeff says, he wet some tissue paper with gas and threw it onto the embers.

"Nothing happened right away, so he blows on it and it flares up. Then it dies back down, so that plan didn't work. Then he pours the gasoline into the cup he eats out of and throws it onto the fire," Jeff says, as we both laugh. "He did that about four times and it kept flaring up and dying down. After the fourth time, gas splashed onto his boot and glove.

"It flares up and his boot and glove are on fire. He starts stomping his foot up and down, but doesn't see his glove. People yell, 'Your hand's on fire! Your hand's on fire!' He sees it and starts patting it on his hip. He didn't give up until the gasoline was gone."

Both of us kept laughing and, when I finally settle in for the night, I fall asleep thinking about the story and smiling.

In the morning, I haven't gone far when I'm caught by Max, 28, a German backpacker who also spent last night at Tri-Corner Knob Shelter. Max, the first foreign backpacker I've met, says he's from a town near Hanover and decided to thru-hike the trail after graduating from law school in Germany.

I tell him I've got a law degree from the University of Wisconsin, but had only practiced for about six months when I quit my job as a public-interest environmental lawyer because I decided I'd rather stay home to care for my newborn son. I say I liked the intellectual challenge of law school and learning new things every day, but found practicing law boring and tedious, and didn't like being cooped up in an office.

So, for six years I mainly took care of Craig, who now loves being a public-interest environmental lawyer, and I also delivered newspapers, officiated sporting events, and took courses at the UW for a master's degree in journalism. I then started working as a reporter at the *State Journal*, where I mainly covered courts. I tell him I liked writing about law because I could learn a lot about one topic, write about it, and then move on to another.

Max, like several other backpackers I've spoken with, says he learned about the trail from a documentary and decided to hike it solo because backpacking didn't appeal to his friends: "I have no friends that like this way of traveling. They like hotels for two or three weeks."

So, he flew into Atlanta on his first visit to the United States, left Springer on May 24, and hopes to finish by early October. He's enjoying his first time backpacking: "I like it. It's good to be out in nature and just hiking. It's pretty hard sometimes."

Max says one of his most memorable experiences was seeing a rattlesnake on the trail about five miles after leaving Springer: "I saw something, but didn't realize what it was. But then she rattled and I moved back."

Also memorable, but less exciting, he says, was his time in Gatlinburg: "I never visited a tourist town like Gatlinburg – all the attractions. It's a lot like a circus."

Like me, Max doesn't have a trail name: "It's not that important. It's about the trail, not the trail name."

We hike together and take a break after 7.7 miles at Cosby Knob Shelter, where a guy sitting at the table tells us to be ready to leave quickly because a helicopter is soon going to be delivering a new privy and then we won't be able to leave until the copter leaves. He says his name is David "Starchild" Koehler and that he's a ridge runner hired by the Appalachian Trail Conservancy to patrol a section of trail during the busiest part of the hiking season.

Starchild asks to see our park permits and I ask him why this shelter is getting a new privy to replace the old one, while the other shelters I've stayed at in the Smokies have no privy at all. He doesn't know.

Max leaves, while I stay to ask Starchild, 43, about his job and his life. He says he was living in Taghkanic, a small town in eastern New York and running his telecommunications business when he spent time on the trail in 2012 talking with thru-hikers to see if such a hike was right for him.

"I had never experienced anything like that in my life," he says, and I knew I needed to experience that." So, he decided to close his business because it was failing and he wanted "to seek a new direction in life."

He started seeking that direction by thru-hiking the trail from south to north last year. He says he started at Springer because he wanted to be part of the big hiker bubble.

"I needed that sense of community in my life and sense of acceptance, and I got that in overwhelming quantities," he says, adding that the hike changed his attitude toward life.

"I learned kind of a different philosophy – to take it one day at a time and don't look past your next resupply. Be flexible and the magic happens time and time again."

Starchild (photo: Maury Hall)

After he climbed Katahdin on September 1, he didn't want to return to a traditional lifestyle, Starchild says, so he got a job as a ski instructor at Ski Butternut, a Massachusetts ski resort next to the trail, and applied for the ridge-runner job, which runs from early June to early October. He spends five days a week on the trail in the park talking with hikers, clearing debris and cleaning shelter areas.

"Unfortunately, also cleaning up the privies," he says, "but it's not that bad."

I leave Starchild in time to beat the helicopter, which I soon hear and see. After hiking a couple miles, I also see Jeff and David, who say the copter couldn't find the shelter before it ran low on fuel; then refueled and had the same problem the second time.

They're headed 18.4 miles to Standing Bear Farm, a hostel just off the trail where they spent the night in a small cabin and then left their car before getting a shuttle to the south end of the park. I'm also planning to stay at the hostel, which they say is quite a place and shouldn't be missed.

The last five miles of the trail through the park descends about 3,000 feet and much of it is wide and fairly flat, so the Formans start running and I run just behind them. Now that I'm running, I think Blaze Runner, the trail name Chef suggested, might be appropriate.

About a mile before the park's northern boundary, we reach Davenport Gap Shelter and stop to take a look at the only shelter in the Smokies that still has a chain-link fence in front to keep bears out. I linger for a while to take a look, while David and Jeff keep hiking.

As I'm leaving, Nick Melton, a park wildlife technician arrives to check a camera that's focused on the shelter to see how often bears approach it. He says there's been a sow with cubs in the area. The park has left the shelter fenced, unlike others where the fences were removed, Nick says, because there are no suitable trees for bear cables.

It's still 3.5 miles to Standing Bear Farm, so I start hiking again and soon hear the roar of traffic on Interstate 40, quite a contrast from the trail, where the loudest sounds are usually the calls of various woodpeckers.

I walk under the interstate and then, about a mile before the hostel, I'm passed by Flutes, the thru-hiker who was "on a roll" and didn't stop to see Charlies Bunion two days ago. Flutes also spent the night at the shelter with me and is heading to the hostel.

When I arrive, I'm greeted by Rocket, the manager, who has a drink in his hand. Rocket tells me to put my pack in the nearby bunkhouse, where beds are $15 a night, and says he'll give me and Flutes, the only backpackers here, a tour of the place.

The old bunkhouse, which looks like it might have once been a horse barn, is dark, dingy and dreary and the mattresses look like they're nearly as old as the building. I ask Rocket, whose name fits because he seems lit up on liquor, if I can stay in a cabin, but he says they're saved for couples.

Rocket says the indoor shower is out of order, but there's lots of hot water for the one outdoors. There are no toilets, just one smelly overloaded outhouse, even though the couple who own the hostel live on the property in a house that I presume has indoor plumbing. There's also a washboard for hikers to wash their clothes in a sink before using an actual dryer. Rocket shows us the available food, which can be cooked in the outdoor kitchen. It includes frozen pizzas that sell for $10, which I consider exorbitant.

I conclude that the Formans are right when they say the hostel is quite a place, but I also think it's quite a rip-off and that the owners can get away with it because it's the only place near the trail to spend the night and buy food in the 108 miles from Fontana Village to Hot Springs.

So, I decide not to stay, even though I'm short of food, it's 5:30, I've already hiked a long day, and I've got to hike 7.1 miles, including a 4.4-mile climb of nearly 2,500 feet before descending to the next shelter. Probably not the best choice.

I get some water from a nearby stream and then start a climb that seems endless, with many false summits. Finally, after more than three hours, I reach the top of Snowbird Mountain at sunset. I take a few minutes to enjoy the great view and then start the descent to Groundhog Creek Shelter.

I try to hike fast in the twilight, but it soon gets dark, so I put on my headlamp and hike at night for the first time. When I reach the shelter, there are two hikers inside who seem to be sleeping.

But they hear me and look up. One is Max and he tells me where to get water. The other is "Just Tim," who's backpacked the entire AT in sections and is hiking from shelter to shelter for a few days to test his new knee replacements. He says he thinks the climb I just did is tough. I know it's the toughest I've done, so far. I get water, drink a lot and start to prepare dinner, while Max and Just Tim go back to sleep.

I'm very hungry and very tired because I've hiked 25.3 miles, the most I've hiked in a day on the trail.

10

ALEX HAWKINS AND ROBIN KING love to volunteer on the Appalachian Trail, love to hike the trail, and grew to love each other after meeting while working on the trail together. Alex tells me his love story when I meet him after a rainy night and dawn.

I'd left the shelter in Deep Gap early, after the rain stopped, and have hiked only about a mile when I see Alex, who left even earlier from his home, about a 40-minute drive away.

Alex says he's been maintaining the 2.9-mile section of trail from Deep Gap to Brown Gap for 22 years, the last 10 with help from his wife, Robin, whom he met in the fall of 2000, when they were both volunteering with the ATC's Rocky Top Trail Crew in Great Smoky Mountains National Park.

Alex, 67, who's retired from his job of evaluating timber, and Robin, 58, a nurse practitioner, are members of the Carolina Mountain Club, whose volunteers maintain the 103.4 miles of trail from Davenport Gap to Erwin, Tennessee, where I hope to be in about a week. I ask Alex about the trees and he tells me the predominant ones are red oak, chestnut oak, red maple, black cherry and poplar.

"I just love to be up here," he says, adding that he expects to work six to seven hours today, and that he works on his section four times a year, sometimes with Robin, to clear blowdowns, clean water bars, repaint blazes and cut back vegetation.

He says he and Robin also love to hike and have done lots of it in the 11 years they've been together. They married three years ago, after Robin's birthday.

"I said: 'What do you want for your birthday?' She said: 'Let's get married.' I said: 'OK.'"

Alex says Robin has backpacked much of the AT and that he had planned to thru-hike last year, but stopped after about 300 miles because he had "blisters on top of blisters" and had lost eight toenails, despite trying five different pairs of shoes.

I wish Alex good luck and haven't gone far when I meet Carolina Mountain Club volunteer Ann Hendrickson, 62, who wants to talk about Wisconsin politics, since she lived in Madison for 27 years before her marriage to Bill Otto, also a trail volunteer, brought her to Black Mountain, North Carolina, 12 years ago.

She asks me if I think the Democrats can beat Wisconsin Republican Gov. Scott Walker in November. I tell her that I think they've got a great candidate in Mary Burke, and that my nephew's wife is running Mary's campaign. I also tell her that she looks a lot like Mary and she agrees.

Ann, a research scientist with master's degrees in wildlife ecology and business, says she drives just over 3 hours round trip to work on her trail section every six weeks and also volunteers every Friday on a weekly crew and on a quarterly crew.

"We're big hikers," Ann says of herself and her husband. "We hike a lot, so we're giving back."

Today, she's brought her friend Mary Swain, 65, also of Black Mountain, to help her. Mary, who just started volunteering last month, enjoys the work. "I like it," she says. "It's challenging."

My day is also going to be challenging because I'm hoping to hike 26.2 miles, the length of a marathon, to Hot Springs, which is known for catering to hikers.

I could run the distance on the road in four hours, on a good day. But this day I've got to climb up and down three mountains and I'm low on food, so I know I might not make it. There's a shelter 3.2 miles before town, though, and I plan to stop there, if I run out of energy, or daylight.

Max Patch, the first mountain, is a bald, and the view is beautiful, as is the bald itself, which is blanketed with yellow flowers. I stop a couple miles past the bald and have lunch at a shelter, but all I've got to choose from are bread crumbs, salmon, almonds and dried blueberries. I eat the salmon and bread crumbs and save the blueberries and almonds for snacks and for dinner, in case I don't make Hot Springs by nightfall.

By late afternoon, I reach the top of Walnut Mountain, the second of the three, and think of stopping at the shelter just below. But it's crowded with members of an extended family who'd climbed the 13.1 miles from Hot Springs. I don't think I can make the town by dark, even though, after I climb Bluff Mountain, much of the last 10 miles is downhill. So, I aim for the shelter close to town.

That turns out to be a mistake, since I'm tired and nauseous much of the way, and occasionally stand with my backpack leaning against a tree and my eyes closed for a little rest.

I'm still about four miles from the shelter when a thunderstorm hits about sunset. I put on my headlamp, but it's still a little hard to follow the trail in the dark and the rain. Suddenly, I see a tent right next to the trail and apparently startle the guy inside, who yells, "Who's there?"

I say I'm headed to the shelter, which I figure is about an hour's hike away. By the time I get to the 0.2-mile side trail to the shelter, the rain has stopped, but it's still misty and I have trouble following the trail. So, I find a flat, grassy, soft patch of ground, put out my tarp, pad and bag, lie down and quickly fall asleep.

11

Elmer Hall is a man of few words, but he doesn't have to say much because his splendid Sunnybank Inn tells you much of what you need to know about him.

Elmer, who, at 77, is the same age as the Appalachian Trail, has run his inn in the trail town of Hot Springs for the benefit of backpackers for nearly half of his life.

The trail goes right through the town of about 600 and is easy to follow, with the AT symbol inscribed in diamonds on the sidewalk. Near the center of town, the trail passes Elmer's imposing inn, which stands out with its Victorian Italianate structure, and is a welcome site for hikers, like me, who have heard that the inn, built in the 1840s, is one of the finest places to stay on the trail.

I get there in mid-morning and plan to take a "nearo" day, what hikers call a day when they hike few miles. I see Deacon, Avatar and Tic-Tac, who have spent last night at the inn. Deacon plans to stay another night, while Avatar's waiting for his wife to pick up him and Tic-Tac and take them home to Atlanta. I ask the two what they thought about their 108-mile hike.

"It was good," Avatar says. "We had a good time. He loved it."

"I'm glad and sad at the same time," says Tic-Tac. "It's hard work, but I'll miss nature."

I go to the back door to check in and meet Jesse Garlick, who has left the trail to work for Elmer. He says the price has recently risen from $20 to $25 for the summer, and then shows me around the beautiful place before leading me to my single, second-floor room, one of seven bedrooms in the inn with curtains on the windows and quilts on the beds. The inn also has a music room with instruments for guests, a common room, two dining rooms, and a kitchen with pots hanging from the ceiling and a cast-iron stove, which Elmer uses to cook vegetarian meals for hungry hikers.

The place has lots of stained glass and shelves full of books nearly everywhere, including just about every book and professional video about the trail. There are also six porches, perfect for hanging wet clothes and equipment, and a beautiful yard with a garden and pecan trees. It's easy to understand why Jesse would decide to stay a while.

Elmer only cooks his $10 dinner if at least four people sign up, so I do so and then leave to explore the town. It's quiet on a Wednesday, but I imagine that changes on weekends, when visitors come to hike the trail, soak in hot mineral water and raft the French Broad River, which flows by the edge of town.

There are rafting businesses, an outing-goods store and a few bars and restaurants in town. There's also Hot Springs Resort and Spa, which pipes the hot underground mineral water to Jacuzzi-like tubs along the banks of the French Broad and Spring Creek. I check out the tubs and then cross the street to a convenience store with a bakery, where I buy fresh bread and thick brownies baked by Glenda Dolbeare, a massage therapist who's recently moved to town from New Hampshire. She says she really likes the outdoorsy town and so do I.

By then, it's about time for dinner, and I head back to the inn. There aren't four signed up, so I walk across the street to the Smoky Mountain Diner, where Deacon sees me and invites me to join him and two other thru-hikers who are staying at the inn. They're Josh "Underdog" Hall, 27, of Marlton, New Jersey, and Robert "Wolvereng" Eng, 30, of Spring Hill, Florida. I order a vegetarian pizza and then learn a little about Wolvereng and Underdog.

Wolvereng, who was a sales rep for Bausch + Lomb, says he'd always wanted to hike the trail and is doing it now because, "I was "killing myself in working every day and not getting anywhere."

In April, his mother bought him *A Walk in the Woods*, Bill Bryson's bestseller about backpacking part of the trail, which is being made into a movie with Robert Redford playing Bill. Two weeks later, without even reading the book, he quit his job, bought backpacking equipment and headed for Springer Mountain.

"It's the experience of a lifetime," he says.

Underdog, who started his hike with a 65-pound pack and three weeks' worth of food, says he quit his job as a sales rep for L.L. Bean to do the hike and has set up a Facebook page called "2200 Miles for Leukemia." He hopes to raise $20,000 for the Leukemia Research Foundation. He's got a story to tell about Chef John Wayne and another about an unnerving bear encounter in the Smokies.

He'd bought a can of olives and was looking forward to eating them at the Top of Georgia Hostel before he noticed they were gone. "Oops," said Chef, who had thought they were for anyone and had used them in a ramen noodle and mashed potato stew. "He shared the stew with me because he stole my olives," Underdog says. "Oh man, it was so good."

Underdog shows us the video he shot of the bear after he spotted it about 40 yards ahead of him on the trail. He says the bear also spotted him and entered the woods, only to emerge about 20 yards in front of him. He clicked his hiking poles together, but the bear didn't leave, so he turned around and ran, which is exactly what you're not supposed to do when confronted with a black bear. Nevertheless, he survived unscathed.

The pizza is great. I eat some, give each of the others a piece and save the rest for the trail. Then the waitress surprises us with apple cobbler, on the house, for dessert. It's delicious. I think this diner is great, as apparently do other hikers, many of whom sent thank-you cards with pictures of them at the top of Katahdin. I scan the cards, which are on a wall, to get some ideas for my picture, if I make it.

In the morning, I eat breakfast at the inn with Jesse and Elmer and learn a little more about Elmer. He got a degree in religious studies at Northwestern University, then spent time in the Peace Corps, where he was a high-school teacher in Singapore and made many Buddhist and Taoist friends who inspired him to live a simple life.

After returning from the Peace Corps, he went to graduate school at Duke in Durham, North Carolina, where he taught religion and was a university chaplain. In the early 1970s, he and some friends opened Somethyme, the state's first vegetarian restaurant, in Durham. By 1976, he had tired of working 70 hours a week and took a break to hike the AT.

He spent several days at Sunnybank during his hike, did most of the trail, and then returned to Hot Springs, where he worked as a farmer on a commune outside of town and also helped out at Sunnybank. In 1978, the owners offered to sell it to him for a song, if he'd keep it as a hiker haven. He happily agreed and has run the place since as a nonprofit for hikers and members of his Sunnybank Retreat Association.

Elmer has neither a computer nor a cell phone and doesn't allow people to use cell phones in the inn. I tell him that's not a problem for me because we've got the lack of a computer and cell phone in common, and that, like him, I don't eat meat and try to live a simple life.

In the association's spring newsletter, Elmer writes: "Living here on the outer margins of Mallville and Macworld, amidst snake handlers and vigilantes, we have continued to try and create a workable synthesis of good place, right work, and simple living. Inspired by the ancient hospitality traditions of Taoist and Zen mountain inns, we will continue to provide shelter, sustenance, and sanctuary to those who come our way."

But not to everyone who comes their way, I learn on Wednesday evening, after taking a zero day to write on computers at the library and an outing-goods store.

I'm sitting in the kitchen when a brassy woman walks in and asks if I'm Elmer. No, but I think he might be somewhere in the inn, I say. She brushes past me and goes inside to look. By the time she returns, Elmer's in the kitchen and she says that two of her group need a place to stay and two others just need a shower.

Elmer's says he's sorry, but that the place is full, even though I know it isn't. After she leaves, I ask him if he just didn't like her vibe. He didn't, he says, and adds that the place is going to be full during the weekend, when there's going to be a bluegrass festival in town.

That's why I'd been asked to move to a room with two beds, which I'm excited to do because there's a plaque on the door saying that Earl Shaffer slept in the room in 1948, when he became the first person to thru-hike the Appalachian Trail, to the disbelief of many, and slept there again in 1998 when he was 79 and became the oldest thru-hiker then, finishing two weeks before turning 80. That record stood until 2004, when Lee Barr finished his thru-hike at the age of 81.

Shaffer, who died in 2002, hiked the trail from Katahdin to Springer in 1965, when he became the first person to thru-hike in both directions. He wrote the book "Walking With Spring" about his first hike and "Ode to the

Appalachian Trail" about his third.

Since Shaffer's third hike, the Hostel at Laughing Heart Lodge has also opened for hikers in Hot Springs. That's where I'd met Mitch "Truck" Zinck when I first entered town. Truck, 20, of suburban Chicago, who's managing the hostel, says he had planned to thru-hike when he climbed Springer on March 11, but had fallen in love with the town, and had agreed to return in June and take the hostel job when the owners offered it to him at the end of March.

"It was an opportunity I wouldn't have again," he says. "I really liked hiking. I really liked this town."

But first, he wanted to hike farther north, which is why he was on 6,200-foot Roan Mountain, at about the 376-mile mark of the trail, in mid-April after a rainy day turned into a sleety evening and snowy night, and ice covered his tarp and sleeping bag, which was only supposed to keep him warm if the temperature stayed above freezing.

"I was up all night walking around," Truck says, "because I was afraid my feet would freeze."

He asks me to be sure to mention Rob Bird, a trail angel whom he credits for rescuing him in the morning when he was "dead on my feet." He called Rob, whom he'd met two days before, and Rob picked up him and another hiker at a road crossing and took them to a restaurant to warm up and fill up.

Truck says the night on Roan Mountain was the worst of his hike, but not the only one with sub-freezing temperatures. On the second night, he and 14 others endured a hard freeze at Gooch Gap. And it rained or snowed nearly every day of his hike through the Smokies.

He says he went into Gatlinburg to escape driving rain and awoke to find the road back to the park closed because the rain had turned into 6 to 8 inches of snow. Nevertheless, when the road opened in the afternoon, he returned to the trail and hiked through drifts that reached his knees.

"Snow isn't too bad because you can walk through it and you can brush it off," he says. "Slush is the worst because it gets into everything." Plenty of other early thru-hikers shared the snow and slush and 25 kept each other warm in Icewater Spring Shelter, which is meant for 12, three miles north of Newfound Gap.

"Why," I ask, "did you start so early?"

Hattie and Underdog

"You get itchy feet," he says. And he also wanted to finish in time to go to school in the fall and study to become an emergency medical technician. Now, he plans to work at the hostel until December, go to school in the spring and then return to where he left the trail in southern Virginia, after hiking about 670 miles, and do the rest next year.

I hope to do it all this year, so, after two days and two nights in hospitable Hot Springs, I get up early; eat a more than filling skillet breakfast, with eggs, cheese, potatoes, peppers, onions and mushrooms, at the Smoky Mountain Diner; and then start the 2,200-foot climb up Rich Mountain, with energy to spare.

12

IN 1996, WHEN HATTIE AND FRED Kinsley opened a store at what's become Hemlock Hollow Inn and Paint Creek Cafe, they knew the Appalachian Trail was nearby, but had never thought they'd be hosting hikers in a year.

Hattie, 73, says she and Fred, 74, were hoping to attract hunters, anglers and NASCAR fans heading to Bristol Motor Speedway in nearby Bristol, Tennessee.

Now she prefers backpackers over her other guests.

"I'd rather have hikers than regular people," Hattie says. "You guys don't complain."

Underdog and I speak with Hattie after spending the night in the comfy, rustic bunkhouse, complete with a microwave and refrigerator, that the couple and their son, Mark, 51, built a couple years after opening the place.

We'd arrived after dealing with a wet afternoon on the trail from Hot Springs. The morning, though, was warm and sunny, and I enjoyed hiking along the French Broad River and watching its rapids, before climbing to Lovers Leap Rock, with a beautiful view looking back at the river and the town.

Later in the morning, I stop to take pictures of patches of white Indian pipe on the forest floor. It has no chlorophyll and doesn't need sunlight to grow because it gets its nutrients from trees via fungi connected to the roots. Each plant has a single stem, about six inches high, with a nodding flower on the top.

By the early afternoon the sky grows very dark and a thunderstorm is just starting when I'm lucky enough to reach Spring Mountain Shelter, 11 miles from Hot Springs, in time to avoid the lightning and the downpour.

William "Professor" Smith, 70, of Knoxville, Tennessee, has arrived just before me. He'd also spent the night at Elmer's Sunnybank Inn and says he's backpacking the trail in sections. Last year, he hiked nearly 240 miles from Springer to the Pigeon River, 44 miles south of Hot Springs. Now, he's planning to hike about 228 miles to Damascus.

Professor, who teaches history at a community college in Knoxville, says he's doing the hike for his health, for the challenge and "because I'm crazy."

He did a day hike on the trail with friends in December 2012 and "just got the bug."

"I said, 'You know what: I'm going to hike the AT.' "

While he hikes, Bunny, 69, his non-hiking wife of 50 years and the mother of their three children, waits and worries at home.

"She said she misses me," Professor says. "She worries about me."

He and I are at least safe and dry now, while the storm rages around us. But Underdog isn't and he's drenched when he reaches the shelter, about half an hour after the rain started.

When it finally stops in the late afternoon, I point out that it's only 5.3 miles to Log Cabin Drive and then another 0.7 mile to the inn and cafe, which sound pretty nice in the guidebook. There are cabins for three for $50, beds in the bunkhouse for $20, a store, and a free ride back to the trail.

Professor, though, says he's going to stay at the shelter. Underdog says he'd come with me, but he doesn't want to spend the $20. I tell him I'll treat him and be both a thru-hiker and a trail angel. After all, I've learned that he's a Packers fan, like me, which is to be expected, since I grew up in Green Bay.

I also tell him the season tickets that my parents had since Lambeau Field, then called City Stadium, opened in 1957 are in my name now, and I'll take him to a game sometime. I add that I delivered the newspaper of legendary Packers Coach Vince Lombardi, sold programs at the famous Ice Bowl in 1967, and still have bunting from the press box that I grabbed after watching the Packers win that dramatic NFL Championship Game.

So, I think he's suitably impressed, and he decides to go to the inn, too. He leaves before me, and I tell him I'll meet him there.

The rain has stopped, but there are still puddles on the trail, so I try to walk on the edge of it and avoid them. I'm walking along a deep ravine on my left, when I walk on the left edge of the trail, which suddenly gives way, nearly tossing me into the ravine. I grab some bushes to stay just off the trail and manage to survive with no injuries, just a muddy rain jacket.

After a few hours, I reach the inn about 7:30 and find Underdog, who got his trail name because his friends don't think he'll make it to Maine, sitting on the steps outside. He says the door is locked and nobody's there, even though the red "OPEN" sign is lit up. He's been there about half an hour. We knock again and then also knock at a house next door, but only hear dogs barking.

We wait another 20 minutes and then I tell Underdog about my experience on the second night of the trip, when I arrived at Mountain Crossings around sunset and found the place closed; then slept outside and learned from Deacon in the morning that the hostel had been open.

I say the bunkhouse might also be open here and suggest we explore the place and find out. That turns out to be a good idea when we find an unlocked bunkhouse and a building with showers and toilets nearby. We decide to stay and pay in the morning. I go to take a shower, but find, to my chagrin, that there's no water.

There is, though, picturesque Paint Creek just outside our door, so we get water to drink there. Underdog then lies on a bed and reads "The Republic" by Plato, quite likely the only hiker on the trail with that title in a backpack. I heat a couple slices of pizza in the microwave.

Then we hear a motorized cart outside and an older woman opens the door. She's Hattie and I tell her that we found the bunkhouse open and figured we'd pay in the morning. She says she'd been in town, that lightning last night had knocked out the water pump, and that we'd have to get water from the creek. I say we already did and we agree to meet her at the store at 7:30 and pay.

In the morning, she tells us that she and Fred had just sat down for dinner when they saw a blue-white light, heard a snap, crackle and boom, and then discovered that they had no water. A lightning bolt had knocked out their water pump, which is 550 feet underground, and it won't be back in operation for at least a few days.

Otherwise, she says, the cafe would be open and she would have cooked anything on her tempting menu, including her Friday special of fresh salmon, for supper last night and also cooked breakfast this morning. That's sure disappointing, but at least she's got energy bars and other food for sale in the store.

Hattie, who has ancestors who came to America on the Mayflower, says the store is the first building she and Fred built after buying the land and a house, and moving in 1995 from Florida, where Fred worked for Tampa Electric. They built their first cabin in 1997, which is when hikers started arriving after learning about their place in a popular trail guide, which was written by Dan "Wingfoot' Bruce, who thru-hiked the trail seven times.

"Wingfoot called me and asked me about becoming a hostel," Hattie says. "I told him the only hostels I knew about were in Europe. He asked if I knew about the Appalachian Trail."

She told him that she not only knew about it, but had grown up near it in New Jersey, and had started hiking it there with a great-great uncle when she was 8. He gave her the trail name "Sparrow" because he thought she sounded like one when she was learning to whistle.

By the time she was 21, she'd hiked the trail through New Jersey, New York, Massachusetts, Vermont, and Pennsylvania, which she says, hikers called "Rocksylvania" then, just as they do now, because of the very rocky trail in the state. Back then there were no hostels, and she stayed in churches, farms, and the backs of stores, then did chores in the morning for coffee and food. She says her best backpacking advice is "never carry more than 27 pounds. "

Wingfoot gave her the names of other hostel owners, including Sunnybank Inn owner Elmer, to contact for advice about opening one. After that, she and Fred kept building, adding cabins, the bunkhouse, a bathhouse, a pavilion, and the cafe.

Hattie says she and Fred have really enjoyed running the place and meeting the hikers, but that it's now for sale.

"It's great, but now that we're older, we want to retire."

Underdog and I tell Hattie, we really enjoyed talking with her, and then she calls her son to give us a ride back to the trail. As we're leaving, she introduces us to AT, her friendly Siberian husky that a backpacker left when it was a puppy nine years ago.

Mark drops us off at the trail and, just like yesterday, we start the day with a climb – this time nearly 2,400 feet, over 4.6 miles, up Camp Creek Bald.

13

WHEN ROBERT "SNAPPER" SAGEBIEL passes me around noon, he's hiking quickly with what looks like a daypack, so I assume he's out for a speedy day hike. But I'm way wrong. He's out for a speedy thru-hike and plans to finish in less than three months. That's very, very fast.

It's less than half the six months it takes an average thru-hiker to finish and at least two months less than the five months I expect to take. And I think I've been hiking quite quickly. I tell Snapper I'm a reporter and would like to talk with him about his hike, so he slows down a bit and I speed up a lot so I can learn a little about his trip.

Snapper, 31, says he grew up in Hamburg, Germany, but is living in Montreal, where he's an aeronautical engineer and manages engineering projects for P3 Voith. When he finishes a project, he asks for extended leave to pursue his passion of long-distance backpacking. This time, he asked for June, July and August off, so he'd have the best weather for hiking the AT.

He left Springer on May 31, nine days after me, and hopes to climb Katahdin around his birthday on August 18, about two months before I hope to finish. To do that, he'll have to average 27.3 miles each day overall. That's more than a marathon a day, if he takes no zero days. And from here, he'll have to average 29 miles a day because he's off to what, for him, is a bit of a slow start.

As fast as he is, though, he still won't come close to the record for an unsupported hike, when hikers carry their own equipment and supplies and have no support crew. The record of 58 days, nine hours and 38 minutes was set in 2013 by Matt Kirk, who was then a 32-year-old teacher from Brevard, North Carolina. He started at Katahdin and averaged 37.7 miles a day in reaching Springer on August 7.

Jennifer Pharr Davis, of Asheville, North Carolina, set the record for a supported hike in 2011 when she averaged 46.8 miles a day in hiking from Katahdin to Springer in 46 days, 11 hours and 20 minutes, finishing on July 31. Her husband, Brew Davis, provided most of her support and, in addition to plenty of encouragement, supplied her with food, drink and a place to rest and sleep when she needed one.

Jennifer wrote *Called Again* about her record hike and *Becoming Odyssa* about her first AT thru-hike in 2005, after she graduated from college. She's the hiker who influenced my decision not to carry cooking equipment on the trail. In *Becoming Odyssa*, she writes that she decided she didn't like cooking and then saved weight by mailing her stove and pot home.

Like Jennifer, Snapper is a very experienced hiker, having backpacked many trails around the world, including the Pacific Crest Trail in 2012, which he plans to do again. That's where he got his trail name after one of his hiking poles snapped early in the hike.

That won't happen on the AT because, unlike nearly every other thru-hiker, Snapper isn't using poles. One of the advantages, he says, is that he can forgo rain gear and carry only an ultralight umbrella, so he doesn't get wet, or sweaty, when it rains.

His 14-ounce pack was made in Logan, Utah, by Ultralight Adventure Equipment. His pack's base weight is 10 pounds, a pound less than Deacon's pack and 10 pounds less than mine. He carries a lightweight alcohol stove and about three pounds of food, at most.

He carried no stove on the PCT, where he ate a lot of instant mashed potatoes, rice and couscous. He puts a staple in water in the morning and it's ready to eat for dinner. He says boiling water isn't necessary, it just speeds the "cooking." He also feasted on convenience-store burritos after they were heated in the mountain sun.

Like me, Snapper likes to run long distances and road races, so I ask him how a hike of many months affects his running. He says he has more endurance, but less speed. So, if it works the same for me, I think I'll take advantage of the extra endurance and look for a marathon to run after I finish.

We talk a little more after stopping for lunch at Jerry Cabin Shelter, where Underdog catches us. Chef John Wayne becomes part of the conversation and Snapper says he also has a Chef story. He saw Chef accidentally spray his face and chest with pepper spray when he put his pack down, which sounds reminiscent of when he set his boot and glove on fire.

Snapper (photo: Maury Hall)

Snapper has strong opinions about other hikers and he's not a fan of crowded trails, and of "slackers, party people" and those who depend on support from trail angels.

"It's come to the point that people rely on trail angels, which is pathetic," he says.

In that case, I tell him that he'll probably like "Leah (no trail name)," who's been about five days ahead of me since Springer. She's become one of my favorite thru-hikers because of her witty, enthusiastic messages in trail registers in which just about everything is still "awesome." She's hiking alone and seems to be in her 20s and quite independent.

That's when Snapper tells me about "pink-blazing," which is trying to catch a woman on the trail, not to be confused with "blue-blazing," which is taking shortcuts on blue-blazed trails, or "yellow-blazing," bypassing a section of trail with a ride. Snapper's going to stick to following the white blazes and, when he leaves, I don't expect to see him again.

I do expect to see Underdog, who leaves the shelter after me, at Flint Mountain Shelter, which is 5.9 miles of fairly easy hiking ahead. When I stop for the night, there's still plenty of light. So, I think Underdog will spend the night at the shelter, too. But, neither he, nor any other hiker arrives, so I have the place to myself.

As usual, I check the shelter register for interesting and/or amusing tidbits and find a message left this morning by Deacon in which he appears to crave company on a trail with few hikers these days. He wrote: "Deacon stopped for early morning snack. Been all alone for 3 days now. Gotta keep going."

A message left by a hiker named Elusive on April 7 makes me feel better about the couple times that I've had to double back after accidentally taking a blue-blazed trail and the time I hiked 2.3 miles in the wrong direction on the AT. Elusive wrote: "Hiked 4 miles past Flint MTN when I realized I left my food bag on the bear cables. So, I came back. 8 extra miles. I probably won't make that mistake again."

I put my food bag on the cables and note that there are instructions on how to use them attached to the trees to which the cables are hooked. That's also been the case at some other shelters in North Carolina, which has made me feel a bit less stupid about not knowing how to use them at Springer on my first night on the trail.

14

A MISSTEP ON THE APPALACHIAN TRAIL can send a hiker plunging into a deep ravine with a very steep and difficult climb back to the top, even if the hiker survives in good enough shape to make the climb. Botanists Caitlin Elam and Brenda Wichmann climb into and out of such ravines many times every day.

The two are resting near their campfire at Bald Mountain Shelter when I arrive, very thirsty after a strenuous 18.9-mile day with lots of climbs and descents, and little water. They direct me to a nearby spring, where I drink lots of cool water and then return to the shelter and get to know the women.

Caitlin, 33, and Brenda, 37, say they're working for NatureServe, a scientific conservation organization that's surveying plant communities along the entire trail for the National Park Service. The NPS has had the communities mapped by plane and has asked NatureServe to assess the accuracy of the results along a corridor that averages about 160 yards wide.

The women are randomly given spots along the trail at which they describe the plant communities. Their results are then compared to the results reached from the air. They say they spend entire days going up and down slopes, often full of brush, with a 35 percent to 40 percent grade. I ask how they do it.

"We just walk or crawl," Caitlin says. "It's really hard, but it's really fun."

She says they'll work from June to September or October and cover about 475 miles of trail from just north of Hot Springs to the middle of Virginia. There are three other teams covering the other 1,700 miles.

I ask them if they saw the small patch of red Indian paintbrush, a wildflower that I've mainly seen on western mountains, on beautiful Big Bald, which is covered with daisy-like yellow ragwort and offers magnificent views in all directions from 5,516 feet. They say they did and were excited to see it.

The views and the women are highlights of a day, in which I also enjoy meeting Bob and Cathy van der Meer, who devised a flip-flop hike to avoid most of the hiker bubble and still have plenty of time to hike the entire trail in good weather.

Bob, 63, and Cathy, 48, drove their truck from their home in Hayesville, North Carolina, to Boiling Springs, a small town about 25 miles north of the trail's midpoint. They left the truck at a bed and breakfast and started backpacking south on the trail, which goes through Boiling Springs. When they reach Springer, they plan to head to Katahdin and then hike south to where they started.

"It seems like a good way to manage the weather, bugs and time," Bob says. "There's no pressure to get to Katahdin."

When I ask whether a finish in Boiling Springs will be anti-climactic, Bob says, "Yes, but I'm kind of contrary, anyway."

The couple decided to do the hike after Bob, a former doctor who had recently retired from his job as a risk and claims manager for Kaiser Permanente, started watching YouTube camping and hiking videos. After seeing videos of Appalachian Trail hikers, he told Cathy about them, and the two decided to attend a three-part seminar on the trail at an outing-goods store.

At the first seminar, they were called "dreamers" when they said they were thinking of thru-hiking the trail in 2015. In February, they decided to do it in 2014, instead.

Cathy says she quit her job as a saleswoman for an electrical distributor, and then she and Bob started planning and buying equipment. She takes off her cap to show me hair that she had colored blue and purple just before her last day on the job. She says she knew it would irritate her boss. "I knew he wouldn't like it. I did it because I wanted to."

When I hear that, I'm not surprised to learn the two are members of the Hash House Harriers, an international running and drinking club with groups around the world.

In Madison, hashers run together every Saturday, sometimes in outlandish dress, on varied and interesting routes of about five miles, often on trails. Every run includes stops on the route to drink beer from coolers stashed nearby, and a party with food, more beer and bawdy songs at the end. I've run with them several times, but not regularly, because there's too much drinking and not enough running for me, even though the food is always good. The Madison hashers also sponsor two annual road races, which I usually run.

I'm also not surprised that the hike has enhanced the couple's relationship, even though I've been told that it does the opposite for many couples. "We had a good relationship coming in," Bob says, "and it's just been great the whole time."

Other than Bob and Cathy, I meet only two other hikers all day, and I'm very lucky to meet them. I'd passed up a spring because it was 0.3 mile off the trail and was running low on water when I meet two day hikers on the short blue-blazed trail leading to a nice view at High Rock. The young men had accidentally left the AT and ask me where they are. I tell them and offer them Clif Bars for water. They say that they have more than enough to share and that I should keep the bars.

I'm very glad to have the water because the three springs in the next 9.5 miles to Bald Mountain Shelter are dry. That's why I'm so thirsty when I meet Caitlin and Brenda. I probably should start carrying more water, but I've managed to survive, so far, and I really don't want to carry the extra weight.

15

Thru-hikers Molly "Stick Ninja" Carlson and Catharine "Pixel" Kosinski headed north on the Appalachian Trail from Erwin, Tennessee. Then, after 3.5 miles, they turned around and headed back. They've had enough backpacking, since starting April 1, and are heading home.

The women are sitting at a picnic table at Uncle Johnny's Nolichucky Hostel when I arrive in the early evening, after hiking 16.4 miles, mostly downhill, from Bald Mountain Shelter. Deacon, who's taken a zero day in Erwin, is also at the table and the first thing I do is ask him to show me where to get water because, once again, I haven't carried enough.

After drinking, I return to the table, where Deacon, tells me I should talk to the women because they've just quit the trail. I've heard tales of thru-hikers who have quit, but these are the first I've met, and they're happy to tell me their story.

Stick Ninja, 27, of Reidsville, North Carolina, and her girlfriend, Pixel, 23, of Kinston, North Carolina, have been taking lots of time to enjoy the trail, hiking 341.5 miles since leaving Springer. But they aren't enjoying it anymore.

"We just sat down. I said, 'I just don't want to walk anymore,'" Pixel says of their decision to quit. "When it's not fun anymore, then we shouldn't be doing it. It's still fun, but it will be more fun to do small portions. I want to drive places, so it takes 30 minutes, instead of three days."

Stick Ninja says much the same: "I'm tired of walking. I'm tired of nature. I just think that it would be more fun, if we could do it in small sections." She also says that she misses cable TV and air conditioning.

When they left Erwin, they were carrying food for five days. Pixel's pack weighed 38 1/2 pounds and Stick Ninja's weighed 35. That's much less than they carried at the start, when Pixel's pack weighed 53 1/2 pounds and Stick Ninja's weighed 46.

However, the packs were still quite heavy and, realistically, the women were hiking much too slowly to make it to Katahdin by mid-October, anyway. But they didn't care. In fact, Pixel says, they had planned for that possibility from the start, having their picture taken at Springer looking really excited, as if they had just finished a southbound thru-hike.

"Our plan was to really take our time to explore," Pixel says. "Get to know people. Not just rush into it."

For example, one day they hiked only two miles before reaching Wayah Bald, which has spectacular views at the trail's 119.9-mile mark in North Carolina. Then, after drinking some moonshine, they decided to stay the day.

The women say that early in their hike they met many other backpackers who planned to thru-hike, but quit because "it's just not what they're expecting."

Pixel says a woman in her 20s, who injured her knee, and her mother's friend, who'd had back surgery before the hike, quit at a hostel after hiking just 21 miles from Springer, got a shuttle to Atlanta, and flew home to Florida. The younger woman then flew back to Atlanta a couple weeks later, got a shuttle back to the hostel, hiked for three days and quit again.

Pixel recently graduated from Appalachian State University with a degree in photography and journalism. On the second day of the hike, she got an offer to work as a photographer for a paper in Goldsboro, North Carolina. But she turned it down because she had "too much time and money invested" in the hike.

I tell her that I was a reporter and copy editor and that if she's willing to go anywhere, she shouldn't have a problem finding a job at another small-town paper. I tell Stick Ninja, who was working at a chicken factory before the hike, and, like Underdog, is a Packers fan, that I'll take her to a game if she ever makes it to Wisconsin when I'm home.

The hostel's on the outskirts of Erwin, a city of about 6,000, so a hostel employee takes the women and me, Deacon and two other hikers in a van to Los Jalapenos, a Mexican restaurant, where I order two different dinners. The waiter points out that I'm ordering two dinners and I say I know and explain that I'm hiking the Appalachian Trail.

On the way back, I get out at the Mountain Inn, about a mile from the hostel, because I want to use the computer and also take advantage of the all-you-can-eat breakfast. I like the place and I want to write, so I decide to take a zero day. For lunch, I walk to Pizza Plus, a chain with mediocre pizza, but lots of it, along with a salad bar, at the all-you-can-eat buffet.

While I'm filling up with pizza, Underdog walks in and says he arrived at the hostel this morning. I ask him why he didn't make it to the shelter three days ago. He says he stopped because he got tired.

He also says that he's in no rush because he's got two weeks after today, until July 1, to hike the 126 miles to Damascus. His girlfriend, who's been sending him food packages, wants to meet him then because it will be the first anniversary of the day they met. He says it's really important to her, but he doesn't think it's a big deal. I think, but don't say, that with that attitude, he might be an underdog in his chances of keeping his girlfriend, too.

There's an IGA across the street from Pizza Plus, so I buy some food for the trail and a couple ears of fresh sweet corn, one of my favorite foods, and the first I've found on the trail. I take it back to the inn and cook it in the microwave for a delicious dinner.

In the morning, after another big breakfast, I walk past the hostel on my way to the trail. The van is full of backpackers, including Professor, who are going to a restaurant for breakfast. I ask if Underdog is already on the trail hiking. They say he's sleeping. So, I figure I probably won't see him again unless he comes to Wisconsin for a Packers game. Maybe Stick Ninja will come, too.

16

ALL THRU-HIKERS SMELL, many thru-hikers snore, and thru-hiker Michael "CAT" Jen couldn't take it anymore.

CAT knew he might not be warmly received when he decided to air his grievances in the Roan High Knob Shelter register. But he decided AT backpackers need rules to sleep by, and he was going to suggest them.

"I hope not to become public enemy," CAT wrote, "if I honestly write my feelings and thinking here."

I'd often seen CAT's register entries, and, until now, I'd always seen the same thing. CAT, who started his hike on April 4, his 58th birthday, writes in English and Chinese that he hopes to become the first Chinese American from Taiwan to thru-hike the trail. I don't know if he'll actually be the first, if he makes it, but I doubt it.

CAT, of Diamond Bar, California, then always adds: "My trail name CAT represents three important places in my life. C means CHINA, my ancestor's land; A means America, my living land; and T means TAIWAN, my born land. CAT is a very gentle animal and I sincerely wish these places always PEACE NO WAR."

He'd made it 376 miles to the Roan shelter, the trail's highest shelter at 6,194 feet, which I'd reached two days and 34.5 miles after leaving Erwin. But it looked like he might not be making many more.

"I always have nightmare when staying at hostel or shelter," CAT wrote on May 10. "One person snore, whole 'house' nightmare. Since hiking AT, I become a light sleeper. This is my personal problem, but odor, smelling and snoring noisy sound causing my sleeping bad."

He did have solutions, though: "We shall have hand sanitizer to 'wash' our foot to reduce odor filtered in the air and put our shoes, socks which produce the most odor, outside the shelter. I think hikers who have snoring habit constantly, shall give up voluntarily to stay at hostel, bunkroom or shelter, he/she shall tent always."

The shelters haven't seemed smelly to me, even though hikers certainly smell. Maybe I'm just used to it. But I can relate to his problem with snorers, since a few have kept me awake and I've been told occasionally that I snore. Some hikers use earplugs to block out the noise. I just sleep outside the shelter, as long as it isn't raining.

CAT also writes that he does "absolutely not relate to discrimination."

Neither do I, and I'd seen none of it on the trail. That's because hikers are nearly all very tolerant and live-and-let-live people. We know that we're all in this together, and support each other.

So, I'm guessing that if CAT suffered any discriminatory treatment, it had nothing to do with the fact that he's Chinese American, and everything to do with the fact that he's not only writing his complaints, but maybe also speaking them. I'll be curious to see if he keeps hiking.

I'd reached the shelter after seeing my first red efts, the life stage of the red-spotted newt when it lives on land. The fascinating efts, which are a few inches long, were wandering along and on part of the trail. They develop from larvae that look like tadpoles and then live on land for two to three years before returning to the water and transforming into aquatic adults. The efts contain a poison called tetrodotoxin and their orangish-red color is a warning to predators that can see color, especially birds, not to eat them.

Joining me at the shelter, the first I've seen with four walls and a door since Blood Mountain, are ridge-runner Fletcher "Gravy Crocket" Meadema and thru-hikers Kevin "ManCalves" Grant and his brother Kameron "Shortbus" Grant.

Gravy Crocket, 26, who runs long-distance trail races, says he'd never backpacked before he took time off after his junior year at Virginia Tech in 2010 to hike about 1,350 miles of the AT in two sections. He left Springer on March 7 and regrets his timing: "I would never go to Springer and hike north at that time again. Too many people."

But he doesn't regret the hike, which led him to change what he wants to do for a living. He got his architecture degree in 2012, but says he won't be an architect because he "doesn't want to be in an office developing things."

Instead, he wants to pursue a career in natural resources and, since last year, has been working seasonally for the Appalachian Trail Conservancy, putting up with the smells and snoring in shelters for $10 an hour and a bonus: "I get to be out here."

Also out here are the Grants, of suburban Chicago, who began hiking the Springer approach trail on April 14, backpacked about seven miles a day at the start, and are now doing 10 to 15.

ManCalves, 28, a pharmacist, says he'd never backpacked before and wanted the challenging adventure of a lifetime: "I have challenged myself mentally my whole life and I wanted to do something physical."

He's 6-foot-2, weighed 307 pounds when he left Springer and doesn't know how much he's lost. Shortbus, 19, who'd been going to college before his first backpacking trip, is 6-foot-1, weighed 280 when he left Springer and 240 by the time he got to Hot Springs.

"I was in the worst shape of my life," Shortbus says. "I can't say I've enjoyed it the entire time. I have learned not to take things for granted at home."

The brothers say their brother Keegan was a 6-foot-2, 305-pound guard on the Northwestern University football team. Their goal is to hike 643 more miles to the ATC headquarters in Harpers Ferry, from which they can take a train to Chicago.

They ask if I've met Stick Ninja and Pixel. I say I have and that the women decided to quit in Erwin because they were tired of hiking. That's not the only reason they quit, the Grants say. They also had said that they missed their cats.

17

THE EARLIEST SOUTHBOUND thru-hikers leave Katahdin at the end of May or early June, so I don't expect to meet any until August. That's why I'm really surprised when I meet shirtless, bronzed, bearded, southbound thru-hiker Harley "Gnarly Harley" Houston.

It's late in the afternoon on the day I've left the Roan High Knob Shelter and I'm just past the summit of Hump Mountain, which has hardly any trees and several false summits, when I meet Gnarly Harley climbing the northern side.

"How far to the top?" he asks. "Not far. I just passed it," I say, before asking him where he started and where he's headed.

When he tells me he left Katahdin last August, hiked through much of the winter, and is heading to Springer, I'm amazed and ask him if we can talk.

Sure, he says, and I climb back to the summit with him, so we can both enjoy the 360-degree views, while he tells me his story.

Gnarly Harley, 30, of Lake Park, Georgia, says he was working a construction job last summer when he decided he wanted to thru-hike the trail.

"I wanted to live out in the woods," he says. "I'd heard of people hiking the trail and I knew people who had done it."

He also knew that it was too late to leave from Springer, but he did some Internet research and learned that some backpackers leave Katahdin as late as August. So, he headed for Maine, climbed Katahdin on August 3, and hit the trail without doing too much planning, like me.

"Some people plan stuff to the nth degree," he says, "then are disappointed if things don't work out. If you take it as it comes, it's more enjoyable."

Gnarly Harley was in New Jersey when the first snow fell and in Pennsylvania by late November. He was backpacking with Billy

"Trashburner" Wendel, who had been his hiking partner since they met in southern Massachusetts.

Trashburner's father picked them up in November and took them to Philadelphia, where they celebrated Thanksgiving and took a week off the trail. They took another break around Christmas, when Gnarly Harley's mom and other family members rented a cabin in Pennsylvania's Gifford Pinchot State Park.

Gnarly Harley says the weather was sometimes very cold.

"We'd been hiking in snow and freezing. If you'd stop for 10 seconds, you'd freeze."

He says he and Trashburner returned to Philadelphia for another break, but that he didn't want to quit.

"I wanted to finish it, however long it took me. I didn't want to get off the trail and have something come up where I wouldn't finish it. Something might tempt me."

He did want to live to hike, though.

He says that he and Trashburner were able to hike on a trail covered with two feet of snow topped by 1/4 to 1/2 inch of ice because the ice softened during the day in the sun. But it hardened at night and one night in March he lost his footing and went sliding down an icy slope when he was headed to the privy at a shelter. By then, they'd hiked about 1,100 miles and were in southern Pennsylvania when they decided to take another break in a hotel near Chambersburg.

"When we got to those hotels," he says, "it was like heaven."

He dealt with the long, cold nights by putting his free-standing tent up in a shelter to conserve warmth, and then lying in his sleeping bag and listening to music. He says the stars were spectacular in the clear, cold winter skies. And getting water wasn't a problem because the springs didn't freeze.

Trashburner quit at the end of March, but he kept hiking. I ask if the hike has changed him.

"I haven't had an epiphany or anything," he says, adding that he doesn't want to do construction the rest of his life and might return to school. He also says he's a scuba divemaster and might get a job leading scuba divers.

Before meeting Gnarly Harley, I'd climbed three other balds in the Roan Highlands with spectacular views, including Round Bald, which had patches of beautiful flame azalea shrubs covered with large, funnel-shaped, bright orange flowers.

In Yellow Mountain Gap, I read a sign marking a trail that was used during the Revolutionary War by the Overmountain Men, frontiersmen who lived west of the Appalachians. They were headed to battle the British.

Nearby is a 0.3-mile trail to the Overmountain Shelter, a converted barn named for the men, and I decide to take a look at it.

Five adventurous teenage boys who have recently graduated from high school in Charlotte, North Carolina, have stopped at the very nice shelter on a four-day backpacking trip. They say they have plenty of food and give me a granola bar and a bagel with peanut butter and honey, making me glad I hiked the side trail. I tell them my name is Cary and they say the extra bagel I ate had been meant for a sixth boy, also named Cary, who had to cancel.

In the register, Leah had rated the place: "Awesome shelter here … Looks like it's going to be a one!" But she didn't sign it Leah (no trail name) She signed it "Stumbles." So now she has a trail name. But she's been misnamed, as far as I'm concerned. I would have named her "Awesome," after the word she writes most often.

After leaving the shelter, I climb Hump Mountain, where there's a plaque dedicated to the memory of Stanley Murray, who, as chairman of the ATC from 1961 to 1975, was instrumental in bringing the AT to the Roan Highlands. He was also the founder and director of the Southern Appalachian Highlands Conservancy, which protected thousands of acres in the Highlands, where there's also a shelter named after him.

In the evening, after talking with Gnarly Harley, I arrive at Highway 19E and walk 0.3 mile to the Mountain Harbour B&B/Hiker Hostel, where I hope to spend the night indoors. There I meet Elaine "Vagabond" Gregory, 71, of Chattanooga, Tennessee, who says she thru-hiked the trail in 2013, and is now managing the hostel for the owners.

Vagabond, a burly woman, says she helped out during the four days she spent at the hostel during her thru-hike and has returned to help out again. In 2012, she started a thru-hike, but had to quit because of ankle and knee injuries. She had arthroscopic surgery on an ankle and got a knee replacement. Then, last year she started her hike on March 27, three days before her 70th birthday, and climbed Katahdin on September 30.

She also had tried to thru-hike in 1994, but had to quit after hiking nearly halfway, to the Pennsylvania state line, when her daughter had a miscarriage. She has three other children, 10 grandchildren and two great-grandchildren.

I ask why she didn't start in 2013 where she stopped in 1994, or at least skip the part she hiked in 2012.

"I wanted to do a thru-hike, all at one time," she says. "It's all or nothing."

"Isn't it a little boring," I ask, "doing the first 1,060 miles again?"

"Nothing's boring," she says. "There's always new things."

The oldest woman to thru-hike the trail is Barbara Allen, of Knoxville, Tennessee, who was 71, when she thru-hiked in 2012. This year, Nan "Drag'n Fly" Reisinger, of Camp Hill, Pennsylvania, who's ahead of me, is trying to thru-hike at the age of 74.

The first woman to thru-hike the AT was Mildred Norman, who was 44 when she completed the first flip-flop hike with Dick Lamb in 1952. The couple hiked from Georgia to Pennsylvania, then traveled to Maine and climbed Katahdin before hiking back to Pennsylvania. In Vermont, they also hiked the entire Long Trail.

In 1953, Mildred set off from the Rose Bowl Parade in Pasadena on New Year's Day after naming herself "Peace Pilgrim" and saying she was "walking coast to coast for peace." She was on her seventh cross-country trip when she was killed in 1981 at the age of 71 in a car crash in Indiana when she was being driven to give a talk. She wrote the book *Peace Pilgrim: Her Life and Work in Her Own Words*.

The first woman to thru- hike the trail solo was Emma Gatewood, who was known as Grandma Gatewood, and hiked it in 1955 at the age of 67. She wore Keds sneakers and carried clothes, but no tent or sleeping bag, in a homemade denim bag slung over one shoulder. She did a second thru-hike in 1957 and finished a section hike in 1964. She was the first person to hike the trail twice and the first person to hike it three times. Her story is told in the book *Grandma Gatewood's Walk*, which was published in April.

Vagabond says the hostel is full with seven women who plan to do a day hike Saturday on the section I'd hiked today. The B&B is also full, so I pay for a spot in the campground.

The owners have set up a huge tent and nobody is using it, so I decide to sleep inside because the sky's cloudy and it looks like it might rain. But there are roots under most of the floor and no flat spot big enough for my pad, so I sleep outside until the middle of the night, when the rain starts. For the rest of the night, I sleep fitfully on roots.

18

AT BACKPACKERS AND MOUNTAIN HARBOUR owners Mary and Terry Hill have a symbiotic relationship. Backpackers provide the cash to keep the bed and breakfast, hostel and campground afloat and the Hills provide a bountiful breakfast to give hikers more than enough energy for a day on the trail.

But, it wasn't always that way. When the Hills bought the bed and breakfast in 2003, they knew nothing about hikers and hikers knew nothing about them.

That changed on a frigid February day in 2004, when the Hills were struggling to stay in business and four Appalachian Trail hikers showed up looking for a place to stay at the B&B.

"Four hikers with icicles in their beards landed on our doorstep in February," says Mary, adding that they hadn't been expecting guests.

"My husband said, 'I can't cook them breakfast.' My brother said, 'Take their money, I'll get Egg McMuffins.'"

Mary says Terry did manage to fix breakfast, after all, and that has led to a thriving business that caters to hikers with what's become known as the best breakfast on the trail.

"Those four hikers literally took care of us," she says, as they spread the news about Mountain Harbour, which has three rooms for guests in the B&B. "The hikers found us. We really couldn't cover the mortgage on three rooms at the time."

Mary, 67, tells me her story while bustling about the kitchen, after rising well before the sun to get cooking.

She and Terry, 68, who have been married for 49 years, grew up in Southern California and were living there in 2003 when Mary was a nurse and Terry was laid off from his manufacturing job five years before he planned to retire.

Mary says they decided to look for a bed and breakfast and, after searching the Internet, decided that Mountain Harbour "was the most cost-effective."

Mary and Terry

The place had been closed for two years, after the young previous owners, who were in business for nine months, gave up and moved to Long Beach, California, where they bought a yacht to sail around the world.

After reopening the B&B, the Hills found it wasn't so cost-effective, after all, because they didn't get the business they had expected from NASCAR fans going to Bristol Motor Speedway and from skiers in the North Carolina mountains. That's why hikers have become their mainstay.

They turned a 100-year-old barn into a hostel, which opened in 2005, and started a campground on their 18 acres.

Mary says long-distance hikers usually stay in the hostel for $25 a night or the campground for $10, rather than the bed and breakfast, where two of the rooms cost $125 and the third is $165.

But, she says, "Sometimes they splurge because they can't take the snoring in the shelters one more night."

Mary says the business "just sort of evolved, one thing after another. Hikers appeared and you got things done."

She started offering breakfast to the hikers who were staying in the hostel or camping and they spread the word. As we're talking, this morning's breakfast also evolves and it's quite an impressive homemade spread.

There are cinnamon rolls, scones and a variety of other pastry; quiche and scrambled eggs; French toast with pecan syrup; a potato dish; tomatoes, cantaloupe and blueberries; and orange juice and coffee. I eat a lot of everything and everything's delicious, and a bargain at $12 for all you can eat.

Mary says the couple will continue operating the place "as long as we need to pay the bills," but don't expect to ever be fully accepted by their neighbors, who generally don't welcome outsiders.

She says many longtime residents were upset in the late 1970s and early 1980s when the National Park Service forced some to sell their land for the trail and its protective corridor. The folks that owned the Hills' land fought a three-year battle to keep their property and ended up losing three acres.

"The mentality here is we're all outsiders. If you didn't own land here for six generations," she says. "The best you can hope for is to be the oldest of the outsiders."

After breakfast, I talk a bit more with Rush, 50, a thru-hiker who had camped near me last night. He says he had been working for Google shooting street scenes and had some free time in April, when he learned about the trail.

"I had a hole in my schedule and saw a trail documentary on Netflix and I thought I should do this," says Rush, who, like me, has also done lots of long-distance bike touring.

Rush says he left Springer on May 3, but has been slowed by foot problems and by what I dub "off-trail pink-blazing." He says that he kept his profile on OkCupid, an online meeting site, while he hiked, and that a wealthy heiress and artist from Asheville had driven to meet him at Fontana Dam because she thinks AT hikers are hot.

He says they had a great day together and that he later got a ride of about 65 miles to Asheville, where they spent a week together. That, of course, makes it less likely that he'll make it to Katahdin, but he has other priorities.

19

IN 2012, TOM WELLS SURVIVED a heart attack caused by a blocked artery called the widow maker.

In 2013, his wife died after living her last nine years with cancer.

In 2014, he quit his job, sold his house and is now trying to thru-hike the Appalachian Trail, while his former cardiologist, now his girlfriend, works and waits in Colorado.

"I think for me, I just want to do whatever I can with the time I have," says Tom, 53. "I can't put things off."

Tom, who doesn't have a trail name, tells me his story after we meet at the Mountaineer Shelter, 9.3 trail miles from Mountain Harbour, where we've both stopped for a break late in the day.

He was living in the Denver suburb of Littleton and training for the Deadwood Marathon in 2012 when he went out for an 11-mile run in mid-November. When he returned, his arms ached, but he never thought he was having a heart attack. His wife, Darsey Gordon, gave him some aspirin and drove him to the hospital.

There, he learned that his left anterior descending artery, which supplies blood to the front wall of the heart, was totally blocked. He survived because he was in great shape from running and because Spencer, the youngest of his three sons, has trouble with math.

Tom and Spencer had been planning to climb a mountain with a peak above 14,000 feet the day of Tom's heart attack, but they canceled their plan after remembering the teen had a meeting scheduled with his math tutor. So, Tom went for a run, instead.

He says that when Spencer visited him in the hospital, the first thing he said was: "Hey dad, I bet you're glad I suck at math."

Tom was able to return to his job of 17 years as tax director for a private investment company, while Darsey, an accomplished kayaker and downhill skier, worked as conference sales manager for a mountain resort, while living with leiomyosarcoma, smooth muscle cancer, which was diagnosed in 2004. Last September, she died at 54.

Tom says he had tired of his job long ago, but kept at it because the company was good at letting him have time with Darsey when she was getting treatment.

After his wife's death, he was ready to quit. Spencer was a high school senior and there was enough money from Darsey's life insurance to pay for college for their two sons and his son from a previous marriage.

And Tom wanted to pursue his dream of more than 40 years to thru-hike the Appalachian Trail.

"I wasn't put on this earth," he says, "to sit behind a desk."

He says he's wanted to do the hike since he was 11 or 12 and living in Portland, Maine. His father had taken him and other Boy Scouts to Baxter State Park and they had climbed Katahdin. He saw the sign saying Springer Mountain was more than 2,000 miles away and decided that he was going to thru-hike the trail.

"I said, 'Someday I'm going to do that.'"

The Scouts climbed Katahdin every year and Tom climbed it three more times. He's dreamt about thru-hiking the AT and now he's living the dream.

He gave his employer seven weeks notice and worked his last day on May 2. On May 21, Spencer graduated high school. On May 29, Tom left Springer and is hoping to finish the trail in 100 days. I tell him that's a pretty ambitious goal, since I hope to finish in five months and we're hiking about the same pace. He started a week after me, but I've taken more days off.

Back in Colorado, his girlfriend, Susie, follows his progress and sends him supplies. She'd been his cardiologist in Littleton, but had moved across the state to Durango.

Tom says he had a crush on Susie and signed up for a course in avalanche training in Durango, so he'd have a reason to contact her. He asked her to lunch and she agreed to meet him, not realizing it was a date. Now, they're a couple and they plan to spend four days together in two weeks around July 4.

That might give him time to get better footwear and let the many blisters on his feet heal a bit. He's wearing hiking boots and has battled blisters since the day he started. I tell him I've had no blisters because I've been wearing the shoes I run in and suggest that he hike in the shoes he runs in, too.

When I ask him why he keeps hiking, he says: "For me, the big part of it is the physical and mental challenge of doing it. I'm not out here to find the meaning of life."

I tell him that I feel the same way about the hike and that we've got a lot in common, in addition to the fact that we've both thought of doing the hike for more than 40 years. We also both run marathons and we both biked cross country to Los Angeles when we were college age. He was 19 when he started in Portland and I was 21 when I left from Green Bay.

Tom says he's been hiking with "Birdman," who's about his age, and "Gearhead," a guy in his mid-20s. The three were thinking of staying at the shelter, but I point out that the Vango/Abby Memorial Hostel is just a short hike off the trail in less than four miles. So, we agree to meet there.

Tom leaves and then I pack up and leave, too. But I hike about 200 yards on the wrong side trail. I turn around and return to the shelter, where I see another backpacker. He's Gearhead and I tell him that Tom headed to the hostel. He says he's going to stay at the shelter, so I say goodbye and leave again.

Meeting Tom has been the highlight of a day of fairly easy hiking, but earlier I'd also enjoyed talking with Tim "Mountain Squid" Stewart and Dave Clark, who were spending Saturday doing trail maintenance with two other volunteers and an intern from the Appalachian Trail Conservancy. The volunteers are from the Tennessee Eastman Hiking & Canoeing Club, which maintains 133 trail miles.

Mountain Squid, 48, says he hiked the trail from 2004 to 2006, after retiring from the Navy. Since then, he's hiked about 75 miles of the trail every year from Highway 19E to Damascus, which I'm looking forward to reaching in about four days. He's been a maintenance volunteer since 2005 and tries to work at least once a week.

Dave, 70, of Bristol, Tennessee, says he's been maintaining trails for three or four years and enjoys it.

"I just like to get out in the woods hiking the trail," he says. "And you can't beat God's beautiful earth and the scenery through this area. "

I'd like to spend more time talking with the men, but it starts to rain. So, I keep hiking and they go back to work.

Just before the trail to the hostel, there's a beautiful view, which hikers can sit and enjoy on a bench placed, according to words inscribed in the bench, "in loving memory of Ron G. Frey "Vango" who received so little yet gave so much." I hope to learn Vango's story at the hostel and also that of the owner, who, according to the guidebook, has hiked more than 14,000 trail miles, including three thru-hikes of the AT.

20

The third time Scott "Scotty" Van Dam thru-hiked the Appalachian Trail he included it in a hike that started in Key West, Florida, and ended at the tip of the Gaspe Peninsula in Quebec.

Scotty, 52, the owner of the Vango/Abby Memorial Hostel, says that the 3,650-mile hike he did over eight months in 1999 was a wonderful experience.

"It was one of the best years of my life. I was in excellent health. I didn't have a care in the world."

Scotty tells me about his many long-distance hikes while we sit in his small home, about 400 yards off the trail. He was cutting the grass when I arrived, then shut off the mower and gave me a Coke before we talked.

Scotty, a Star Trek fan, took his trail name from the chief engineer on the Starship Enterprise. He says he liked James Doohan, who played Scotty, and uses his trail name off the trail, too.

He decided to thru-hike the trail when he was in eighth grade in Elizabethton, Tennessee. His teacher had asked the students what trip they'd like to take and the girls had said they wanted to hike the nearby AT.

"We hiked and everyone had a wonderful time. I knew that, if this trail went all the way to Maine, I'm going to hike it."

He thru-hiked it the first time in 1993, after he was laid off from his job as an electrical engineer for NASA in Cape Canaveral, Florida. By then, he had read *Blind Courage*, a book by Bill Irwin, who was blind when he amazingly thru-hiked the AT in 1990 with his guide dog, Orient. He says Bill, who died March 1 at 73, and his eighth-grade hike inspired him to tackle the trail.

In 1995, he finished his job as a consultant for an aerospace company and thru-hiked the trail again.

"It was an escape from the real world of engineering and politics," he says. "I enjoyed escaping into the woods. It's a miniature lifetime compressed into six months—all the people you meet, just being close to nature."

In 1998, Scotty read a magazine story about John Brinda, who in 1997 became the first person to hike from Key West to Springer, in part on the Florida Trail; then thru-hike the AT; and finally thru-hike the International Appalachian Trail, which was then still being built, and went from just outside Baxter State Park to Cap Gaspe, the easternmost part of Quebec in Canada's Forillon National Park.

"I thought," he says, "I'm going to do the same thing."

So, he left Key West on February 3, 1999, and hiked through the Keys and part of mainland Florida until he reached the Florida Trail, which starts in the Big Cypress National Preserve in southwest Florida. He hiked through much of Florida on the trail, where he got lost many times. He then followed small roads and old railroad routes through Georgia, reaching Springer on April 23, after hiking about 850 miles. He reached Katahdin on September 3, after hiking about 2,150 miles, and then hiked about 650 more miles to reach Cap Gaspe on October 3.

Scotty says the IAT, which goes through northern Maine and New Brunswick, before reaching Quebec, was difficult to follow.

"I got seriously lost a couple times," he says. "I hardly passed a soul."

Scotty had also gotten Lyme disease after being bit by a deer tick in Pennsylvania. The disease was diagnosed in New Jersey and he was given an antibiotic. But he didn't take the last two weeks of pills because they melted in the heat. That, he thinks has led to his health problems today, including arthritis in his right hip and thumb, which keeps him from hiking now.

In 2003, though, he was able to hike Vermont's Long Trail, and, in 2004, he hiked about 60 miles of the C&O Canal Towpath Trail from Washington, D.C., to Harpers Ferry. His favorite hike has been the Pacific Crest Trail. He backpacked it in 1997 and loved the many stunning views.

"It was more rugged, but it's gorgeous in the High Sierras."

Scotty bought his home in 2005 and in 2007 built the hostel, which sleeps six on the first floor and has a private room with a queen bed upstairs. He named it for his friend, Ron "Vango" Frey, a retired tool and die maker from La Crosse, Wisconsin, and Vango's dog, Abby.

Scotty says he met Vango in Shenandoah National Park on his 1995 thru-hike. Vango, who enjoyed traveling and socializing with backpackers, had parked his RV near the AT and helped hikers as a trail angel. He helped care for Scotty's home and hostel until dying in 2008 at the age of 75.

Scottty's rates are a bargain at $9 for a bed in the hostel, or $12 with heat, and $15 single or $25 double for the private room.

The first thru-hiker this year, a rugged North Dakota woman with a husky, arrived February 1, after leaving Springer on New Year's Day.

"I was surprised that anybody was thru-hiking," Scotty says, noting that there was a foot of snow on the trail and that snow on the trees made the blazes hard to see.

He says he enjoys being close to the trail and to hikers.

"It brings back many good memories. The years that I was hiking were some of the best years of my life."

It's getting late, so I say good night to Scotty and walk across the yard to the hostel, where Tom and I are the only occupants. We've hiked 405 miles of the AT and I think my next stop will be Hampton, Tennessee, 14.7 trail miles away.

21

Terry "Birdman" Martin first hiked part of the Appalachian Trail when he was 6 and plans to finish it this summer, 49 years later.

Birdman, 55, of the Cleveland suburb of Berea, says his parents first sparked his interest in the AT when they took him and his sister to hike part of it in the Presidential Range in the White Mountains of New Hampshire. A few years later, they climbed Katahdin.

"I have vivid and prized memories of those climbs, which indeed kindled my desire to hike the AT," he says. "In addition, one of my cousins hiked the AT in the early 1970s and an uncle of mine hiked it in the mid-1990s at the age of 65. I often heard it mentioned and those stories planted a seed."

Birdman, an English professor at Baldwin Wallace University in Berea, tells me a little about his life after he and Alex "Gearhead" Harps, Tom's hiking partners, catch me on the trail after spending the night together at the shelter before the hostel.

He says his parents introduced him to backpacking when the family would often spend a day backpacking into the Adirondack Mountains in New York and set up a base camp for a few days so they could take day hikes to climb high peaks nearby. Birdman, who's divorced, says his daughter, Nikita, 18, and son, Ivan, 17, like hiking, but aren't interested in backpacking.

"They haven't wanted to accompany me on the AT. The backpacking gene seems to have bypassed my children."

He started backpacking the AT in 2008 and has hiked about 1,700 miles of it in section hikes. He plans to complete it by finishing the southern third of the trail and then driving to northern Vermont and hiking to Katahdin. He got his trail name because he loves photographing wildlife, especially birds.

"Photography has transformed the way I hike," he says. "I used to be focused on getting to my destination, but now I am much more attuned to natural beauty and I will stop for any good photo op, no matter how tired, cold, wet, or hungry I am."

He says he loves just about everything about the trail, including "the high that one experiences on a mountaintop" and "the peaceful, cool sense of being immersed in the deep woods of the valleys."

"I likewise love the camaraderie, the many opportunities to observe wildlife, the sight of the golden light filtering through the trees at dawn and dusk, the feeling of living more intensely and the deeply meditative state to which hiking is so often conducive. Hiking the AT has been one of the most joyful experiences of my life."

Gearhead, meanwhile, who's in his late 20s, is a fast hiker with a big agenda that I hear about while hiking quickly with him for a couple miles. He plans to thru-hike, but has to leave the trail occasionally to report to the Air National Guard in Little Rock, Arkansas.

He also plans to take a break from the trail in July to climb Mount Rainier in Washington and then visit his girlfriend, a University of Wisconsin graduate, in my hometown of Madison for the first time. I tell him he'll love living in Madison, but he says he expects her to move to be with him.

Gearhead tells me that his job in the military was to help track people targeted for death by U.S. drones. When I ask him if he's bothered by the innocent civilians killed in drone attacks, he says: "That's war."

I slow down and then reach lovely Laurel Falls, 40 feet high and 50 feet wide. I enjoy the fabulous falls on a sunny Sunday with Birdman after hiking 13.2 miles from the hostel. We're joined by many day hikers who make the 1.2-mile hike to the falls along the AT from a parking area.

Birdman, who teaches nature writing, among other courses, and is also passionate about landscape photography, uses me to put a little perspective in his photos of the falls. I keep hiking after we see the falls, while he stops to take more photos; but he catches me by running. Like me, he's been running since he ran cross country in high school.

We hike together and leave the trail on a side trail to Hampton, a small town with two hostels, a grocery store, and a few restaurants. We hike a mile on the side trail and a half mile on the highway before reaching Brown's Hardware and Grocery in the evening. We're tired and hungry, so we're disappointed when we see it's closed on Sunday. We start discussing which hostel sounds best when Sutton Brown, who owns the store, and his two sons step out the door.

Sutton says he'll open the store for us, and, by the way, he also owns Braemar Castle Hostel, just a couple blocks away. He says it's a great place, so we finish our shopping and follow him to a fine fieldstone building, which housed top officials of the Pittsburgh Lumber Co., as well as a commissary and post office, more than 100 years ago in what was then called Braemar.

Sutton

Sutton, 60, started working in the store with his father after graduating from college. He lives in half of the building with his sons and his wife, Beverly, a biologist. The couple operate the other half as a hostel. It's beautiful with mostly hardwood floors, two rooms with bunks downstairs, private rooms upstairs, and kitchens on both floors. It was named after Braemar Castle in Scotland.

We leave our packs in the hostel and Sutton gives us a ride about a mile, or two, across town to a Subway. There's a long line, so Sutton says he'll be back to pick us up. I order three foot-long veggie subs, figuring I'll have at least one for dinner and the rest for breakfast and lunch. I also order an extra-large Coke, and then see Tom, who has walked to the restaurant from the other hostel in town, which is near the grocery store, and also has an extra-large Coke. Neither of us drinks much soda when we're not backpacking, but we both crave Coke now.

Tom had left the hostel before me this morning, but had to take a short side trail to another hostel to pick up supplies that Susie mailed him from Durango. Many hikers like Tom, Deacon and Marmie, pick up food and other supplies at hostels, motels, post offices, and other places near the trail. But I don't want to plan for such stops, so I'm only going to have new running shoes sent to me. And I haven't needed a new pair, yet.

Tom says the other hostel in Hampton isn't great and that there were a couple people there smoking. He hasn't paid, so I tell him he should join us, and we all ride back with Sutton, who invites us into his place to watch the U.S. soccer team battle Portugal in the World Cup. Birdman and I enjoy the game and the delicious Key lime pie that Beverly gives us for dessert, while Tom gets his pack from the other hostel and then stays outside to call Susie.

Later, Sutton comes over to the hostel to talk and lament Portugal tying the United States, 2-2, with a goal in the last seconds of stoppage time. Tom joins us for a while, but spends much of his time outside talking with Susie again to help keep her awake as she makes the 340-mile drive home across Colorado from Denver to Durango.

Sutton tells us that the bears near the Watauga Lake Shelter, which we'll pass tomorrow, have become a problem because locals have fed them. That's why signs posted along the trail have ordered backpackers not to stay at the shelter or camp anywhere nearby. After Sutton leaves, I read the hostel register, in which a few hikers write about bears that have scared them off the trail near the shelter, so I know I'll have to be more cautious near there.

Before we go to bed, I tell Tom he should call Susie again to make sure she arrived home safely. "Really?" he asks. I say she'll probably appreciate it, but add: "Who am I to be giving advice? I'm the one without a girlfriend."

Tom goes outside to call her and when he returns, says: "You were right."

In the morning, Birdman and I head to the store to buy a few more things, while Tom lingers to call Susie again. I smile at him. "I'm whipped," he says.

The sign on the side of the store, which dates to 1909, says "IF WE DON'T HAVE IT, THEY PROBABLY DON'T MAKE IT." That's an overstatement, of course, but the well-stocked hardware store does attract customers from nearby states looking for hard-to-find items, such as hardware designed to fit plumbing and electrical fixtures from the 1920s and 1930s

The whole place reminds me of the small department store started by my Jewish grandfather, Charlie Segall, a Polish immigrant, in Pulaski, a village with mostly Polish Catholics, about 20 miles from Green Bay. My father, Sol, and his brother, Harold, worked in the store with my grandfather, while I was growing up. But, unlike Brown's, it closed, like most similar small-town stores, because it couldn't compete with big-box discount stores on the outskirts of nearby cities, like Green Bay.

After Tom arrives, Sutton offers to drive the three of us to a restaurant for breakfast. Tom and Birdman go with Sutton, but I decide to start hiking because I'll be climbing 1,722 feet over 2.5 miles when I start the trail this morning and I want to get a head start on the pair, so I might be able to spend a little more time with them later.

The steep climb is difficult and the descent is about the same distance on a warm, sunny day, so I'm a little tired when I get to Shook Branch Recreation Area on the shore of Wautaga Lake, where I eat a vegetarian sub in the shade and drink lots of water before hiking along the lakeshore, toward the shelter. I'm alone, so I'm a little nervous, but I see no bears and then start another long climb away from the lake.

On the way up, I pass Rush, the off-trail pink-blazer whom I last saw two days ago at Mountain Harbour.

"Hi, Rush, how'd you get here?" I ask. "Did you yellow-blaze?"

"Yeah," he says. "I'm doing every color of the rainbow."

I keep climbing and look for the spring, which the guidebook says is 7.2 miles from the recreation area, where I last had a drink because I didn't think I needed to carry water. But it's dry, so I head 1.7 miles to the next shelter, where there's supposed to be a spring 0.3 mile down a steep trail.

I'm quite thirsty when I get to the shelter, but the two hikers there say the trail to the spring is difficult and the water lousy. I've still got a few hours of light, so I decide to keep going. The guidebook says there's a spring in 3.8 miles and another one 2.8 miles after that, 0.2 mile before the next shelter.

I'm on my way to the first spring when Birdman, who's also thirsty and out of water, passes me, anxious to get to the spring. But that's also dry, so we keep going. It's nearly dark when we get to the spring before the shelter. It's flowing, but barely, so, for the second time on the trail, I use the scoop I made by cutting the end off of a disposable plastic water bottle and leaving the cap on. Birdman also uses it and so does Gearhead, who arrives after we do.

I drink a lot, but I'm still dehydrated and quite tired after hiking 23.1 miles, so I set my pack near the shelter and put my tarp, pad and sleeping bag on the ground, then take a nap before dinner. When I awake, I find that Birdman has hung my food bag and that he and Gearhead are about to go to sleep in the shelter. Birdman helps me get the bag down and I eat before going to sleep myself.

It's still dark and I'm still sleeping when a light rain wakes me. I lie there a while, hoping it'll stop. But it doesn't, so I gather my stuff and walk to the shelter, where Birdman's already up and eating, and tells me it's only about an hour to dawn. I get my food to eat and Birdman waits for me. But I tell him to take off because I'm still beat and I plan to take my time, while I know that he and Gearhead will probably try to hike the 25.8 miles to Damascus.

I'm going to shoot for Abingdon Gap Shelter, which is 9.9 miles from Damascus, and then hike the rest of the way, which is mostly downhill, tomorrow morning. I'm about four miles from the shelter when Tom catches me and says he didn't make it to the shelter last night because he had walked an extra mile out and back on a road after missing the blaze for the trail. The guidebook says the trail is on the road for only 0.4 mile, so I'm guessing he was thinking about Susie, and not reading the guidebook or looking closely for the blaze.

From left, Birdman, Gearhead and Tom (c.p.)

When we reach the shelter, it's evening, and I stop for the day. Tom, who often hikes at night, decides to keep going, so I have the shelter to myself.

In the register, there's an entry from CAT, the hiker who wrote in the Roan High Knob Shelter register that hikers should leave their smelly shoes and socks outside shelters and use hand sanitizer on their feet, and that those who snore shouldn't sleep in shelters or hostels and should always use their tents. I was wondering how long he'd keep hiking, and now I know he's hiked at least 81.2 more miles.

CAT wrote on May 16: "Last night I tent in front of the shelter. It was heavy rain."

So, I guess that he's decided to sleep outside the shelters, regardless of the weather, to escape the smells and the snores.

MARYLAND
HARPERS FERRY
FRONT ROYAL
WEST VIRGINIA
SHENANDOAH NATIONAL PARK
WAYNESBORO
McAFEE KNOB
BUENA VISTA
DALEVILLE
CATAWBA
PEARISBURG
MARION
VIRGINIA
GRAYSON HIGHLANDS STATE PARK
USPS
DAMASCUS
TENNESSEE
NORTH CAROLINA

22

CHUCK "WOODCHUCK" BISSONNETTE grew to love the Appalachian Trail lifestyle so much while hiking it that he bought a house near the trail and turned it into a hostel.

"It keeps me in touch with the trail and hikers. It's interesting to meet people and get different perspectives," Woodchuck says during my stay at his hostel, about 200 yards off the trail in delightful Damascus.

Woodchuck, 66, who hiked all but 162 miles of the trail in 2012 and finished it the next year, says he started thinking about opening a hostel after his 2012 hike, then saw the house for sale in one of the favorite towns of AT thru-hikers and bought it last year.

"This house and property caught my eye. It seemed like a good layout for what I'm doing."

What he's doing is providing hikers just about everything they want in a hostel, including comfortable beds and a good breakfast, and also giving them the option to camp in his big, grassy yard.

"I'm really hiker-centric in my thought process," he says, explaining that the money he makes from the $25 he charges for one of nine beds and the $10 for camping will be used to improve the place for future hikers.

"I have to make a profit to continue to serve the hiker. There are lots of ways to maximize things that I don't do. I want to provide a good service for what I'm charging."

Now, for example, he's paying Timber, 50, a master carpenter who says he spends most of his time living in the woods, to build a hiker pavilion.

Woodchuck, who sleeps in his two-car garage, says he's housed lots of hikers, since he came from Montana and opened the hostel in March. He plans to be open each year from March 15 to October 15, and return to Montana for the winter.

"It's been really good," he says. "Not everybody knew about me and the response has been positive."

Woodchuck

Woodchuck retired in 2012 from a career teaching school in Montana, Michigan and Alaska, and selling real estate. Then he learned what hikers want and need during the hike he started on the Springer approach trail with his sister on February 1, 2012.

"It was a lifelong dream that I figured I better get with before I got older."

He says he started so early "because I knew I was going to be a slow hiker. The weather looked pretty darn good, so I thought I'd do it. It was a warm winter and, with the exception of two or three snowstorms, it was good hiking."

He was hiking on his own, though, because his sister quit after 21 miles. But she stuck around and supported him through nearly 200 miles, so sometimes he could slackpack, like Marmie did with the help of her husband. Other hikers slackpack by paying for support from hostel owners and shuttle drivers. I don't plan to slackpack or yellow-blaze. So far, I've been what AT hikers call a "purist," a thru-hiker who carries a backpack the entire way and doesn't take shortcuts.

Woodchuck was in Vermont in late August when he went to see a doctor in Rutland because he was growing increasingly fatigued. He was diagnosed with Lyme disease and prescribed an antibiotic, and took about two weeks off. Then he hiked to the trail's 1,887-mile mark, a few miles east of Gorham, New Hampshire, where a friend from New Jersey picked him up and drove him north so he could be sure to climb Katahdin while it was open for the season. He then hiked part of Maine and finished New Hampshire before quitting in Maine on October 12.

He says he stopped because snow and ice made the Maine mountains too dangerous. He was also discouraged after a night when the temperature dropped to 20 and his boots froze because he had forgotten to put them in his sleeping bag. He thawed them out with boiling water and then had to hike in cold, wet boots. He returned last summer and finished the trail.

He says the experience changed the way he approaches life: "It made me aware of the moment and less concerned about external possessions that don't mean much. Your life is reduced to eating, hiking and sleeping and I think when you get your life simplified, it has more meaning. I'm enjoying life more and I'm more accepting of the simple things and I'm more content."

I end up at the Woodchuck Hostel, in part, because Dave's Place, where I had planned to stay, is temporarily closed. The clerk at Mt. Rogers Outfitters, which runs the hostel, says it's just been treated to get rid of bedbugs. I'm surprised she tells me that because I think that letting hikers hear about bedbugs will be bad for business.

Outside the outfitters, a boy on a bike rides up to me and asks if I want to camp for free in his backyard. He's Dante, 10, and he says his parents like backpackers. I tell him thanks, but I don't have a tent, so I'm looking for a hostel.

I'm happy to be in Damascus, considered a milestone by hikers because it caters to them and they've hiked 467.1 miles, after entering Virginia 3.4 miles before town. Thousands of hikers flock here each May for Trail Days, a weekend celebration of hiking and the AT.

Damascus is known as Trail Town, USA, because seven hiking, biking and highway trails pass through town. One of the bike trails is the TransAmerica Trail, which stretches 4,262 miles from Astoria, Oregon to Yorktown, Virginia and is the one on which I biked about 3,000 miles with Craig in 2001 and the rest solo, after Craig left to return to college.

I've told a few hikers that, if I had to choose between long-distance backpacking or long-distance biking, I'd choose biking. On a long bike trip, you carry nothing on your back; the scenery changes frequently; you usually don't have to carry much food, if any; and you can coast downhill. I've never thought of quitting a bike trip. I don't plan to quit this trip, either, but I do occasionally think about it, like most AT thru-hikers.

After learning about the bedbugs, I head to the library, where I find Tom, Birdman and Gearhead using the computers. I tell Tom that I've got a great trail name for him.

"What?" he asks. "You named yourself in Hampton on Monday," I say. He thinks for a moment before saying "Whipped?" He laughs, and sticks with Tom.

I also use a computer and find a message from Deacon, who says he's in Damascus, where he's finished his section hike. He's leaving this evening and says I should come over to Crazy Larry's hostel to see him. I go to the hostel and talk with Deacon, as well as Crazy Larry. I tell him that I'd stay at his place, but I'd rather find a place with a computer. He then calls Woodchuck, who says he has a computer I can use.

While I'm there, trail legend Adam "Baltimore Jack" Tarlin, walks in to see Larry. Baltimore Jack, 55, first tried a thru-hike in 1995, but had to stop in Maine when he fell and broke three ribs. He finished the trail in 1996 and then thru-hiked it northbound seven straight times from 1997 to 2003, the record for consecutive thru-hikes. He had to give up thru-hiking because of bad knees, but has continued to live his life connected to the trail by helping hikers and volunteering at hostels, as he follows hikers north. He's also a popular and prolific writer on WhiteBlaze, an AT discussion site, and writes the site's most read article, a guide on to how to resupply along the trail.

I say goodbye to Baltimore Jack, Crazy Larry and Deacon and walk across town to meet Woodchuck, who gives me a room to myself and a computer with Internet access. I want to use it to write when the library's closed.

I plan to take a zero day in Damascus tomorrow after my nearo day today. I want to write, watch the United States play Germany in the World Cup and do a little personal business, including getting a new pair of running shoes shipped to me. I bought five pairs of New Balance 940s before leaving Madison, and left four at Movin' Shoes running store. Employees there said they'd send me new shoes when I need them

I look in the guidebook for a place about a week away that holds packages for hikers, and at which I'll want to stop. I settle on Woods Hole Hostel, about 155 miles away at the 620.9-mile mark. I ran about 100 miles on the shoes I'm wearing before I left, to break them in, so I'll have about 720 miles on them by the time I get to Woods Hole.

I've been looking forward to picking up my first package of the trip at Adventure Damascus, an outing-goods and bike-rental store that holds packages for hikers. Rock Slide, the woman who picked me up hitchhiking in Great Smoky Mountains National Park, has emailed me to say she's baked me cookies and mailed them to the store.

When I get there in the morning, though, an employee can't find a box for me. So, I walk a couple blocks to the Post Office, where Postmaster Mark Sheets says there's no box there, either. I'd really like those cookies, so I walk to the library and email Rock Slide to tell her the bakery is missing. She calls the Post Office and store, without success, and then sends me the tracking number, which indicates the package arrived in Damascus eight days ago on June 18.

I go back to the Post Office, tell Mark that the package has arrived in Damascus and ask him what happened. He says that when a package arrives for Adventure Damascus, a notice is placed in the store's Post Office box. After the package is picked up, the notice is scanned to show the date, and there's no record that the cookies have been picked up. So, I leave disappointed.

I do, though enjoy the rest of the day in Damascus, including great food at the Blue Blaze Cafe, which sells huge brownies at a bargain price. I buy several to pack, instead of Clif Bars, as well as a pizza for the trail.

Bill

The next day, on my way out of town, I stop at Adventure Damascus again, even though I know it's almost certainly a cookieless gesture.

When I walk in, a guy with a white beard who was sitting in the store playing a guitar yesterday, is sitting and playing again. He looks at me and says: "Your package is here."

"Really. Are you kidding me?" I say.

"It got here just after you left," he says. "Chris ran up and down the sidewalk looking for you. He said, 'Where the heck do you think that guy went?'"

The guy with the guitar turns out to be Bill Leonard, a co-owner of the store and a member of the band "Steel Trestle." He says his co-owner had been gone for a week and had picked up my package at the Post Office yesterday before I checked there, and dropped it off at the store minutes after I left.

I wondered why the Post Office records hadn't shown the package had been picked up, so, I walked back to the Post Office and asked the postmaster. He said that's because all of the notices are scanned closer to the end of the day.

The cookies Rock Slide has sent me are chocolate chip, my favorite, and she has included her favorite pasta dish and a small, light backpacking towel. I walk to the library, so I can send her an email to tell her I got the package, after all, and thank her. I also want to tell her that the cookies are scrumptious.

Then, I head for the trail again, and am across the street from Crazy Larry's, when I hear him yell: "Hey, Cary!"

I talk with him a while and he says that I'll likely outlive him. I say that might not be true because he's 10 years younger than me and can get in shape. Then, he says that he's recently been diagnosed with cancer and that he's ready to die at 54. I ask what he knows about his cancer and if he has insurance. He says he doesn't know much yet, has no insurance and hasn't told his friends.

"Do the people in Damascus like you?" I ask.

"They love me," he says.

I tell him that then he needs to go public with his diagnosis and that residents will most likely hold fundraisers to help him pay for his treatment. And that perhaps he'll still live a long time.

As I walk away, he yells, "Thanks for the encouragement!"

23

WHEN ICONIC AT THRU-HIKER Grandma Gatewood got caught sleeping in the rain, she rolled up in the shower curtain she carried in her homemade denim sack. Or at least that's what Deacon told me.

We talked about the first woman to thru-hike the AT solo 29 days ago when we were eating breakfast at a restaurant in Franklin. I'd just showed him a newspaper article about the new book *Grandma Gatewood's Walk.*

So, when I wake up to rain in the middle of my second night after leaving Damascus, I try doing the same thing with the tarp underneath me because there's no shelter nearby. It might have worked for Grandma Gatewood, but it sure doesn't work for me.

The rain is light at first, but then it starts pouring and I'm soon lying in puddles while wrapped in my tarp, while my down bag soaks up more and more water. There's not much I can do, except try to sleep, which isn't easy, and wait until dawn.

Fortunately, when the sky lightens, the rain stops, and I pack up without getting even wetter. I manage to stuff my formerly 29-ounce bag, which now weighs much more, into its sack, pack the rest of my stuff and start hiking.

I'd slept next to the half-mile side trail to Mount Rogers, Virginia's highest mountain at 5,729 feet. I mistakenly hiked part way up the trail last night when it was misty and dark, and I was trying to reach Thomas Knob Shelter, 0.4 mile north. I turned back, but then had trouble finding the AT, so I'd decided to just sleep here.

This morning, I decide not to hike to the summit because I'm wet and the guidebook says there's no view. So, it's still early when I reach the shelter, which sleeps 16, and find that it's full and everyone's sleeping. I figure that it's packed with day hikers who hiked to it from a parking lot three miles away and climbed Mount Rogers yesterday or plan to climb it today. So, I might have had to sleep in the rain, even if I had made it to the shelter.

I keep hiking on a section of trail that's been beautiful much of the time since I left Damascus, with many blooming rhododendrons. For several miles outside of Damascus, the trail parallels a pretty stream and the Virginia Creeper Trail, a 34.3-mile rails-to-trail bike path. The Virginia Creeper Marathon is held on the path every March and I plan to run it as my Virginia marathon. I hope to run one in all 50 states and Washington, D.C.

I'm soon passed by WT, a backpacker I met at a shelter two days before I reached Damascus. We talk a little and then he takes off ahead of me. I've hiked about a mile, when I'm surprised to see him hiking toward me from the north.

I tell him that somehow he got turned around and is hiking south, so he follows me and we soon slip through a rock tunnel called Fatman Squeeze and realize he turned the wrong way after exiting the tunnel.

WT heads north and I'm behind him again, when I meet Marty "Recycled" Cain heading south. He tells me that several days ago he met a mom who's hiking from Springer to Harpers Ferry with her 4-year-old twins. I find that hard to believe, but, if it's true it'll be a great story and I hope to catch them.

I take my time, though, to enjoy the 2.7 miles of trail through stunning Grayson Highlands State Park, which I enter shortly after meeting Recycled. The trail drops from 5,017 feet to 4,410 feet through the park, and I enjoy great views from beautiful balds with large rocky outcroppings. There are a few trees and blooming rhododendrons, but most of the balds are covered with short vegetation, such as grass and shrubs, which are grazed by wild ponies brought to the park to keep the vegetation under control.

I see several ponies and pet one, but I'm not quite as excited to see them as are other hikers because I've seen plenty of their ancestors at Assateague Island National Seashore, a barrier island off the coast of Maryland and Virginia, where I worked as a ranger-naturalist in the summer of 1976. The ponies were brought to the park from Assateague.

Shortly after leaving the park, I reach the trail's 500-mile mark and half a mile later stop at Wise Shelter, where I eat lunch and try to dry out my waterlogged bag, pads, tarp and clothes. I wring lots of water from the bag before hanging it at the front of the shelter.

I read the register and learn that Stumbles (aka Leah), has joined a gang and changed adjectives from "awesome" to "magical," at least in this entry, with five stick-on stars, which she wrote eight days ago and titles "THE PEACHES GANG." Then she substitutes "we" for "I" in part of a lyric from "I'm Gonna Be (500 Miles)" by The Proclaimers in writing: "And we would walk 500 miles, and we would walk 500 more, and 500 more, and 500 more..." Then, she writes: "Rained all day except one hour of sunshine, which was MAGICAL! Saw some ponies, which made my whole day, and got to pet some ponies, also magical!"

Engineer, a talented artist who draws charming black-and-white sketches in registers, drew one on May 30 of a backpacker in Grayson Highlands singing, "And I would walk 500 miles and I will walk 1685.3 more." The sketch has been colored with what appear to be colored pencils by Color Bandit, who is hiking behind Engineer and coloring his sketches.

I'm still reading when ridge-runner Jonathan Lemberg arrives to check on the place and we chat a bit. Jonathan, 38, has a degree in botany from the University of Montana and pretty much lives to backpack.

He's thru-hiked the AT and PCT, and spent part of three summers hiking all of the 3,100-mile Continental Divide Trail from Mexico to Canada. Completing the three trails is considered doing the Triple Crown of Hiking. He's also backpacked many other trails, including the 800-mile Arizona Trail from Mexico to Utah and the 296-mile Superior Hiking Trail on rocky ridges above Lake Superior in northeastern Minnesota.

Jonathan's worked as a ridge runner since 2009 and patrols about 100 miles of trail from April to July. Then, he drives to Baxter State Park and works there until mid-October. He says that it's best to climb Katahdin by the end of September because October weather is iffy and the mountain trails can be closed due to ice. When that happens, he says, thru-hikers usually wait at a hostel in Millinocket, about 35 miles from the Katahdin trailhead, and then get a shuttle from the hostel to climb the mountain if it reopens.

Jonathan isn't enthralled with thru-hikers and points out graffiti left on the shelter walls by a few. He says he thinks too much attention is paid to thru-hikers and not enough to the volunteers who maintain the trail. I tell him I'm writing about both and have interviewed several volunteers.

I ask him if he's seen the mom and twins and he says he hasn't, but that he's heard about them. He says that there are more children than usual thru-hiking this year and that he's seen eight or nine pre-teens thru-hiking and being homeschooled.

Before leaving, he tells me that there's "a very nice ridge runner" named Regina working a section of trail that starts about 140 miles north of here, along the Blue Ridge Parkway, and that I should interview her. I say I will, if I meet her.

Then, he says: "Actually, she's my girlfriend."

He says they met in Maine in July 2007, when they were both thru-hiking southbound. They hiked together most of the way and finished together in January 2008. Since then, they've hiked many miles together, and Regina joined Jonathan on most of the PCT. She's going to Maine with him in July and they plan to hike southbound on the AT for a while in October.

"How old is Regina?" I ask.

"In her 50s," he says.

"Really! What part of her 50s?" I ask.

"Boy, you're nosy," he says.

"That's my job. I'm a reporter," I say.

"Well, she's got a very important birthday coming up," he says.

"Really! She's going to be 60!" I say. "I guess that's fine, as long as you don't want to have children and you're having fun together."

I tell him that I'd love to meet an older woman who'd like to backpack with me, but women over 50 who like backpacking, or even camping, are rare. The only older female backpacker I've met on the trail is Marmie, but she's married. So, I say, if Regina has any single, backpacking friends looking for a male hiking companion, tell them to contact me.

Jonathan leaves and then I pack up my gear, which is still wet, and hike farther into Virginia, where I'll be backpacking 553.5 miles, more than a fourth of the trail's miles and the most of any state the trail passes through. I've heard that the hiking's a little easier in Virginia, so I'm hoping to pick up my pace and average about 20 miles a day.

Engineer's sketch

Today, though, I only hike 11.4 because I stop early at Old Orchard Shelter, after seeing a pretty patch of purple fireweed, to give my sleeping bag and other gear more time to dry. I'm the only hiker here, and I've hung my stuff all around the shelter, when I hear a loud group of kids coming from the north. But they stop to camp about a quarter mile before the shelter, and nobody else shows up. So, I've got the place all to myself.

24

IF COLLIN "VICEROY" SANDOE hadn't had sharp eyes, I wouldn't have enjoyed a delicious all-you-can-eat lunch buffet at the Pizza Hut in Marion, Virginia.

I'd met Viceroy, 24, a sous chef from Minneapolis, at Trimpi Shelter, where I spent the night after hiking 14.1 miles from Old Orchard Shelter on a rainy day, including two thunderstorms.

The highlight of the day for many, if not most, hikers would have been the two cans of Miller Lite that someone had left at Hurricane Mountain Shelter, where I stopped for lunch. But I don't love beer, so the highlights for me were the rhododendrons, some with pink flowers and some with white, and the many colorful and interesting-looking mushrooms.

I leave both cans for a hiker, or hikers, who'll really appreciate them, and I read the shelter register while eating. Snapper left a brief entry on June 23, so he's gained a week on me in just 16 days. Maybe, he really will climb Katahdin around his birthday on August 18.

Viceroy's also a fast hiker and we both plan to hike 10.6 miles quickly tomorrow morning, so that we can get to the Mount Rogers Visitor Center in time to catch the 11 a.m. Marion Transit bus for the six-mile ride to the town of about 6,000. If we don't make it, we'll have to wait for the last bus at 2:30 p.m.

I get up before dawn, so that I can get an early start, and I've hiked about three miles when I come to a clearing with a canopy covering a chest and two chairs placed there by the Valley View Baptist Church Youth Group. The chest holds a variety of food for hikers, including ramen noodles, crackers, pretzels and trail mix, as well as tissues, lotion and Bibles. I'm guessing the Bibles don't go fast, since a backpacker would have to be desperate for reading material, or really religious, to add a Bible to a pack. Maybe day hikers grab some.

A sign says that the youth group has been supplying hikers since 2010 and that last year more than 6,000 signed the guestbook. It doesn't say how many Bibles hikers took. I sign it, too, and then grab some snacks, and keep hiking so that I can stay ahead of Viceroy, who soon catches me. Then, I pick up my pace and even run some of the downhills, so that I can keep him in sight.

We arrive at the visitor center by 10:30, and Viceroy notices a phone outside the center and a sign that says the bus only makes the trip to the center if someone calls for a ride. I had misread the guidebook and thought a call is only necessary for the 2:30 bus, so we're lucky that Viceroy sees the sign in time to call.

A few minutes later, I learn that we're even luckier than we thought when I try to call a few Marion motels and get no dial tone. I've just hung up the phone when a man walks around the corner of the building, sees me, and asks if the phone is dead. I say it is and he says he thinks he just accidentally cut the phone cable while trying to fix a sewage problem.

I ask a visitor center employee if there's a cell phone I can use to call motels and she tells me that there's no cell-phone service here. So, if Viceroy hadn't called when he did, we wouldn't have had a bus ride to Marion.

Viceroy plans to hike all of the trail, except the nearly 200 miles he hiked in a previous year from the visitor center to Daleville. So, he's used Craigslist to find a guy who'll drive him the 107.5 miles from Marion to Daleville on Interstate 81. I want to spend the rest of the day and the night in Marion so that I can eat a lot, buy some food for the trail and watch the United States play Belgium in the World Cup.

Viceroy and I are the only two passengers on the bus, which costs us 50 cents each for a ride anywhere in Marion. I tell the driver about the phone outage, and then we ride through town toward the motels on the outskirts. Viceroy gets off at a Taco Bell, and I think he's made a mistake when, just a quarter mile farther, we pass a Pizza Hut with a sign advertising a lunch buffet. I get off in another quarter mile at an America's Best Value Inn, where I get a room and take a quick shower before walking back to the Pizza Hut.

I eat as much as I can, then walk across the street to the Food Lion grocery store. I see Viceroy there and he says that his ride to Daleville fell through. So, I tell him he can stay in my room, if he wants, and look for another ride to Daleville. I say his best bet will be to ask hotel guests at breakfast if they're going as far as Daleville and if he can get a ride.

He decides to stay and we watch the soccer game together for a while. Then he tells me he really isn't interested in soccer, but he's gay and just likes to look at the players. He watches them a little longer, then leaves, and I watch Belgium beat the United States, 2-1, in a thriller.

After the game, I buy Viceroy dinner at a nearby Mexican restaurant. He says he grew up in Rochester, Minnesota, where his father is an exterminator. He says his dad has backpacked much of the trail and gave him money for the hike, but probably won't hike with him. When I ask him if motels have bedbug problems, he says some have and that his dad knows which ones they are and needs to keep that information confidential.

In the morning, an older couple in the lobby say they'll give Viceroy a ride to Daleville, and I get the early bus to the visitor center, where I arrive about 9 and find the phone's still not working. I guess hikers who arrive today won't be able to get a bus to town, unless the driver decides to make the trip, regardless, because the phone's out. It's a good thing there are few hikers on the trail now.

That's also probably why I find lots of ripe blackberries, the first of the trip, before I get to the Relax Inn, a dumpy motel at an Interstate 81 exit, where's there's also a gas station/convenience store and The Barn Restaurant, which is known for its one-pound Angus "hiker burger." I get a room at the motel, where my mother and three sisters would absolutely never stay, and then take a shower before I walk to the restaurant and find that it closed already.

I still look at the menu on the door and see that about all it serves is meat and that there's no salad bar. So, I'm not disappointed and settle for Hot Stuff pizza slices and chocolate milk from the convenience store. The pizza is pepperoni, but I'm OK, in this case, with pulling the pepperoni slices off and eating what's left.

In the morning, I return to The Barn and find plenty of meaty omelets on the menu. When I ask if I can get a veggie omelet, the waitress looks at me dumbfounded, as if I've asked for something almost unimaginable, and says the place doesn't serve one. So, I settle for a cheese omelet, potatoes and pancakes, and then hit the trail.

After about 10 miles, I meet WT heading south again. He tells me that this time he hasn't made a mistake and has decided to hike back to Marion, rent a car and drive home.

"Why?" I ask.

"No people. No water," he says, adding that he spent the last three nights alone at shelters and that he doesn't like carrying water. He also says that he wasn't heading for Katahdin, anyway; had planned to hike only another 44 days, until August 15; doesn't really like camping; and misses his family.

"What do you think about all day?" he asks.

"I pretty much went through my entire life in the first few days," I say, "and now think mainly about the people I interview and how to write about them. That's a big part of what makes the hike fun and interesting for me."

"You're lucky to have a project," he says, and I agree.

When I ask how he got his trail name, he says he named himself and that WT could stand for many things, such as "wet traveler" or "without trekking poles." WT, who hikes with a cane, says his real name is Larry Burdon and that he's a 65-year-old retired pharmacist from Princeton, Kentucky. He left Springer on May 7 and hiked 341.5 miles to Erwin in three weeks.

"I was flying" he says. "I wanted to get in shape." He says he had hiked nine 20-mile days and two days of 32 miles, 6.7 miles longer than my longest day. Then, he took a break and returned home for a bit, which is why I'd met him on the day I left Hampton, nine days ago, at a shelter at the trail's 434.5-mile mark, even though I had left Springer 15 days after him.

WT warns me that there's no water at the next shelter, about four miles away, where I plan to spend the night. He says the only water before the shelter is in the Holston River, about a mile ahead, and in a little stream that I need to watch for carefully. But he says that there's foam on the river and that the stream runs through a field with grazing cows, so it might be unsafe to drink.

I thank him and continue to the river, where there is lots of foam. But I'm thirsty, so I filter some water and drink it, anyway, and then carry more than a quart. When I get to the stream, I decide the water looks cleaner, despite the cows; so, I drink more, then dump the river water and carry the stream water, instead.

There's no water at Knot Maul Branch Shelter, as WT had said, and also nobody, except me, spending the night. I bought the Bristol paper today and the Roanoke paper yesterday, so I'm looking forward to reading them. And I've also got a beautiful setting to savor because I'm going to sleep outside the shelter with blooming magnolias all around me. And after dark, the first eastern whip-poor-wills I've heard on the hike start singing continually. I'm quite content.

25

Nigel "Trubrit" Collins got divorced and gave up most of his money and his construction business before opening a campground for backpackers near the Appalachian Trail.

"I had enough of chasing the dollar. I decided I wanted to completely change my lifestyle," Trubrit, who's in his mid-50s, says, in explaining why he left a 10-year marriage, let his former wife keep most of a million dollars, and closed Abacus Home Improvements in Joliet, Illinois, before moving to a piece of land in southwest Virginia.

I meet Trubrit while I'm taking a break near lovely Laurel Creek on the day after I left Knot Maul Branch Shelter. He sees me near the gravel road and stops his Land Rover with a license plate that says "T-Brit" on the back.

I know who he is because I've seen signs on trees along the trail this morning advertising his Fort Bastian campground, about 1.5 miles down the road. For $7, he picks backpackers up at the trailhead, lets them camp on his land, takes them five miles to the Dollar Store in Bland for supplies, and cooks them a breakfast of bacon, eggs, pancakes and coffee.

He says the $7 just covers his costs and he plans to make a living by developing a wilderness school and outdoor education center at which he'll teach people the survival skills he learned when he was in the British special services.

"I've got all these skills and I want to impart them. Now, I'm happier living in the wilds."

He says he bought land near the trail and opened the campground in 2012 because he loves hikers and is one himself, having hiked many thousands of miles in 36 countries. Last year, 882 hikers, about 600 of them thru-hikers, camped among his pines, got water from the creek that flows through his land, and partied at night under a tarp with a fire burning and guitars available for hikers who want to play. He runs a generator to provide power that hikers use to charge their phones and cameras.

The place sounds tempting, but I've only hiked 4.8 miles and I hope to do 23.8 on this sunny, warm day. In that case, Trubrit says, carry lots of water because there's no reliable source near the trail until Trent's Grocery, 25.5 miles away. If I'm lucky, he says, there might be water in seven miles left by a church group.

So, I get about two quarts from the creek and head north. I've carried lots of water, since I left Knot Maul Shelter on July 4, because I've learned water sources are unreliable now in Virginia. There was only one good source yesterday, and that was near the halfway point of my hike of 19.1 miles.

I get lots of water then from what's called a piped spring because the water comes out of a pipe. The spring is near Chestnut Knob Shelter, which is made from concrete blocks and is the third enclosed shelter I've seen.

I read the register and find that someone this morning has climbed 890 feet over 1.3 miles to the shelter from a dirt road to the north. The hiker wrote: "Hiked up to shelter and to open meadow to clear my head. Lost my best friend of almost 13 years yesterday. Rest in peace, Brodie J. You were a great dog and friend."

The shelter's on a bald with patches of beautiful Turk's-cap lilies and orange butterflyweed. There's also a wonderful view of Burke's Garden, an oval valley about 8 1/2 miles long and four miles wide. In the late 19th Century, Vanderbilt family members picked the valley, also known as God's Thumbprint, as their first choice for an estate. But the local farmers didn't want to sell, so the Vanderbilts built their Biltmore Estate near Asheville, instead.

Burke's Garden is surrounded on all sides by a high ridge, including one that I'll follow for 8.7 miles today to Jenkins Shelter, where I plan to spend the night. Much of the trail in Virginia is along the sides and tops of such ridges, and there's a lot of climbing in getting up a ridge, and even more walking the ups and downs of the trail along them.

I hike down to the road, climb the ridge and haven't gone far when I stop and talk briefly with four hikers, including two thru-hikers who met on the trail. One's a woman from California and the other's a man who graduated a few years ago from the UW in Madison and is living in Chicago. He says he loves Madison and is trying to find a job there so that he can move back. I tell them I hope to talk to them more this evening at Jenkins Shelter, which is about eight miles away.

By the time I get to the shelter, it's nearly dark and the only hiker there is sleeping in a hammock nearby. I get water from a creek and then eat alone because the couple apparently stopped before the shelter. I hear, but can't see, Fourth of July fireworks from a nearby town, which I assume is Bland. After the fireworks end, I fall asleep again to the sound of eastern whip-poor-wills.

In the morning, I get two quarts of water from the creek and, when I leave, the hiker in the hammock is still sleeping. I hike about a half mile before I meet a guy who'd spent the night in a tent and is hiking south. I ask him if there's water in Laurel Creek, about four miles north. He says there is, so I dump my water and hike with a pack that's four pounds lighter.

After reaching the creek and talking with Trubrit, I head for Jenny Knob Shelter, 19 miles away. I climb another ridge and hike nearly seven miles before descending the ridge and finding seven bags full of soda and water that I presume was left by the church group. I take a Coke and a bottle of water, then hike about a half mile farther on a gravel road before I meet two guys in a pickup truck. They give me a can of Natural Light and two more bottles of water. I drink about half of the beer while it's cold and dump the rest, figuring I've got enough liquid left for tonight and part of tomorrow.

Shortly after meeting the men, I meet a section hiker and his dog heading south. He tells me he spent last night at Jenny Knob Shelter with the mother who's hiking north with her 4-year-old twins. He says the mom's trail name is Mama Bear, her son's name is Strong Man and her daughter's name is Little Butt.

He says the twins talked non-stop and had fun celebrating Independence Day, playing with sparklers brought by two women who also stayed at the shelter. So, now I know the mom and twins are at most a day ahead of me and I hope to meet them, hike with them and write a story about them.

I climb about 500 feet up another ridge and hike about seven miles along it before descending. By then, it's about half an hour to sunset and

I've still got 2.8 miles of hiking, including a climb of 416 feet up Brushy Mountain before reaching the shelter.

I hike faster, but then slow down when I see a skunk ahead of me on the trail. The skunk sees me, too, but instead of leaving the trail, as I expect it to do, it ambles ahead of me. I slow down to stay behind the skunk, as the sun sets, and then, after about half a mile, it finally leaves the trail, and I speed up again.

About a mile before the shelter, I put on my headlamp so I can better see the trail and won't miss the sign for the side trail. By the time I see it, it's nearly dark, and once again I've got the shelter to myself. Tomorrow night, though, I hope to be sharing a place with Mama Bear and her twins.

26

DORTE LOWMAN, 72, her daughter Kerstin Rhinehart, 45, and her granddaughter Annika Rhinehart, 16, had never backpacked two weeks ago. Now, they're experienced backpackers on the Appalachian Trail.

I meet the three hikers 14.2 miles after leaving Jenny Knob Shelter, when I take a short side trail to Wapiti Shelter to see if Mama Bear and her twins are there. They're not, but the A-OK trio have stopped in the late afternoon and plan to spend the night.

I've got to hike 7.2 miles on the trail and a half mile on a road to reach Woods Hole Hostel, where I figure I'll likely find the mom and twins. But when Dorte, Kerstin, and Annika tell me a little of their story, I want to hear more.

I tell them I haven't seen even a mother and daughter backpacking the AT and the oldest woman I've met is Marmie, who was 62, and I haven't seen three generations of any family. So, I think they're quite exceptional.

Dorte, of Abingdon, Virginia, says she and her husband have lived along the Virginia Creeper Trail, near the AT, since 1997, and she's wanted to backpack it since then.

"I've been wanting to do it all along and my husband won't do it, so Annika decided to organize it for my birthday on July 24."

Annika, who hadn't even camped before, says she wanted to do something special for her grandmother: "We sometimes take hikes as a family and I enjoy it a lot, and since oma (grandmother in German) wanted to do the trail, I thought it would be fun."

Kerstin, who hadn't camped since she was a child, agreed and spent a year planning the hike that the three started 13 days and 146 miles ago in Damascus.

Kerstin, of Arlington, Virginia, a real estate investor and Coast Guard reservist, says she read "every book I could get my hands on" and took a course from a guy who'd backpacked the trail

"It's a lot more challenging than we thought it was going to be with the rocks, the elevation," says Kerstin. "I had us going 20 miles a day the second week. That's not happening."

Instead, they're hiking about 10 to 12 miles a day and having a great time. They plan to hike for 36 days, in all.

"Being divorced from reality is very nice," Kerstin says.

"I'm not on my phone when I'm out here," says Annika, who'll be a high school senior in the fall.

"I'm enjoying it very much," says Dorte.

I say goodbye to the trio and hike faster because now I've got only about three hours of light and what looks like a difficult hike, including a 1,277-foot climb to the top of a ridge, to reach the hostel. Along the way, I meet a hiker heading south who says he spoke with Mama Bear and she told him she was headed to Woods Hole.

It's nearly dark when I reach the gravel road that leads to the hostel, which, like Mountain Harbour, includes a bed and breakfast, a bunkhouse and a place to camp. I meet two women outside the bunkhouse who say they supplied the sparklers for the twins two nights ago. One of them shows me where Mama Bear and her children are camping.

Mama Bear is just getting Strong Man and Little Butt settled in the tent for the night when I meet her. She says her name is Lisa Murray, that her children, Tess and Cole, really are 4 and that they really have hiked from Springer. I tell her that I think what she and her children are doing is incredible, that I'm a thru-hiker and former reporter, and that I'd love to write a story about them.

"Oh, you're sweet," says Mama Bear.

"No, I'm not sweet," I say. "I just think you and the twins backpacking the Appalachian Trail is a great story and I'd like to write it."

I ask if I can hike with the three of them tomorrow, so I can see them in action, and she says that would be OK.

I say that's great and that I'll meet them in the morning. Then, I return to the rustic bunkhouse, where there are 14 mattresses in the loft, and downstairs there's a table, refrigerator and lots of reading material about the interesting history of Woods Hole. There are also cookie bars baked by

Neville Harris, who owns and runs the place with her husband, Michael Lasecki.

The two met in 2005, when Michael stayed there while thru-hiking and Neville was helping her grandmother, Tillie Wood, run the bunkhouse that she and her husband, Roy Wood, opened to AT hikers in 1986. Roy died a year later and then Tillie ran the place until she died in 2007 at the age of 89.

Michael and Neville kept in touch through emails and phone calls and in 2006 he returned to Woods Hole and told Neville that he loved her. In 2009, they married and reopened the bunkhouse. They also opened the bed and breakfast, where they offer dinner and breakfasts that their guests in the B&B, bunkhouse and campground can help prepare and then help clean up.

I eat several of the $1 cookie bars for dinner and then climb the stairs to the loft, where a dog with the women is unhappy to see me. But it soon settles down and stops barking, and I fall asleep.

In the morning, I go to see Mama Bear and find that the twins are still sleeping. Breakfast isn't being served today because Neville and Michael are leaving on a trip, but Neville still makes me a smoothie in the kitchen and sells me a hunk of cheese and a loaf of her homemade bread. She says she likes running the hostel because she likes helping hikers. But she says she and Michael still need to run the place as a business, unlike her grandmother, who didn't charge much and was mainly a trail angel.

"I like serving the people in the atmosphere we're working in," says Neville, 35, who seems sweet and soft-spoken. "If they have a need, I like figuring out how to get to it."

Also in the kitchen is Ron "Stone Bear" Shields, who'd been hiking the trail before deciding to stay at Woods Hole for a while and help run the place.

Stone Bear, 66, a retired tobacco company sales manager, says he lives in a houseboat on Lake Guntersville in northeast Alabama and suffers from chronic obstructive pulmonary disease that he got from smoking from the age of 16 to his 40s. He decided to try thru-hiking the trail after meeting a woman on Facebook who inspired him to try something he didn't think he could do because his lung capacity is 68 percent of normal.

He started at Springer on March 8 because he thought the hike would take him six months and he wanted to be done by the end of August so he could attend his father's 90th birthday party. But he had trouble breathing above 5,000 feet in Great Smoky Mountains National Park and left the trail for a while at the 206.8-mile mark at Newfound Gap.

Stone Bear

"I felt like I'd be a casualty on the trail and have to be rescued," he says.

He yellow-blazed and hiked about 110 miles to reach Damascus, and then got a shuttle to Woods Hole, where he planned to stay for two days. But Neville and Michael needed help and offered to pay him to stay and work. He agreed to volunteer for a couple months, but hasn't accepted any money.

"There's no way they could pay me enough to do this, unless I loved it," he says. "My motive is to serve people, just like Neville."

So, he spent about 15 hours a day gardening, cleaning and doing other housekeeping, and slept on a mattress on the floor of a steel shed. He left on June 16 and went to Maine, planning to hike the trail southbound. But he had a problem with bronchitis and his father was battling an infection, so he flew home. He returned to Woods Hole on July 5, two days ago, and plans to stay for 10 days, so Neville and Michael can go on vacation. Then, he plans to hike more of the trail.

Stone Bear gets me the box with the shoes that Movin' Shoes shipped to the hostel, and I'm sitting on the porch opening it, when I hear Neville telling Stone Bear that she doesn't think Michael, who's left on an errand, is cut out to run a hostel.

Mama Bear, Strong Man and Little Butt at Wood's Hole Hostel

I'm still on the porch with my shoes and the box when Michael, who hasn't met me, returns, and says, gruffly, "What are you doing here?"

"I slept in the bunkhouse and just picked up shoes I had mailed to Woods Hole," I say, figuring that he thinks I shouldn't be on the porch because I didn't stay in the B&B. I think he's unfriendly and jumps to conclusions, and that Neville's right.

By mid-morning, Mama Bear and the twins are ready to hike. Mama Bear introduces me to Strong Man and Little Butt, who are known as the Cubs on the trail. They're both very cute and seem happy to have company as we start hiking.

27

WHEN HIKERS SEE MAMA BEAR and the Cubs hiking the Appalachian Trail, they smile. Then, they gape in astonishment when Mama Bear tells them that she and her twins, who were 3 when they started their hike on May 4, are backpacking 1,019 miles from Springer to Harpers Ferry.

"So many people will say, 'You're just out for a day hike.' They're seeing me from the front and not seeing my pack," Mama Bear says. "I say, 'No, not really, actually, we've come from Springer.' Then, there'll just be silence. They're like, 'Oh, really?' I always hear in the distance: 'Did you hear how far that woman came?!'"

Mama Bear, 46, of Naples, Florida, tells me her story while I spend one delightful day and half of another on the trail with her and her engaging, energetic Cubs. She's 5-foot-10 and weighs about 145, but is carrying a heavy pack with most of the equipment, food and water for three. She says she doesn't know or want to know how much it weighs.

"My pack doesn't bother me – the weight of it. It's manageable. Only on extreme uphills; then it bothers me. Or when carrying an extra gallon of water swinging on the back."

Little Butt, who weighs 36 pounds, and Strong Man, who weighs 40, wear daypacks that weigh about five pounds each. They each carry water, a sleeping pad, a rain jacket and a headlamp. Strong Man also has two Matchbox cars, while Little Butt has an Aristocats plush.

Mama Bear says Cole, who has a small, lean, muscular build, called himself Strong Man and Tess asked to be named Little Butt after they saw a rock along the trail called Big Butt.

The twins celebrated their fourth birthday a day late on May 20 at the Nantahala Outdoor Center in North Carolina, 137.3 miles from Springer. Mama Bear says they all had two full meals in the center's restaurant; then dessert with candles, and everyone in the place sang "Happy Birthday."

The Cubs seem to be having a great time and have no problem when we start the morning with a 490-foot climb over 1.3 miles, after a half mile hike to the trail. They hike quickly over the rocks and the roots and the many shorter climbs and descents. So, even though their feat sounds incredible, when they're seen in action, it's easy to understand how they and their mom, who all wear running shoes, usually hike 10 to 14 miles a day.

"Up and down, up and down. Rock steps," Little Butt says with a lilt in her voice. "Tunnel," they both say, when the trail is enclosed by rhododendrons. "Slide," they yell, when Strong Man slips and falls backward onto the trail. Sometimes they sing together and they stop for the butterfly wings and bird feathers they collect, and stuff them into their packs.

Little Butt says her favorite part of the trip has been "seeing the horses" at Grayson Highlands State Park and seeing cows. Strong Man says he loves "the flat," referring to when the trail's not going either up or down. Mama Bear says all three of them like the sunny open spaces, when they hike through an occasional pasture, prairie, or mountain bald.

"Obviously, we're from Florida," she says, "so we crave sunshine."

She likes "encountering all these nice fellow hikers" and all of the new experiences: "It's a break from society and reality. I enjoy seeing new things every day and not knowing what the day will bring. I enjoy meeting the people and the small towns."

She thinks the Cubs feel much the same.

"Even at their young age, they enjoy experiencing things they normally wouldn't. We don't need all those toys and fancy gadgets the world embraces."

Strong Man, who walks with kid-size hiking poles, "will fall 20 times a day," says Mama Bear. "Cole's always falling because he has to look at everything else but where he's going, but never hurts himself."

She says Little Butt, who doesn't use poles, falls about twice a day.

"They just kind of bounce because they're so low to the ground." But she says that Little Butt did get hurt once when she cut her lip while climbing a big, wet boulder and somersaulted backward before Mama Bear caught her.

"They're little daredevils," says Mama Bear, who keeps them well back from cliffs that provide beautiful views, and is afraid of heights herself.

That fear, though, as well as the age of the twins and the many people who advised her not to attempt the trip, didn't keep her from trying to tackle the trail she was inspired to hike after seeing a National Geographic special on it about six years ago.

"I filed it in the back of my mind that that was something I wanted to do someday," says Mama Bear, a single mom who owns a condo in Naples and has a master's degree in education. But she cleans houses three days a week, instead of teaching, because she wants to care for her kids full time. She brings them with her on the job. "I've come to enjoy it because it's super physical. I try to do it as fast and as well as I can."

She says she thought of hiking the entire trail this year after seeing how much the twins loved hiking many miles along the Gulf Coast beach in Naples in southwest Florida. Mama Bear says she brought the twins hiking with her because they got too heavy to push in a stroller, and she needed exercise. They did six miles at first; when they started doing 10, she says, she started thinking of taking them on the trail.

"That's how I judged that it was a rational thing that could happen. Then, we would walk in dry sand to make it more intense. We did six, and then ten. It was still working."

Mama Bear, who had camped with the Cubs, but never backpacked, says that in February she called the Appalachian Trail Conservancy to get the names of parents who had hiked the trail, or large parts of it, with young children, so that she could get their advice. All of the children had been 10 to 12, except for one 8-year-old who had thru-hiked.

She says nearly everyone she called for advice told her not to do it.

"When I told the people I called the ages of my children, all of them, except one, expressed major doubt about 3-year-olds on the trail."

The one is Dennis Pendleton, of Delray Beach, Florida, who thru-hiked the AT with his son when he was 10.

"He was super positive," she says. "I think he's just that way. He really encouraged us to give it a whirl. 'What do you have to lose?' he asked. 'You can always come back.'"

Pendleton became her mentor and advised her on every detail during several phone conversations. In April, she decided for sure to do the hike, despite the doubts of her friends and relatives.

Cary and the Cubs (photo: Lisa Murray)

"I had a bunch of doubters. They already knew I was out-of-the box. I've always surprised people with my choices. The one who was most worried was my 20-year-old son."

But they couldn't dissuade her, and she bought backpacks, sleeping bags and pads, a tent, backpacking stove and other necessary equipment.

Then, she convinced her ex-husband, who she says is "super cautious" and said "no way" at first, to let their 10-year-old son, Tuck, hike with her and the twins until he had to go to a sailing camp taught by his dad. The twins' father is out of the picture.

Chad, the 20-year-old, drove the four of them, along with Mama Bear's two Chihuahua-mix mutts to the Springer trailhead, and hiked 31.7 miles with them to Neel Gap in three days, faster than many thru-hikers. He then hiked back for the car and met his mom and half siblings to get the dogs.

Tuck, who got the trail name Spicy Guy because he loves spicy chips, carried a regular backpack with all of the kids' sleeping bags, all of the snacks, his clothes and water. He hiked to Damascus and was upset when he had to leave, Mama Bear says.

"Tuck wanted to go from the get-go. Tuck was crying when he left us. He didn't want to go. He could go the whole way. He was slowed down by us."

She says there were about 20 people planning to thru-hike who left Springer with them, and they didn't expect them to keep hiking and make it to the next shelter.

"At the end of every day, they were surprised that we would make it again. They were astonished. A lot of them were college kids who were kind of surprised we were still hanging with them. Humbling, I guess. Starting in mid-May, I think they expected us to show up every day. But then they got their trail legs and took off."

Mama Bear says one hiker she met at Springer, called "Puddin," "had a belly like Santa Claus."

"He said he was going all the way and we said we were out here for at least a few months. We sized each other up the first day. We looked at each other and thought, no way."

When they all reached Damascus together, after seeing each other nearly every day on the trail, Puddin's belly was mostly gone, she says, and they laughed about their initial impressions.

She says she had thought of trying to thru-hike with the Cubs, and figured she could make it by mid-October by averaging 15 miles a day on days when they hiked, and also taking occasional zero days.

"In theory, the math makes sense. But, in reality, when you're on the trail, you realize how hard it is, at least for us, to keep that pace day after day."

She says that on ideal days they hike 10 to 14 miles from 10 a.m. to 7 p.m. So, she's set her sights on Harpers Ferry, and, if they make it there, she says they might hike the rest next summer or another time.

In the late afternoon, after we've hiked about seven miles, we see a flat open space in the woods ideal for camping. Mama Bear wants to stop because the next town, Pearisburg, is about 3.5 miles ahead, and the miles are mainly downhill, where there usually aren't good places to camp. She prefers camping to staying in towns.

She sets up her tent and then makes dinner for the Cubs. She also boils some water for me so that I can eat the pasta dish that Rock Slide sent me. It's my first hot meal on the trail and tastes great. She says she and the twins eat a lot of rice, couscous, instant mashed potatoes, Little Debbie snack cakes, corn chips and Slim Jims, much like many of the other backpackers.

After dinner, the three hang out in the tent, where, Mama Bear says, they usually tell stories, watch movies on her smart phone and play card games, such as Old Maid and Go Fish, before the Cubs fall asleep.

After they're sleeping, Mama Bear and I talk a while. She thinks the hike has been good for the Cubs and she doesn't think it's been dangerous.

"Really, when you think about it, it's more dangerous when you put kids in a car and bring them to a mall, or on vacation."

She says the hike's been great overall, but it wasn't great one time when the twins and their brother all threw up in the tent in the middle of the night.

"It was all over the place. It's funny now, but I didn't think it was funny at the time."

She thinks the twins will remember the hike, despite their age.

"I think they'll remember, only because it's such a large chunk of time, and the photos, and people will talk about it. It teaches the children that they can experience things that aren't the norm, and persevere."

The twins sleep well past dawn, and, after they and Mama Bear eat breakfast, we leave mid-morning and stop at Angels Rest, where there's a beautiful view of Pearisburg, the New River and the mountains beyond. Mama Bear keeps the Cubs well back from the edge of the cliff.

From Angels Rest, the trail descends 1,900 feet in 2.5 miles to Pearisburg in a series of long, wide, fairly smooth switchbacks. I start running down them and Little Butt surprises me by running right behind me. Strong Man stays right behind us by cutting the switchbacks, which is generally frowned upon, and smiling, as he does it.

As we walk the road into the town of about 2,700, we stop often to eat wild strawberries and Little Butt holds my hand, reminding me why I wish I had a daughter, in addition to my son. I treat the three to an all-you-can-eat lunch buffet at Pizza Plus and then get a room at a motel, where I plan to write about them because I think it's an amazing story and I want to find a newspaper to publish it.

Mama Bear wants to keep hiking, but first goes to a grocery store across the street with the Cubs and buys food for five days. Then, the three return to my motel room and she somehow crams the food into her pack. I try to lift it and find it's hard to even budge off the floor. I guess it weighs 60 to 70 pounds.

But Mama Bear manages to get the pack on her back, and I tell her and the Cubs that I enjoyed hiking with them and hope to catch them and see them again. Then, I start working on their story.

First, I call Laurie Potteiger, information services manager at the ATC, and tell her about Mama Bear and the Cubs. I say I'm writing what I hope becomes a newspaper story about them and ask if any other children as young as the twins have hiked a large section of the trail.

She says the youngest she knows of is Christian "Buddy Backpacker" Thomas, of Crested Butte, Colorado. He was 5 when he hiked the trail with his mother and her boyfriend from April of 2013 to this January.

But, unlike Mama Bear and the Cubs, the three had a Jeep Cherokee that Buddy's mom used to support her son and boyfriend so that they could slackpack or carry less food and equipment when they backpacked. They also skipped around for the best weather and the easiest ways to hike, such as Buddy being driven twice to the top of Mount Washington, a very difficult mountain to climb in New Hampshire, so that he could hike down both sides.

Laurie says two-6-year-old boys have also hiked the entire trail in a year, as part of a family. But she says the ATC doesn't publicize such young hikers or promote such hikes because it doesn't want to encourage people who might be unprepared to try the same thing.

"It should only be undertaken by parents who are very experienced in backpacking," Laurie says. "With children, you don't want to take the same risks that adults would take. We encourage families with young children to explore the AT, but start off small with day hikes."

After talking with Laurie, I take a zero day to write a story on the motel's computer and send it to *The New York Times* because I think it's of national interest and to several other newspapers, including the *Naples News* in Mama Bear's hometown and the *Roanoke Times*, which I've been reading lately and which covers the area we're hiking through.

I wrote two court stories for *The New York Times* when I was a reporter for the *State Journal*, but that was 20 years ago and I have no contacts at the Times now. So, I doubt editors there will be interested in a story that sounds incredible from someone they don't know. But an editor at the Naples paper says he's interested and will get back to me. Then, I stuff myself at the Lucky Star Chinese Restaurant's all-you-can-eat buffet so that I have lots of energy to hike tomorrow. In the morning, I check to see if any other editors have emailed me. They haven't. So, I figure I'll check again after hiking 96.2 miles to Daleville, the next town the trail passes through.

28

WAYNE "DRIFTWOOD" HAYWARD HIKES, writes and hitchhikes. I meet Driftwood my second day out of Pearisburg when I stop for the night at Laurel Creek Shelter. He's 70, but he's very fit and doesn't look it, with his muscular build, ruddy complexion and long brown hair. He and I are alone at the shelter and he tells me a little about his wandering lifestyle.

Driftwood spends five months of the year sleeping in a tent in the 63-square-foot shack he built with scrap wood 20 years ago on a sandbar in the Florida mangroves, on the Gulf side of Scout Key, about 30 miles northeast of Key West.

For much of the rest of the year, he hitchhikes around the country and stays with friends, including one in Beaver Dam, Wisconsin, about 40 miles from Madison. So, I tell him he can stay at my place the next time he's in Wisconsin. Sometimes, he backpacks, and when he has free time, which is a lot of the time, he sometimes writes.

I tell him I did some of the same in my late teens and early 20s, but never thought of making a lifestyle out of it. And, unlike Driftwood, I've never written a novel.

The novel's name is *Frank*, and it's based on the 1903 partial collapse of a mountain that buried part of the Canadian town of Frank in what is now Alberta. The landslide is the deadliest in Canadian history and killed 70 to 90 people when it dumped 121 million tons of limestone rock on the town.

Driftwood says he was encouraged to write it by a friend on Big Pine Key, and he read it to her, as she was dying of cancer. The 714-page paperback, which he self-published in 2009, is $18 on lulu.com.

He says that when he first saw mostly uninhabited Scout Key, 25 years ago, he knew it was the place for him. He spends some of his time with friends, but spends most of it savoring the solitude at the shack he reaches on a hard-to-see, half-mile path he made through the mangroves.

Driftwood

He keeps his clothes, food, reading material and other supplies dry in 5-gallon buckets. And he gets around the area with friends or public transportation. He picks up packages on a nearby key at a UPS store in a strip mall with a library that has computers he uses to keep in touch with relatives and friends.

Few people have found their way to the shack over the years and, remarkably, when he returns each December, he finds the place undisturbed.

So, Driftwood leads a very simple life, but he thought even that might be in jeopardy once, when he mistakenly burned wet wood and sent a lot of smoke rising from the mangroves. The sheriff and a deputy were called, saw the smoke and followed the path into his camp to see where it was coming from. They were surprised by what they found and Driftwood thought his shack might go up in flames, too.

But, after checking him out, Driftwood says: "The sheriff took out his wallet, handed me a twenty, and said, 'Here, I think you can use this.'" Life is often like that on the Keys and on the trail. So, Driftwood fits in fine in both places.

He keeps a fire going here, too, and we keep talking, as the sky grows dark and the flames keep burning. He plans to hike the entire trail in sections and averages about 10 miles a day, from shelter to shelter. In 2008, he hiked about 240 miles from Springer to Standing Bear Farm. This year, he plans to hike much of the 778.2 miles from Standing Bear Farm to Harpers Ferry.

I tell him that I might drive down to the Keys on a camping trip this coming winter, and he says I can find him by going to Coconuts Bar on Big Pine Key and asking for Cyndee. I tell him there's a good chance I might do that. Then, he gives me his card, which was written by his son, Wayde. It says he's a "SOJOURNER/AUTHOR" living a "casual, carefree, chosen lifestyle," "following the sun when able," and "able to travel at a moment's notice."

Sounds pretty good to me, I say, before lying down on my pad outside the shelter to sleep, while Driftwood keeps the fire going.

Driftwood has been the highlight of the last two days, but, as usual, there are plenty of other interesting people on the trail. The day I leave Pearisburg, I meet Sam "Sam-I-Am" Lewis, who teaches me about ranger beads. He's headed south on a long section hike and keeps track of the distance he hikes with the beads on a cord that hangs from his pack.

He says that a hiker, for example, can count the number of paces it takes him to cover 100 meters going uphill, downhill, and on the level. Then, when hiking, he counts his paces and when he reaches the number for 100 meters, he moves a bead on the bottom of the cord. When he's moved 10 beads, and hiked a kilometer, he moves a bead on the top of the cord.

I think it's a clever way to measure distance and counting paces would certainly give a backpacker something to focus on while hiking. But I think it also would be quite monotonous and I'll keep focusing on the trail and the people I meet, and continue relying on the reliable mileage numbers in the guidebook.

After meeting Sam-I-Am, I stop at a shelter to eat lunch and read the register. Then, Paul, a high school math teacher from nearby Blacksburg,

Virginia, and his dog, Abba, stop, and we hike together. He says he's just out for a couple days because his wife told him it would be a good idea for him to get out of the house for a while.

Paul, in his mid-30s, says he used to make a good living playing poker and trading stocks. But he's enjoying teaching now. I've been trading stocks since I was in seventh grade, so, for the first time on my hike, I talk to someone about various stocks and trading and investing, which I'm mostly giving up on the trail. I do, though, keep track of the market on computers in towns along the way. One of the reasons I'm glad I don't have a smart phone is that it keeps me from checking on my stocks and trading much more frequently.

Instead, I track berries and, shortly after meeting Paul, I find my first blueberries of the trip. A few miles after that, and about 10 miles from Pearisburg, we meet two German backpackers who are the opposite of Snapper, the speedy German hiker I met many miles ago.

Friends Olaf Winkler, 28, and Janina Maciejek, 25, are getting their master's degrees in geoscience from the University of Bremen in Bremen, Germany. They plan to study and write about the geology of the trail from Pearisburg to the northern end of Shenandoah National Park, which is about 330 miles of hiking. They're novice backpackers and carrying packs that must weigh more than 60 pounds each.

They're really struggling and they're surprised that Paul and I have hiked as many miles in most of a day as they've hiked in most of two. I tell them they'll be much better off if they return to Pearisburg and either give up much of their stuff, or mail it home, before resuming hiking.

I'm hiking a little faster than normal to keep up with Paul, which is probably the reason I stumble over some rocks and fall. I've fallen other times during my hike, but I'm usually going so slow that I escape with just cuts and scrapes on my legs. This time, I break my fall with my left hand and my palm is bruised and bleeding.

If I'd been alone, I'd have stopped and rested, at least until the bleeding stopped. But I want to keep up with Paul, so I grab a big leaf, press it between my palm and pole, and keep hiking.

Paul and I spend the night at a shelter together and hike together much of the next day before he hikes ahead to get picked up by his wife. I stop for the night and meet Driftwood. When I leave at dawn, he's still sleeping, and the fire is still smoldering.

In about four miles I find Mama Bear and the Cubs camped in a grassy meadow, next to the Keffer white oak. It's the largest oak tree on the AT in the South and is from 18 feet to 19 feet around, about 60 feet tall, and over 300 years old.

Strong Man and Little Butt are sleeping, so I talk with Mama Bear until they wake up and I can talk with them again. They're as cute as ever and I take a picture of them and their mom in front of the tree.

Just past the oak, there's a steep climb of about a mile up another ridge, I take my time and stop to rest occasionally on the switchbacks. Mama Bear and the Cubs pass me and keep climbing without stopping. They just keep amazing me. The hike along the ridge is rocky and difficult, with great views, and I stop often to enjoy them, and to eat black raspberries and blueberries growing in sunny patches along the trail.

When I catch the three again, they've stopped for lunch. Little Butt sees me first and yells, "Hi!" Then, Strong Man also yells "Hi!" I really like these kids. I keep hiking, but stop in the early evening at Niday Shelter because it looks like rain and it's 10.1 miles to the next shelter.

I'm here for just five or ten minutes when two guys in their 20s also stop. We all hike down a hill for water and find a trickle flowing from a spring. I use my homemade water-bottle scoop and one of them uses it, too.

By the time we return to the shelter, there's thunder in the distance, and the two guys discuss whether to stay. They started at Springer separately in June and are both trying to thru-hike in less than three months, like Snapper. And, also like Snapper, they've got ultralight packs with base weights of less than 10 pounds. One has a pack made mostly of springy mesh that he ordered while on the trail.

The other one advises me, as I advised the Germans, to get rid of everything I really don't need. I say I've already done that and that much of my added weight is in my heavier pack itself and sleeping bag. I'd also like to travel lighter, but to do it, I'd also need to order new gear from the trail. And my pack, which now has a base weight of 18 pounds, feels pretty light, as it is.

The guys wolf down some food and decide to keep going because they've got a plan and they plan to keep it. Mama Bear and the Cubs also decide to hike past the shelter because it's still a few hours until dark and they've got a tent. I decide to play it safe and stay. So, I've got a shelter to myself once again.

29

Don "Lost Bard" Krause felt trapped. He was taking care of his 89-year-old mother in his home, but he wanted to backpack the Appalachian Trail.

Then, his brother was seriously injured when he crashed his motorcycle. He was recuperating in Lost Bard's home in Tampa, Florida, when Lost Bard saw a way out.

Lost Bard, 64, a retired appraiser, tells me his story while we're relaxing in the Four Pines Hostel, a three-bay garage in the country with couches, chairs, cots and a bed scattered about, a bathroom with a shower, and a wood stove.

He says he decided to see if his brother was capable of caring for his mom on his own, so he took a short camping trip. When he returned, everything was OK, so he took a longer trip, and when he got back, everything was OK again. Then, he figured his brother could handle the job and he decided to backpack the trail.

In April, he told his brother that he wanted to hike some of the Appalachian Trail. His brother asked how long he was going to be gone and Lost Bard said he wasn't sure. Then, after he left Springer on April 18, he called his brother and told him he had decided to hike the whole trail and he'd be back in about six months.

His brother wasn't happy and neither were two of his four sisters who live in the Tampa area. They were getting their mother ready for church once when Lost Bard called, and one asked: "Couldn't you have waited until she passed?"

No, he couldn't. He's got lots to do and not much time to do it. After he finishes the trail, he might try to sail around the world.

He and I also talk about Dragon's Tooth, a 35-foot-tall, quartzite rock monolith on the top of Cove Mountain, which I climbed today.

Climbing the mountain from the south was hard; descending was a tough, treacherous and scary 0.8-mile rock scramble with tricky steps from rock to rock and arrows painted on the rocks pointing the way. Near the top, there were two sections of U-shaped iron bars embedded in the rock to use as steps and handholds, and below that was a 20-foot cliff with ledges several inches wide to use as toeholds. I was relieved when I made it down what I consider the hardest, most dangerous descent so far.

So, I'm worried about Mama Bear and the Cubs doing that descent. Lost Bard has also met Mama Bear and the Cubs, who are behind us, and we agree that she shouldn't try to take them over that section of trail. We don't see how the three of them can safely make the descent without at least one other hiker there to help. They might get help because the climb to Dragon's Tooth is a popular day hike, but we're still concerned.

I'd talked with Mama Bear again in the morning, a couple miles after leaving the shelter, and, when I left her, the Cubs were still asleep. I'd heard her ask hikers heading south what they thought of the trail near Dragon's Tooth, so I knew she was aware of the difficulty. But the hikers had told her that, if the three had handled the rest of the trail from Springer, they could do it. So, I figure they'll be hiking it tomorrow.

I've got her phone number, so Lost Bard calls her and texts her to let her know we don't think she should try it, and that someone from the hostel can pick her and the Cubs up in the morning at the lot where day hikers park before climbing the mountain from the south, but he gets no response.

After I saw Mama Bear, I'd climbed Brush Mountain, where I saw a monument to Audie Murphy, who was the most decorated U.S. soldier of World War II, receiving every military combat award for valor available from the Army, as well as French and Belgian awards for heroism. After the war, he was an actor for 21 years before dying at the age of 45 when the small plane in which he was a passenger crashed into Brush Mountain on May 28, 1971.

By the time I made it down from Dragon's Tooth, it was nearly dark, and I was walking about a third of a mile to the hostel when a couple guys in a van headed the same direction stop and ask if I need a ride. They're AT hikers and say the van belongs to Joe Mitchell, the hostel owner. He lets hikers take it a little less than a mile to the Catawba Grocery, where they've just been.

Sure, I say, and then they offer to turn around and take me to the grocery, too. I'm grateful because I'm very hungry and very thirsty. I drink several cups of water at the store, and then get two veggie pizzas baked there, one for dinner and one for the trail. I also get a quart of orange juice, five big brownies, two scoops of chocolate Moose Tracks ice cream in a waffle cone and the Sunday *Roanoke Times*.

I thank the guys for waiting and then we return to the hostel, where there are several hikers outside drinking beer with Joe. It's the biggest group of hikers at a hostel or shelter I've seen since the Smokies, and the first thru-hikers I've caught up with since then, too. I'd like to interview amiable Joe, but he's partying with the hikers. He charges nothing, but asks for donations to keep the place going.

I'm sitting outside eating pizza when one of the thru-hikers comes over and says he heard I'm from Wisconsin and he's from Wisconsin, too. He's Jason "Nuke" Green from Sparta, about 115 miles northwest of Madison. Sparta calls itself the "bicycling capital of America" because it's at one end of the 32-mile-long Elroy-Sparta Trail, the first rails-to-trail bike path in the country, known for its three long tunnels. The city also has what's almost certainly the world's only combination space and bicycling museum, which honors Deke Slayton, a rural Sparta native and one of the first astronauts.

Nuke says he left Springer on May 8, two weeks before me, but took a week off the trail to attend a friend's wedding in Wisconsin. His parents picked him up in Pearisburg and then drove him back to the trail. He got his trail name because he was a submarine nuclear reactor operator in the Navy, where he spent six years after graduating from high school. He wanted adventure before going to college and plans to study mechanical engineering at the UW campus in Platteville, about 70 miles southwest of Madison. I ask him if he'd like a piece of pizza, and he says no thanks.

After I finish the pizza, I go into the garage, where I meet Lost Bard. After we talk, I'm tired, but most of the hikers are still outside drinking. I ask the few in the garage if I can turn off the lights and they say OK. So, I do, and then fall asleep on a couch.

In the morning, I get up at dawn again and leave while everyone's still sleeping. I walk back to the trail and have hiked about 1.5 miles when I meet Jim Webb, 64, and Dave Horst, 62, volunteer AT maintainers from the Roanoke Appalachian Trail Club, which cares for 123 miles of trail.

They're removing a stile, which consists of wide ladders on both sides of a fence, so that hikers can cross, and they're building a dodgeway to replace it. The dodgeway is a fence opening that hikers can walk through, but cattle can't. The Appalachian Trail Conservancy is having all of the stiles on the trail replaced with dodgeways because some hikers have been seriously hurt falling forward when descending stiles. The club's section of trail had 21 stiles when club members started replacing them in the spring and there are five left.

Jim, who's moved from Buffalo, New York, to Roanoke after retiring, is the club's assistant trail supervisor and spends about 16 to 20 hours a week working on the trail, sometimes hiking five miles just to remove fallen trees.

When I ask why he does it, he says: "I'm retired. What else do I have to do?" But he doesn't backpack because he's got a bad back, arthritis and "likes clean sheets and hot showers too much."

After leaving the men, I meet the first father and daughter I've seen hiking the trail together. Cacie "Banana Woman" Thompson, 23, and Mike "Spreadsheet" Thompson, 65, both of Raleigh, North Carolina, started near the trail's midpoint in Pennsylvania's Pine Grove Furnace State Park and have hiked about 400 miles southbound. They were originally headed to Springer, but now might stop in Damascus after hiking about 230 more miles.

"It was his idea, but I jumped on board pretty quickly," says Banana Woman, who just graduated from Georgetown University.

"This is on my bucket list. I've been wanting to do it since I was a teen," says Spreadsheet.

"I wouldn't trade it for anything. It's a great adventure," he adds. "The challenge is a little more than I expected. You get a sense of accomplishment. The thing that impresses me the most is that it's a totally different environment than the real world."

After leaving the two, I reach Highway 311 and the parking lot for the 3.7 mile climb on the AT to McAfee Knob, known as the most photographed spot on the trail. Gwen, a hasher from Pennsylvania, is about to do a day hike to the knob with her teenage daughter. She gives me a bottle of beer and a bottle of water, and she says the two plan to spend the night at Four Pines Hostel. I think Gwen will fit right in.

Cary on McAfee Knob (photo: Jason Green)

Nuke catches me on the hike through a forest of mainly oaks and hickories to the knob, a rock outcropping with a spectacular 270-degree view of the Catawba Valley. We enjoy the view and take each other's picture sitting on the edge of the knob, recreating a shot that's most likely been taken of nearly every hiker who's been there and isn't afraid of heights.

By now, it's early evening and I don't know if there's water at the shelter less than a mile away. The shelter after that is six more miles, so I know I've got to hike quickly. As I leave the knob, I see Gwen and she gives me more water; so, I've got enough, for now.

The nearby shelter doesn't have water, so I pick up the pace and get to Tinker Cliffs close to sunset. I enjoy more beautiful views of the valley, while walking half a mile along the cliffs. In reaching Dragon's Tooth, McAfee Knob and Tinker Cliffs, I've completed the Triple Crown of Virginia hiking.

Then, I arrive at Lamberts Meadow Shelter at dusk. A couple staying in a tent tell me there's a little water in a nearby stream. I use my water-bottle scoop to get some and then eat dinner and read yesterday's paper, while the only hiker in the shelter is fast asleep.

30

BACKPACKING THE APPALACHIAN TRAIL with a dog is difficult when the dog doesn't want to walk. That's why Theo "Beach Bum" Gray and his mostly pit-bull mutt are sharing my motel room in Daleville.

I'm taking time off the trail the day after I enjoyed the magnificent views from McAffee Knob and Tinker Cliffs. I want to try again to get my story on Mama Bear and the Cubs published, mail a few things home and do some shopping.

I'm using the computer in the lobby of the Howard Johnson Express when I see Beach Bum, 26. I'd spoken with him at Woods Hole and I ask him how is hike is going. Not good, he says, because his dog is tired of the trail and has often been simply sitting and refusing to walk. So, he plans to hitchhike home to Florida on the interstate, which runs past the edge of Daleville, about half a mile from the motel.

I say it'll likely take him a long time to hitch to Florida, since he's a Black man with a backpack and a dog known for being aggressive. I tell him, as I told Viceroy in Marion, that he'll likely have better luck asking motel guests at breakfast if they're heading south and if he and his dog can come along. And I say he and the dog are welcome to stay in my room. He likes my suggestion and decides to stay till morning.

Then, I try again to interest an editor at the *Roanoke Times* in my story about Mama Bear and the Cubs, since Daleville is only about 15 miles from Roanoke and Mama Bear and the Cubs aren't far behind me. I send an email and the story to the paper's managing editor, Michael Stowe. I tell him that I was a reporter at the *Wisconsin State Journal* and ask him if he'd like to publish my story.

"Thanks, Cary," he replies. "Do you know where she and her kids are now? Have they gotten to Daleville yet? I'm wondering if I can get a photographer out to meet them. How much will you charge us if we use the story?"

I tell him he can use the story for free, but that I want to keep the rights to it and that Mama Bear and the Cubs will likely reach Daleville tomorrow. I also give him Mama Bear's cell-phone number and email address so that a photographer can contact her and arrange to meet her and take pictures.

In the evening, Beach Bum and I walk to Country Cookin', near the interstate, for the all-you-can-eat buffet. There's also a Shoney's, which I liked in Gatlinburg. But the hotel clerk says Country Cookin' is even better, and she's right. There's lots to choose from and it's delicious.

Beach Bum also orders sweet tea, which costs extra, and I get water. When the waitress keeps refilling his glass and not mine, he tells me that's because the sugar in the tea is filling and results in guests eating less from the buffet. Now, I understand why Pizza Plus servers have kept refilling my glass with soda, which is free with that buffet. So, from now on, I'll drink only water at all-you-can-eat places, so I can fill up with food.

In the morning, Beach Bum sits in the motel lobby with his dog and backpack and asks guests for a ride. He's getting discouraged when the breakfast crowd has gotten slim and he still hasn't gotten a lift. But then he asks a guy who says he got up early this morning just so he could hike a bit on the AT.

Andy Haddock's from Maine and knows about the trail, and he's headed for New Orleans. Beach Bum's father lives in Atlanta, which would be about an 85-mile detour, but Andy says he'll take him there. I say goodbye to Beach Bum and then check to see if Michael has written me back to tell me if he's going to use the story.

He hasn't, so I leave and in 1.5 miles pass the side trail to Troutville, where I spent the night of September 18 during my cross-country bike trip on the TransAmerica Trail in 2001. I remember the date because it's Craig's birthday and I called him from there.

Later I meet Debbie Wroten, of Florida, heading south and she tells me about the Ursack she uses to store her food. She says bears can't chew or claw through the bag, so she doesn't have to hang it and can just tie it to a tree. I plan to look into getting one.

In the evening, I reach the Blue Ridge Parkway, which runs 469 miles from Great Smoky Mountains National Park to Shenandoah National Park, with frequent beautiful views. I've driven part of it and I biked part of it on my cross-country trip, but never walked it. Now, I'll be walking a little of it several times in the 120.3 miles from here to Shenandoah National Park.

It's nearly dark when I arrive at Bobblets Gap Shelter, after hiking 18.5 miles. I'm using my headlamp to look around, when the only person in the shelter, says, "It's me." It's Nuke and I'm surprised to see him because he left Daleville yesterday afternoon. But he says he's been taking his time and tells me where to find water.

In the morning, I leave first, but Nuke passes me after a few miles when I'm climbing a mountain slowly and stopping often to eat blueberries. In ten miles, I reach Jennings Creek, where I take off my tech T-shirt, soak it and then wring the water out before putting it back on. That helps keeps me cool and my shirt kind of clean, so I've been doing it on warm days whenever I can.

I climb and descend another mountain to Cornelius Creek Shelter, where Nuke's stopped for the day after 18.4 miles, and I stop, too. There are also a couple backpackers out for a few days here, so we've got others to talk with.

In the morning, I've hiked five miles and I'm near the Thunder Hill Shelter when I meet trail crews putting the finishing touches on about two miles of new trail that will open tomorrow.

The trail relocation has taken nearly a decade from the time it was first proposed to deal with erosion problems on the current trail, says Jason Hammer, 38, trail supervisor for the Natural Bridge Appalachian Trail Club, which maintains 90 miles of the AT. He says the work in the woods started about four years ago, and the club is now planning relocations for the summer of 2019.

Jason, of Lynchburg, who hiked the entire AT over 2000 and 2001, says he's been volunteering since then and worked about 300 hours on the trail last year because of his "love of the AT and nature and the outdoors."

Assisting the club is the Appalachian Trail Conservancy's Konnarock Trail Crew. Davis Wax, 23, of Concord, North Carolina, an assistant crew leader, says the crew relies heavily on volunteers who work five-day shifts and get food, housing, camping gear, and training. Wax says "the work is the most fun, interesting and challenging I've done." He says he hopes to do it year-round by also working on other trails.

Nancy Thornhill Hauser, 45, of South Pasadena, California, says she volunteered after an AT backpacking trip she planned with her daughter fell through. Her daughter and husband didn't want her to hike solo, so she volunteered, instead. "I've loved it," she says.

By evening, I've hiked 17.7 miles to Matts Creek Shelter, where Nuke has called it a day. But I decide to hike 3.9 miles more to Johns Hollow Shelter because the hike looks fairly flat and easy, and then I'll be only 20.1 miles from the highway to the city of Buena Vista, where I plan to spend tomorrow night.

The trail parallels the wide, placid James River for a mile before crossing the river on the stunning 623-foot-long James River Foot Bridge, the longest pedestrian bridge on the trail. The bridge, which eliminated a dangerous bridge crossing, is named after the late Bill Foot, who thru-hiked the trail with his wife, Laurie, in 1987, and then became passionate about improving it, because, said Laurie, "He wanted everyone to be able to enjoy the trail as much as he did."

The couple helped make the bridge possible and were known as "The Happy Feet." In 1997, they were the first people to complete the American Discovery Trail from Cape Henlopen, Delaware to Point Reyes, California, which they did by hiking and biking.

Bill, who had been a past president of the Natural Bridge Appalachian Trail Club and a past member of the ATC Board of Governors, spent the last years of his life raising $1.5 million to build the bridge. He died in the spring of 2000 of cancer at 53 in the couple's home in Lynchburg, Virginia. The bridge was dedicated on October 14, 2000 in his memory.

As I cross the bridge, I enjoy beautiful views of the Blue Ridge Mountains and then follow a sparkling stream, full of rapids and waterfalls. It's dusk when I reach the shelter and find a tent set up inside.

In the tent are a young couple about to go to sleep. We talk briefly and they say that they're thru-hikers and left Springer on May 22, which is the day I left. I think this is the first time I've seen them, but they say they were arriving at Woods Hole when I was leaving and we said hi to each other then. They also say they hiked about 330 miles with Monica, the woman I shared the Springer shelter with and haven't seen since.

They're tired and want to sleep, so I say good night and eat dinner. I also read the register and find a note written on July 14, five days ago, by Regina, the ridge runner whom I've been curious about and hoping to meet since her boyfriend, Jonathan, 38, also a ridge runner, told me that she was about to turn 60 and that I should interview her because she's very nice.

Regina wrote: "HI from Regina the ATC Ridgerunner. Thanks for a great season class of 2014. Sorry I missed you after today. Thanks for being good stewards of the trail by packing out all your stuff and hanging your food. Happy Trails. Regina ATC Ridgerunner."

So, I guess that if I get to meet her, it'll be in Baxter State Park in Maine, where Jonathan told me they're heading.

 In the morning, the couple in the tent leave before me, but I catch them in the early evening, where they've stopped at a shelter 1.8 miles before the highway to Buena Vista, and we talk about their trip.

Christine "BrightSide" Villa, 22, of Pleasantville, New York, graduated in the spring from Fairfield University in Fairfield, Connecticut, while her boyfriend, Jeff "Ascender" Loselle, 22, of Westport, Connecticut, has finished his junior year at the University of Connecticut in Mansfield. They plan to hike 1,362 miles from Springer to the border of New York and New Jersey, before Ascender has to return to school.

They say they've been together for nearly two years and that "when we told people we're doing the trail, they said then you'll know for sure if it will last."

So far, BrightSide says, they're "very happy." One reason she's happy is that Ascender is carrying about 55 pounds, while she carries 20. That, Ascender says, is "because I love her."

We haven't met until now because they stopped before reaching Springer on May 21, when I arrived, and left Springer about five hours after me the next day. Then, they took five days to hike the 31.7 miles to Neel Gap that Deacon and I did in two.

They say Monica's trail name is "Wild Fire" and that they met her their third night and hiked with her to Erwin. They also say that Monica battled shin splints in the beginning and got compression socks to help deal with the problem.

Like me, they also saw the note left in Muskrat Creek Shelter for a woman named Monica by southbound hikers on December 6. But she told them it was for a different Monica.

We talk a little about hikers' opinions of Mama Bear and the Cubs and they say comments vary from it's "the best thing ever" to someone should call social services to protect the twins. But they say "most people thought it was a good thing – better than other things you could do with your kids."

After leaving them, I hike faster because I've got only about an hour of light and 1.8 miles to hike to the highway, where I plan to hitch 9.3 miles to Buena Vista. Then, I fall and bruise my left quadriceps. It's sore, but I still make it to the highway before dark.

There are few cars on Sunday evening, but a nice local couple stop and give me a can of Coke, a Baptist tract, and a ride to the Buena Vista Motel. My quad hurts, but, after I get a room, I still manage to limp about a mile round trip to get a Domino's pizza for dinner.

31

Shuttle driver Aubrey "Piney" Taylor has been "helping hikers since 1959." When Piney, 72, of Buena Vista, sees me and my backpack in a wayside along Highway 60, he stops his pickup truck to see if I need help, too. I don't because I've just gotten a ride from Buena Vista to the AT trailhead.

I do, though, want to learn a little about Piney, who makes a living driving hikers from place to place. He says he started helping hikers 55 years ago when he was logging near the trail. Back then, he gave them water and many ate supper with him in the woods.

In 1980, he started shuttling hikers and he says he's enjoyed it enough to have kept at it for 35 years.

"It's all right. Sometimes it gets frustrating when you drive 50 miles to pick someone up and they're not there. A lot of them don't leave, but some will leave."

Piney says some people who planned to thru-hike call him for a ride when they decide to quit.

"Some get hurt. Some run out of money. Some just get tired of walking."

Piney says his most notable passenger has been Bill Bryson, the author of *A Walk in the Woods.* He says he shuttled Bryson in 1996 from Reeds Gap, 36.1 trail miles north of here, to a motel in Waynesboro, 19.2 trail miles north of Reeds Gap.

He reaches into the truck and picks up a well-worn badge that journalists from the *Atlanta Journal* and *Atlanta Constitution* gave him 19 years ago when they and reporters and photographers from four other newspapers were working on *Appalachian Adventure*, a coffee-table book about the AT that includes a picture of Piney sitting on the back of his truck.

"It's been hanging in my truck since 1995," Piney says.

I tell Piney I plan to hike the 56.2 miles to Shenandoah National Park in three days, and he says there's no way I'll do it in three because the hike includes tough climbs over The Priest and Three Ridges Mountain. But I tell him I'm pretty sure I can make it.

I'd taken a day off in Buena Vista because my quad still hurt after my night in the motel. In the morning, I limped the mile from the motel to the Blue Dog Art Cafe to eat breakfast and get a bed at the hostel that the helpful cafe owner, Susan Hogan, runs next door. After eating, I'm standing outside the cafe when Ascender, BrightSide and Nuke arrive and we all get a spot in the hostel.

Then, I walk to the library, where I want to see if Michael Stowe, the managing editor of the *Roanoke Times*, has emailed me about my story. He has and I don't like what I read in the email he sent me after I left Daleville.

"Thanks again for the heads up on this story," he wrote. "We have a reporter and a photographer trying to meet up with Lisa and the kids tonight around Daleville/Troutville. We may use parts of your story, along with our own reporting, but will make sure to give you credit in some form if we do. I appreciate you reaching out to Laurie Potteiger for context from the Consevancy. (sic) We'll be happy to share our photos to any other newspaper that picks up your story."

So, he decided to take the story that I'd put lots of time and effort into and told him that he could publish for free, but not that he could use parts of it and pass it off as the work of his own reporter. That's stealing a story and is a blatant breach of journalism ethics. When a freelancer offers a newspaper editor a story that the paper's editors and reporters wouldn't have known about otherwise, the editor can buy or not buy it, but not ethically send his own reporter to write it.

Then, I read the story with the byline of rookie reporter Amy Friedenberger published Thursday. I find that she filched many facts from my story and combined them with a few things Mama Bear said about her last few days in basically rewriting my story into a much shorter version with eight mistakes, including getting the number of days Mama Bear and the Cubs have been on the trail wrong and the Cubs' birthday wrong, because she couldn't even steal from my story correctly. A line at the bottom of the story, says I "contributed" to it.

Amy, who graduated from the University of Pittsburgh last year and just started working at the paper in April, did what she was told to do, so I don't blame her. But I think Michael is a discredit to journalism.

When I return to the hostel, I find BrightSide looking for a place to do laundry and I tell her she might want to try my method. I say I think it's a waste of time, money and resources to wash just a few pieces of clothing in a machine. So, I've never used one on my hike. Instead, I've kept soaking my clothes in running water and wringing them out in a sink until there's little dirt left. Then, I hang them to dry.

When she asks if they smell, I let her smell the tech T-shirt I wear every day and "washed" last night. It smells fine she says, and adds that she might try my method.

From the hostel, I head to the hardware store to get something to fix my shoes. I had no problems with my first pair of New Balance 940s, but the shoes I picked up at Woods Hole, 181.7 miles ago, are a new model with redesigned soles, and parts of these soles are coming apart. I've been holding them together with duct tape and want to get something better.

A guy at the hardware store recommends contact cement, so I buy some and then explore the rest of the city of about 6,700, which, I'm surprised to learn, is home to a Mormon university in an area with few Mormons and mostly Baptists. A group of Mormons bought a failing women's college in 1996 and now successful Southern Virginia University occupies stately Main Hall, a Virginia historic landmark, and the other buildings on University Hill, which overlooks Buena Vista.

By evening, my quad feels OK, and Nuke tells me I can ride back to the trail with him and a friend from high school who's going to hike with him for a distance to be determined. He says he and Amber, who enlisted in the Army for four years out of high school, reconnected on Facebook. She lives nearby and wants to join him on the trail.

I ask Nuke if he thinks Amber will slow him down and cost him the time he needs to reach Katahdin.

'She might," he says. "Maybe it's worth it, though. We'll see."

In the morning, Amber arrives in a pickup truck driven by her friend and I see why Nuke is willing to take the risk. If I were 24, I'd probably make the same decision. Nuke and I ride in the bed of the pickup and it reminds me of when I was a kid and my sisters and I rode in the bed of the pickup driven by my father.

Nuke and Amber put on their packs and hike away. Ascender and BrightSide arrive in another vehicle and follow them, while I sit and talk with Piney.

All of us, except Piney, gather at Seeley-Woodworth Shelter after a 14-mile day that includes a 1,994-foot climb to start and several other shorter climbs and descents. I ask Amber what she thinks of the trail and she says she doesn't love all of the ups and downs, which the rest of us have gotten used to after 816.6 miles.

After we talk and eat, then get ready for sleep, I hear Nuke say to Amber: "I sleep in the nude. I hope that's OK." "OK," says Amber. "I was kidding," says Nuke.

32

Long-haul truck driver Roger "Islander" Carter is trying long-distance hiking, instead, for his health. Islander, 56, who was born on Prince Edward Island in Canada and lives in Mocksville, North Carolina, hopes to lose many of his 255 pounds and deal with diabetes by backpacking the Appalachian Trail.

He started in Tennessee 32 days ago on June 21, and, when he weighed himself on an outfitter's scale in Daleville, 271.6 miles later, he was down to 230. He doesn't know how much he's lost since then, but he does know he feels good and likes trail life.

"I like the no stress, no TV, all that,' says Islander, who also had spent last night at Seeley-Woodworth Shelter. "But I was listening to NPR this morning."

Islander and I are the only ones up at the shelter and we talk a little more before I get another early start.

He says he spent five days backpacking the trail in Tennessee last year and learned a lot. His main goal this year is Hudson, New York, where he has family. Hudson is north of the trail on the Hudson River, which the trail crosses. If he makes it to the river, he'll have hiked another 583.1 miles from here.

Yesterday, we passed a cardboard sign nailed to a tree along the trail wishing Mama Bear and the Cubs "best of luck from a nearby landowner cheering you on!"

Islander disapproves of Mama Bear taking the Cubs on the trail. "I think it's a bad idea," he says, noting the danger of falling and getting hurt and the damage he thinks it might do to their bones and tendons.

I leave Islander and head for The Priest, which is 7.1 miles of mostly rolling trail, with a final 800-foot climb to the 4,063-foot summit. The hike is relatively easy because I did most of the climbing yesterday.

But the rest of the day's hike is tough with a 3,093-foot descent to the Tye River and then an arduous 3,014-foot climb up Three Ridges Mountain, which includes several false summits. Piney was right when he said the climb would be difficult.

I take a break to watch a beautiful swallowtail butterfly feeding on a patch of Turk's-cap lilies, and I meet Eric Giebelstein, 32, a wilderness ranger who works from May through September patrolling six wilderness areas, including The Priest Wilderness, for the Southern Appalachian Wilderness Stewards, a project of The Wilderness Society. He says that he shared a place this year with ridge-runner Regina, when they weren't on the trail, and that she had turned 60 and left yesterday for Maine with Jonathan.

It's dark when I reach Maupin Field Shelter after a 20.4-mile day and find Ascender and BrightSide in their tent. They say they blue-blazed and avoided the 7.3 miles up and down Three Ridges on the 3-mile-long Mau-Har Trail, part of which follows Campbell Creek. They say the trail along the creek was beautiful with many waterfalls and pools. I would have taken it, too, if I didn't want to hike the entire AT.

I hear a guitar being played in the shelter, and then meet the Honeymooners: David "Guitarzan" Bowen, 45, and Heather "Hard Headed" Collins, 51. Guitarzan guesses that I'm 55 and when I tell him I'm 64, he plays "When I'm Sixty Four" by the Beatles and keeps playing while I eat dinner on a picnic table and then go to sleep outside the shelter. But I move inside when it starts raining in the middle of the night.

In the morning, Ascender and BrightSide hit the trail, while I stay a while to talk with the Honeymooners, who married three years ago, but were working then and didn't have time for a honeymoon. So, they're taking it now by thru-hiking the trail.

Hard Headed says she'd heard about the AT in high school and had thought about hiking it after moving in 1994 to Georgia, where, as a Unitarian Universalist, she was the head of pastoral care and education at the Atlanta Medical Center, a city hospital, before she left on the hike.

But, she says, she and Guitarzan, a professional musician, didn't think seriously about thru-hiking until two years ago, when they were driving from Kentucky to Georgia in mid-November and stopped for the night at Standing Bear Farm Hostel, where I decided not to stay after hiking through Great Smoky Mountains National Park. She read comments of hikers from all over the world in the hostel's log, and then she and Guitarzan took a short hike north on the AT.

"We learned that we both entertained the idea of hiking it for a long time," Hard Headed says. "Now that we found each other, we could do it together."

She and Guitarzan had camped by car, but never backpacked. And she says she was in lousy shape from commuting 30 miles each way to her job in Atlanta.

"I figured if I didn't get into shape, I would never be able to do it."

Guitarzan says he plays and sings mostly blues, jazz and classic rock, and also writes and plays spiritual and nature-based songs for his wife's ministry. That's a big change from the time his band, Shaky Dave and the Barstools, was the house band for the Outlaw Biker Gang in Davie, Florida.

"I couldn't go six months without playing the guitar," he says. So, he bought a 2-pound Martin Backpacker guitar for the trail.

The couple left Springer on April 16, hiked five to eight miles a day at first and now do eight to seventeen. By Erwin, after 341.5 miles, Hard Headed had lost 40 pounds and they'd doubled their daily mileage. Guitarzan says his waist size has dropped from 40 inches to 32, the thinnest he's been since high school. They plan to hike north until September 1, then flip to Maine, climb Katahdin and hike south.

They say the scariest moment of their hike was just before midnight on May 12, just north of the Smokies, when they were lying in their tent in a rainstorm and a tree branch, 10 feet long and six inches in diameter, fell on them.

"It was horrifying," Guitarzan says. "I heard the crack of the branch. The next thing I heard was 'ouch.'"

The branch had hit Hard Headed, leaving her dizzy with a mild concussion, her right eye swelled shut and a large lump on her head. Her cell phone was also broken, but she says the poles of their Big Agnes tent, which got bent, saved their lives.

One of their favorite trail times was at a crowded Spence Field Shelter in the Smokies on a cold and rainy night. Five of the other hikers were good guitar players and they took turns playing Guitarzan's guitar around a fire, while one also played the harmonica, as they sang.

Guitarzan and Hard Headed (photo: Terry Martin)

"We're enjoying the people we meet, the towns we go through," says Hard Headed.

They say the hike has been good for their marriage.

"I think it's great," says Guitarzan.

"I think it's been really good," says Hard Headed. "You can't avoid things by going to work every day. Now, we're together all the time."

33

"HOW OLD ARE YOU?" I ask Norman Anderson, as he gives me a ride to town.

"Ninety-one. Ninety-two in September," says Norman, while driving the 4.5 miles from Rockfish Gap to Waynesboro, Virginia, as he's done countless times for AT hikers for 40 years.

Norman, who doesn't look his age and is a fine driver, tells me he and a friend founded the Waynesboro program in which many area residents give free rides to hikers to town and back from the gap, just south of the southern entrance to Shenandoah National Park.

I learn about the shuttle service when I arrive at the gap the morning after the morning I spoke with Guitarzan and Hard Headed. There's a sign at the trailhead with the names and phone numbers of 25 people who will provide rides "to town when their schedules permit."

Since I don't have a phone, I hike about a half mile up a steep hill to the Rockfish Gap Trail Information Center, where center volunteer Richard Bronski calls Norman for me.

About 15 minutes later, he rolls up in his 2003 Buick Le Sabre Custom, which he's driven about 66,000 miles, many of them carrying hikers. He says he makes 130 to 140 round trips in a hiking season from Waynesboro to the gap.

"In the peak season, I'm up and down the mountain a lot," says Norman, who's lived in Waynesboro for about 60 years and used to run a Sherwin-Williams paint store.

He says he and a friend had post office boxes in the 1970s and started offering hikers free rides after seeing them at the post office. They found a few other residents willing to join them and posted a sign offering rides, with the names and phone numbers of drivers, at the post office, library and YMCA. In the late 1970s, the city tourism office took over the project.

Norman says he keeps giving hikers rides "because it's one of the civic things I do and I meet a lot of interesting people."

Norman

He drops me off Downtown at the Quality Inn, and I plan to spend the day in Waynesboro, a city of about 21,000, where chemist Joseph Shivers invented spandex in 1958 in a DuPont laboratory. DuPont named the synthetic fiber Lycra.

I've nearly gotten here in the three days I'd told Piney it would take me. I'd hiked the final 5.1 miles early this morning, after spending last night at a shelter with Guitarzan, Hard Headed and two boys who'd just graduated from high school and were out for a few days of adventure with monstrous packs. We told the boys how to pack light. Hard Headed suggested that I take the trail name "Clark Kent."

"That's a clever idea," I say. "But I'm not Superman."

Earlier yesterday, I'd been resting at a roadside picnic area when two retired guys stopped their touring bikes, with little gear, and told me they were nearly done with the TransAmerica Trail. I was surprised to learn I was sitting next to the same road I'd ridden when I completed the cross-country bike route in 2001.

The bikers were inspiring because they also had thru-hiked the AT in 2010 and one had also thru-hiked the Pacific Crest Trail and Continental Divide Trail. Like Jonathan Lemberg, he'd done the Triple Crown of Hiking. They rode on and I continued hiking on a day that featured lots of blueberries and a few hours of heavy rain in the afternoon.

In Waynesboro, I check in to the motel and then check my email on the computer in the lobby. I've gotten a few messages from credit card companies asking me to call because there were recent charges on my cards that appeared fraudulent. I was sure they were fraudulent because they were made on cards that I'd left in a drawer in my bedroom dresser.

When I call one company, I'm told that whoever made the purchases has my card. I live in a low-crime neighborhood and I doubt anyone has broken into my house, but I call Elis Wilson, my new housemate, to find out what might have happened. When I hear that her phone is no longer in service, I know, and figure her name is an alias.

I had rented Elis two vacant rooms and a bathroom in the back of my house, with a private entrance, a couple months before I left because I wanted someone reliable living there and taking care of the house and garden while I was gone. I'd advertised the place on Craigslist and she called me to say she was moving from Santa Fe, New Mexico, to Madison and was interested in the rooms. She was in her mid-40s and seemed fine when I checked her out and when she arrived, so I rented them to her.

I call my neighbor Scott Hirschler, who has a key to my house, to see if she's moved out. He checks and tells me she's left, so I spend much of the afternoon calling credit card companies to cancel cards, and my bank to close my checking account because my checks were in the drawer, too. I learn that Elis has gotten thousands of dollars worth of cash and merchandise, and I call Madison police to report the crimes. Then, I walk around Waynesboro and try to enjoy the rest of the day.

In the evening, I walk to Ming Garden, where a sign on the door of the Chinese restaurant advises hikers that there are free showers at the YMCA, a few blocks away. I enter to find the best all-you-can-eat buffet I've ever seen, including stir-fry meals made to order, baked salmon, pizza and ice cream.

In the morning, I buy food at the grocery store, but not much because there are restaurants and food at campground stores in Shenandoah National Park, where the 102.2 miles of the AT generally follow Skyline Drive, which runs along the ridge of the Blue Ridge Mountains through the park, which is about 70 miles long and from less than a mile to 13 miles wide, with the Shenandoah River Valley to the west and the Piedmont to the east.

Then, I walk over to the Saturday farmers' market, where Guitarzan had said he might play for tips. But he's not there, possibly because there are few farmers and few shoppers. So, I walk back to the motel and call a few people on the driver list to see if I can get a ride back to the trail.

Carol Sloan, 69, picks me up and says she's been ferrying hikers since a year after she moved to Waynesboro in 2002. She says a friend who worked at the visitor center and provided rides had recommended that she do it, too. She often gives rides from mid-May to the end of June, sometimes many times a day.

"It's easy. I can pick you up and return in twenty minutes," she says. "It's interesting. People who hike the trail are not the people you expect to hike the trail. I've picked up a woman with a nine-year-old kid and a dog."

Carol drops me off and I'm excited to start backpacking through Shenandoah, which was established in 1935 from private land acquired by the state of Virginia and given to the United States. Nearly 40 percent of the park's 208 square miles is designated as wilderness and plenty of black bears roam the park, with the number varying from the low to high hundreds, depending on the availability of food, especially acorns, and other factors, such as the amount of hunting on adjacent lands.

I get a free backcountry permit at the self-registration station and then hike into the park, where I cross Skyline Drive twice in the first 4.5 miles and then climb Little Calf Mountain, where I enjoy seeing a field full of purple monarda and mountains in the distance. After seven miles, I reach Calf Mountain Shelter and stop because it's early evening and the next shelter is 13 miles away.

The only hiker here is Bobby "Peterman" Hunt, 61, of Calabash, North Carolina, who tells me he hiked 1,900 miles of the trail in 2009, before tearing the meniscus in his knee when he slipped in Maine's Mahoosuc

Notch, which is filled with huge boulders and is often called the most difficult mile of the trail.

Then, he says, "I found the quickest way out and I took it."

In 2011, he climbed Katahdin and hiked south to finish the trail. Last year, he hiked the 212 miles through New Jersey, New York and Connecticut again, and this year, he plans to hike about 165 miles from just south of Waynesboro to Harpers Ferry.

So, now he's a backpacking veteran; but, when he started the trail in 2009, he was a retired Yonkers, New York, police lieutenant who'd never backpacked and hadn't camped since he was a kid. Then, his son, Matthew, who was about to graduate from the University of Tennessee in Knoxville, decided to thru-hike the trail and asked his dad to join him.

"I thought it was cool. Why not? Spend time with my son. I said, 'Let's do it and see how far we go.'"

Matthew had neither camped, nor backpacked, but had been inspired to hike the trail after reading *A Walk in the Woods.*

Peterman did all of the research and planning, and then the pair left Springer in mid-May. Peterman enjoyed the hike, but Matthew didn't.

"If it was raining, he was miserable. If it was hot, he was miserable. He went through more trail names than anyone I know."

One was "Silver Toes" "because every single toe was covered with duct tape because of blisters. He had blisters over blisters." Among the many others were "Bee Sting," after his whole leg swelled up and "Turtle Stomper" when he didn't see the turtle.

Matthew made it to Damascus before he quit. His fraternity friends picked him up and brought him back to Knoxville.

"He'd just had enough," Peterman says. "He just wanted to party. I don't think he'll be out here for five days again."

"I was enjoying it," says Peterman, who got his name because he looks like the "Seinfeld" character. So, he kept hiking with other thru-hikers for company.

He says Matthew did return to the trail for a day in 2011, when he took his dad to Katahdin. They climbed the mountain together and then Matthew left.

We also talk about other things and Peterman tells me he's a big football fan and has been to every NFL stadium. When I tell him I'm from Green Bay and have been a Packers fan since I was a kid, he says: "I hate Packers fans."

"Why?" I ask.

Because, he says, he's a Bears fan and "the Packers dominate the Bears."

We're still the only two at the shelter around sunset, when Nuke and Amber arrive. They'd stopped briefly in Waynesboro for food and are in good spirits. Amber is enjoying the hike now and Nuke says she's talking about hiking to Harpers Ferry. It's dark when Islander shows up, followed by a college-age couple, who are just hiking for a few days and have the fixings for s'mores for all.

Soon, there's a campfire going and we enjoy an unexpected trail treat.

34

Maria "Groceries" Icenogle and Jason "Boy Floyd" Jacobs met at an Appalachian Trail shelter three years ago and have been together ever since.

"We just decided to walk together and never stopped deciding that," says Groceries, after I meet the couple while they're enjoying the late-afternoon sun and the splendid valley view from a rocky Shenandoah overlook on their honeymoon.

They say they met on June 11, 2011, when they both stopped for lunch at Icewater Spring Shelter in Great Smoky Mountains National Park.

"I found her there on a lunch break," says Boy Floyd, 37. "I walked into the shelter and happened to see a pretty gal. I was nervous and didn't know what to say. I was just happy she'd talk with me and wanted to hike."

"It wasn't a romantic connection immediately," says Groceries, 32. "It was: 'He's a cool guy. Our hiking styles are similar. Let's see what he's all about.'"

She became intrigued by the Appalachians when she was 10 and her family took a trip to Appalachia, where her grandmother was born. Then, when she was 16, she took her first backpacking trip, which included a little of the AT.

Groceries was a hospice counselor in Colorado when she decided to thru-hike the trail. She named herself after the nickname that Elizabeth Gilbert, the author of *Eat, Pray, Love*, wrote about in her book. Gilbert wrote that a friend gave her the nickname because she loved food.

Groceries left Springer on April 23, but injured her knee early in the hike and spent three weeks recuperating at the Nantahala Outdoor Center in North Carolina. So, she'd hiked just 210 miles when she met Boy Floyd.

Boy Floyd, a college math instructor in Prescott, Arizona, had hiked the entire trail in sections from 2006 to 2009, and had returned to the trail to hike a section starting at Springer.

They hiked north together and a few weeks later Groceries told Boy Floyd that she hoped to be near a phone on July 4, so she could talk with family members at their annual Fourth of July reunion in French Lick, Indiana. Boy Floyd suggested that, instead, they leave the trail in Erwin, get his car in Franklin, and drive to French Lick. Which is what they did.

When I tell Groceries that I bet I'm one of the few people on the trail who know that French Lick is the childhood home of former NBA star Larry Bird, she tells me that her father played pickup basketball with the older brother of "The Hick from French Lick."

After the reunion, Groceries was way behind schedule for a thru-hike, so the two decided to take a road trip, instead, including a stop in Maine, where they hiked the last 151 miles of the trail from Caratunk to Katahdin. Along the way, they spent a couple weeks at The Lakeshore House in tiny Monson.

The House's owner, Rebekah Anderson, attended the couple's wedding on July 6, three weeks ago, in the trail town of Duncannon, Pennsylvania, where Boy Floyd's family is from. Boy Floyd says Rebekah said at the wedding that "she observed us fall in love in Room Three."

After the honeymoon, the two are returning to Prescott, where Boy Floyd teaches at Embry-Riddle Aeronautical University and Groceries, who wrote magazine articles about her hike, is returning to college.

When I meet them, I've hiked 17.4 miles since leaving Calf Mountain Shelter at dawn, and plan to hike 26.2 today, the length of a marathon and my highest mileage day on the trail. The hiking is easy in the park because there's not much climbing and the trail is very well maintained by the Potomac Appalachian Trail Club. At times, I feel almost like I'm walking on a dirt sidewalk.

Before meeting Boy Floyd and Groceries, I spoke with ridge-runner Lauralee "Blissful" Bliss, 51, of Charlottesville, Virginia.

Blissful, a former nurse, says she'd wanted for 30 years to thru-hike the trail before she did it northbound in 2007 with her son, Joshua "Paul Bunyan," who turned 17 on the trek.

"It was really great," she says. "We had our moments, as any mother and son. He thinks of it as the highlight of his life."

Blissful says she hiked the entire trail southbound in 2010 and 2011 and has written a book about her hikes. She's been a ridge runner for three years and has hiked all of the more than 500 miles of trails in the park. She backpacks from Friday through Monday and spends each night in a shelter. On Tuesday, she does office work.

I ask her if she's heard about the mother who's hiking north with 4-year-old twins. When she says that she's heard rumors of the trio, I tell her that I've met and written about the three and that she might get to meet them, too.

But, I say, I've learned that they might rent a canoe in Waynesboro and take the river route to Harpers Ferry, which is called aqua-blazing. Blissful says she doesn't think that will happen because the water is very low and they would have to make too many portages.

Three miles after meeting Boy Floyd and Groceries, I buy some groceries myself at the Loft Mountain Campground store and then hike 5.9 miles to Pinefield Hut, where I plan to spend the night. All of the shelters, except last night's, are called huts in the park and, unlike last night, I've got this one to myself. The others at last night's shelter must have stopped at, or before, the campground.

35

BRIAN "BILBO" CLARK BATTLED biting insects when he started his Appalachian Trail thru-hike last month in Maine.

"The black flies and mosquitoes were very bad," Bilbo says of his time hiking south after he and 11 other thru-hikers climbed Katahdin on June 1.

"A lot of people quit early. Two of them got injured. A few didn't want to be on the trail anymore."

Bilbo, 60, of Sweetgum, North Carolina, says he's at a Shenandoah hut now because sprained ankles forced him off the trail in New Hampshire, and he then decided to change his backpacking plan.

He's alone at Bearfence Mountain Hut and falling asleep when I arrive at dusk, but he gets up and tells me a little of his AT tale.

Bilbo got his trail name because, like Tolkien's Bilbo Baggins, he's a "reluctant adventurer," even though he's backpacking the trail, and has finished about 12 Ironman triathlons and four 100-mile trail runs, including two of the toughest, the mountainous Wasatch Front in Utah and Hardrock 100 in Colorado. He decided to try the AT after retiring from his job as a chemist.

"It's just something I've always wanted to do," he says. "I retired and it gave me the opportunity."

He decided to start at Katahdin, unlike the vast majority of thru-hikers, because he wanted to get the toughest part done first and liked the idea of hiking toward home.

So, he and his wife, Linda, made a vacation of their 10-day drive to Maine, and then he headed south with a group of 12. He was the oldest and the next oldest was 37.

Bilbo says he had sprained ankles when he started, but he kept hiking because he expected them to get better. Instead, they got worse. So, after 319.4 difficult miles, he left the trail in New Hampshire's Pinkham Notch, took a bus from Gorham, New Hampshire, to Boston, and flew home. He started heading south a week ago in Harpers Ferry and plans to hike to Springer, then hike from Harpers Ferry to Pinkham Notch next year.

I let Bilbo go back to sleep and I eat dinner, but not nearly as much as I'd like, because I got to the Lewis Mountain Campground store after the 7 p.m. closing time. That's because, for the second time on the hike, I climb a mountain twice.

This time, I climb 653 feet over 1.6 miles from Swift Run Gap up Saddleback Mountain. Then, following in Baby Steps' footsteps again, I somehow turn around and hike back to the gap. I'm very surprised and disheartened to see a scene I just saw less than two hours ago.

So, even though I advanced 20.4 miles on the trail today I actually hiked 23.6. It's a good thing the hiking is fairly easy and my pack is light because I'm not carrying much food. I had told myself, after I made the same mistake in North Carolina, that I'd never do that again. I was wrong.

In the morning, I hike 7.1 miles on the trail and an extra 0.8 mile round trip to the restaurant at the Big Meadows Wayside, where the bean burger and vegetarian chili are great. In the evening, I hike a couple miles along a rocky ridge and enjoy many magnificent views of the valleys to the west, and the sunset, before reaching the Pinnacles Picnic Area at dusk.

There's nobody here and the place has restrooms, water, picnic tables in a small pavilion and soft grass to sleep on. So, I stay on what becomes an unusually chilly night in late July, even though I'm at 3,420 feet. It feels like it's in the 40s, so I put on my three tech T-shirts, my running tights, raincoat and my hat before burrowing into my down bag and pulling the hood over my head.

The grass is wet with dew at dawn and I'm still alone when I continue hiking past beautiful ferns, mountain laurels and rhododendrons, along a ridge with more great views of the Shenandoah Valley. After 3.5 miles, I reach the 3,514-foot summit of Mary's Rock and enjoy more spectacular views.

On the way down, I see lots of day hikers making the steep climb of 1,210 feet over 1.7 miles to the mountaintop on numerous switchbacks from the Panorama parking lot. Many of them are struggling and some wearily ask me how much farther it is to the top.

One of the hikers is wearing a red University of Wisconsin T-shirt and I ask him where he's from. He says he's from Appleton, a city near Green Bay, and went to UW Medical School. He's doing his pediatrics residency in

Charlottesville and says he's looking forward to returning to Wisconsin because the people are much nicer and friendlier there. I tell him about Mama Bear and the Cubs and ask him what he thinks about 4-year-olds hiking the trail. He says he doesn't think the hike will hurt them, but he questions whether they'll remember it.

When I reach the parking lot, I tell a few people about to start the hike that, if they don't want to do the difficult climb and want to enjoy many beautiful views on a hike that's twice as long, they should drive to the Pinnacles Picnic Area and hike north to the summit. And I add that they don't have to hike far for great views. They decide to take the easier and longer route to the mountaintop.

In the late afternoon, I buy some food at the Elkwallow Wayside convenience store, then take a break and eat. At dusk, I reach Gravel Springs Hut, where there are several backpackers out for a few days in the park, and I see Ascender and BrightSide for the first time in five days. After 952.2 miles and 70 days since they left Springer about five hours after me on May 22, we're still hiking at the same pace overall.

36

Retired Army Gen. John "Web Breaker" Hedrick now commands a committed corps of Appalachian Trail volunteers.

When I meet the general, he's armed with a tool he's wielding to cut back wayward vegetation from one of the two sections of trail he maintains when he's not doing office work, as president of the Potomac Appalachian Trail Club.

Web Breaker, 72, a big man who's sweating heavily in his bib overalls on a warm day, takes a brief break to tell me about his many hours of volunteer work for the 7,200-member club that he's led for 3 1/2 years, and about his AT thru-hike.

The thru-hike was in 2000, seven years after he retired from the Army after a 28-year military career. He was a vice president at Lockheed Martin in 1999 when Joanne, the youngest of his three daughters, suggested they hike the trail together.

"My daughter had finished one year of college. One day, she came to me and said: 'Dad, we should hike the Appalachian Trail.' I was still working, so it wasn't like I could just take off."

But he did, and on April 14, 2000, he and "Jo" left Springer. The trail was tough on Jo and a poor diet and physical exertion might have caused the irritable bowel syndrome that led to her ten bouts of diarrhea a day.

When the two got to Hot Springs, they went to a dispensary that was crowded with ailing hikers. Web Breaker says the number of hikers had increased 45 percent over the previous year due to the popularity of *A Walk in the Woods*, which was published in 1998, and many were unprepared.

"There were hikers all over the floor sick, beaten up. It looked like a war zone," says the general. "The doctor said: 'Dad, you take this child off the trail. I don't know what she has.' My wife picked her up. She was crying like a baby. She was a good hiker, very strong."

Web Breaker, though, never thought of leaving the AT.

"I was committed. I had no thought of quitting. I just approached it as a job."

It was a job that he started earlier each day than the other hikers, which is why he got his trail name. Like me, he was usually the hiker who broke the webs that spiders had woven across the trail overnight.

"There were some days that were bloody awful with the weather, the heat, the bugs," he says. "Some days were fun. The people were interesting."

When he climbed Katahdin on Sept 28, Jo climbed with him, having driven there with her mom to bring Web Breaker home.

Web Breaker, who lives just east of Shenandoah, has had the same commitment to the PATC that he had to hiking the trail, volunteering about four hours a day at what he says is almost a full-time job.

"I knew I wanted to give something back to the recreation users. If you're going to take a job, do it right."

He says club volunteers, less than 10 percent of the members, maintain 240 miles of the AT and 1,000 miles of other trails. The club also has 39 rental cabins in four states and pays five ridge runners to patrol its part of the trail. He was a ridge runner himself in 2006 and 2007 and has written the *Appalachian Trail Guide to Shenandoah National Park*, which also covers 400 miles of other trails in the park.

The trail section he's working on today is 1 1/2 miles long and the one he maintains in Shenandoah stretches 2 1/2 miles. He also does corridor monitoring, in which he bushwhacks from the trail to the edge of the trail corridor to make sure nothing is encroaching on the National Park Service land.

"Without volunteer support, you wouldn't have an Appalachian Trail," he says. "Parts would be closed within two years. To me, trail magic is good maintenance."

I thank him and tell him that the Shenandoah trails were in the best shape of any on my hike.

Web Breaker is the first general I've met, and a few miles later, I meet my first colonel. Maston Gray, 68, of Vienna, Virginia, who retired from the Army in 1992 after a 25-year military career, is also a PATC volunteer doing trail maintenance. He's volunteered for 10 years and works on his two-mile section about every three weeks, most of the year.

"I do it because I enjoy being outdoors," he says. "I like the work. I enjoy meeting other people and I like helping the PATC."

Maston says he's never backpacked on the AT, but is thinking of doing a thru-hike next year.

I meet the retired officers the day after I leave Gravel Springs Hut, and 9.8 miles after leaving the hut, I also leave Shenandoah.

That's when I meet thru-hiker Pete "NoBigDeal" Smith, 55, of Doylestown, Pennsylvania, who retired from his job as a chemical engineer in December. He says he and his wife, Rebecca "Racquet" Smith, who left her accounting job to care for their four children, headed north from Harpers Ferry on April 21.

NoBigDeal says the children gave them their trail names. They chose his name because whenever he calls them and leaves a message, he starts with "no big deal," so he doesn't worry them. They chose Racquet's name because she's an avid tennis player.

Racquet, who had problems with plantar fasciitis, quit after 450 miles and NoBigDeal continued to Katahdin, which he climbed on July 20. He left Harpers Ferry three days ago on July 28 and is headed for Springer.

"It's a fantastic way to see small-town America," he says. "The trail community is unique, very trusting."

For example, he tells me about the time he and Racquet were in a hostel in Palmerton, Pennsylvania, and saw a note telling hikers to call Soul Flute for a 1.5-mile ride back to the trail. They called and a man in his early 20s with dreadlocks and an old beater showed up in the morning.

He said he'd thru-hiked the trail last year and that the path just ahead was difficult. So, he suggested the couple slackpack and said he'd leave their backpacks at the Beer Stein, a bar 20.1 trail miles ahead in the town of Wind Gap, which was on his way to work.

The pair had five minutes to decide whether to trust Soul Flute with their packs.

"We said, 'OK, let's do it.' Very trusting, when you think about it."

They tipped Soul Flute $10 and hit the trail with just daypacks.

"When we got to the Beer Stein, all our stuff was there," NoBigDeal says, "and we were able to get a beer and a sandwich."

After talking with NoBigDeal, I hike to Highway 522, where I hitch for half an hour, before Bonita Rose picks me up and gives me a 3.5-mile ride to Front Royal. I'm familiar with the town of about 14,500 because I stopped at a sports bar here last October to watch the Packers beat the Vikings, when I was on my way to run and hike trails in Shenandoah.

NoBigDeal and Racquet (c.p.)

I get a room at the Quality Inn, then email the Movin' Shoes manager, Shalon Holbeck, and ask her to ship shoes for me to Pine Grove Furnace State Park, 132.3 miles away and 5.7 miles north of the AT halfway point. After that, I buy Shoe Goo to repair my soles because the contact cement hasn't worked any better than duct tape. I also buy a bottle of Smartwater because I've learned from other hikers that my Sawyer MINI water filter screws perfectly onto the bottle. I can fill the bottle with water from a spring or stream, screw on the filter and then drink right from the bottle through the filter.

In the morning, the motel's 82-year-old gardener gives me a ride back to the trail. For the first time on the AT, I'm wearing running tights, instead of shorts, because I've read that deer ticks are much more common under 1,650 feet, which is where I'll be hiking most of the time until I reach Massachusetts, which is 536.7 miles away.

37

Ridge-Runner Hal "Kite" Evans was a fat, materialistic software developer before the Appalachian Trail changed his life.

Kite, 62, who lives in a rural area near Shenandoah National Park, says he first thought of hiking the trail to get fit.

"I got motivated because of health reasons. I was very heavy, very out of shape. I lost weight before hiking the trail or I never would have made it," says Kite, who's in great shape now. "It was life changing for me for that reason alone."

In addition, he says, the trail taught him that he doesn't need much to live a happy life.

"It changes your outlook on living. It makes you realize what you need and what's really important. Basically, you need 50 or 60 liters of stuff and you can go anywhere."

And he learned before the hike that his wife, Wendy "Sandpiper" Evans, wanted to hike the trail, too.

"My wife says, 'I've always wanted to hike the Appalachian Trail.' We'd been married for 20 years and I never realized that. I didn't think she'd use the privy and sleep on the ground."

But she did and they hiked the entire trail in three sections in 2007, 2008 and 2010. Now, he's in his third year of working as a ridge runner.

When I meet him, he's filling in for the caretaker at the Blackburn Trail Center, where I've stopped in the afternoon to look around and get some water, three days after I leave Front Royal. The center, which is owned by the Potomac Appalachian Trail Club, includes a cabin with bunks for backpackers.

Kite tells me that on a clear day people can see the Washington Monument from here, and that visitors on July Fourth can see the fireworks all around the horizon, including those over Washington.

The previous night I'd stayed at the beautiful Bears Den hostel, an historic stone lodge 3.9 miles before the north end of The Roller Coaster, 13.5 rugged miles with numerous climbs and descents.

A sign at the southern end, says: "WARNING!! YOU ARE ABOUT TO ENTER THE ROLLER COASTER!! BUILT AND MAINTAINED BY THE "TRAILBOSS" AND HIS MERRY CREW OF VOLUNTEERS HAVE A GREAT RIDE AND WE WILL SEE YOU AT THE BLACKBURN TRAIL CENTER (IF YOU SURVIVE)"

So, I was worn out when I arrived at sunset at the 8,000-square-foot hostel, which was built in the 1930s as a private stone mansion to model a European castle. It's owned by the ATC and operated by the PATC. I really appreciate the comfortable beds, hot showers, Tombstone pizza, Ben & Jerry's ice cream and self-serve, all-you-can-eat pancakes for breakfast. I enjoy the hostel with Ascender and BrightSide, along with German graduate students Janina and Olaf, whom I'm very surprised to see after last seeing them struggling with heavy backpacks 360 miles ago, 10 miles north of Pearisburg.

I suggested then that they return to Pearisburg and lighten their load. They say they left the trail and got a ride to Pearisburg, where they rented a car and drove to Waynesboro, before hiking through Shenandoah.

Janina, 25, a graduate student in marine geoscience and her friend Olaf, a graduate student in geoscience, are writing a geological guide to the national park, as part of their master's degree requirements at the University of Bremen. From here, they're going to hike to Harpers Ferry and then take a train to Washington.

When I leave, after a filling breakfast of pancakes and a pint of Ben & Jerry's chocolate fudge brownie ice cream, I hope to hike the 19.8 miles to Harpers Ferry by nightfall. After 0.9 mile, I reach the 1,000-mile milestone and two miles later I reach West Virginia.

After talking with Kite, I'm slowed by a thunderstorm, so I'm still a few miles from town in Harpers Ferry National Historical Park when it gets dark. The storm's over and the sky's clearing, so I find one of the few spots nearby without big rocks and lay out my tarp, pads and sleeping bag. Then, I sit on a rock, eat dinner and read a newspaper.

In the morning, the sky is blue and the view beautiful when I approach historic Harpers Ferry, a town of about 300 nestled between the Shenandoah and Potomac rivers. I'm looking forward to visiting the ATC headquarters, which I visited once before, when I took a train to Harpers Ferry in 1986, and then backpacked the AT across Maryland.

I'm hoping to meet Laurie Potteiger, the ATC spokeswoman I interviewed when I wrote the story about Mama Bear and the Cubs in Pearisburg. But she's taken Monday off, after working on Sunday.

Visitor service representative David Tarasevich says that I not only just missed Laurie, but that I also just missed Mama Bear, Little Butt and Strong Man, who arrived yesterday after managing to aqua-blaze from Waynesboro, despite the low water that ridge-runner Blissful said would keep them from making the canoe trip.

David says the three survived the canoe capsizing and dumping them into rapids, as well as the portages when the water was too low for canoeing. He says Laurie, who had told me that the ATC didn't encourage or publicize parents hiking with young children, enjoyed meeting the trio, nevertheless. Little Butt was sweet, he says, while Strong Man was a bit grumpy when their pictures were taken. I'd like to see them again, so I ask David if he knows if they're in town, but he doesn't.

The ATC takes pictures of the backpackers who visit and places them in a book, arranged by date and color coded as to northbound thru-hikers, southbound thru-hikers and section hikers. I enjoy looking through the book and seeing how a few hikers I've interviewed are doing and seeing the pictures of hikers whose entries I've been reading in trail registers.

I learn that Tom, who had survived a serious heart attack and told me he was "whipped" over his cardiologist girlfriend, arrived on July 28, a week before me, and decided not to take the trail name "Whipped," when I told him he had named himself. Instead, he chose "Cardioman."

Snapper, the speedy hiker I met on June 14, arrived on July 12, and had averaged 24.26 miles a day since starting on May 31. He had told me that he hoped to climb Katahdin around his 32nd birthday on August 18. To do that, he'd have to average about 31.6 miles a day from Harpers Ferry to the finish, and the hiking is much harder in New Hampshire and Maine. So, he'll most likely not make his goal. But, if he maintains his current pace, he'll come pretty close by finishing around August 30, which is still very fast.

I'm surprised when I see that Lost Bard, whom I'd last seen in Daleville on July 15, had registered as a northbound thru-hiker on July 23, 12 days ago, even though I'm hiking faster than him. I guess that he probably got a ride to Harpers Ferry and plans to return here after climbing Katahdin to hike the section he missed. Now, I can try to catch him again and ask him what happened.

And I find that Stumbles, the evidently effervescent backpacker who liberally uses the word "awesome" and stick-on stars in her register entries, is Leah Thomas and that she grew up just off the AT in Pomfret, Vermont. She's written that she's flipping to Katahdin from Harpers Ferry and then hiking south. So, if I do meet her, we'll be hiking in opposite directions.

I'm still looking through the book when BrightSide and Ascender, who spent last night in town, walk in and join me.

Harpers Ferry, known for abolitionist John Brown's raid on the U.S. Armory and Arsenal in 1859, is a pretty place with many historic buildings preserved by the National Park Service, and I see some of them as I follow the trail through town, along the Shenandoah River. I stop at Jefferson Rock to see the confluence of the Shenandoah and Potomac, a view that Jefferson said is "worth a voyage across the Atlantic."

In the quaint town center, I see Ascender and Brightside again and they say they're going to spend another night here, so I say goodbye, in case I don't see them again on the trail. Then, I get a little taste of home at a shop that sells real frozen custard, a popular Wisconsin treat, before leaving on the C&O Canal Towpath, along the Potomac. I share the path for 2.5 miles with walkers, runners and bikers, before climbing into the mountains of Maryland.

At the top of the Weverton Cliffs, I stop for a look back, then head to the Ed Garvey Memorial Shelter for the night. The shelter was built in 2001 by the PATC and named for the AT icon, who thru-hiked the trail in 1970, wrote *Appalachian Hiker: Adventure of a Lifetime* about his hike, and then spent much of the rest of his life working to protect and preserve the trail.

The impressive shelter has a second-floor loft with big windows and pictures of Ed, who died in 1999 at the age of 84. I've got the place to myself, so I relax, read the paper and enjoy a couple slices of the great Greek pizza I bought for lunch and dinner at the Cannonball Deli in Harpers Ferry.

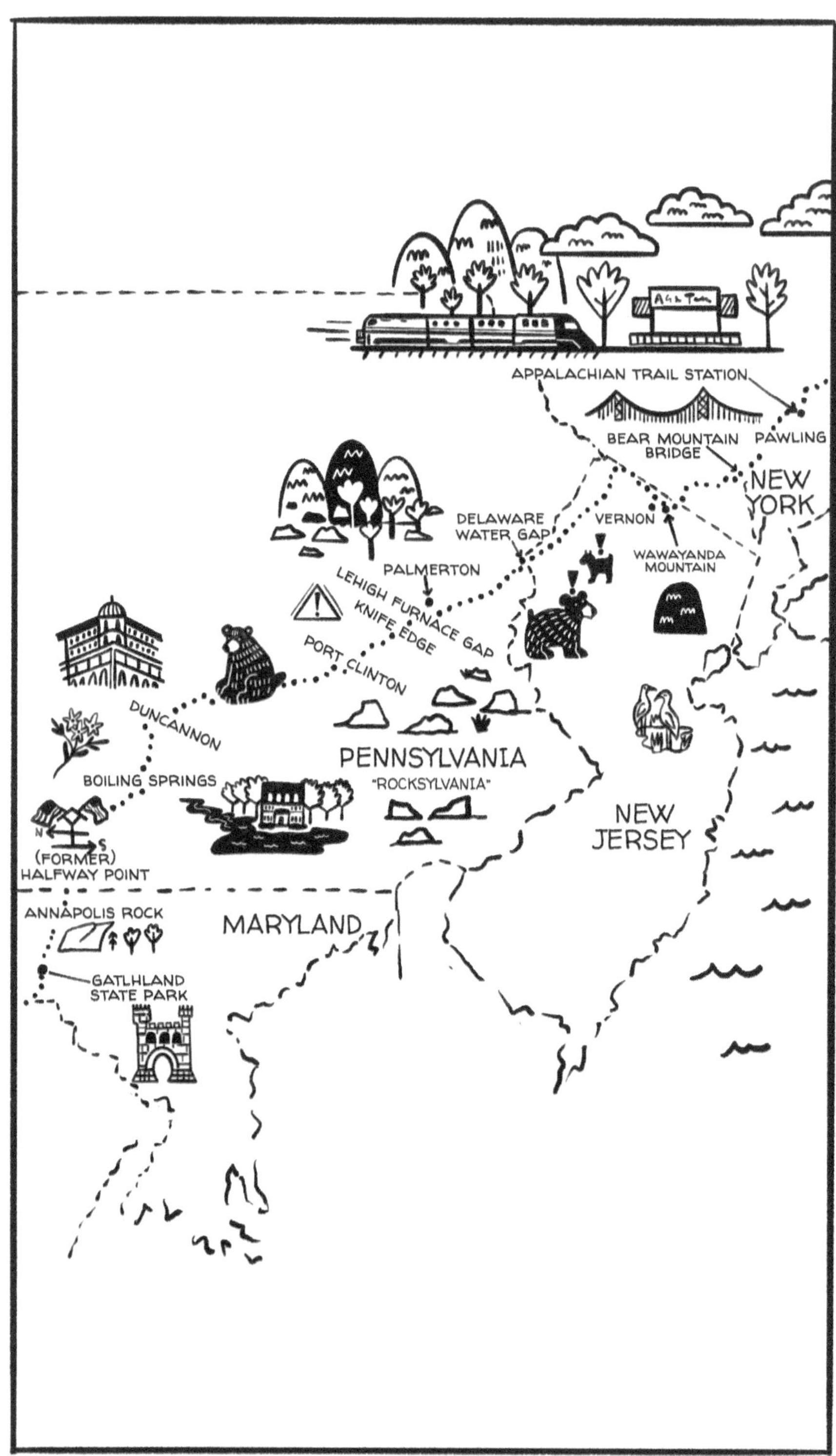

APPALACHIAN TRAIL STATION
BEAR MOUNTAIN BRIDGE
PAWLING
NEW YORK
DELAWARE WATER GAP
VERNON
PALMERTON
LEHIGH FURNACE GAP
KNIFE EDGE
WAWAYANDA MOUNTAIN
PORT CLINTON
DUNCANNON
PENNSYLVANIA
"ROCKSYLVANIA"
BOILING SPRINGS
NEW JERSEY
N
S
(FORMER) HALFWAY POINT
ANNAPOLIS ROCK
MARYLAND
GATHLAND STATE PARK

38

BILL "MAGELLAN" SOUSA WAS RUNNING on the Appalachian Trail when he saw bear scat, then "a little ball of fur running at me."

"My first thought was, 'bear cub, where's mama?'"

He turned around and ran, and so did the goat. Yes, a goat. Magellan says two goats that escaped from a farm have become feral and have been living for a long time just north of the Ed Garvey Memorial Shelter.

This morning, he stops on his run to the shelter, which he and another volunteer maintain, along with 7.5 miles of trail, to ask me if the goats were at the shelter.

"Sometimes, they hang around the campers and get fed," he says. "They love pineapple and they love ginger snaps."

Magellan, 51, of Burkittsville, Maryland, says he's an air traffic controller, but has a poor sense of direction on the ground. He still does 100-mile trail runs, though, and this morning he's running 4.1 miles south from Crampton Gap to check on the condition of the trail and the shelter. He and his fellow volunteer also care for the 3.4 miles of trail from the shelter to the C&O Canal Towpath.

He's running with a 14-inch saw and a 21-inch saw attached to his daypack. He says that he uses the saws to cut up trees blocking the trail and that he's been doing the volunteer work for about five or six years "to give back to the community."

"It'd be a shame living just a mile off the trail and not be out here helping maintain it."

He says he loves running the trail, but doesn't backpack.

"I like my creature comforts. I've had back and neck issues. I like sleeping in a bed, when I can."

The trail in Maryland is wide and there's not much climbing so it doesn't take me long to reach Gathland State Park, 0.4 mile before the gap. The interesting park is on the former estate of noted Civil War correspondent George Alfred Townsend, whose pen name was Gath.

Magellan

The park holds the impressive 50-foot-tall and 40-foot-wide War Correspondents Memorial Arch, built in 1896 and the first monument in the world dedicated to journalists killed in combat.

The park also has interesting museums about the Civil War Battle of South Mountain, which was fought in Crampton Gap and two other gaps, and about Townsend, who was a well-known journalist and novelist in the mid-to-late 1800s.

In the late afternoon, I reach Washington Monument State Park, where much of the first completed monument to George Washington was built in a day on July 4, 1827 by the citizens of Boonsboro, Maryland. The original 30-foot-tall monument has been restored twice since then, and is now a 40-

foot-tall stone tower built by the Civilian Conservation Corps and dedicated on July 4, 1936.

I ask a caretaker if he knows the weather forecast, and, after checking his smart phone, he tells me there's no chance of rain overnight. So, I decide to hike 1.6 miles past Pine Knob Shelter and stay at Annapolis Rock, where there's an expansive view of the setting sun and the mountains and valleys to the west.

I think the view's beautiful, at first, but I'm not so enthused as I see thunderheads build in the distance and watch as a thunderstorm gradually moves toward the rock ledge on which I'm sitting. I'd already set up my tarp, pads and sleeping bags, and this time I wasn't going to make the mistake I made near Mount Rogers, in Virginia, when I tried rolling up in my tarp during a storm in the middle of the night.

Instead, I make the mistake of taking the tarp out from under the pads and bag and then lying under it. That doesn't work any better, and once again my down bag is soaked and I have to wring the water out of it. If I'm caught in another storm without shelter at night, I'm going to put my bag in its stuff sack and just sit under the tarp until the rain stops.

But tonight, I've got to sleep again in a wet bag. I'm glad the weather is warm.

39

FELIX SCHMIDT HAS BEEN HIKING the Appalachian Trail for more than four months with a pickup truck, a scooter, a camper and a daypack.

Felix, 65, of Ruidoso, New Mexico, says he wanted to hike the trail after retiring in December from his job as a county water and septic tank inspector. But he doesn't like backpacking.

"I day hike all the time," he says. "Backpacking I haven't done much at all."

And he doesn't want to start doing much now.

So, he towed a Little Guy teardrop camper and carried a Genuine 50cc scooter when he drove his Toyota Tundra pickup to the Springer trailhead and started hiking on March 25. He rides the scooter to a trailhead about a day's hike away. Then, he hikes back to the truck, picks up the scooter and sleeps in the tiny camper, which he calls "a tent on wheels." He carries a daypack and hikes about 10 to 15 miles a day.

Felix says his daily distance is determined primarily by where a road crosses the trail.

He's hiked 720 miles, including all of Georgia and Virginia. He says he skipped most of Tennessee and North Carolina because he's not ready to backpack, and the trail in those states isn't suited to his method. Now, he's heading north, but hiking south, through Maryland.

"Some of it's been a pain in the ass – finding trailheads, where to camp," he says.

He says he's been reluctant to sleep in the camper at trailheads. I say that's where I'd sleep, and I doubt if anyone, including law enforcement officers, will bother him.

He says another disadvantage is that he doesn't get to talk to other hikers much because he's not spending the night at shelters. He's not sure how much of the trail he'll hike, but says he'll backpack when necessary.

"My plan is when I do have to backpack, I'll backpack."

Felix and I talk in the morning after the thunderstorm at Annapolis Rock. We've both been dodging puddles on a trail that's very wet.

Felix

While we're talking, Spoons, a college-age gal who's thru-hiking southbound, stops briefly, but she has little time to chat because she's tackling the Four-State Challenge. She started in Pennsylvania and plans to hike 43.3 miles in 24 hours through Maryland and West Virginia, before stopping in Virginia.

"Go, go, go," says Spoons.

A short time later, her backpacking companion, Toey, a college-age guy, also hustles by.

The two are the first southbounders I've met who've left Katahdin this year and are hiking straight to Springer. They say they started on May 31 and have hiked 1,140 miles, more than halfway, in 67 days.

I get going, too, on a trail that involves little climbing, except for the 749-foot climb to the High Rock summit. On the way down, I fall, and cut and bruise my shin. It's still sore when I reach Pen Mar County Park, 0.3 mile before the Maryland border.

The park has a huge, covered wooden overlook, with a spectacular western view that includes the city of Waynesboro, Pennsylvania, in the foreground and Tuscarora Mountain, 20 miles away, in the distance.

Near the deck is a dance pavilion, where big bands draw big crowds on Sunday summer nights. Few people are in the park tonight, though, and the sun is about to set, so I decide to sleep on the overlook. I enjoy the pretty sunset, then unpack my wet gear and clothes and hang them on the overlook railing to get them somewhat dry.

In the morning, I awake before dawn and decide to get an early start, as usual, even though I've only got enough food to last through lunch and there are three places to buy groceries within a few miles.

But I'm heading to Caledonia State Park and the guidebook says there are vending machines and a snack bar open until 7 at the park and an Italian restaurant less than a mile away.

So, I cross the Mason-Dixon line and start my 229.4-mile trek across reputedly rocky Pennsylvania.

Today's trail, though, isn't any rockier than the rest of the AT, and there's only one difficult climb, so I've hiked 18.2 miles and it's still light when I get to the highway that leads 0.4 mile to the restaurant. Problem is, I realize before walking to the restaurant that it's probably closed.

The guidebook says the place is open from 11 to 1:30 from Tuesday through Thursday, and today's Thursday, so I'd figured this morning that I'd eat dinner there and pack enough pizza for breakfast and lunch tomorrow, when I plan to spend the night at a hostel with food.

But I hadn't noticed the guidebook also says the restaurant is open until 10:30 on Friday and Saturday. I figure it wouldn't be open later on Thursday than on Friday and Saturday, so I conclude it was open today just for lunch, and I don't want to walk an extra 0.8 mile round trip to find a closed restaurant.

There's a grocery store 1.7 miles away in Fayetteville, but the guidebook doesn't list its hours and I figure it might be closed, too. So, I decide to hike the half mile to the park and rely on the vending machines, since the snack bar will also be closed. But, when I get there, near dark, I find the guidebook is wrong and there are no vending machines, which leaves me with a small supply of almonds and chocolate for tonight and tomorrow. I eat half for dinner, save the rest for breakfast and go to sleep hungry.

In the morning, I eat more of the almonds and chocolate and save a few nuts and a little chocolate. I then walk the pretty side trail, along a stream lined with rhododendrons, back to the AT. After 2.2 miles, I reach Quarry Gap Shelter, which is the most well-maintained shelter I've seen on the trail.

Jim "Innkeeper" Stauch designed the place and helped build it in 1994. It's really two shelters that each sleep four, separated by a picnic table covered by a roof with a skylight.

Innkeeper, a PATC volunteer, has gone all out to give the place a homey feel with a gate, bench, sundial, knickknacks, hanging pots with flowers, newspapers and tarps that can be rolled down for windbreaks. The spotless privy has the book *Nature Calls* for users' reading pleasure, and there's a box for hikers to store food to keep it away from bears.

In the register, one hiker wrote on July 18 that he was in the area to attend the July 6 wedding of Boy Floyd and Groceries, the honeymooners I met in Shenandoah, in Duncannon, 62.1 miles from here.

But what interests me the most are the three single-serving packets of instant oatmeal I find in the shelter. I've never eaten uncooked oatmeal before, but I eat a packet now, and it's not bad, especially since I'm very hungry. I save the other two for later. Fortunately, for me, there are lots of wild blueberries on this section of trail, and I stop often to eat them.

So, I'm not desperate when I catch Dan Riley, 43, of Dover, Pennsylvania, who's backpacking 57 miles from Pen Mar County Park to Boiling Springs with his sons Benjamin, 11, and Daniel, 15. He says they plan to take four or five days and that the trek is a "shakedown cruise" for longer trips to come.

Dan was a fire inspector for a military contractor in Afghanistan from 2010 to 2011 and worked to keep U.S. bases safe. He says the trail's a snap compared to that.

"Everything here is easy because people aren't trying to kill you."

I tell Dan I've got little food, and, for the first time on my hike, ask another hiker if he has a couple extra energy bars I can buy. He's nice enough to give me a handful of nuts and a couple granola bar two-packs. So, with the oatmeal and blueberries, I've got enough food to last until tonight.

Dan, Benjamin and Daniel

Shortly after speaking with Dan, I meet Edwin Wallace, 65, of Peekskill, New York, who first backpacked a section of the AT in 1971, a year before I did, and finished section hiking it in 1976. Since then, he's backpacked other trails and parts of the AT again, as he's doing now. Edwin says trail names weren't common in the 1970s, when about 100 miles of the trail were on roads. They started being used more often in the 1980s and 1990s, he says.

Ten miles later, when I meet a group of hikers who have driven to a trailhead, and are hiking a short side trail to a PATC cabin, I ask again if I can buy a couple energy bars, and I'm rewarded with a granola bar, and a cheese cracker packet. So, now I'm really set.

At the trail's 1092.65-mile mark, I reach the marker for this year's official halfway point. At the 1,098-mile mark, I enter Pine Grove Furnace State Park, where I plan to spend the night in the Ironmaster's Mansion hostel.

The park is also the home of the Pine Grove General Store, which is known for the "half-gallon challenge," in which backpackers who eat that much ice cream get a small wooden spoon stamped with the words "MEMBER OF HALF GAL CLUB" commemorating their accomplishment after hiking half the trail.

You'd think that since I'm quite hungry, love ice cream and am from the dairy state and a city where the University of Wisconsin and the Chocolate Shoppe make some of the world's best ice cream, I'd chomp at the challenge. But you'd be wrong. Eating a half gallon of ice cream at one sitting just doesn't appeal to me under any conditions.

But it does appeal to many thru-hikers, says Peggy Stiegelman, 58, who's sitting outside the store, which has closed for the day, and has been a cashier there for two years. She estimates that seven of every ten hikers buy a 3-1/2-pint ice cream tub, since Hershey's cut the size, plus an extra pint to take the challenge. She says about five of those finish a half gallon, one of those five gets an upset stomach and many of those throw up.

"They hang out a while until they get better," she says, "and then eat something hot, like a burger and fries."

She says the store records the time it takes each hiker to complete the challenge, as well as where the hiker is from and the flavor of the ice cream.

After talking with Peggy, I walk over to the mansion, an English Tudor-style red-brick building built from 1827 to 1829 by Peter Ege, the owner of Pine Grove Iron Works. It was closed in 2010, renovated and restored beautifully by the Central Pennsylvania Conservancy with 5,000 hours of work by volunteers, and reopened in 2011. It's managed for the conservancy by Roger and Kathy Stone and the cost is $25 a night for a bed and breakfast. I've got the men's dorm to myself.

Roger, 63, and his wife, Kathy, 57, have been the innkeepers since March 2013. They get to live in the mansion for free and are paid minimum wage for 40 hours per week. Roger says he and Kathy find the job "a lot more work than we thought it would be." But they enjoy the job and the hikers, who make up 95 percent of the guests.

"They're very good," Kathy says, "about taking care of their belongings and trash, and picking up after themselves."

"We love them," Roger says. "It's fun talking to people from all over the world."

He says one of the more interesting thru-hikers this season was Guy "AstroGuy" Gardner, 66, who was the pilot on two Space Shuttle missions. He says "AstroGuy" was a great guy and said that he likes to do a new challenge every two years.

Edwin

The mansion sells the same ice cream sold in the general store for $5, but a hiker completing the challenge here doesn't get the wooden spoon and his or her name recorded. I buy 3-1/2 pints of chocolate fudge to eat after my cheese pizza. I manage to finish about a third of it and save the rest for morning, when I eat another third for dessert after a breakfast of Grape Nuts and toasted waffles.

I'd like to visit the Appalachian Trail Museum, which is in the park, but it opens late and I want to leave early. I've picked up a new pair of shoes at the hostel, after putting 477 trail miles on the pair I got at Woods Hole. So now I'll have solid soles to handle the rocky Pennsylvania trail.

40

CARSON "TOONS" POTTER IS BACKPACKING with books that weigh three pounds and a guitar and case that weigh four.

Toons, 22, of New Orleans, is a singer-songwriter and graduated from Northwestern University in June with a degree in computer science. He says he won't give up the things that mean the most to him just to save weight on the Appalachian Trail.

"I play every day. It's how I relax and how I think," he says, reminding me of Guitarzan, when I ask why he brought the guitar. "It would seem totally heinous that I wouldn't bring a guitar. For me, a huge part of the trail is self-exploration, being with your thoughts in the tranquility of nature."

Books are also important to him, which is why he's carrying books that include *Walden, On the Road,* and *The Stranger* in a pack that has a base weight of 25 pounds, including the books and the backpacking guitar and case.

Toons started 625 miles ago in Hanover, New Hampshire, which is where he met Spoons, his friend from high school and the woman I met in Maryland when she was trying the Four-State Challenge with Toey.

He says Spoons, who just graduated from John Hopkins University, and Toey met when they climbed Katahdin and are hiking very quickly.

"She's go, go, go," he says.

But, he says, after they finished the challenge, they planned to hike the section of trail again so they could take more time to see and enjoy it.

Toons says he managed to keep up with the two for about 10 days, but then slowed down. He's excited about his dad, Tom Potter, a Nashville lawyer, meeting him in Boiling Springs, where I spent last night after hiking from the Ironmaster's Mansion hostel. The two are going to hike together to Harpers Ferry, which is when Toons is going to leave the trail and head to Southeast Asia with his girlfriend.

Toons (c.p.)

"I'm having a blast," he says. "It's been incredibly rewarding."

Yesterday, about five miles after leaving the hostel, I meet ridge-runner Sam "Shoofly Reibman, 21, of Emmaus, Pennsylvania, who says this is his second year patrolling about 75 miles of trail from the state park to Rausch Gap. Today's Saturday and he says I'm the first thru-hiker he's seen this week.

That makes sense because few southbounders have made it this far and I think I'm one of the last thru-hiking northbounders who left Springer and are this far south. I think nearly all of the rest are either ahead of me, have flipped to Katahdin and are hiking south or have quit. The last thru-hiking northbounder I talked with was Nuke and that was about 240 miles ago in Shenandoah. That's why I've got the trail much to myself these days.

Shoofly says he's a student at Ithaca College in Ithaca, New York, and is studying outdoor adventure leadership. He spends ten days on the trail and then takes four days off, and enjoys the job, especially "meeting people from all walks of life."

He tells me that several days ago he met a northbound woman who, I've noticed, writes detailed accounts of her personal life in shelter registers. Her trail name is Seeks Chaya, which means "life" in Hebrew, and she's from Deerfield, New Hampshire. She's about 10 days ahead of me and I've recently started reading her entries and become curious about her.

Shoofly says she's in her 30s, has a degree in biology and has worked in a lab and a restaurant.

"She was very friendly, very outgoing and she told me pretty much her whole life story," he says. "The sun was setting and I wanted to get back to my tent and she still had a mile and a half to go to town. She sat and we chatted for a half hour or so. She said she's trying to figure out life by going out on the trail. She really wanted to tell me her whole story."

I wish Shoofly good luck and then start hiking quickly because I want to get to the Allenberry Resort Inn & Playhouse in Boiling Springs in time for the buffet dinner and a show. After 18 miles I descend South Mountain, the northern tip of the Blue Ridge, and feel like I'm back in Wisconsin when I enter the Cumberland Valley and start hiking along a cornfield.

After 1.4 miles, I reach Boling Springs, a charming place of about 3,200 named for natural artesian well springs in and near the town in which the water looks like it's boiling when it's pushed to the surface, even though it's only about 55 degrees. The town has buildings that date to the 1700s and is a site of the Network to Freedom, a collection of numerous noteworthy sites along the Underground Railroad, which helped slaves escape to free states and Canada.

I walk quickly along seven-acre Children's Lake in the town center and pass the ATC Mid-Atlantic Regional Office before reaching the northeastern edge of the town and the resort, 0.4 mile off the trail. It's 7:15 and I've got just enough time, if I hurry, to shower and stuff myself at the buffet before the start of "Oklahoma" at 8. So, I'm a bit chagrined when the hotel clerk says she isn't sure if she has a room available on the busy Saturday night.

But, after a few anxious minutes for me, she finds one and I manage to clean up and eat in time to enjoy the show.

In the morning, I fill up again at the big buffet breakfast and continue my 13.9-mile hike across the Cumberland Valley. I walk along fields of corn and soybeans, which farmers are allowed to plant on National Park Service land. I see area runners on the flat trail and wish I was running with them.

In the evening, I climb Blue Mountain and speak with Toons, before reaching Darlington Shelter, where I'm going to spend the night. I've got a shelter to myself again and I see that someone has left most of Saturday's *Sentinel*, the daily paper in Carlisle, Pennsylvania. I enjoy reading it and notice that it's owned by Lee Enterprises, the same company that owns the *Wisconsin State Journal*, where I used to work.

I also read another in-depth entry from Seeks Chaya in which she filled half a page in the register. She wrote: "Seeks Chaya stopped at 2:47 p.m. on 8/2 for snack. Hoping to make it into Duncannon by evening. If I do, it will be my first hike over 20 miles. Keeping fingers crossed and breaks short. Special thanks to Sourpatch and Chef Jeff for assisting in finding my lost wallet, to Lost Bard for his hospitality. (I am keeping fingers crossed that your hernia doesn't send you off trail.)"

I think Seeks Chaya might have a penchant for losing stuff because in the register at the Quarry Gap shelter, she'd written that she had a late start because she "lost a pair of smart wool socks and obsessed over finding it, unsuccessfully 'til nearly 9 a.m.. Normally I prefer a 7:30 start."

Today's August 10, so now I know that I'm about eight days behind Lost Bard, who must be slowed by that hernia, and that I've picked up about four days on him since I left Harpers Ferry six days ago. I've now hiked 71.3 miles in Pennsylvania and the trail still hasn't been particularly rocky.

I rarely write in registers, but tonight I decide to do something useful for southbounders and write a list of my favorite places to eat and stay between here and Springer.

In the morning, I've hiked 4.8 miles to a point where the guidebook says the trail will be "very rocky" for the next 6.1 miles, when I'll reach the town of Duncannon. But the trail still doesn't get really rocky, so I'm beginning to wonder when the trail in Pennsylvania will become especially hard.

41

The legendary Doyle Hotel has fantastic food and rustic rooms that only a backpacker could love.

"We tell people we don't have any stars, we might have an asterisk, here or there," says Vickey Kelly, 59, who owns the Duncannon dive with her husband, Pat Kelly, 72.

The Kellys, who have been married for 35 years, bought the historic hotel in 2001 and have since catered to AT hikers, who consider the place a mandatory stop for at least a meal, as they follow the trail through the Pennsylvania borough of about 1,500.

The original three-story wooden hotel was built in the 1770s and served travelers following the north-south route along the Susquehanna River. It burned down in 1803 and was replaced by a four-story brick hotel, which once hosted Charles Dickens. The hotel was purchased in 1880 by Adolphus Busch, the co-founder of Anheuser-Busch, who bought many hotels as outlets for his company's beer.

Busch died in 1913 and his company sold the place when Prohibition started in 1920. It became the Doyle after Jim "Doc" Doyle won $444,444.44 in the Irish lottery in 1944 and used some of it to buy the place. Doyle operated it into the 1990s and it then had two more owners before the Kellys took over.

Pat, who had left the cable TV industry, had been working at the hotel as a cook for just a week, when the couple who owned it decided to close. The Kellys bought it on a whim.

"That's when we went insane," says Vickey.

They got rid of the down-and-out drug addicts and alcoholics who lived there, bought mattresses and sheets and did some painting. Then, they offered the 17 rooms with battered furniture, and a bathroom down the hall, almost exclusively to AT backpackers. Four hundred stopped the first year and now about 1,200 stop each hiking season. About half of them stay the night in a room that costs $25.

Vickey and Pat

"It's still a dump," Vickey says, "but at least it's a clean dump."

I stop for a second lunch at the hotel after hiking 11.3 fairly easy miles from the Darlington Shelter. At Hawk Rock, I enjoy a pretty view of Duncannon and the Susquehanna, before descending 608 feet to town.

I'm greeted by big, bright orange "APPALACHIAN TRAIL DETOUR SIGNS," bigger than the ones you'd see for cars, that route hikers a couple blocks around bridge construction, through a park to a pedestrian bridge over a creek.

First, I stop at Zeiderelli's Pizza & Subs and get a large vegetarian pizza. I eat two slices, pack the rest and then walk a block to the Doyle, which has a "WELCOME HIKERS" sign above the front door.

Pat's standing just outside the door and follows me inside, where a few southbounders are lounging around. Pat says he enjoys this time of year more because there are fewer hikers and more time to get to know them. Most backpackers visit from mid-May to mid-July, he says, with June being the busiest month.

"Our locals tend to avoid us at that time" says Vickey, referring to the bar and restaurant, known for a good beer selection and fine food prepared by Pat.

Most of the hikers are great, Pat says, but some of those in their 20s and some in their 40s "reliving their college days" do like to party.

"We get tired of that," he says.

For the most part, though, Vickey says: "Hikers have respect for the building. You can't treat it like a Holiday Inn. The pipes are old. The windows are old. The owners are old."

I order a wild-caught salmon patty and home-cut fries. Pat says that's what he'd order and goes into the kitchen to make it for me. The fish and fries are delicious. Besides enjoying the food, I get to read today's *USA Today* and Pat tells me I can take the weekend edition.

When I get ready to leave about 4, the sky has turned cloudy and it's become windy. Vickey tells me that the forecast is for 2 inches of rain, starting tonight. I say I better get going then, and ask them how long they plan on operating the place. They say they have no plans to leave.

"It's a tossup on what floor I'm going to die on," says Vickey.

"We're going to die here and haunt it," says Pat.

I say goodbye and then hike two miles through town, stopping briefly to buy a big tube of Shoe Goo at a hardware store. Then, I climb 856 feet over 2.4 miles to Clarks Ferry Shelter, where I plan to spend the night. There are three young locals here, though, cooking canned food over a campfire. I decide to let them have the place to themselves, even though it's 6.7 miles to the next shelter and I've got at most two hours of light.

The trail, though, is fairly level and still not rocky, so I can hike fast. I'm doing just that when I see a big black bear sitting on the trail, about 20 yards ahead of me. I don't have time to waste, so I growl and start hiking toward the bear. It looks up, sees me, and runs into the woods.

I hustle past, put my headlamp on and hike the last 2.9 miles to Peters Mountain Shelter in the dark. It starts to sprinkle about an hour before I reach the shelter, where I find one person sleeping. I'd hiked 22.3 miles for the day and I'm hungry, so I eat a few slices of pizza and then go to sleep, as it starts to pour.

The rain has let up a little in the morning, when I meet the guy I saw sleeping last night and three other backpackers who were sleeping on the second level of the spacious shelter, which sleeps 16. They're two retired men from Ohio on a 10-day section hike, along with one's daughter-in-law and her female friend, who are out for two days on their first backpacking trip.

I hike much of the day in the rain on a trail that often becomes a stream, and I see only two other backpackers, a northbound section hiker who's stopping early and a thru-hiker heading south. I'm quite tired and wet, even though I'm wearing a high-quality rain jacket, by the time I reach Rausch Gap Shelter, after 18 miles. The shelter is the one that Baby Steps spent the night searching for before finally arriving around sunrise and reuniting with his son, Chris. I hang my stuff up around the place, so it can get somewhat dry. The Ohio backpackers don't arrive, so I figure they must have gone to a hotel with the women, who were leaving at a highway 11.3 miles back. So, once again, I spend the night alone.

42

RICH "SHARK" EDWARDS WASN'T LOOKING for a companion on his Appalachian Trail thru-hike in 2011.

"I had no intention of hiking with anyone else," says Shark, 32. "I was enjoying doing my own thing."

Laura "Thimble" Edwards felt the same way on her thru-hike the same year.

"I was in loner mode," says Thimble, 39.

The two had each hiked about 1,230 miles solo when they met while spending the night at a Pennsylvania shelter.

"We probably ran into each other three or four times that week," Thimble says, "but then he got a little ahead of me."

Then, they didn't see each other again until they'd reached the trail's 1,565-mile mark in Massachusetts.

That night, it looked like a storm was brewing, so they both decided to stay in Cheshire at St. Mary of the Assumption Church, where backpackers are allowed to sleep for free.

"He was the only other person," Thimble says. "I asked him to go to eat and we had a good conversation."

"There was some common ground that made sense," Shark says, such as them both being introverts. "There were a lot of real similarities there. She's in the same mindset."

Shark left first in the morning, but they met again that afternoon on top of Mount Greylock, the highest mountain in Massachusetts, and had lunch together.

In Rutland, Vermont, 115 miles later, they stayed together at the same hostel and by then the die was cast.

"After that," Shark says, "we pretty much hiked together to Katahdin."

After finishing the trail, the two went to Pittsburgh, where Thimble owned a house. Shark, who'd been a professional poker player, played online poker, while Thimble worked as a software testing consultant.

Thimble, Shark and Mary (c.p.)

In December 2012, they married and six months later moved to a house on the trail, where they're living with their 21-month-old daughter, Mary. They're expecting a son in December.

I meet the couple at the 501 Shelter after hiking 17.5 miles from Rausch Gap. The shelter is near a highway, so the National Park Service wants people to live in the house it owns next door. Shark and Thimble get to live in the house for free, in exchange for caring for the shelter and keeping an eye on two nearby viewpoints on the trail.

"When we got off the trail, we wanted to do something linked to the trail," Thimble says. "We like the trail culture and want our daughter exposed to it."

In addition to caring for the shelter and viewpoints, Thimble does software testing at home and Shark is a mailman in nearby Myerstown because he "wants to keep on walking."

Thimble says that couples who meet on the trail and stay together, like them and the honeymooners I met in Shenandoah, Groceries and Boy Floyd, are the exceptions.

"Lots of people couple up," says Thimble, "but only for a trail relationship."

Thimble says she'd gotten divorced before she started the hike, but that the main impetus was her brother's death at 39. He survived two rounds of chemotherapy for colon cancer, but then died in a motorcycle crash. She was then a company software development manager and realized she needed "to do the things I want to do now."

Shark says the trail also ends relationships, especially when one member of the couple stays home and the other thru-hikes. He and Thimble know of three such relationships that are no more.

The shelter they care for is one of the nicest on the trail. It's a spacious wooden building with screens and a large skylight. There are six double bunks and a picnic table inside and a solar shower outside, and I've got it all to myself.

The place is just a few miles from the town of Pine Grove and Original Italian Pizza, which delivers to a parking area on the highway, near the shelter.

I'd read about the pizza place in the guidebook, so, when I got to the highway, I asked a young couple stopped there if I could use a phone to call the restaurant. Sure, said Dave Celentano, who also gave me a couple peaches that he and Sue Yeon had just picked. I ordered lots of food and ate much of it in the shelter before talking with Shark and Thimble.

In the shelter register, I see a comment written on July 7 by CAT, the thru-hiker who wrote in the Roan High Knob Shelter, 813.6 miles ago, that hikers should leave their smelly shoes and socks outside shelters and use hand sanitizer on their feet, and that hikers who snore constantly shouldn't sleep in shelters or hostels. Now, I know he's apparently adapted to trail life and kept hiking.

CAT writes: "This is a very famous shelter, so I decide to write down this statement even (though) I didn't stay here overnight."

The trail had been especially scenic today after the heavy rain because the creeks were full and rushing through rapids. One spot, where a fallen tree served as a bridge over a normally placid creek, was scary because the creek was running fast and deep, and I could have gotten hurt, or even drowned, if I'd fallen.

Unlike the rest of the trail since Springer, today's section often passed through thick vegetation that hadn't been cut back, which hiking club volunteers, like Web Breaker and Maston Gray of the Potomac Appalachian Trail Club, had done on the rest of the trail I've hiked. Sometimes the trail was actually hard to see and I hoped I didn't get any ticks in walking through the undergrowth.

Shark and Thimble say they've heard similar complaints about the trail maintenance by the Blue Mountain Eagle Climbing Club, of Reading, which cares for the trail section I hiked today and the next 45.1 miles to the north. They say the problem is that the club doesn't have enough volunteers.

That makes me appreciate the volunteers I've met, and all the rest of them, even more. I hope they've done a better job on the section I'm going to hike tomorrow.

43

ANDY "CAPTAIN BLUE" NIEKAMP has backpacked the entire Appalachian Trail three times in sections and is now on his fourth.

"The Appalachian Trail is like an old friend who doesn't change very much," he says, when I ask him why he hikes the same trail over and over again. "When I come out here, I know what to expect. I know where things are. It's nice to see the subtle changes in the trail."

I meet Captain Blue, 53, of the Dayton, Ohio, suburb of Kettering, a few miles after leaving the 501 Shelter. He says he started backpacking in the Boy Scouts and first hiked the AT in 1989, not long after he heard about it, and backpacked 35 miles in Great Smoky Mountains National Park in five days. The hike was tough because he was out of shape and he had a heavy backpack, including canned food. But he still loved it and was hooked.

He returned the next summer and hiked the entire trail in the Smokies and Shenandoah National Park. A couple years later, he hiked from Springer to the Smokies and first thought of doing the whole trail.

He finished it in 1998, which was also the year he got heat exhaustion in Connecticut when the temperature was in the mid 90s. He had spells of vomiting and falling and became a little delirious, but he managed to make it to a farmhouse, where he rented an air-conditioned room and stayed until he recovered.

He hiked the trail the second time from 2000 to 2004. In 2003, he had to quit sooner than he planned when he was diagnosed in Vermont with trench foot after days of hiking in rain and mud.

He did the trail the third time from 2006 to 2010, and then, after finishing on Katahdin, he celebrated by driving to Harpers Ferry and hiked with a friend the Four-State Challenge. They finished the 43.3 miles in 17 hours.

He says he backpacked during his four weeks of vacation and unpaid leave from his job as an information technology specialist for 26 years at

Electronic Data Systems and Hewlett Packard. He left Hewlett Packard in 2010 after his job ended and started Outdoor Adventure Connection, a Dayton company that provides backpacking workshops and guided backpacking trips. He's also started Dayton Hikers, a club with thousands of members.

Captain Blue began his fourth AT hike in 2011 and has backpacked the 1,060.5 miles from Springer to the Maryland-Pennsylvania border. He's hiking the 229.4 miles of Pennsylvania on this trip from north to south and has finished about 90 of them.

"I go different directions, different times," he says.

Captain Blue says he got his trail name in 1994, when friends teased him because he was wearing blue long underwear.

"Friends were going to call me Blueberry. I said call me Blue, Captain Blue."

Today, he's wearing a blue headband, blue sleeveless T-shirt and brown shorts, and is carrying a blue backpack.

He actually enjoys the rocks in Pennsylvania, which I haven't experienced yet, after hiking about 140 miles in the state.

"The rocks aren't bad the second time. The third time they're kind of fun and the fourth time they're a delight. It's a challenge and you know you're going to hit it."

Captain Blue says he's backpacked several other long-distance trails, including the Long Trail, the 486-mile-long Colorado Trail between the Denver suburb of Littleton and Durango, and the 319-mile-long Sheltowee Trace Trail, mainly through the Daniel Boone National Forest in southeast Kentucky. In 2011, he was the first person to complete a solo thru-hike of the 1,444-mile-long Buckeye Trail and the seventh overall to thru-hike the loop trail through Ohio.

But many people still question why he keeps hiking the AT and he tells them that it keeps him young.

"I get a lot of condescending comments from people who ask, 'Why are you doing it?' I tell people that hiking the AT is my personal fountain of youth. I can come out here and get great exercise, commune with nature. I can live healthy and feel young again."

Captain Blue

I tell Captain Blue that I admire his backpacking ability and dedication to the AT. Then, we head in opposite directions on a trail that hasn't had much elevation change today.

I'm hoping to make it 24.1 miles to the tiny town of Port Clinton, where there's a free pavilion for hikers. But I'm still a few miles from town around sunset, so I decide to sleep under the stars in the woods, since the sky is clear and it doesn't look like rain.

In the morning, I make a steep descent of nearly 1,000 feet over a mile to town, and the Little Schuykill River, and meet a day hiker with a backpack climbing. He tells me he's trying to get into better shape for the steep climbs on the AT in the White Mountains of New Hampshire, where's he's going to backpack soon.

I'm low on food and I'm hungry, so I walk nearly a mile off the trail to 3C's Restaurant, known on the trail for its great breakfasts, and I can see why when I devour my delicious three-egg veggie omelet, home-fried potatoes and pancakes. The fantastic food is well worth the walk. There's no grocery store in Clinton, so I ask the waitress if I can buy a loaf of bread. She asks the cook and he agrees to sell me one.

Then, I get some dried fruit, almond butter, fresh-roasted peanuts and homemade chocolates at the charming Port Clinton Peanut Shop, which also sells an incredible variety of what was called penny candy in the 1960s, when the shop was founded. Its appearance doesn't seem to have changed since then.

Fortified with fresh food, I'm glad I don't have to walk or hitch nearly two miles in the opposite direction to get groceries in the bigger borough of Hamburg. I make the steep climb out of town and the trail gets rockier before I reach Pulpit Rock and a beautiful view of the Lehigh Valley below. I enjoy it with a day-hiking couple from nearby New Jersey, who give me some fresh fruit. Then I hike 2.2 miles quickly to The Pinnacle for a splendid panoramic view of the valley at sunset.

There are several overnight hikers camped near the side trail to The Pinnacle on this Friday night in mid-August, and I decide to camp near them and sleep under the stars again, since the next shelter is 5.5 miles away and the sky is clear.

44

Top ultrarunner Karl "Speedgoat" Meltzer is chasing the Appalachian Trail speed record.

I run into Speedgoat on August 17, when he'd run 937 miles in 21 1/2 days and I'd hiked 1,248.3 in 88 1/2.

I knew he was heading south from Maine and I was hoping I'd at least see him speed by. Then, I get lucky enough to actually sit and talk with him and his crew.

Two days after I leave Port Clinton, I've spent much of the day picking my way along a trail filled with pointy rocks and scrambling along cliffs filled with huge boulders. I have to constantly and carefully jump from boulder to boulder to boulder and I'm ready for a break in the late afternoon when I reach Lehigh Furnace Gap and Ashfield Road and see a white van and a few people nearby.

"Where are you from?" I yell to the guy closest to me. "Utah," he says. "What are you doing?" I ask. He says they're supporting a runner trying to break the Appalachian Trail speed record.

I tell him I'm also a runner and I'd love to meet Speedgoat. I also say that I'm a reporter writing about my hike and ask Larry O'Neil, 48, of Salt Lake City, also an ultrarunner and Speedgoat's crew chief, if he's got time to talk with me.

Sure, he says and tells me that Speedgoat, 46, of Sandy, Utah, has won 100-mile races 35 times and "is the greatest 100-mile trail runner ever." He also says that breaking the AT record is important to Speedgoat because he ran the trail while growing up in Auburn, New Hampshire, where he was the state cross country champion in high school.

Speedgoat ran for the AT record the first time in 2008, when it was 47 days, 13 hours, and 31 minutes, and missed by more than seven days, finishing in 54 days, 21 hours, 12 minutes. This time, he's chasing the record of 46 days, 11 hours and 20 minutes set by Jennifer Pharr Davis in 2011. To beat her, he'll have to average more than 46.8 miles a day.

Speedgoat

Larry says Speedgoat is eight miles and four hours ahead of the record pace. He summited Katahdin at 4:20 a.m. on July 27 and headed south through Maine, which, Larry says, has been by far the toughest state.

"There's water, roots and bogs everywhere," says Larry, who ran about a third of the first 10 days and 450 miles through Maine and New Hampshire with Speedgoat for safety reasons, while another runner joined him for the other 300 miles. Speedgoat, Larry says, called his seventh day on the trail in Maine the "hardest day of his life."

While I'm talking with Larry, Eric Belz, 36, of South Lake Tahoe, California, the crew chef and also an ultrarunner prepares a table full of wraps, sweets and fruit for Speedgoat to choose from. Eric also works on Speedgoat's feet at night.

Larry says they meet him at road crossings five to seven times a day, if possible, and that about every eight to ten miles is ideal. He says Speedgoat tries to take in 500 to 1,000 calories at each stop, and grabs more food, such as energy shots and gels, for the trail. He says Speedgoat is dealing with feet that have deep blisters, surface blisters and bone bruises.

Then, a haggard Speedgoat emerges from the woods with a fellow ultrarunner, sits down next to the table and starts eating, while Larry works on his Hoka One One trail running shoes. Speedgoat says "Rocksylvania" has lived up to its name and that his feet "really hurt."

"Then, why are you doing this?" I ask.

"Because I know I can break the record, if everything clicks," he says. "It hasn't all clicked to this point."

If he succeeds, he says, "It'll be a cool stamp on my career." Then he adds, "I wouldn't mind taking a little nap."

That's understandable, since he's been up since 5:30 and won't be going to sleep until 9 or 10 in the van he bought for his AT run. Instead, he heads back to the trail with Lou D'Onofrio, 36, an ultrarunner from Wallington, Pennsylvania, whom Speedgoat coached and who'd come to support him.

Lou's taking the place of James Brennan, 35, of Indianapolis, another ultrarunner Speedgoat coached and who'd run 27 miles with him on Saturday and 18 on Sunday.

"He was very impressive," James says. "He kept picking up the pace."

He says that Speedgoat always wants to be in front and isn't real sociable on the trail.

"It's not like he's very talkative," he says. "It's sigh, sigh, sigh. I need to take a piss."

Nevertheless, he says he's happy to be running with him.

"If he was to accomplish this," James says, "it would be the highlight of my life to be part of it. This is the thing he wants to die with."

But Larry says that, unlike in 2008, Speedgoat won't keep running if he gets injured or if his feet get infected and he realizes he has no chance at the record.

"He says he's not here to just finish."

The day before I meet Speedgoat, I leave my campsite near The Pinnacle, hike the trail down an old road and see a high school cross country team running the opposite direction early on a Saturday. Seeing them, I think about how much I miss running and that I'd like to be running with them.

When I reach a parking lot after two miles, I realize that I missed the spot where the AT leaves the road and I walk back nearly half a mile, where

I find a tree with two white blazes, one on top of the other, which indicate that the trail goes right or left. I'd missed it because the blazes were partly covered by branches.

I follow the trail to the left and reach Hawk Mountain Road, which leads to Hawk Mountain Sanctuary. The place is popular with birdwatchers who come to see some of the 18,000 raptors that migrate past it each fall. I've been there twice, most recently in 2012, and thought it was great.

I take a short walk on the road to see the Eckville Shelter, which is where Shark and Thimble, the 501 Shelter caretakers, met. The shelter, like the 501 Shelter, is in an enclosed building and there's also a caretaker living in the home next door. The shelter is the only one I've seen with a flush toilet nearby, other than the Fontana Hilton in North Carolina, and, also like the 501 Shelter, it has a solar shower.

I read the register and see that Lost Bard and Seeks Chaya, who wrote another detailed account of her hike, both signed in on August 10. She wrote that Lost Bard and two other hikers went to a Deadhead festival the previous night. I'm six days behind them, so I've picked up two days on Lost Bard since I left the Darlington Shelter five days ago, and figure I might catch him again in two weeks.

From Hawk Mountain Road, the trail climbs 900 feet to Dan's Pulpit, a rocky, broken ledge with a view south across rolling fields and woods to The Pinnacle. Then, the trail becomes more difficult with many patches of big boulders.

But there's not much elevation change to Highway 309 and Blue Mountain Summit, where AT backpackers can camp for free and buy dinner and drinks, too.

Ken Lalik, 56, the owner of the bar, restaurant and bed and breakfast, says he didn't know his place was just west of the trail when he bought it in 1996. But he learned all about the trail when backpackers started arriving in droves, after he opened a year later.

Ken put a water spigot for hikers on the back of his building and doesn't charge them to camp in his big grassy backyard, next to the forest. He says thru-hikers almost always camp and that section hikers are more likely to spring for one of the three rooms in his bed and breakfast. He says the hikers have been good for business because they often eat in the restaurant, which is open from Thursday through Sunday.

But, Ken says: "It's not about the money. It's about helping people, if I can. Ninety-nine percent of you guys are awesome."

I eat a splendid seared salmon dinner in the restaurant and talk to the only other backpacker here tonight, a section hiker headed south. He tells me he had a difficult time today handling the Knife Edge and often sat as he navigated the trail. Then, I fall asleep on the soft grass.

In the morning, I wait for a brief shower to end before I hike 3.1 miles to the Knife Edge and see why it's treacherous on a dry day, and even more so this morning, when it's wet. It's a mountain summit with sharp drop-offs on both sides of a scary trail that's less than two-feet wide in spots and about a quarter mile long. Making a mistake could lead to a long fall and serious injury or death. I sometimes sit down, too, as I slowly and carefully make my way along the edge.

Five miles later, I get to Lehigh Furnace Gap, where I meet Speedgoat. In the evening, I reach Highway 248 and decide to walk the 1 1/2 miles along the busy highway to Palmerton, where there's a free hostel, even though the guidebook advises hikers to take a side trail nearby. I've walked a bit on the shoulder when a couple boys biking along some nearby railroad tracks tell me the tracks lead to town.

I take the tracks, but, when I get to Palmerton, I find that the old depot is now a private home with a chain-link fence and a no-trespassing sign between the tracks and town. I climb the fence, though, because I see no other option, and walk through the yard to Palmerton, where I plan to stay at the Jail House Hostel in the basement of Borough Hall. The guidebook says to check in first at the police station after 4 p.m. and on weekends.

Nobody answers the doorbell at the station, so I cross the street and try the door to the hall, but it's locked. Then, I walk to nearby Bert's Steakhouse & Restaurant and ask a worker if she'll call the police station for me. She does and the dispatcher says he'll send an officer to the hall.

I wait about half an hour before two teen-age boys see me and tell me that the basement door to the hostel is often unlocked. They show me the door, which is open, so I enter the hostel and find lots of hard bunks and one backpacker. He says he's a thru-hiker, but is probably going to quit here because of knee problems.

Then, I walk a few blocks through the vibrant downtown to Tony's Pizzeria to buy us both a pizza. When I get back, I realize I don't have my hiking poles. I check the spot where I waited for the officer and also check the pizza place, but can't find them. I can't check at the restaurant because it's closed.

I tell my fellow hiker that I'll buy his, if he quits and I can't find mine, or a place in the borough of about 5,500 where I can buy them. They're especially useful for balance in Pennsylvania when the trail is rocky.

But he doesn't want to sell them, so I'm relieved in the morning when I walk into Bert's and the smiling waitress hands me my poles and also serves me a great breakfast in the '50s-style diner. Then, I walk to the Country Harvest grocery store, where the owner, Richard Nothstein, 76, is greeting many of his customers by name at the door.

He tells me to take an apple for free and says he's given thousands of apples to hikers, since he started doing so at his former store in 1979. He also offers me a ride back to the trail. I thank him, but say I want to spend time at the library, first.

I also stop at Shea's Hardware to see if I can buy biking gloves to protect my hands, especially my left palm, which has been cut and bruised a few times from braking falls. Speedgoat was wearing biking gloves to protect his hands and I think that's a good idea that I wish I would have thought of before I started my hike, or at least after I first hurt my hand.

When I enter the store, I'm carrying three scoops of ice cream in a waffle cone from Claude's Creamery. Bernie Shea, the store's owner sees me and asks, "Do you know the rule in Palmerton when you walk into a store with ice cream?"

"No," I say.

"You have to get everyone in the store ice cream," he says.

So, I offer everyone a lick. Then, I look for biking gloves, but find none; so I buy cotton garden gloves, instead. There are also no hiking poles at the only place in town that might have had them.

Bernie then gives me an extra-large gray cotton T-shirt with the store's name on it. I don't want to carry it on the trail, but I'd like to keep it as a souvenir, so I stop at the post office and mail the shirt and a few other things home.

I've enjoyed my time in Palmerton, but life here in the recent past hasn't been so pleasant because of zinc mining that started in 1898. The New Jersey Zinc Co. operated here and the town was named after Stephen Palmer, once the company president. The company's zinc smelting released heavy metals, including cadmium, lead and zinc into the air and water, and killed off vegetation on 2,000 acres of Blue Mountain, above the town.

The town has abandoned factories and a smelting residue pile called the Cinder Bank that's 2.5 miles long, over 100 feet high and 500 to 1,000 feet wide. Palmerton and its surroundings were declared a Superfund site in 1983, and cleanup of the town, Blue Mountain and the Cinder Bank have been ongoing since 1987, with much success.

On the edge of town, I find a spot to climb up a bluff to the railroad tracks, without cutting through the private yard, and head back to the trail. But, after walking a couple miles, I reach a tiny town and realize I walked the wrong tracks. I decide to try asking people leaving a restaurant if I can pay for a ride back to the trail. I don't have to wait long because the first person I ask, the Rev. Edward Unangst, gives me a ride to Lehigh Gap for free.

From the gap, the trail climbs 914 feet over 0.8 mile of huge boulders. The extremely steep trail is hard to follow and I realize shortly after starting that I must have missed a blaze and that I'm off the trail.

I figure I'll just climb to the top and find the trail there, but, after climbing about a rugged quarter mile, I know I've made a stupid mistake and slowly climb down and look for a blaze. I've retraced much of my climb before I see a blaze on a boulder below me. I continue to descend, then follow the blazes to the top with difficult hand-over-hand climbing most of the way. From here, the trail follows a ridge north and skirts land defoliated due to the zinc smelting. As I walk, I watch the sun slowly set over Palmerton and other towns in the valley. There's no rain in the forecast, so I find a flat place off the trail, enjoy the beautiful sunset, and then set up my tarp, pads and bag for the night.

45

When a black bear started chasing their dog, then turned on them, thruhikers Blue Velvet and The Gardener were terrified.

Roland "The Gardener" Schumann, 22, says he, Amy "Blue Velvet" Fissmer, and Sasha, their 8-month-old Australian cattle dog, were hiking south through New Jersey about 9 a.m. eight days ago, when Sasha heard a noise in the bushes about 20 yards ahead.

"She ran ahead to see what it was," The Gardener says. "Before I could tell, she was running off into the woods with the bear chasing her. The bear was bounding through the woods after her, but she's pretty quick, actually.

"I panicked. I was naturally pretty horrified seeing this unfold. I took off running after the bear at an angle, yelling at it. It stopped and turned toward me and charged up to me, stopping 8 to 10 feet away, bellowing. I thought I was going to get eaten by a bear. I put my hands above my head with hiking poles, trying to look big and yelling.

"It waited for a second. Sasha came wide around the bear to get to us. The bear saw her coming back and started chasing Sasha. I ran after her again, cracking off my trekking pole to make into a point. It was really close to her, right on top of her. It stopped again and turned toward me. I backed up toward Amy, so we could be more intimidating together.

"It came right up to us and did false charges. It was growling and we were yelling and yelling at it. Then, it took off running a third time after Sasha. They disappeared into the woods."

The couple started looking for Sasha, but, The Gardener says, "We thought she had been eaten. If she got away, we thought she'd be thirsty and might have made it to water, three-quarters of a mile back."

Then, they saw a guy they'd met the night before and he told them he'd seen Sasha at the creek.

"We ran as fast as we could to the creek and found her a little way off the trail, her tail between her legs," The Gardener says. "We hiked the rest of the day with her on a leash. We were pretty shaken up."

Shortly after that, they hitched to Washington, D.C., for a wedding, and, since they've been back on the trail, Sasha's been on a leash and they're carrying bear spray. They're the only backpackers I know of doing so.

I meet the couple, who are from Blacksburg, Virginia, in the Church of the Mountain Hostel in Delaware Gap, Pennsylvania, two nights after I slept along the trail above Palmerton. The Gardener has a degree from Virginia Tech in philosophy, while Blue Velvet has gone to Virginia Tech for two years.

The Gardener says the couple didn't expect to take a dog on the trail, but that before they left Blacksburg he had seen on Craigslist that someone was giving one away.

"Roland came over to my house and said there's this dog on Craigslist," Blue Velvet says. "I said we should visit the dog."

"I fell in love with her," says The Gardener.

So, they took her along and the three of them have covered 895.7 miles, since leaving Katahdin on June 4.

I've hiked 1,289.6 miles and have finished the trail across Pennsylvania. The last two days and 35.7 miles the trail has been as rocky as predicted. Much of it is covered with small pointy, angular rocks, so on many miles I have to be careful where I place my feet with every step.

After leaving my campsite overlooking Palmerton, I hike 17 miles before reaching the highway to Wind Gap, which is one mile east. I've heard that the Beer Stein, a bar and cafe in town where NoBigDeal and Racquet stopped, lets hikers camp for free and also make their own breakfast for free from leftover food. But it's just late afternoon, so I decide to keep hiking.

First, though, I walk to a house near the trail and ask for water. The owner gives me some and then I return to the trailhead to find Tim Shane returning from a day hike. He asks me if I need anything and I say I'd buy a few energy bars, if he has any. He's got boxes of Clif Bars and gives me a few.

I make the steep 605-foot climb from the highway and hike a few miles when, for the first time on the hike, I feel a sore spot on the bottom of a foot. I stop to take a look at my right foot and see the beginning of a blister, which, I think, might have been caused by the pointy rocks. That scares me and I don't want it to get worse, so I stop at the first nice spot I see and set up camp in the woods. Then, I put petroleum jelly and a bandage on the spot and hope it'll get better overnight.

In the morning, it feels fine, even though the trail is still full of rocks. When I reach Wolf Rocks, I see there's a bypass trail, but I want to stick to the AT, so I hike over and around the big boulders and enjoy the valley view.

Then, I stop for lunch at Kirkridge Shelter, where Seeks Chaya wrote six days ago that she stopped for "a late afternoon snack" and "had a behemoth breakfast at Beer Stein." A backpacker named Ginja Ninja from Quincy, Massachusetts, left a phone number and a note on July 25 saying he or she lost a clear plastic bag with debit and credit cards, money and a driver's license.

In the evening, I reach Delaware Water Gap, a charming town of about 750, and stop at the nice hostel in the basement of the Presbyterian Church of the Mountain, which was dedicated in 1854.

The hostel was started in the church basement in 1976 by a part-time church pastor who enjoyed hiking. It's the second-oldest hostel on the trail after The Place, which was started in Damascus in 1975 by the First United Methodist Church in a separate building.

The Rev. Sherry Blackman, who became the Church of the Mountain pastor in June, says she's heard that church members had seen hikers packing and unpacking gear and going to the post office, and had let hikers spend the night in their homes before the church turned the basement into a hostel.

The hostel has eight wooden bunks covered with carpet, a large living room with a couch, tables and chairs, and a shower with shampoo, soap and towels. Hikers are also allowed to pitch a tent in the church's yard and about 1,300 spend the night here every year. On Thursday nights from June through August, the church has a potluck dinner for backpackers.

Church members wash the towels and keep the place clean. The hostel is free, but the church welcomes donations.

Hikers looking for entertainment can walk next door to the Deer Head Inn, which is the oldest continually operating jazz club in the country and lets hikers come as they are.

I take the only backpacker here when I arrive, a recent Bible college graduate who's spreading the word of God on his hike, out for pizza. Then, I stop at the Village Farmer and Bakery, where I buy its signature apple pie, cannoli, a pecan bar and three giant chocolate chip cookies.

When we return to the hostel, we meet Blue Velvet, The Gardener and one other backpacker. I listen to the bear story and give everyone a piece of pie, which is delicious.

Tomorrow, I'll cross the Delaware River and enter New Jersey, where there's a good chance I'll also see a bear because there are about 2,500 in the small state. I just hope I don't get charged by one.

46

Justin "Wazi" Warrington has thru-hiked the Appalachian Trail once. Now, he's doing it again, so he can hike it with his dad.

Wazi, 31, of Manchester, New Hampshire, says he had wanted to thru-hike the Pacific Crest Trail this summer, but his friend didn't want to join him.

Then, his dad, John "Dreamer" Warrington, told him he was going to retire this year and thru-hike the AT. He says his dad has a bucket list and thru-hiking the AT is on it. Wazi says he asked his dad, who had planned to go solo, if he could join him, and told him he wanted to hike with him at his pace.

Dreamer, 62, of Suffield, Connecticut, said sure, and worked his last day as a middle school principal on June 6. Wazi, an environmental engineer, took a leave from his job. The two got to Baxter State Park on June 7 and climbed Katahdin a day later.

Wazi says they started together, but it didn't take Dreamer long to decide that he wanted Wazi ahead of him and out of sight.

"He wants the wilderness experience, and that doesn't involve me next to him."

But Wazi is still having a great time with his dad.

"I'm glad to be out here. I'm enjoying the southbound experience," says Wazi, who hiked northbound in 2010. "I love thru-hiking."

I ask him if he's got any advice for me and he tells me to do lots of pushups before reaching the steep trails and rock scrambling of the White Mountains. I started doing lots of pushups in January, so I think I'm ready for the challenge.

I meet Wazi after entering New Jersey at the southern end of Delaware Water Gap National Recreation Area. After hiking about 10 miles in the state, I notice the sole of one of my shoes coming apart and I've stopped to repair it with Shoe Goo when Wazi stops to speak with me. A couple miles later, I meet his dad.

"You must be Dreamer," I say. I tell him I interviewed his son and ask if I can interview him, too.

OK, says Dreamer. He says he's glad his son joined him.

"I like the company. I like the encouragement. I think he motivates me. I don't think I would be close to New Jersey, if I was doing it myself. It's almost as if our roles have been reversed. He's taking care of me."

Dreamer says that at first the two met for lunch and dinner, but now he prefers to have the day to himself and have Wazi get to their destination first. Then, they eat together, discuss their experiences, and sleep in separate tents.

Dreamer tells me that many southbound thru-hikers, just like those headed north, start with packs that weigh too much. But, unlike the northbounders, they don't have a convenient place on the trail early in the hike to mail stuff home because, after descending Katahdin, they hike 9.4 miles in Baxter State Park and then enter the 100-Mile Wilderness. The first town is Monson at the trail's 114.5-mile mark.

"They get in there and they find their packs are way too heavy."

He saw a tent, clothes, hatchets, knives and machetes, among other things, ditched along the trail early in his hike.

"You could open a supply store," Dreamer says, "with what people discard going into the 100-Mile Wilderness."

After talking with Wazi and Dreamer, l step up my pace because the hiking's easy and I hope to do a 24.8-mile day and reach Brink Road Shelter. But an early evening thunderstorm slows me down and I'm still about seven miles from the shelter when it gets dark and keeps raining.

I decide I better stop when I reach a spot where the trail climbs wet rocks because I don't want to fall. So, I stand next to a tree and wait for the rain to stop. But it keeps raining and I get wet, despite wearing my rain jacket.

When I start to feel chilled, I know hypothermia is a risk. So, I dig my tarp out of my pack, drape it over me and put two dry tech T-shirts on under my wet one. Then, I sit on a big rock under the tarp and eat the three giant chocolate chip cookies I bought last night. So, at least I have a delicious dinner, while I wait for the rain to end.

It stops after about an hour and then I set up my tarp, pads and bag and go to sleep, while sprinkles still fall from the trees around me.

47

WHEN ERIC "PAPA WOLF" WOLF was diagnosed two years ago with a cancer that weakens bones, thoughts of backpacking the Appalachian Trail didn't cross his mind.

"I didn't know if we'd ever be able to hike again," Papa Wolf, 48, says, while thru-hiking with his son, AJ "Sinatra" Wolf, 22, and AJ's best friend, Tavis "Moses" Robertson, 23. All three live in Southern California. I meet them the day after I talk with Wazi and Dreamer.

Papa Wolf says he was a Marine stationed at the U.S. Embassy in Mexico in 2012 when one of his vertebrae collapsed while he was out for a run. He was flown to San Diego, where doctors used a titanium cage and pins to repair his spine.

They also did a biopsy and found that he has incurable, but treatable, multiple myeloma, a cancer of plasma cells, which are found in bone marrow. Myeloma cells cause a variety of problems, including bones that are easily broken because the cells interfere with other cells that keep bones strong.

Papa Wolf says that in December 2012 he had a stem-cell transplant and, after he recovered, he and Sinatra "wanted to do a long hike."

They decided that either the AT or the PCT would be long enough and chose the AT, says Papa Wolf, because Sinatra, who got his trail name because of his singing, "mistakenly thought the AT would be easier than the PCT."

Since then, Papa Wolf, who's been backpacking since fourth grade, says they've learned from hikers that have done both that they're about equally difficult and both have advantages and disadvantages. They decided to go southbound because they needed to wait for Sinatra to finish college. He graduated in May from Point Loma Nazarene University in San Diego.

Papa Wolf, who retired in April after 30 years in the Marines, says they wanted to raise money for a worthwhile organization on the hike: "We wanted to do it for a cause, not just spend five months pummeling ourselves."

Moses, who's majoring in journalism at Point Loma Nazarene, had been involved with friends in filming "The Drop Box," a documentary about a South Korean pastor who wanted to address the problem of abandoned babies in Seoul.

Sinatra and Papa Wolf

Pastor Lee Jong-rak built a padded, heated, baby-sized box on the side of his home for unwed mothers to leave babies that otherwise might be left to die. Other mothers leave babies with disabilities.

The film led to the formation of Kindred Image, a Los Angeles-based Christian organization that's raising money to build a rescue center for the mothers and children.

The three decided to try to raise $10 a mile, or $22,000, for the rescue center during the hike. They named their effort "Hike for a Home" and are telling people they meet on the trail about their cause.

When I meet them, they've hiked about 870 miles and raised $2,600, since starting on June 11 by climbing Katahdin, then hiking through

Maine, which, Papa Wolf says, "has lots of mosquitoes, lots of wet, lots of bogs."

A day after talking with Papa Wolf, Sinatra and Moses, I meet Ricky "Badweather" Adams and his son, Tucker "Tall Milk" Adams, who are also thru-hiking southbound.

Badweather says his daughter, Amber "Dandelion" McDermid, and her husband, Stacey "Fire Squirrel" McDermid, are thru-hiking with them and are a few miles behind.

Badweather, 52, says the hike is his idea. He says he's wanted to thru-hike the trail, since he was a teen. He retired on May 28 as police chief in Pittman Center, Tennessee. So, now he can do it.

"It's been my lifelong dream. I went on a hike when I was 13 with my best friend. He asked me on a hike on the Appalachian Trail. I just fell in love with the trail when I was a kid."

Since then, he's hiked all of the trails in Great Smoky Mountains National Park, which has about 800 miles of trails.

He says Tall Milk, 18, who graduated from high school May 28, always assumed he'd thru-hike with him. Dandelion, 25, grew interested in the trail while hiking at Carson-Newman University in Jefferson City, Tennessee, and Fire Squirrel "married into it."

Badweather says Dandelion, who did marketing for a bank, and Fire Squirrel, a teacher, quit their jobs to do the hike and hope to celebrate their first anniversary in Harpers Ferry on September 13. He says that after the hike they're probably going to move to Colorado.

Badweather says the four climbed Katahdin on June 2 and, like other southbounders, he says that the "mosquitoes were terrible" in Maine.

Still, he says, "We wanted to go north to south because it's like walking home."

When I meet Badweather and Tall Milk, it's late afternoon and they've set up their tents where there's a beautiful view. I've got 4.1 miles to hike to reach High Point Shelter, two nights after I sat on a boulder in the rain. The trail is still quite rocky and I hike a bit more carefully because I bruised my left little toe on the rocks of Pennsylvania, and it hurts a little every time I hit a rock the wrong way.

After talking with Badweather, I meet a day-hiking couple who talk with me about the trail and give me granola bars.

Then, I get water at High Point State Park. New Jersey's highest point at 1,803 feet on the summit of Kittatinny Ridge is in the park. Atop the high point is the 220-foot-tall High Point Monument, which was built from 1928 to 1930 and is dedicated to New Jersey veterans. I climb the 220 stairs inside the obelisk and get splendid views of Pennsylvania, New Jersey and New York.

After I hike through the park, I meet another couple out for a day hike, Lou and Kerry Panarella, of New York City, who give me a bag of granola bars. I've hit the jackpot today.

Lou, 61, a retired New York City police sergeant, says he's read many books about the trail. Kerry, 49, a social worker, says that I'm very thin and guesses that I weigh 125. I haven't weighed myself lately, but I think I'm more likely closer to 140, which would be 18 pounds less than when I started the trail and 15 pounds less than what I used to think was my ideal running weight.

So, I guess I can gorge on granola bars and I eat several before I reach the shelter, where two southbound thru-hikers are also spending the night.

48

Thru-hiking the Appalachian Trail isn't enough of a challenge for Swiss backpacker Daniel Eichenberger.

Daniel, 33, of Bern, Switzerland, the first Swiss hiker I've met on the trail, is lying down and reading in High Point Shelter when I arrive. He says he quit his environmental engineering job on May 15 and is southbound. He says he wanted to do a long bicycle trip or hike.

"I chose hiking because you're closer to nature."

But first he spent 10 days cycling about 600 miles from Bern to Amsterdam. Then, he took a train home and flew to Bangor, Maine. He left Katahdin on June 16.

When he'd hiked 487.3 miles and reached the point in Vermont where the AT merges with the southern 102.5 miles of the Long Trail, he met a woman at a hostel in Rutland and decided to hike the northern 166.8 miles of the Long Trail with her, which took eight days.

Then, he got a shuttle to Burlington and a bus to Montreal to visit a Swiss section hiker he met on the trail who lives there. After that, he took a trip to the Gaspe Peninsula in Quebec with a woman he met in Montreal and returned to the AT 17 days and 364 miles ago on August 6.

So, he's definitely making time and the most of the six months he can spend in the United States.

Daniel says he's liked Maine the most: "What I really liked were the ponds in Maine, the shade of the trees, the shelters, and the weather was great this year."

In the morning, I watch a pretty sunrise from the shelter. Then, I say goodbye to Daniel and hike a section of trail that's fairly level and fairly easy.

After 9.1 miles, I reach a road and meet Angie "Talkie" Shirley, 28, and Brad "Walkie" Shirley, 29, who are thru-hiking southbound. When Talkie says she's from Wisconsin and got a degree in legal studies from the University of Wisconsin, we talk a little about home. She's thinking about a career in journalism, so we talk a little about that, too.

Walkie and Talkie (c.p.)

Talkie says she grew up in Stevens Point, about 110 miles north of Madison and met Walkie in the Marines. They had their wedding celebration on Madison's Capitol Square during an annual Labor Day weekend festival called the Taste of Madison, where festivalgoers sample food from a wide variety of restaurants, listen to bands and drink lots of beer. She says she chose the Square because it's a beautiful spot on an isthmus between two lakes and the festival because she "wanted the weekend to be a big party for the people who traveled to honor us."

Talkie says thru-hiking the AT has been the longtime dream of Walkie, who grew up in the trail town of Hanover and graduated from Williams College in Williamstown, Massachusetts, another trail town. She says they trained by climbing a few New Hampshire mountains, including the highest, Mount Washington, with Walkie's dad, Eric, a retired doctor, who drove them to Maine and climbed Katahdin with them on June 15.

"We wanted to hike south because the timing worked best for us and because we thought there would be fewer hikers to compete for resources around shelters and campsites," Talkie says. "Although it's immediately more physically grueling to start north, that challenge inspired us and we were not disappointed."

She says Maine has been their favorite state and that they saw a bull moose there.

"We'd been arguing and its hefty presence cut us short of our silly bickering. It struck the fear of God in us, too. It was huge and awesome and not quite a stone's throw away. It stood in a pond and munched on pond mush."

She says they've earned their trail names because she likes to talk, which slows them down, and her husband would rather just walk.

After talking with Talkie, I meet Dave "Iceman" Martin, a section hiker who lives nearby and has driven here to meet a southbound hiker whose blog he's been following. Iceman got his trail name in June 2012 when he was at a trailhead and met a 12-year-old girl who was thru-hiking with her father. The girl had fallen and broken her arm and Iceman gave her ice from his cooler to put on her arm until help arrived. She called him "Iceman." He says she took two days off and then went on to finish her thru-hike.

Iceman, 63, an estimator for a masonry contractor, says he started section hiking the trail in 2010 and has finished 689 miles. He plans to do it all. He gives me a Coke and asks if I'm a purist because the trail is on two roads for the next 0.7 mile and he's willing to give me a ride. I say I am, so I thank him for the Coke and the offer and start walking.

I'm glad I didn't take the ride because just before the second road, I look to the left and see a bear with three cubs having a bite to eat about 100 yards away. I'm thankful the bite isn't me. The bear looks at me and resumes eating with her cubs. I'm glad I'm not between her and the cubs and enjoy watching them for a while.

Then, I see many great egrets feeding in a stream before the road ends at the Wallkill River National Wildlife Refuge, where the trail follows the refuge edge for two miles. The scene reminds me of Everglades National Park, where I saw many great egrets and other wading birds when I was a ranger-naturalist there in my mid-twenties. At another road crossing, a trail angel has left a box full of treats, including soda, chips and fruit.

I eat a little and then walk through a beautiful marsh on a 1.5-mile boardwalk and impressive suspension bridge over Pochuck Creek, and then on puncheons through a pasture. I walk fast because Heaven Hill Farm is just a mile from the end of the boardwalk and I hope to eat ice cream and buy bakery and vegetables there. The guidebook says Heaven Hill is open until 7 six days week, but closes at 6 on Sunday and today's Sunday. I don't have a watch, but I can tell by the sun that it's early evening.

I'm disappointed when I arrive to find Heaven Hill has just closed. Then, I stand in front of it, hoping to hitch 2.4 miles on Highway 94 to the St. Thomas Episcopal Church Hostel in Vernon, New Jersey. Two people leave Heaven Hill in separate cars heading toward Vernon. I think one of them will likely pick me up, since most backpackers stop there to eat. So, I'm surprised when they ignore me and I decide I won't stop there when I return to the trail.

Then, two teenagers headed away from town stop, turn around and give me a ride to the hostel. Maryjane Fitzgerald-Perez, 17 and Morgan Elia, 19, say they decided to help me out because, if they were in my situation, they'd want someone to do the same for them. I thank them, give them $10 for gas and then get settled in the hostel, where there are a few southbounders, before going out for pizza.

In the morning, I decide to spend a day in Vernon because the comfy hostel, which requests a $10 donation and has a shower and refrigerator with free treats, also has a computer and I want to write stories about Speedgoat and about Papa Wolf, Sinatra and Moses.

I've spoken a couple times with Jonathan Beverly, the editor of Running Times magazine, and I think he might be interested in a story about the ultrarunner. I want to write about the other three because I think some people reading my stories might want to donate to their cause.

I also need to email Shalon at Movin' Shoes and ask her to send me a new pair of shoes, and call Black Diamond in Utah to see if I can get a new pair of metal tips for my hiking poles. I hadn't noticed until recently that the tips had worn out and that I was wearing away the pole itself.

But first I go next door to the Mixing Bowl Restaurant for what's one of the best breakfasts I've had anywhere. The owner is also the cook and he doesn't scrimp on anything, so my omelet is full of vegetables and it's delicious. The blueberry pancakes are loaded with blueberries and are great, too.

After breakfast, I walk to the nearby Municipal Center, where a clerk lets me use a phone to call Black Diamond. An employee there says he can ship me the parts I need and I ask him to send them to Peter Becks Village Store, which is 142.4 trail miles away in Salisbury, Connecticut, and accepts packages for AT backpackers. I email Shalon and ask her to ship my shoes to the same place.

Then, I walk to a hardware store to see if I can find something I can glue to the bottom of my poles to keep them from deteriorating further before I reach Salisbury. The employees there don't have any suggestions, but one at H & H Auto Parts brings me two tiny hard rubber cup-shaped parts that will work perfectly. I use Shoe Goo to glue them to the bottom of the poles and I'm set.

I go to the Mixing Bowl again the next morning and then return to the hostel, where Bill "Friar Tuck" Shapiro offers to drive me and two others back to the trail.

Friar Tuck, 68, a retired high school math teacher who says he hiked much of the trail in sections in the 1980s, drives six miles from his home to the church three or four times a week during the hiking season to give rides to backpackers. He says he likes to help.

"It's my church. It's a way to give back and hikers help hikers. That's the most important thing."

I thank Friar Tuck and then climb 890 feet in 1.4 miles on the Stairway to Heaven up Wawayanda Mountain, named from an Indian word that means "winding waters."

At the top, I take a 0.1-mile side trail to Pinwheel's Vista for a fantastic view of Vernon Valley and some of the section of New Jersey I've hiked through. Hikers can sometimes see High Point Monument, 21 miles away. The vista is named for Paul "Pinwheel" DeCoste, who helped build this section of trail. Climbing the mountain to the vista was his favorite hike.

Then, I hike 7.7 more miles to finish the 72.1 miles through New Jersey and enter New York, where a painted white line on a flat rock marks the border. The guidebook says the 89.7 miles in New York will be tougher than they appear: "Despite the unimposing profile, rocks, abrupt ups & downs make this section challenging."

Shortly after crossing the border, I reach Prospect Rock, which is the highest point on the trail in New York at 1,433 feet. Then I walk a couple miles more across a rocky ridge before I decide to stop for the night a little before sunset. I find a flat, grassy spot on the ridge and enjoy the view while eating dinner. Then, I read the paper and go to sleep.

49

When I see Christine "Sparrow" Bachetti hiking toward me the second time Wednesday, she stops and tells me what's going on.

Sparrow, 34, of Milford, Pennsylvania, who works at a spa, says she plans to hike the entire Appalachian Trail in sections and do much of it with day hikes. Today, she drove about 35 miles from Milford to hike 6.6 miles in two out-and-back hikes.

Sparrow says she started hiking the trail last year and hikes every Wednesday, Thursday and Friday. She also backpacks, but prefers to spend her nights off the trail.

"I like backpacking because I get to meet people on a different level. But I was always uncomfortable being dirty and tired. So, I think day hiking is the way to go. Day hiking, I'm much happier. I can enjoy the trail."

Nevertheless, in June she took more time off work and backpacked the 102.5 miles of trail in Vermont that the AT shares with the Long Trail. She met some of the first northbound thru-hikers then. In July, she met thru-hikers in the second northbound wave in New Jersey.

"The first ones are a little arrogant," she says. "They're in a rush. I don't think they're really enjoying the trail."

She's completed 350 miles of the AT and hopes to do it all by the time she's 40. By then, she hopes to be married to her boyfriend and then thru-hike the trail with him as an adventure they can do together.

"Some people don't realize how hard it is," she says. "What a mile of rocks feels like underfoot."

Sparrow got interested in the trail by reading journals of those who hike it.

"I started reading people's online trail journals, as a hobby, and it was very inspiring. I also saw a video from start to finish on YouTube."

Now, she says, "The Appalachian Trail is my second home."

Sparrow has posted photos from her hikes on Instagram. I wish her good luck and continue hiking on the day after my night on the rocky ridge after I entered New York.

Before I meet Sparrow the first time, I find a note left on a tree by an apparently and understandably elated and excited section hiker named Shaupie who wrote: FINISHED MY AT SECTION HIKE HERE! 30 YEARS, 8 MONTHS, 3 DAYS, 25.5 HRS! THANK YOU AT FOR AN AWESOME JOURNY (sic)! AND THANKS TO ALL THE PEOPLE, PLACES & FACES! IT TRUELY (sic) HAS BEEN ABOUT THE SMILES ALONG THE MILES! HAPPY TRAILS TO ALL!

That's an average of about 71 miles a year, so Shaupie could very well have the record for the longest time to section hike the AT. Perhaps, Shaupie used an abbreviated version of Sparrow's hiking strategy.

Shaupie wrote the note at 1:30 p.m. on August 3, 24 days ago, on a page torn from the 2014 edition of the "Appalachian Trail Thru-Hikers' Companion," another popular trail guide, and left it at the trail's 1365.8 mark, where Sparrow was heading and where the 0.8-mile Village Vista Trail leads to the town of Greenwood Lake. The paper is still in perfect shape, so I assume it hasn't rained here since the note was left and I better carry water.

When I meet Sparrow the first time, it's mid-morning and I'm looking forward to ice cream at Bellvale Farms, just 0.3 mile west of where Sparrow started her first day hike. But when I arrive about 11, I find it doesn't open until noon. I don't want to wait, so I'm disappointed, just as I was at Heaven Hill Farm three days ago, when I arrived a bit late. I settle, instead for a Pepsi and chips from a hot dog stand, just west of the trailhead.

In the evening, I find four gallons of water left for backpackers, near a road, by John and Susan, "hikers of 30 years." They also left their phone numbers and email address on cards offering "a soft bed," "a hearty meal" and "shower and laundry." It sounds great and I'd call them, if I had a phone. But I don't, so I drink a lot of water and take a lot, too.

Then, I hike 1.7 miles to the next road, where I find eight gallons of water left by The Tuxedo Trail Angels from St. Mary's-in-Tuxedo Episcopal Church in Tuxedo, New York, about four miles from here. The angels started leaving water for hikers in 1999, after a former resident hiked the trail and then asked her mom and dad to become trail angels to repay the kindnesses she had received.

So, when I stop for the night alone in the woods, after hiking about 13 miles, I've had plenty to drink and I've got plenty of water.

In the morning, I've hiked less than a mile when I reach another road and find four gallons of water, muffins, fruit, Bibles and a register left by a trail angel whose trail name is Headley.

Headly writes, "Help Yourselves Oh Weary Hikers." I do and enjoy an unexpected breakfast. I see that Snapper, the speedy backpacker I met in North Carolina, signed the register on July 25, and that CAT, the backpacker who complained in Virginia about snoring hikers and about those with smelly shoes, socks and feet, signed it on July 18. CAT also noted that there's a video on YouTube about him on the AT.

Less than two miles farther, at Highway 17, The Hikeman has left many gallons of water. Since I started hiking much later than all but a few northbounders, I haven't, until the last five days, seen the type of stashes left by trail angels for the waves of thru-hikers who started in late winter and early spring. Now, I've got a better sense of how great most northbounders are treated.

When I lay my pads and sleeping bag on the top of Black Mountain, I've only hiked about 14 miles, one more than yesterday. That's because the guidebook was right when it said that the trail in New York would be challenging with climbs and descents over many ridges. I've also got the start of a blister on the bottom of my right foot, only the second of my hike.

I treat the incipient blister and then enjoy the magnificent view. I can see the Hudson River below and the Manhattan skyline in the distance. It looks stunning when it glows at sunset and sunrise.

50

"REMEMBER ME?!" ASKS ICEMAN, when he sees me hiking toward him, after I cross the Hudson River.

Of course, I remember him, and I'm surprised to see him. He's the section hiker who gave me a Coke and offered me a short ride, when he was parked at a road crossing last Sunday, five days ago.

He says he's hiking more of the trail this Labor Day weekend and that his wife, Barb, is dropping him off and picking him up at trailheads. They're staying at a nearby hotel. We talk a bit more and then hike in opposite directions.

Nearly two miles later, I see him again. Barb has picked him up and they've driven to a road crossing just to meet me and give me another Coke. I thank them and he says we might see each other again tomorrow because we're going to be hiking the same section of trail.

Before meeting Iceman, I pack up on Black Mountain and soon reach the Palisades Parkway, a busy four-lane divided highway, where I see a road sign that says "N. Y. City 34."

In the afternoon, I climb Bear Mountain and enjoy the panoramic view from 40-foot-high Perkins Memorial Tower in Bear Mountain State Park. The tower was built from 1933 to 1934 and named for George Walbridge Perkins, the founder and first chairman of the Palisades Park Commission.

At the bottom of the mountain a nice woman at a snack bar gives me a salad and then I hike through the Trailside Museum and Zoo, where the bear cage is the lowest point on the trail at 124 feet, before reaching the busy Bear Mountain Bridge over the Hudson River.

Then, I meet Iceman and plan on hiking 5.8 more miles on the trail and then 0.4 mile on a road to the Graymoor Spiritual Life Center, a monastery that lets hikers sleep for free in a picnic shelter with water and a shower.

But, a mile from Graymoor, I reach Highway 9 and the appealing Appalachian Market, which is open 24 hours a day and serves a wide variety of food, including pizza. It also sells newspapers and has a place to sit, eat, and read. It's getting dark, so I decide to spend a couple hours here eating and reading, then sleep nearby in the woods.

I'm not here long, when another backpacker walks in. He says his name is Chayse "Sciencetooth" Zay and he's thru-hiking northbound. Sciencetooth, 21, of Inverness, Florida, says he left Springer on March 23, two months before me. But he met a backpacking art instructor from Madison, Wisconsin, who suffered a groin injury and he'd taken lots of time off the trail to be with her. He then hiked with her to Harpers Ferry, when she returned to Madison. I tell him that I'm from Madison, that it's the best place in the country to live, and that he should move there to be with her after he finishes the trail.

He says he got his trail name because he often talked about nature and science facts and loved his dark chocolate and Sour Patch Kids candy. Some hikers wanted to name him Bill Nye the Science Guy, while others preferred Sweet Tooth. They decided to combine the two.

Sciencetooth is also heading to Graymoor, but it's dark now, so I suggest that he also eat at the market and sleep in the woods. He thinks that's a good idea, so we go set up camp, then return to the market. I get us my usual, a large vegetarian pizza.

Later, we return to the woods to sleep and, when I wake up, it's still dark. I don't know the time, but I'm wide awake and figure I can eat breakfast at the market and start hiking before dawn. I pack up my stuff, walk to the market and am surprised to find it's only 2:30. I order a big breakfast and read the paper until it gets light. Then, I get an early start.

Sciencetooth catches me a few hours later and then we both stop at a little roadside park with water. We're not there long when Iceman arrives from the north. I ask him if I can use his phone to call two pizza places that deliver to the RPH Shelter, where I plan to spend the night after hiking 19.4 miles.

Wisconsin is playing LSU tonight in the college football season opener and I want to find a place to watch the nationally-televised game. I'm hoping I can order a pizza and then pay the delivery driver for a ride to the pizza place and then back to the shelter after the game.

But one place is closed and the other will close well before the game will end. Iceman says he'll pick me up at the shelter and take me to a place to

Sciencetooth (c.p.)

watch the game, if I'd like. I think I might as well get a hotel room to watch it and ask Sciencetooth if he wants to join me. Sciencetooth says he would and Iceman says he'll pick us up at the shelter, which is 10.7 miles from here.

When we reach the shelter, we find the biggest crowd I've seen since Shenandoah. I figure that most of the hikers, if not all, must be out for the long weekend. A little later, Iceman arrives and we head to a hotel. But his hotel and several others are full. Iceman is nice enough to keep looking and finally we find one that has vacancies. Sciencetooth and I get a room, and Iceman says he'll pick us up in the morning to bring us back to the trail.

Sciencetooth orders us a couple pizzas and I rinse out some of my clothes and take a shower before the game. I'm surprised how skinny I look. Maybe I am down to 125, as day-hiker Kerry guessed last Saturday, but I doubt it. Both of my feet have a sore spot on the sole, so I put a little petroleum jelly on them and watch the game, in which the Badgers blow a 17-point lead in the third quarter and lose by 4. That's disheartening.

After the game, I start thinking about leaving the trail, which hadn't even crossed my mind until I met Sciencetooth. He told me he's going to take a commuter train to visit New York City from a train stop right on the trail in 19.9 miles. I realize I could take the train to New York, fly or take the train home and return to the spot I left by commuter train next summer.

Today's August 30 and, when I reach the train stop tomorrow, I'll have hiked 1,444.8 miles, nearly two thirds of the trail, and have 740.5 miles to go. I'll be 6.9 miles from Connecticut and 341.8 miles from the White Mountains, when the hiking will be much more difficult the last 394.9 miles to Katahdin. Hikers have told me to expect my average day's mileage to be cut in half in the Whites and much of Maine.

I'm also hiking fewer miles a day because the days are getting significantly shorter and will get shorter still by mid-October, when Katahdin could be closed to climbing. Baxter State Park closes the trails that lead to Katahdin from mid-October through November to protect them from damage from hikers who use spikes on their shoes to deal with rime ice. The park reopens the trails from December through March, when they're covered with snow, then closes them again until late May because they're muddy. The park recommends that hikers finish by October 14, which leaves me 44 days after tomorrow.

I figure I can average 18 miles a day until I reach the Whites, which means that I'd get there about September 19, if I take no zero days. That would leave me 25 days to climb Katahdin by October 14, and I'd have to average nearly 16 miles a day, with no zero days, to do that.

So, I'm unlikely to be able to finish by October 14, and even, if I could, that would mean not taking an occasional day off in small towns, which is an enjoyable part of the hike that I don't want to give up. And it would mean rushing through the spectacular White Mountains, the marvelous mountains of Maine and the wonderful 100-Mile Wilderness.

Worst of all, I wouldn't be able to spend much time interviewing people and hearing their stories, which is my favorite part of the hike, even if I manage to find many people to interview. I meet few hikers these days because Sciencetooth and I are quite likely the last northbound thru-hikers this far south. And nearly all of the southbounders are south of us.

The few thru-hikers I'm likely to meet are those who have flipped to Katahdin. I could do that, too, but that would take a couple days and be complicated and expensive.

So, flipping doesn't appeal to me and I'd much rather finish on Katahdin. And if I did flip, the weather could be getting bad by the time I reach the Whites, with cold, snow and ice, which sometimes happens even in the summer.

In addition, I'm not enjoying the longer nights and I especially won't enjoy them as they get even longer. I've camped in New England in four Octobers when I took short backpacking trips, hiked and ran marathons, most recently last October, when I ran marathons in Vermont and Maine. I also hiked a little of the AT in Maine and met one person, a northbound thru-hiker.

But on those trips, I had a car and, when I wasn't backpacking, I could spend part of the long nights in a bar watching football or baseball before going to a campground, many of which were already closed.

I've also been spending almost all of my time, day and night, alone, and I think it'd be much more fun and interesting to have more hikers around. Finally, my feet are also a bit of a problem for the first time on the trip, with my tender little toe and occasional sore spots on my soles.

I want to thru-hike, but I want to enjoy the hike even more. And I know I'll enjoy it much more, if I return to the trail next July and take my time when the days will be longer, the weather will be better, and there will be more hikers, including many other northbounders, to talk and hike with.

So, I'm most likely going to be happy hiking a LASH (long-ass section hike) this year and finishing the trail with a shorter LASH next year. I don't want to make a snap decision, so I'll sleep on it and decide tomorrow.

In the morning, Iceman picks us up and takes us back to the trail. I thank him and say goodbye to him and Sciencetooth, who takes off ahead of me. Then I start hiking and think more about what I want to do. By the time I stop after 5.1 miles at the Mountaintop Market Deli for a great brunch, I've concluded that heading home is the right choice and I'm happy with my decision.

In the evening, I reach the south end of beautiful and ominously-named Nuclear Lake. The trail runs for nearly a mile a little west of the lake, which was named by the United Nuclear Corp. The company had a research plant on the south end of the lake and in 1972 an explosion at the plant broke windows in a building and scattered plutonium dust.

The plant was then closed and the site was cleaned up over two years. The trail in the area was on roads then and the Department of the Interior paid nearly $1 million in 1979 for 1,100 acres that included the lake so that the National Park Service could move the trail onto the site.

The NPS took the trail off roads to where it is now, despite an investigation that found the company might have dumped radioactive waste water in the lake and the objections of area residents, who said a trail through the site was a serious health hazard. But in 1994 the Nuclear Regulatory Commission declared the site safe for unrestricted use and today it's a popular spot for fishing and swimming.

After leaving the lake, I end a 16.8-mile day of easy hiking at the Telephone Pioneers Shelter, which, like the shelter I stopped at last night, is crowded with weekend backpackers.

In the morning, I hike 3.1 miles to the Appalachian Trail Station, which was built in 1990 for hikers and where the Metro-North train stops only on Saturdays, Sundays and holidays, twice going north and twice going south. It's 65.9 miles from here to Grand Central Terminal in New York.

I take the train a couple miles to Pawling, where I plan to spend the rest of Labor Day because I want to use a library computer on Tuesday to email the editor of Running Times, who wants to run my story on Speedgoat, find a place to stay in New York, and look for the best way to get home.

Pawling, a quaint village of about 2,500, was the site of a Quaker movement against slavery that began in 1767 and was the first antislavery movement during the early days of the American Revolution. The Oblong Friends Meeting House, where the Quakers gathered, was built in 1764 and is now owned by the Historical Society of Quaker Hill and Pawling.

But the building that's the highlight of my stay is the one housing McKinney & Doyle, a wonderful bakery/cafe where the small, rectangular, intensely chocolate cakes are addictive.

Cary at the Appalachian Trail Station (c.p.)

Also appealing is the Pawling Tavern, where I have dinner before walking a mile to the outskirts of town and Edward R. Murrow Memorial Park, which is named in honor of the prominent broadcast journalist, who was living in Pawling in 1965 when he died at the age of 57.

The village lets hikers camp for free in the park, which has a small lake and a pavilion. I'm the only person here and I set up my pads and sleeping bag in the pavilion, then read the paper before going to sleep. In the morning, I walk back into town, spend a couple hours at the library, buy more bakery at McKinney & Doyle, and then take the train to New York.

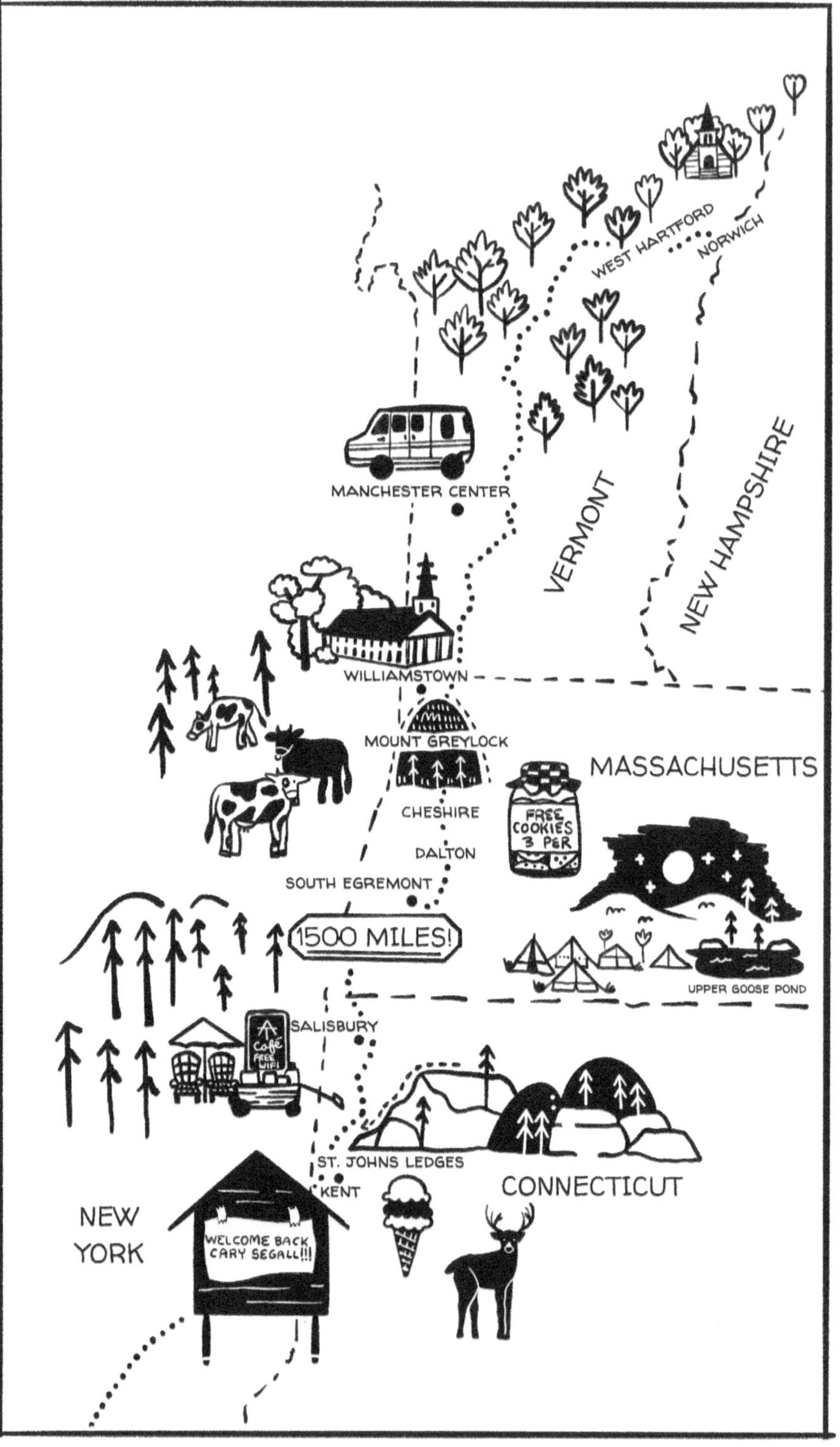
WEST HARTFORD
NORWICH
VERMONT
NEW HAMPSHIRE
MANCHESTER CENTER
WILLIAMSTOWN
MOUNT GREYLOCK
MASSACHUSETTS
CHESHIRE
DALTON
FREE COOKIES 3 PER
SOUTH EGREMONT
1500 MILES!
UPPER GOOSE POND
SALISBURY
Café FREE WIFI
ST. JOHNS LEDGES
CONNECTICUT
KENT
NEW YORK
WELCOME BACK CARY SEGALL!!!

WHEN BILL "TURTLE" FAIR FELL 20 times backpacking down a steep southern Vermont mountain on a snowy day in late November 2014, he thought about taking a break from the Appalachian Trail hike he'd started eight months and 1,643 miles before.

Two weeks and 42 arduous miles later, Turtle, 63, of Huntsville, Alabama, left the trail for the winter in Dalton, Massachusetts, planning to finish it in 2015, like me. He's hiking north to Dalton when I meet him at Native Landscapes and Garden Center, which is next to the Appalachian Trail Station, where I left the trail last Labor Day.

Two days ago, on July 22, I'd taken a bus from Madison to Chicago and the train to New York, then walked from Penn Station through tumultuous Times Square to Grand Central Terminal and caught the 7:54 p.m. commuter train to placid Pawling. I had dinner again at the Pawling Tavern and spent the night again at the Edward R. Murrow Memorial Park pavilion.

In the morning, my day started inauspiciously when I forgot my hiking poles at a convenience store, where I had bought a bagel with cream cheese and *The New York Times*. I ran back to the store and, fortunately, the poles were still there 15 minutes after I had left them. The day got sweeter when I bought small chocolate cakes, chocolate pound cake and other chocolate bakery again at McKinney & Doyle, before heading the 2.6 miles to the trail.

I hitched for a while, then started walking before Pat Dealy went out of his way to give me a ride. "I knew you were only going a couple miles and you don't look like trouble," said Pat, who runs a brewery business in Pawling.

Last year, I was the only hiker at the pavilion. This year, there are several hikers there and many thru-hikers milling about the garden center, where hikers can get water, take cold outdoor showers, use electrical outlets, buy snacks and drinks, pick up mail, and, until a week ago, could camp for free.

Turtle

Turtle, a retired Army medic, says he had never camped or backpacked before he left Springer around March 21 last year, two months before me. He reached Harpers Ferry on July 20 and then flipped to Katahdin, planning to beat winter by hiking south to Harpers Ferry.

"I knew I was slow, but I still thought I could get through."

I'd left Springer on May 22, reached Harpers Ferry on August 4, and kept heading north, figuring I could finish by mid-October.

"Did you meet Guitarzan and Hard Headed?" I ask, referring to the Honeymooners who spent two nights with me at Virginia shelters, just south of Shenandoah National Park, in late July. They told me they had left Springer on April 16 and planned to hike north until September 1, then flip to Katahdin.

Yes, Turtle says, surprised that I met the hikers who had become his friends while they hiked south together through wintry weather after meeting in Gorham. Turtle says he was set to leave the trail in Gorham, just before the difficult White Mountains, when he met the couple.

"I was planning on quitting. I was worn out. It was over. I had my bus ticket and I was sitting in the hostel at night, when in they walked."

He says he and Hard Headed "talked about how hard Maine was."

"We were crying because it was so hard. She wanted to quit, too. Then she says, 'Let's hike together.'"

So, they did. The trio headed through the Whites, where Turtle celebrated his birthday on October 12. They'd hiked about 284 miles from Gorham by the day before Thanksgiving, which is when Turtle kept falling on a steep, slippery descent. They spent the holiday in Bennington, Vermont, before hiking to Dalton. The backpacking was tough, he says, because he'd hurt his toe and some of the time there was too much snow on the trail to hike.

The Honeymooners also left the trail in Dalton, but they returned to Harpers Ferry in late February and sometimes hiked through cold and knee-deep snow before finishing in Dalton on April 14.

Turtle says "Guitarzan was real driven to be a thru-hiker," which is hiking the entire trail within 12 months, according to the standard set by the Appalachian Trail Conservancy. So, the Honeymooners, who left Springer on April 16, made it with two days to spare.

"Me," Turtle says, "the trail's going to be there."

Turtle needs to hike only the 546 miles between Harpers Ferry and Dalton to finish this year, but instead returned to Springer on April 6 and headed north again.

"Why?" I ask.

"Crazy," he says. "I thought maybe I'll try another thru-hike."

But when he got to Great Smoky Mountains National Park, after 167 miles, he thought, "Why see the Smokies now that I've seen the Whites?" So, he yellow-blazed 693 trail miles to Waynesboro, just south of Shenandoah National Park, and has been hiking north from there.

He gets a little tearful when he notes that he has only 120.4 miles to hike before he'll reach Dalton. Maybe, he says, he'll hike 181.8 miles more to Hanover, where there's a place that serves "huge portions" of bread pudding.

"I'm a little melancholy," he says. "I don't know what I'll do next. I like the trail. I like the people. It just seems perfect, a community of people taking care of each other.

"It's life changing. It showed me how good some people can be. The kind of kindness you don't see in everyday life. It made me want to be a better person."

After he finishes, he plans to get together again with the Honeymooners, who are living in Saginaw, Michigan, where they bought a big old home and are refurbishing it.

Inside the garden center, I meet owner Peter "Grin" Muroski, who's helped hikers since he opened the place 15 years ago.

"I want to do what I can for them," says Grin, who's hiked about 300 miles of the trail.

But, he says he decided to end camping at his business after a man threatened hikers a week ago and was taken to a hospital by police for a mental evaluation.

He says he's been worried about liability, as the number of hikers has grown. Some bring cases of beer back from Pawling and a small minority don't respect his property. The latest incident was the last straw.

"We're doing what we can, but it's got to the point where we need to focus on the business."

Problem hikers also caused the closure of the free Jail House Hostel in the basement of Borough Hall in friendly Palmerton, where I stayed last August. I didn't experience any problem hikers or big drinkers last year, when I was one of the last backpackers heading north. I wonder if this year will be different, now that I'm in the backpacker bubble.

I know I enjoy being around lots of other backpackers with stories to tell and I know I'll like the longer days, so I'm glad I decided to leave the trail last September and I'm glad to be on the trail now.

I thank Grin and then start happily hiking again on a warm sunny day.

52

PHIL "RIGHT CLICK" VALENTINE says he "was shaking and quaking in withdrawal from heavy narcotic medication, brutal chemotherapy and intense radiation treatments in late 2010" when God called him to thru-hike the AT.

Right Click says God whispered: "Walk the Appalachian Trail."

"Wait. What? The whole thing?!" Right Click asked.

"Hmmm hm, the whole thing," God replied.

When he told Sandy, his wife of 21 years, she thought he was delusional, and said, "OK, honey, whatever you say. You're so sweet."

But Sandy became a believer when Right Click, 55, of Manchester, Connecticut, who's a recovering alcoholic and drug addict and wasn't a hiker or camper, heeded the call. He had never seen the trail, even though it's only 50 miles from Manchester, but soon started reading books about it, researching gear, planning an AT hike, and taking long walks with a fully loaded pack.

He decided he would hike the trail to spread the message of recovery, which he also does as executive director of the Connecticut Community for Addiction Recovery (CCAR) in Hartford. During the hike, he's been visiting communities to share the message though talks and stories in newspapers and on radio and TV.

Right Click tells me his story while we're stopped at a shelter for lunch during his fifth month on the trail and my first day back. He says he'd been fired from his job as a golf pro running a public course due to his cocaine use, and was "wildly strung out on cocaine" when his first child was born in 1987. Two months later, he prayed for help and has been sober since.

He faced a terrible test, though, in 2010, when he was diagnosed with stage 4 cancer of the tongue, which had metastasized to his lymph nodes and neck. He'd endured a feeding tube, two inpatient chemotherapy treatments and 39 radiation treatments that cured him, when he heard God's call.

Right Click

Two years ago, he asked the CCAR board if he could take a leave from his job to hike the AT, but adds, "I was going to do the hike no matter what."

The board said the agency would pay his salary while he hikes, and he's trying to raise $75,000 for CCAR from people who donate for each mile he walks, from ticks who contribute a penny a mile to bears who spring for a dollar.

"I want to leave a legacy," he says, "that people in recovery from alcohol and other addiction, people in recovery from cancer, we do survive and we go on to do extraordinary things."

Right Click left Springer on March 19, five years to the day after his cancer diagnosis and he's hiked through knee, ankle and foot problems. When he started, he carried 254 pounds on his 6-foot-2 frame, and his right knee clicked when he hiked uphill. Now, he weighs about 200 and the clicking has stopped. He also no longer needs to take drugs for high blood pressure and high cholesterol.

He says other hikers occasionally offer him alcohol or pot, but he knows that if he ever took a sip or a drag, the great life he has would go up in flames.

He says the trail has taught him to value his relationships more and to slow down to better enjoy life. He misses his five children, including his daughter, Sami "Tough Love" Valentine, 19, who met him in Damascus and hiked with him for 23 days and 280 miles, and he misses Sandy, for whom his love has deepened.

"She was so surprised how pure the intensity of my love for her was. It rocked her world."

Right Click has mixed feelings about life on the trail: "At times I'm having the time of my life. At other times, not so much."

I've hiked 5.7 miles when I meet Right Click, including my first AT climb of 2015, and I already feel at home on the trail. I'd started with cotton garden gloves to protect my hands during falls, but had lost one before stopping for lunch. Luckily, Turtle had seen me wearing them when I left the landscape center. He picked it up when he saw it along the trail, and gives it to me at the shelter, while I'm interviewing Right Click.

After we finish talking, I eat bread and cheese curds from the Dane County Farmers' Market in Madison, just like I did last May on Springer Mountain at the start of my hike. I then read the shelter register, while Right Click, Turtle and about 12 other hikers head north.

I find an entry from Gearhead, whom I figure is the same Gearhead I spent a little time with over five days last summer in Tennessee and Virginia, along with Birdman and Tom, who later became Cardioman. All three finished the trail.

Gearhead had told me that he was going to leave the trail to climb Mount Rainier, visit his girlfriend in my hometown of Madison, and then return to finish a thru-hike. He flipped to Katahdin when he came back and was hiking south to Virginia.

"Good to see fireplaces again!" he wrote on September 23. "Bring it on New York!"

Cardioman wrote me in April and said his relationship with Susie, who was his cardiologist after he survived a serious heart attack and then became his girlfriend, had lasted through his hike and that he had moved to

Durango, Colorado, to live with her. He said his "feet were in tough shape for several months" after he finished the trail.

Seeks Chaya, whose entries I found intriguing and amusing last year because she wrote in depth about her hike and her life, left another lengthy message on August 28, four days before I left the trail. I'd wanted to meet her and probably would have caught her in a couple weeks, if I had kept hiking. She wrote, in part: "I did not shower through the whole New York portion – Bleck!"

And Stumbles, who called just about everything "awesome" in her exuberant entries last year and flipped to Katahdin from Harpers Ferry, simply signed the register on October 2, while hiking south. I'd probably have met her, too, if I hadn't stopped.

After leaving the shelter, I hike 1.2 miles to the Connecticut border, where I'm happily surprised. On the sign that says: WELCOME TO CONNECTICUT GATEWAY TO NEW ENGLAND," there's a note that says: "WELCOME BACK CARY SEGALL!!!" and another that says: "ENJOY the MAJIC from SParrow."

I met Sparrow on the trail last August in New York and wrote about how she was trying to finish much of it by doing day hikes. She wrote me four days ago and said she was going to be doing trail magic in Connecticut this weekend, and I replied that I'd be in Connecticut then and maybe would meet her and write about her again.

I don't see Sparrow, but I do enjoy a little of the food and drink she's left for hikers, including Ramen noodles, muffins, peanut butter, grapes, apples, strawberries, soda and Gatorade.

After entering Connecticut, I start feeling nauseous, and it has nothing to do with the state. Rather, I think my nausea might be due to the fish I'd saved from dinner last night and had eaten for breakfast. Regardless, by the time I reach Ten Mile River Shelter late in the afternoon, I still feel lousy and decide 9.7 miles is enough for my first day back.

Turtle has also stopped for the night and we've got the place to ourselves until shortly before dark, when Lucas Gentry, 27, a backpacker from Dallas joins us. Lucas says he left Springer on May 19 and hopes to finish the trail and be home in time to start his junior year at Southern Methodist University on August 20.

He reminds me of Snapper, the speedy backpacker I met last June in North Carolina. Snapper left Springer on May 31 and hoped to finish by his 32nd birthday on August 18. He wrote me in January to let me know that he finished on August 27 and that he didn't have to rush "too much through Maine," which was his favorite state.

Lucas will have to average 29.2 miles a day over the last 731.1 miles, including the toughest sections of the trail in New Hampshire and Maine, to finish by August 18 and be able to get to SMU in time for the start of classes. Lucas, who spent five years in the Navy before starting college, says he welcomes the challenge.

53

STUART "VANILLA THUNDER" RACKLEY is thru-hiking the Appalachian Trail with his son before life gets in the way.

"My fear is if we didn't do it now, he'd be married, have a job and then he wouldn't be able to break away from life to do this," Vanilla Thunder says about Seth "A-Town" Rackley, 22, who graduated from Georgia Tech on May 3 with a degree in civil engineering.

Vanilla Thunder, 53, an Atlanta veterinarian who's using his college nickname as his trail name, is heading south when I meet him on my second day back on the trail. I get an early start, as I almost always did last year, leaving the shelter at dawn, while Turtle and Lucas are sleeping.

Vanilla Thunder says he and A-Town climbed Katahdin on June 3. They decided to hike south, despite the black flies, mosquitoes and wet trails in Maine in June, for psychological reasons, as did a few southbound hikers I spoke with last summer who also live near the southern part of the trail.

"It's easy to bail out for the first three weeks" starting at Springer because it's near Atlanta, he says. And this way, "every step is a step home."

He learned about the trail when he was a child: "As a kid, when I heard about it, I thought hiking it would be really neat."

As an adult, Vanilla Thunder took A-Town backpacking on the Georgia section of the trail when he was a high school student, and they finished the 78.5 miles in the state over three years on one three-day, two-night hike a year. He told his son then that he'd join him and pay for the trip, if A-Town ever wanted to thru-hike the trail. This year, A-Town took him up on the offer.

Vanilla Thunder told his two associates that they'd be on their own for five to six months and got the blessing of his wife, Denise, who's not interested in thru-hiking.

"She's supportive," he says. "She misses me, but she knows it was an opportunity to do this with my son. She enjoys getting out for an overnight, but has no interest in being in the woods this long."

A-Town and Vanilla Thunder

He says A-Town is behind him this morning, but should catch up soon, and that the two are hiking 18 to 19 miles a day.

"He's faster than me, so he'll lag back and do stuff. We'll hike together some and other times say, 'See you down the trail in a few hours.' We both need some space, at times."

Like many other hikers, Vanilla Thunder says one of the highlights of the trail for him is "seeing the positive side of people again. When you're in town, people's generosity and kindness. People give us rides. People give me money for beer. It's nice to see that side of people."

They got the beer money in Hanover, when a man outside the food co-op asked which direction they were headed, said he had a friend headed north in Pennsylvania and then said, while giving them a $20 bill, "Do me a favor and go get yourselves some cold local brews," which is what they did, using them to wash down pizza.

A-Town, who got his name because he's from Atlanta and wears a Braves cap, arrives and calls the trail "a tour of America."

"It's interesting. It's not what I expected, by any means. I started out doing it because I like backpacking and I still do, but it's not an ideal hike."

He says he enjoys hiking with his dad.

"I am incredibly thankful to get to do this, especially with my dad. It's the opportunity of a lifetime for me. It's nice to have someone you can trust completely, but you have to work together, compromise." A-Town says he's writing a blog about the hike.

Vanilla Thunder tells me that backpackers are allowed to camp in the backyard of Country Clothes, a store in the small, posh town of Kent, about five miles up the trail, and that he and his son stayed there last night. I thank him for the info, which isn't in the guidebook, wish him and A-Town good luck and head toward Kent.

As I hike, I think about my cross-country bike trip with Craig after his freshman year of college. I was a reporter at the *State Journal* then and the paper in March 2001 offered newsroom employees up to a year of unpaid leave. Like Vanilla Thunder, I knew that I had better grab the chance to take a long trip with my son, while both of us had the time and freedom to do it.

We'd ridden a 500-mile weeklong group ride through Wisconsin the previous summer and, after it was over, Craig said, "It was fun, but I wouldn't want to do it again." So, when I called to ask him if he'd like to spend the summer biking the TransAmerica Trail with me, I wasn't sure what he'd say.

"Are you really going to do it?" he asked. "Yes," I said. "OK," he said, and then I started buying equipment and planning. Like the way Vanilla Thunder and A-Town hiked, we biked together some of the time and other times biked solo.

The trail today, like yesterday, is fairly easy and mostly below 1,000 feet, with occasional climbs a bit higher. I'm wearing tights, as I started doing after leaving Front Royal last year, because deer ticks are much more common under 1,650 feet and I want to reduce my chances of getting Lyme disease from the ticks. Before leaving Madison this year, I'd also sprayed my shoes and trail clothes with permethrin, which repels and kills ticks. The tights also keep my legs from getting cut and bruised as much when I fall.

Before meeting Vanilla Thunder and A-Town, I'd crossed Ten Mile River on the Ned Anderson Memorial Bridge, which is named for the

Connecticut farmer who spearheaded construction and maintenance of the AT through Connecticut from 1929 to 1948.

I've hiked for a couple hours when Lucas passes me. After a couple hours more, I stop at a shelter to have a bite to eat and read the register. Another southbounder mentions Country Clothes in the register and says it's a great spot to stay. Turtle catches me when I leave the shelter and I tell him that I think I'll walk the mile, or so, on the highway to Kent to check out the place.

He walks with me and we stop at Annie Bananie Ice Cream on the edge of town, where Lucas is eating popcorn. I'm not hungry enough, yet, to get a triple scoop ice cream cone, but I do, anyway, because I learned last summer that I've got to eat as much as possible in towns to avoid losing too much weight. And this summer, I've got less to lose.

Last year, I thought my ideal running weight was about 155 and I weighed about 158 when I climbed Springer. When I returned home, I weighed about 145 and I tried to stay close to that weight after finding I could race much faster when I was lighter. So, this year, I weighed about 149 when I started.

I manage to finish the cone and then Turtle and I walk a couple blocks to check out Country Clothes, where there are several tents and backpackers in the big, grassy backyard. Carol Jalbert, the owner of the boutique with fine clothes for women, says we're welcome to stay, too.

It's only mid-afternoon, but the place looks inviting and I'd like to write about it. There's also a library nearby and I want to check my email, while Turtle wants to buy some groceries. So, we decide to stay and meet later for dinner.

54

Country Clothes owner Carol Jalbert was at a New York City gift show several years ago when a Virginia woman noticed her Kent badge.

"Let me tell you about Kent," the woman said, before detailing her upsetting experience in the upscale weekend getaway for New Yorkers and the home of Henry Kissinger, a former U.S. secretary of state. She said that she and her husband were hiking the Appalachian Trail and wanted to stay at a local bed and breakfast, but were turned away because they were backpackers.

"I started to cry," the woman told Carol, adding that a local resident saw her, asked what was wrong and told her the couple could stay at his house.

"The word on the trail," Carol says, "was negative vibes about Kent. You knew full well the word was out. Don't stop in Kent. I had to make up for that. There are lots of people who welcome the hikers and are glad doing it."

So, Carol and her husband of 54 years, David Jalbert, decided to let backpackers camp for free in the store's big, grassy backyard. Since then, David, 86, has catered to campers and added a few amenities. There's a large shed with books, magazines and a hiker's box, a charging station, a porta potty, and a cold shower with plenty of clean towels.

David talks to me after I get back from the library. He says area residents give old towels to Carol to use as bedding for the stray and abandoned animals she cares for at the couple's home, about seven miles from Kent in Gaylordsville.

"I have a shed at home full of towels. I just get the big ones, wash them and bring them here," he says.

"I call him the cabana boy," says Carol, who also pays for the cost of spaying and neutering cats, as part of her Kent Kats. She's paid for 75 procedures this year and keeps a running tally on a sign in the clothes shop.

David, a retired real estate appraiser, says he likes the backpackers and that helping them out gives him something worthwhile to do.

David

"It's a goal. If I didn't have hikers here, what am I going to do – sit around and play solitaire on the computer? The whole idea is to keep busy."

And, he adds, "The hikers are all very appreciative. They all come in and thank me very much."

He says the hikers also appreciate that, since June 20, they've been allowed to use the only laundromat in town, which had banned backpackers. The owner wasn't happy with hikers cluttering the place with backpacks, spreading dirty clothes over her folding tables and washing sleeping bags. But Charlotte Lindsey, who lives next to Country Clothes and lets injured hikers stay in her house, negotiated with the owner on behalf of backpackers.

Now, they can use the laundromat, as long as they leave their backpacks outside, bring in only the clothes they want to wash and don't wash sleeping bags. Charlotte's husband, Dick, who owns a bookstore across the street, helps the Jalberts pay for the porta potty.

A few weeks ago, David says, the hikers included Mama Bear, her 5-year-old twins, Little Butt and Strong Man, and her 11-year-old son, Spicy Guy.

I tell David that the four are known as Mama Bear and the Cubs on the trail and that they left Springer last year in May, when the twins were 3, and backpacked 467.1 miles to Damascus, Virginia, when Spicy Guy had to leave for a sailing camp taught by his dad.

Mama Bear, Little Butt and Strong Man hiked 390.8 more miles to Waynesboro, Virginia. From there, they canoed to Harpers Ferry. This year, the four left Harpers Ferry on May 23 and are heading to Katahdin. They're now in Vermont.

I visited in February with Mama Bear, Little Butt and Strong Man at a park in their hometown of Naples, Florida, where the twins, as cute and energetic as they were on the trail, remembered me and enjoyed showing me how daring they are on the playground equipment.

Mama Bear, who had never canoed, told me that she decided to aquablaze so that the Cubs could experience something different. They started in the South River, which flows into the South Fork Shenandoah River. The South Fork joins the North Fork near Front Royal, Virginia, then continues as the Shenandoah River to Harpers Ferry. She said it took them five days to go 125 miles.

"It was very challenging with many portages to drag the canoe around, one over a mile. We also encountered whitewater."

She said nobody had warned her about the rapids on the river and that the canoe capsized in rapids once.

"Upon capsizing, we were in water only a few feet deep, but incredible currents and luckily calm, shallow water ahead."

She said that they were rescued by three nearby fly fishermen who heard them screaming.

After they got to Harpers Ferry, a couple who gave them a ride called the police because they were concerned about the Cubs, Mama Bear said. An officer came to check on them and concluded they were fine.

On the same Florida trip, I stopped to see Marmie, the woman who hiked with me for much of a day in North Carolina and had dinner with me and Deacon, a hiker I met on Springer and spent time with occasionally until he left the trail in Damascus. Marmie was volunteering at Gulf Islands National Seashore and lived in a house on the Gulf of Mexico. (Deacon hiked from Damascus to Harpers Ferry this spring.)

I also visited Driftwood, a backpacker I met in Virginia who spends the winter living in a tent in a 63-square-foot shack he built on a sandbar in the mangroves on the Gulf side of mostly uninhabited Scout Key, about 30 miles northeast of Key West. When I told him on the trail that I might visit him in the winter, he said that I could find him by going to Coconuts Bar on Big Pine Key and asking for Cyndee.

When I stopped at the bar in mid-morning, it reminded me of bars in Wisconsin, with a bunch of men having beer for breakfast. I asked if anyone knew Driftwood, and one guy told me that, even if they did, they wouldn't tell me because they didn't know anything about me. The bartender, though, did call Cyndee for me and she had another of Driftwood's friends call me to tell me how to find him.

I drove back to Scout Key and found the half-mile path to Driftwood's shack. He was very surprised when I walked in on him sunbathing in the nude and he said few people wander back to his place. He dressed and showed me around, and then I drove him to a UPS store to pick up packages and to a home on Big Pine Key to meet his friends.

After I finish interviewing David and telling him about Mama Bear and the Cubs, Turtle arrives and we go to an Italian restaurant for dinner. I get my first vegetarian pizza of the hike, half to eat at the restaurant and half for the trail.

When we return to the backyard, Turtle crawls into his tent to sleep. The other backpackers are in about 15 other tents scattered about the backyard. I read the paper for a while before falling asleep under a cloudy sky.

Raindrops wake me in the middle of the night and I wait a bit to see if the rain will stop. When it doesn't, I grab my backpack and sleeping stuff and walk across the yard to the shed. I'm surprised to find a guy asleep on the floor. But there's room for me, so I lie down on the floor and fall asleep, too.

When I wake up, the sky is just turning light and the rain has slowed to a drizzle, so I pack up and head for the trail, while the others are still in their tents.

55

TRAND "ACE" RICHARDS GRADUATED from high school and then headed to Maine to thru-hike the Appalachian Trail. Ace, 18, of Knoxville, Tennessee, is the youngest person I've seen hiking the trail solo and the first recent high school graduate. He was homeschooled and wants to be an underwater welder. He says his trail name is a nickname he got because he's a winner

"I'm good at lots of things," he says, "and I always seem to come out on top."

Ace likes hiking and has taken a couple backpacking trips in Colorado with a youth group. He found hiking "was just always a way to clear (his) head through high school." So, he found the idea of doing the trail appealing.

"I've always been considered an extreme, going-all-the-way type of guy. When a couple said, 'you should hike the Appalachian Trail,' I said, 'you know what, I will.'"

I'm impressed.

He explains why he decided to start in Maine: "I heard it was harder and I also wanted to walk toward home and not the middle of nowhere."

His father, Jonathan, and his father's friend flew with him to Portland and then drove him to Baxter State Park. The three climbed Katahdin together on May 27, before Ace headed south.

When I ask him how he likes backpacking, he says: "It's been good."

Before leaving, I warn Ace about St. Johns Ledges, which he'll have to climb today. For me, it was a difficult, steep descent of nearly a mile over boulders and rock steps on a cliff popular with rock climbers.

The rocks were wet and slippery when I cautiously crept down them alone on a rainy day, 3.8 miles after leaving Kent. But I had to pick up my pace about halfway down, when I was suddenly surrounded by hornets, whose nest I must have passed. I was scared.

After making it down without falling or being stung, I thought of a morning when Craig was a teenager and we were camping along a remote dirt road in the mountains of Tennessee. I got up early, while Craig was sleeping, and ran a couple miles down the road, where I found an unused fire lookout tower. The wooden steps were getting rotten, but I foolishly climbed it anyway, and when I was near the top, I felt stings and realized hornets were swarming around me. I descended fast and cautiously, and then ran back to the tent.

Ace

At the bottom of the ledges, I enjoy a mostly flat, 4.7-mile walk along the beautiful, broad Housatonic River. I take a break along the river to check out the register at a shelter and learn that other backpackers have fallen on the ledges and suffered injuries that forced them to stop hiking.

After I meet Ace, the trail is tougher and I make a few moderate climbs and descents before reaching West Cornwall Road and a stash left by the friends and family of Red Panda, who's a thru-hiker from nearby Goshen, Connecticut, and is ahead of me. They've left snacks, soda, water, apples and various toiletries. I eat and drink a little before walking about 0.8 mile to Pine Swamp Brook Shelter and the end of a 17-mile day.

Several backpackers are outside the shelter and inside there are four loud and obnoxious high-school age boys, nothing like Ace, out for the weekend. They've left trash on the picnic table and taken up all of the space in the shelter, which is supposed to sleep six.

I tell them that I'm going to sleep there, too, and that more backpackers might be coming, so they've got to make room for others. I also tell them to pretend I'm one of their parents or teachers and try to settle down a little. They do and say they've been there much of the afternoon because of the rain. One of them turns out to be a pretty good high school runner, so we talk about that.

Then, suddenly, not long before sunset, they decide to pack up and hike on. I tell them not to leave because of me, but they say they want to be near water, so they can swim. So, by the time it gets dark, I've got the place to myself.

I check out the register and find another entry from Stumbles, and I'm surprised to find that it was written just a little over a month ago, and learn that she started working as a ridge runner two months ago in Connecticut.

"Awesome weather today," she wrote on June 22.

That's awesome, I think. Maybe, I'll actually get to meet her this year.

56

MOKSHA COLOTELO SURVIVED a double lung and heart transplant and was at her mom's home to celebrate when she saw lots of thirsty-looking backpackers walking by on a Connecticut country road.

Moksha, 50, of Delray Beach, Florida, had seen the big orange signs sending Appalachian Trail hikers on a three-mile detour on pavement. Her mom, Abby Moksha, 74, has plenty of clear, cool spring water.

So, Moksha got an old red wagon out of the garage, filled it with a cooler full of food and a three-gallon jug of water, and the roadside "AT Cafe" was in business. It includes Abby's Wi-Fi password, so that hikers can go online, while they eat and drink.

I've walked nine miles since leaving the Pine Swamp Brook Shelter, including most of the detour, which was needed because of construction on a pedestrian bridge over the Housatonic River. The day is sunny and warm, so I really appreciate the water and the food, just like all of the other hikers.

"Hikers stop and say thank you," says Moksha." Everyone is so grateful for the water."

She tells me she's grateful to be alive after suffering allergies and asthma as a child and, when the asthma became severe, being diagnosed with chronic obstructive pulmonary disease in her late 20s. In 2010, she was told she had 12 to 18 months to live, but lasted four years tethered to an oxygen machine before getting the transplant 16 months ago at Duke University Hospital in Durham, North Carolina.

She's slim and looks great, and hosted a party with about 30 friends and relatives this past weekend to celebrate. She's feeding hikers food left over from the party.

"I don't eat very much and there's all this fresh food around," she says. "I was cooking for the party weeks ahead."

Moksha's husband, Peter "Frostbite" Freedman, 53, says that she's hiked part of the AT with him, despite her bad knees, and that he's hiked

450 miles of it. The couple are getting ready to leave after 24 days and Moksha says she'll miss the hikers.

"Everybody's been so pleasant and the conversation's been wonderful. I've been loving the trail names. I wish I was staying longer. I'd do this all summer."

I thank Moksha and think about how lucky I am to be healthy and hiking, while I walk the last quarter mile of the detour before re-entering the woods. I hike a little farther to magnificent views of Great Falls, where the Housatonic flows over a cliff 100 feet high and 60 feet wide.

Moksha

From there, I climb 6.1 miles up and down 1,475-foot Mount Prospect, sometimes walking along and through openings in walls made of rocks that farmers plucked from their fields 200 years ago. The moss-covered walls have been common along the trail since Pennsylvania. In the late afternoon, I reach the bottom of the mountain and the outskirts of the town of Salisbury.

Thunderstorms are predicted for tonight, so I decide to see if there's room for me in the home of Maria McCabe, about a mile off the trail. I see another backpacker and he lets me use his phone to call Maria, who's listed in the guidebook, to ask if she has a bed available. She does, so I say I'll be there soon and then talk to the backpacker, who says his trail name is Detox.

I ask Detox if he got the name for the reason I suspect. He says yes, he's an alcoholic and has been sober on the trail. He says he chose the name so that his fellow hikers help hold him accountable. I'd like to talk to him more, but he wants to beat the storms to the next shelter and I want to get to Maria's. So, I tell him I hope to see him again.

Maria offers me a Coke when I arrive and tells me that Tim "Just Tim" Runfola, a backpacker about my age, will drive me to a restaurant after I get settled. There are three rooms upstairs with three single beds and one double bed and I'm the only hiker up here. Just Tim, who backpacked the entire trail in sections from 2004 to 2011, is a friend of Maria's and is sleeping on the living room couch.

He's a retired Army staff sergeant from Fort Bragg, North Carolina, and is hiking with two artificial knees. He says he backpacked about 250 miles to Maria's on the AT from Hanover, which included the path that the AT and Long Trail share in southern Vermont. He's staying for Maria's 86th birthday in five days on August 1 and is then going to return to Vermont and hike the rest of the Long Trail.

Just Tim drops me off at Mizza's Pizza & Restaurant in nearby Lakeville and says he'll be back to get me later. I check out the menu and find that it's the first Albanian restaurant at which I've eaten. But I opt for vegetarian pizza, which is pretty good. The toppings include eggplant and broccoli, which I haven't seen in Wisconsin, but are common in the Northeast.

Maria, who's spry and doesn't look or act her age, is driving her Toyota Corolla when she and Just Tim pick me up. When we return, I pay her $35 for the night and she shows me around the kitchen. She says I can help myself to three eggs, a muffin, a banana and orange juice for breakfast. Then, she retires to her quarters on the first floor.

Just Tim tells me he thinks we met last summer in the Smokies when he was hiking a trail section to try out his knee replacements. At first, I don't remember him, but then I realize he's the guy who was falling asleep and grumbled when I arrived a little after dark at the first shelter north of Great Smoky Mountains National Park.

I was hiking late because I'd left Standing Bear Farm in the early evening because I'd thought it was a rip-off, and then had made a difficult climb of nearly 2,500 feet over 4.4 miles. Just Tim told me last year that he thought the climb was tough and I agreed.

After talking with Just Tim, I read *The Lakeville Journal*, a weekly paper, and learn that the area is home to many notable people, including actress Meryl Streep, who lives in Salisbury, a town of about 4,000 that was established in 1741.

I also check out the register and learn that Maria grew up in northeastern Italy, near the Dolomites, and had to write letters to German soldiers when she was 12. She emigrated to the United States after marrying an American after World War II. I also learn that many of the hikers who have stayed here think she's wonderful.

"I wasn't homesick till spending a zero with Maria," Antonio, whose trail name is Luigi, wrote last Thursday. "Her kindness and generosity made me feel more like a member of her family than a guest."

Clarity, who stayed here on July 15, wrote: "You are truly the most beautiful soul I have had the pleasure of meeting! You're spunky, lively, funny and truly a kind, generous lady."

Stumbles, who stayed here last September, also wrote about her love for Maria, although she didn't call her "awesome." She did, though, place colored stars around her entry.

57

"Bob the Trail Maintainer" says volunteers like him are a dying breed.

Bob says he's one of four or five people over 50 who do much of the work on the 48.6 miles of the Appalachian Trail in Connecticut, as volunteers with the Connecticut chapter of the Appalachian Mountain Club.

"There are getting to be fewer people like me, says Bob, 64, of Naugatuck, Connecticut. "The younger guys aren't as involved because they've got careers and families. They're more interested in text messages and games. I'm guessing that in five years there will be nobody on this section of trail."

For now, though, Bob, will continue to drive 120 miles round trip about once a week to work on the trail section assigned to him, as he's done for about nine years, even though, he says: "My feet are shot; my knees are shot." He will also keep volunteering most weeks for work parties on other trail sections, which, he says, do attract younger volunteers and will probably end up being the way much of the trail is maintained.

"Once you've done it for so long, you want to keep doing it," he says. "I've been up and down this trail dozens of times. It's become part of me. It's my church and my gym. I like being alone. I like the woods."

I meet Bob not long after leaving Maria's house on a steamy, cloudy morning. It's a good thing he's here early because the sky's supposed to clear and the highs are expected to be in the 90s.

Bob says this is the best place to hike in Connecticut because the trail leads to Bear Mountain, which is the highest peak in the state at 2,316 feet and has beautiful views. The highest point in Connecticut, though, is at 2,380 feet on the south slope of Mount Frissel, which peaks at 2,454 feet in Massachusetts.

Today, Bob's here mainly to cut a path through a tree that's fallen across the trail. A hiker reported it to the club's website and the overseer of trails asked Bob to take care of it. He's backpacked here with about 26 pounds of equipment, including a chainsaw, helmet with a visor, and chaps to protect his legs.

I watch, as he starts cutting the tree, which is more than a foot in diameter. He's cut about halfway through, when the chainsaw gets pinched and stops cutting. Bob asks me to try to lift the tree to free the chainsaw, but that doesn't work, so he cuts down a smaller tree to use as a lever. When that also doesn't work, I suggest he use a handsaw to free the chainsaw. That works.

Bob The Trail Maintainer

When the chainsaw gets caught on a second cut, Bob uses the handsaw again. When it gets caught a third time, he takes two wedges from his pack and uses a tree branch as a hammer to free the chainsaw.

"Why," I ask, "didn't you use the wedges the first time?"

"I didn't follow protocol," he says.

I tell Bob I enjoyed talking with him and helping him, and then make the short, steep climb to 1,712-foot Lion's Head, which is 3.7 miles before Bear Mountain. The clouds have cleared and I get great views of the small towns, lakes, valleys, farms, forests and mountains of Connecticut to the south/southeast and Massachusetts to the north/northeast.

Less than a mile north of Lion's Head, I reach Riga Shelter, which also has great views, and am very surprised to find that Stumbles was here to enjoy them yesterday.

"Ridge Runner Leah (Stumbles) here to enjoy the view," she wrote in the register. "Awesome day for hiking. Come visit me at Sages Ravine, if you're bored."

Sages Ravine is just 3.4 miles away, so maybe I'll finally meet Stumbles today. First, though, I reach a sign marking the 1,500-mile mark of the trail. Then, I get to the top of Bear Mountain and climb a huge pile of big rocks, what's left of a monument built in the late 1800s, and get views similar to those from Riga Shelter and Lion's Head.

The monument was built after Robbins Battell, of Norfolk, Connecticut, who was a prominent banker, musician, philanthropist and adviser to Abraham Lincoln, read in the Encyclopedia Britannica that no spot in the state was over 1,000 feet. That upset him, so he hired a surveyor to prove the article wrong. He then in 1885 signed a 999-year lease for the Bear Mountain summit and five acres around it, and hired mason Owen Travis, of Salisbury, to build a monument on the highest peak in the state.

Owen used oxen to haul 350 tons of native stone to the summit over three years and built a monument that was 20 feet by 20 feet at the base, 10 feet by 10 feet at the top and 22-1/2 feet tall. He topped the monument, which could be seen for miles around, with a 16-1/2-foot-tall lightning rod and metal ball. In the 1960s, the monument partially collapsed. It was restored in 1972, but collapsed again six years later. The ruins were stabilized in the early 1980s.

On the way down the mountain, I enter Massachusetts and at the bottom I walk into the ravine. I see a tent cabin on a hill across a stream, which I assume is where Stumbles is staying. So, I cross and climb to the tent, and see a woman nearby.

"Are you Stumbles?" I ask.

No, says Amanda "Not a Chance" Timeoni, the other ridge runner. She says Stumbles left today for the four days she gets off every two weeks. So, I don't get a chance to meet her.

Not a Chance tells me Stumbles (Leah Thomas), is 23 and, as I learned last summer at the ATC headquarters, is from Pomfret, Vermont. She graduated in May last year from West Texas A&M University in Canyon, Texas, where she was on the equestrian team and got a bachelor's degree in agricultural communications/journalism. So, it makes sense that she writes well and that I've enjoyed the messages she's left since she started the trail not long before me. After finishing her thru-hike, she worked at Eastern Mountain Sports, an outdoor clothing and equipment retailer, before starting her ridge-runner job in May.

I'm disappointed not to meet Stumbles, but I enjoy talking with Not a Chance, who's an accomplished backpacker with an interesting story to tell.

58

Not a Chance got her trail name because nobody thought she could finish the Pacific Crest Trail when she started it at age 23. Now, she's 30 and has thru-hiked the trail four times.

The first time, she had graduated from Western Washington University in Bellingham with a philosophy degree and had thought of going to law school to become a public-interest lawyer. But she decided she'd rather backpack the PCT.

So, she started hiking the 2,653-mile-long trail in late April 2009 and finished the trek from the Mexican border to the Canadian border through California, Oregon and Washington in early October. But she says she wasn't a good backpacker, at least by her standards.

"I wanted to get better at it, more efficient," she says, which is one reason she thru-hiked it again in 2010, 2012 and 2014."I got a little faster each time."

But the main reason she hiked it again and again and again was because: "I just loved it. I loved that trail. I had this insane love for it."

Among her loves were "the views everyday, the desert, alpine, Sierras, volcanoes, trail angels."

"Why don't you hike other trails?" I ask. She says she does and last winter she hiked the 1,864-mile Te Araroa Trail, which stretches the length of New Zealand.

"It was the hardest hiking I've ever done," she says, harder than not only the PCT, but also two other long-distance trails she's hiked: the 1,200-mile-long Pacific Northwest Trail from the eastern edge of Glacier National Park in Montana to the Pacific Coast of Olympic National Park in Washington, and the 770-mile-long Grand Enchantment Trail from 45 miles east of downtown Phoenix to Albuquerque.

When Not a Chance isn't backpacking, she works short-term jobs to get money for backpacking, like the ridge-runner job she's doing now from mid-May to mid-August for $9 an hour. She's also worked on a legal marijuana farm and been a waitress, bartender, and pizza-delivery driver.

"I like to try and work seasonally and save up. I live minimally. I don't have a lot of things, so I can hike one trail each year."

She says she likes being a ridge runner, in which she helps maintain the trail in Connecticut and the campsites in Sages Ravine.

"It's been so mellow this year. People have been so nice."

Not a Chance says she didn't backpack, while growing up in Perry, Ohio, until she was 15, and went to a snowboard school in Northern California. While there, she took a backpacking trip in the Trinity Alps. She also went to snowboard school in Steamboat Springs, Colorado, when she was a teen, and spent time in the Rockies.

"Those schools influenced me," she says.

I think that she and my son would be great together and tell her that Craig is a 33-year-old public-interest environmental lawyer in Sacramento, loves backpacking and would be perfect for her. But she says she recently got a boyfriend, a thru-hiker she met who's headed to Maine. She says he's talking about buying land in Georgia and getting some cattle.

"Why would you want to live on a cattle ranch in Georgia?" I ask, and say I'll send her some info about Craig and Craig some info about her.

Then, I tell her I really enjoyed talking with her and head back to the trail, which parallels a stunning stream, with cascades, waterfalls and swimming holes. It flows through the ferns, eastern hemlocks and moss-covered rocks of very green Sages Ravine.

At the end of the ravine, I start a three-mile climb to the top of 2,365-foot Mount Race. The last half mile of the climb is along a rocky ridge with spectacular views to the east. The sky is clear, rain's not forecast and the sun will set soon, so I look for a flat grassy spot on the ridge big enough for my pad and sleeping bag and far enough from the edge so that I don't roll down into the valley overnight.

I find a good spot, then sit on a rock and enjoy a couple slices of Mizza's pizza, while watching the pink sky darken and the three-quarter moon rise. The evening would be perfect, except that, for the first time on the trail, I'm a bit bothered by mosquitoes. I've got repellent and a head net, neither of which I've used on the hike, and I decide not to use them tonight. Instead, I climb into my bag, keep slapping the mosquitoes around my head and eventually fall asleep.

In the morning, the mosquitoes aren't around while I eat a Clif Bar, hike and watch the sun rise above a layer of wispy clouds in the valley. Then, I climb to the top of Mount Race and climb up and down 2,602-foot Mount Everett before reaching the Guilder Pond picnic area, where a trail angel named Dottie has left 30 gallons of water for hikers in 20 plastic milk containers and two five-gallon jugs. I drink a lot because, like yesterday, the day is sunny and hot.

Just over a mile past the pond, I mistakenly hike a side trail for about a quarter mile before I see blue blazes and realize I'm not on the AT. After I retrace my steps, Finn, a recent college graduate from Ohio, catches me. He says he's going to stop in about three miles at the Appalachian Trail Conservancy New England Regional Office, just east of the trail on Highway 41. He hopes to buy a Coke. I plan to head another 1.1 mile east to the tiny town of South Egremont, where I want to eat lunch at Mom's Country Cafe and buy some food at the Egremont Market, after nearly eight miles on the trail today.

We hike together and talk a bit and then I head to the ATC office with him to look around. But, before we get to the door, an employee who must have seen us coming steps out and says the place isn't air conditioned and there's nothing inside for hikers. He's not the friendliest fellow and tells us the guidebook says the office has no services for hikers. But he does say we can get water from a spigot outside and use outlets on the porch to charge phones.

I check the guidebook and find it has the "info center" symbol next to the office and says nothing about no services. I tell Finn I find it strange that the ATC put an office close to the trail and then doesn't welcome hikers, unlike its headquarters in Harpers Ferry and its Mid-Atlantic Regional Office in Boiling Springs. But, I say, maybe the guy is the only person working there and doesn't like to be constantly interrupted. I invite Finn to come with me for lunch, but he says he wants to charge his phone and take a nap.

So, I walk back to the highway and try to hitch a ride as I walk to town. I've just started walking when I see a car leave the driveway of the building the ATC shares with the Appalachian Mountain Club. There's only the driver in the car, so I figure he'll pick me up. But he speeds by and, after he passes me, I see an AMC sticker on the back, so I figure he probably also works there. I think that maybe the workers there are just plain tired of backpackers stopping by.

I keep walking in the sun, with temperatures in the 90s, and am happy to get to the air-conditioned cafe. I order the veggie burger plate, which includes a salad and cottage cheese and am surprised when the burger comes without a bun. The waitress says the burger plate doesn't include a bun, but she gets me one anyway. It's 1:45 and the place closes at 3, so I ask her if I can pay her $5 for a ride back to the trail when she leaves. She says she rides with the cook and asks him. He says that'll be OK.

After lunch I go the market next door and ask the deli guy for a half pound of Muenster cheese. I also get a loaf of bread and see that he's sliced the cheese. I ask if I can get a chunk because I'm backpacking and it'll last much longer that way. He cuts what must be a two-pound chunk and charges me for half a pound. At least the folks in South Egremont are friendly.

While I'm riding back to the trail, I ask the cook and waitress if Mama Bear and the Cubs ate at the cafe. The cook says they were there two or three weeks ago and tried to hitch back to the trail. I hope they had better luck hitching than I did.

It's now 3:30 and I plan to backpack 10 more miles to the next shelter, so I try to hike fast on a trail that's fairly flat for the first 4.9 miles. But then there's a 1,072-foot climb up East Mountain for three miles, and I'm still a couple miles from the shelter when the sun sets.

I keep hiking, but, when it gets very dark, I have trouble following the trail, even with my headlamp. I'm exhausted, so, even though I'm probably less than a mile from the shelter, I find a fairly flat spot off the trail, skip dinner and lie down. I'm nearly asleep when two backpackers walk by. One is Detox and he says they're headed to the shelter. I say, "Good luck," and fall asleep.

59

MARCIA "TUMBLER" TERRY and Winston "Ratman" Terry were dating when they thru-hiked the Appalachian Trail northbound the first time. They'd been married half a year when they thru-hiked it the same direction on their honeymoon. Now, they're thru-hiking it a third time and, for a change of pace, doing it north to south.

When I meet them, Tumbler, 43, and Ratman, 49, of Jonesville, Virginia, are sitting along the trail munching onion rings from a bag, and are happy to tell me how the trail changed their lives.

They say they'd been dating for four years and had heard about the trail when they went to Springer Mountain in April 2009 out of curiosity and met some hikers.

"On our way back down to the car," Ratman says, "we looked at each other and I said: 'We're going to hike this trail next year.'"

"I said, 'Okay,'" says Tumbler, even though neither of them had camped or backpacked.

"If you'd known this man before we started hiking," Tumbler adds, "you would have said there's no way he'd be out in the woods."

But out in the woods they were nearly a year later, when Ratman, a physical therapist, and Tumbler, who cares for the elderly at home, started their first thru-hikes in jeans, with external-frame backpacks that weighed about 45 pounds each. The packs were filled with the cheapest equipment they could get at Wal-Mart, and plenty of things they didn't need, such as Ratman's bottle of cologne.

"We were going as cheap as we could because we didn't have any money," says Tumbler, adding that they sold a car for $1,000 to get cash for the trip. Ratman's two daughters and two sons, and Tumbler's two daughters and one son didn't join them. They also each have two granddaughters.

Ratman and Tumbler

When they got to Springer, a guy named Many Steps was signing people in. "We thought we had to have a trail name to hike it," Ratman says, "because we were dumb."

He says that he picked Ratman from the nickname, Rat, his dad gave him when he was born and picked Tumbler for Marcia because she had fallen often on their day hikes.

The couple finished the hike in September and were married on Springer a year later on September 17, 2011. They started their second thru-hike as the "Honeymoon Hikers" the next March and summited Katahdin on their first anniversary. They say not all couples are as compatible as they've been on the trail.

"We've seen people married for years and the trail destroyed their relationships," says Tumbler.

"We've also seen a woman meet a guy on the trail, dump her husband, then marry another," adds Ratman.

"We've got a strong marriage," says Tumbler. "But we've had our bad days out here as well."

The two are wearing identical purple T-shirts. Printed on the front of the shirts are the words: "This walk is for Jesus because He made THE WALK for me"

"This trail turned my life around," says Ratman, adding that "he's dedicated his life to the Lord because of all the kindnesses they received."

"He answered many, many prayers," adds Tumbler.

In 2014, the couple started to thru-hike the Pacific Crest Trail in late April, but quit after hiking 454 miles in a month, many of them across the California desert, because they didn't like having to carry 15 pounds of water, or nearly two gallons. When I ask why they didn't just skip the desert they had left to hike and head to the High Sierras, they say they don't like skipping things.

So, this year, they're back on the AT after warming up from May 17 to June 4 by backpacking the Benton MacKaye Trail, which is named after the man who proposed the AT and stretches nearly 300 miles from Springer Mountain to Big Creek in Great Smoky Mountains National Park.

They flew to Maine a week later and climbed Katahdin June 12 on a beautiful day. They're writing a blog about their hike.

Before leaving, Tumbler and Ratman advise me to spend the night at the cabin for backpackers on Upper Goose Pond, even though it's still morning and the cabin is just three miles ahead. They say it's a great spot and that I could meet Seeker, a female friend of theirs whose place they stayed at the last two nights. They say that they met Seeker when she also thru-hiked the trail in 2010 and that she's looking for a guy like me to travel and backpack with her. Seeker is kayaking to the cabin to meet her friend Fly Away, a northbound thru-hiker who also stayed at her place the last two nights and who should be coming along soon.

I head north and within a half mile a young woman passes me. "You must be Fly Away," I say. "Yes," she says, and I tell her how I know her name. We hike together to the cabin and talk about the trail and about Ratman, Tumbler and Seeker, who hiked with her for several days in Pennsylvania. Fly Away says that when she met Ratman and Tumbler she learned that she was born in the hospital in which Tumbler's children were born.

The day before, I'd woken in the woods, where I'd been falling asleep when Detox passed me in the dark. When I got to the shelter, Detox was gone, but Winston, a thru-hiking woman from Florida in her 60s, with a husband at home, was packing up and complained about two loud and obnoxious guys who woke her while shining their headlamps in the shelter and making a lot of noise setting up camp. She said she and the guys swore at each other before she went back to sleep.

She was surprised when I told her one of the guys was Detox, whom she'd met, and she said maybe he was drinking again. She and Gray Goat, 49, a thru-hiker from New Mexico, told me that they were tired of dealing with partying stoners on the trail, something I didn't experience last year when I was one of the last northbounders and haven't experienced this year, either, in the hiker bubble.

I was dehydrated and a little nauseous from not drinking enough the hot day before and thought I'd take it easy and hike only 7.1 miles to Mount Wilcox North Shelter, which is 0.3 mile off the trail. But when I got to the side trail to the shelter, there was an official sign that said: "Aggressive Bear at shelter July 14! Be cautious and hang food well!" A hiker had written on the sign that the shelter spring was dry, and another added: "Abandon All Hope."

So, I kept hiking. I'd gone 8.9 more miles by evening and was looking for a place to stop, when I crossed a road into a field that looked like a good spot. But then I saw a herd of cows about 200 yards away. I crossed the field and entered a pine forest, where the ground was covered with soft pine needles and there didn't seem to be any mosquitoes. So, I stopped, ate some pizza and read part of *The New York Times* while sitting on a log, and then went to sleep.

In the morning, I woke to find slugs all over my tarp, bag and pack, the first time that had happened on the trail. I picked them off, grabbed a Clif Bar and started hiking, before meeting Ratman and Tumbler.

When Fly Away and I reach the cabin, she stops to set up her tent, while I check out the cabin, which overlooks beautiful, glacier-carved Upper Goose Pond. The 60-acre pond would be called a lake in Wisconsin, but small lakes seem to be called ponds in New England. The wilderness area around the lake and the cabin are owned by the National Park Service and managed by the Appalachian Mountain Club, which provides caretakers who each volunteer for a week from Memorial Day to Labor Day.

The cabin has a big gathering room and kitchen downstairs, a room with six double-bunks upstairs and a covered porch. I pick a bed and then talk with a few of the interesting hikers here.

60

REED "DETOX" DILLARD IS DETERMINED to stay sober on his Appalachian Trail thru-hike.

"When I decided I was going to do the trail, I knew this was the trip of a lifetime and I didn't want anything to taint my experience. There would be no chance of me finishing the trail, if I was drinking or smoking," says Detox, 32, of San Diego, who's also been a pothead and got drunk the first time when he was 15.

"There's no party," he says, "that I haven't seen or experienced."

Detox spent last night at Upper Goose Pond cabin and is getting set to leave when I arrive, but stays a while to tell me his tale.

He says he has a degree in communications from James Madison University in Harrisonburg, Virginia, and had been a bartender in San Diego. He grew up in Charlottesville, Virginia, and hiked part of the trail when he was a Boy Scout.

"Hiking the trail," he says, "was a dream of mine since I was a Boy Scout as a kid."

Detox spent much of last year traveling in Australia and, when he returned to San Diego, thought the time was right to live his dream. And he wanted to live it sober.

He says naming himself Detox "was my way of making sure that I hold myself accountable."

"I'm not ashamed of being an alcoholic. It's a part of what makes me who I am and I'm not ashamed of myself. And I'm not ashamed of telling people why I named myself Detox. I don't want to be a hypocrite. It's more motivation not to drink."

He says Winston was way wrong when she suspected him of drinking and complained about the behavior of him and the hiker with him at the shelter two nights ago. He says they shined their lights into the shelter to take a look at it and that Winston had set her tent up inside, right next to the entrance. When she asked them to quiet down, they said they would as soon as they got set up.

Detox

Detox says, though, that staying sober has been "very difficult" on the trail because many of the young hikers party with beer and pot. But he won't even try a beer.

"I know better. I just can't have a beer. It's either no beer or 10 beers."

I ask him if he'll stay sober after he finishes the trail.

"If I want to move forward in my life, I have to stay sober," he says.

"Sobriety," he adds, "I'm taking it one mile at a time."

After Detox leaves, I look around the grounds and see a pier with two canoes for backpackers to use. But I want to go swimming first and I'm in the narrow channel that connects Upper Goose Pond with Lower Goose Pond, when I see a woman around my age kayaking by.

"You must be Seeker," I say.

She's surprised I know her name. I tell her that Ratman and Tumbler told me a little about her. Joanna "Seeker" Ezinga, 65, of Canaan, New York, about 20 miles from here, tells me a little more.

Seeker (c.p.)

Like Ratman and Tumbler, she thru-hiked the trail in 2010, but, unlike them, she hadn't planned to thru-hike when she started. When she left Springer on March 18, she had planned to hike for a little less than a month.

That was all the time that Seeker, a personal trainer and triathlon coach, thought she could take off work and from training for the USA Triathlon Age Group National Championship in September. She'd qualified for the championship in two other triathlons and was hoping to qualify there for the International Triathlon World Championship in Beijing in 2011.

But, by the time she'd hiked halfway through Great Smoky Mountains National Park, her "heart was totally on the trail" and she decided to continue to Katahdin, which she summited on September 16.

This year, she started her second thru-hike on March 18 again, but, after four months and 1,410 miles, she decided to stop because she was limping along with sore muscles and a weary body, found hiking to be a chore, and wasn't having fun. She stopped in New York, about 45 miles south of where I stopped last year.

I tell Seeker that maybe we can talk more later and she paddles away to meet Fly Away. I walk back to the cabin and talk with Alan "Thumper" Breach, the AMC volunteer this week at the cabin, which is free, but donations are welcome.

Thumper, 68, who's hiked about 1,845 miles of the trail from Katahdin to Erwin, Tennessee, over 15 years and plans to hike the rest, says he got his trail name when he pitched his tent in a shelter that was then overrun with porcupines, which were chewing on his tent ropes. He says other hikers heard him trying to scare off the animals and yelled: "Alan, you're making so much noise. Stop thumping on the table."

Thumper says he lives near the trail in New York with Joyce, 68, his wife of 47 years and also a hiker. He maintains about four miles of trail and the High Point Shelter, which is near his home.

At the cabin, he supplies hikers water by paddling a canoe across the pond to a spring, 50 feet from shore. He fills plastic, gallon containers, then brings them back to the cabin, 100 feet from the pier, and has hauled 25 so far today, three at a time. Sometimes, backpackers help. In the morning, he gets up just after dawn and makes coffee and pancakes, with fresh blueberries, when he has them.

"If we're real lucky, some southbound hiker will bring blueberries from the Cookie Lady," he says, referring to the woman who gives hikers cookies and runs a blueberry and raspberry farm just off the trail, 11.1 miles north of the cabin.

Thumper loves the job.

"I meet all these cool people, hear unusual stories. Everybody's generally up and friendly. They thank me up the wazoo for lousy pancakes and not-so-good coffee and they think they're in nirvana. It's a unique place full of unique people."

Also at the cabin is ridge-runner Jim "High Octane" Niedbalski, 55, of Adams, Massachusetts. He teaches journalism at the Massachusetts College of Liberal Arts in North Adams and was a reporter and copy editor, like me. He's hiked all of the Appalachian Trail and Pacific Crest Trail in sections and thru-hiked the Continental Divide Trail. So, he's done the Triple Crown of Hiking. He says working as a ridge runner is "my way of giving back."

"I certainly don't do it for the money," he says, but adds: "It's a great job. You get to meet all the interesting thru-hikers."

By evening, the cabin's full and other backpackers are staying in tents. Most are down by the pond after dark to watch the beautiful blue moon rise above the distant shore in a clear sky. The sky is still clear in the morning, when I get up before dawn to watch the sunrise. But, by the time Thumper has made the pancakes and hikers have devoured them, the sky's become cloudy and, when I'm set to leave, it starts to rain.

Fly Away heads out anyway, and Seeker paddles away in her kayak. But I wait until the rain's let up a bit. It's only sprinkling an hour later, when I head out, too, hoping to meet Cookie Lady.

61

MARILYN "COOKIE LADY" WILEY wants to help hikers eat right. That's why the three cookies she gives each backpacker are oatmeal chocolate chip.

"I figure they need the oatmeal," says Cookie Lady, who has a master's degree in nutrition education. She'll celebrate her 80th birthday in two days, but still works part time as a dietician for Elder Services of Berkshire County.

When I meet her at the house door, inside the garage, she hands me three cookies and tells me that this year she's already handed out 1,800, which she bakes in batches of 150 and then freezes.

"Right now," she says, "the cookies are going pretty fast."

"They're great, I tell her," and then ask how the tasty tradition started.

She says that shortly before she and her husband of 57 years, Roy Wiley, 84, moved to the place, 100 yards east of the trail, in 1984, she read a newspaper story about a woman farther down the road who used to bake cookies for backpackers. About 25 years ago, she thought that since she liked baking and hikers, she'd give them cookies, too.

"Most of the time, I enjoy it," Cookie Lady says. "I like knowing about the hikers. Why they're doing the trail."

And she likes the pleasant surprises, such as a few days ago, when a hiker gave her a card: "It was from his mother who gave me $20 to keep the hikers happy by baking cookies."

What she doesn't like are the rare times "when hikers are rude and don't say, 'thank you.' When they come to the door and say, 'where are the cookies?'"

Cookie Lady grew up in Strawberry Point, Iowa, home of the world's largest strawberry. She met Roy at Iowa State University in Ames, where she got a degree in home economics and Roy got a degree in electrical engineering. They have two daughters, one an anthropology professor and the other a glassblower, and three grandsons.

Cookie Lady and Roy

She says they were living in Pittsfield, Massachusetts, where she was the school system's director of food service and Roy worked for General Electric, when they bought the place here because it had a grass airstrip for Roy's 1949 single-engine Piper Clipper. The place, called Blueberry Hill, has 1,500 blueberry bushes that were planted in 1948 and still produce plenty of berries for people who come to pick them for $2.50 a pound. There are also U-pick raspberries at a pound for $5.

For backpackers, the Wileys also sell hard-boiled eggs, frozen Snickers bars, Klondike bars, Coke and lemonade. And they let hikers camp for free on their grassy yard, although Roy sometimes asks them to mow grass in the yard and the blueberry patch.

"That doesn't happen too often, though," Cookie Lady says, "because they get here too late."

She says that Mama Bear and the Cubs camped here a couple weeks ago.

"They were so little," she says of the 5-year-old twins. "I wondered how they would handle New Hampshire. When I asked them their names, they said, 'Do you want our trail names or our real names?'"

Cookie Lady says she and Roy, who retired in 1990, aren't hikers, but have traveled by bike, and in 1982 biked the popular, annual RAGBRAI ride across Iowa, which Craig and I rode in 2004.

I tell her that she's the second Cookie Lady I've met on a long-distance trip. The first was June "Cookie Lady" Curry, whom I met just east of the Blue Ridge Parkway in Virginia, while bicycling cross country on the TransAmerica Trail in 2001. June, who died in 2012 at 91, started helping bikers in 1976 and later turned an extra house on her property into the Bike House, with food and shelter for cyclists.

After talking with Cookie Lady, I walk over to see Roy, who's sitting in a chair in the old garage and running the U-pick blueberry business.

"The day we moved here was the day we saw our first hiker," Roy says. "They're always looking for water. One thing led to another. First, we gave them cookies. Then, we let them stay overnight."

He and his wife also shuttle hikers to spots along the trail in Massachusetts, Connecticut and Vermont for the nonprofit price of $25 per hour.

Roy says that, when he met Mama Bear and the Cubs, "my initial reaction was it was child abuse, but they seemed to be doing just fine."

I get a bucket and walk over to the blueberry bushes, where I pick lots of plump blueberries and some of the few raspberries left. Then, I pay Roy and walk over to the picnic tables, where Fly Away is packing away some of the food in the package from home she had mailed here.

She's got way too much and plans to put the surplus in the hiker box for other backpackers to take for free. Instead, I give her $10 and pack the food that isn't meat and doesn't need cooking. Pale Rider, a backpacker in his 20s who's recently arrived, takes the rest.

The three of us are talking when Roy walks over and mentions mowing, which we'd rather avoid after hiking much of the day. So, we talk with Roy, instead, and he shows us a little more of the place, including the airstrip and the chickens, which he feeds while we watch. He says he used to fly his plane every August to the annual Experimental Aircraft Association convention in Oshkosh, Wisconsin.

On the walk back, I admire the many flowers and other plants in pots on the deck of the Wileys' home. Cookie Lady loves gardening. Roy shows me the inside of a dilapidated old house he uses to store stuff, including the recumbent bike that he built himself. There's also a toilet and many buckets of water for hikers to use to flush because there's no water connected to the house.

In the morning, I leave at dawn, as usual, before Fly Away and Pale Rider, but they pass me after I've hiked a couple miles. A few miles later, I cross a road, and see a vehicle with socks covering the front windshield, held there by the wipers. A short time later, I meet the men who own the socks.

They're Matt Peters and Eriks Perkons, who like two women I talked with in Tennessee last year, work for NatureServe, a scientific conservation organization that's surveying plant communities along the AT for the National Park Service. The NPS has had the vegetation mapped by plane and NatureServe employees assess the accuracy of the results along a corridor that averages about 160 yards wide.

Matt and Eriks have been randomly given spots to check along about 365 miles of trail in Massachusetts, Vermont and New Hampshire. Many spots in Massachusetts are on boggy land. There are often boardwalks across the bogs for hikers, but not for the two men, who also have to slog through ponds and alder swamps.

"There's no keeping your feet dry out there," says Matt, 35, of Woodbury, Vermont, an ecologist and botanist. But he still likes the job: "It's great overall. I like being outside and seeing what's out here. You find rare species in places. I get to do a lot more of the off-trail stuff I don't normally do."

Eriks, 37, of State College, Pennsylvania, a geologist, says the most dangerous part of the work has been surveying the steep talus slopes in the White Mountains.

"It's interesting for me just meeting other folks along the trail," Eriks says, "and getting a taste of AT culture along the way."

A few miles after meeting the men, I reach Dalton, the town of 6,700 where Turtle is planning to finish the trail, and Guitarzan and Hard Headed finished in April. The trail goes through the center of town, where I stop for lunch at Angelina's Subs, which dates to 1958 and has been rated the best sandwich shop of the Berkshires by the readers of the *Berkshire Eagle*, a daily newspaper in Pittsfield.

When I'm picking the fresh vegetables for my foot-long cheese sub, I say, "It's just like Subway."

"We don't say the 'S' word around here," the two employees behind the counter admonish me. I figure the shop is popular with backpackers because the subs are good and because the condom machine in the bathroom bears an Appalachian Trail Conservancy sticker.

From Dalton, I hike about seven miles, up and down Crystal Mountain, before I reach Cheshire at dusk. I hope to spend the night in St. Mary of the Assumption Church. The Rev. David Raymond lets me in, and I join Fly Away, Pale Rider and a southbound hiker.

The church has been welcoming hikers since 1981, when the Rev. Tom "Father Time" Begley became pastor and started the practice. Father Time was inspired by the backpackers he met to hike the trail himself and completed it after 12 years of section hikes when he summited Katahdin on Labor Day in 1995 at the age of 61.

Father Time considered hosting hikers one of his proudest achievements and, by the time he retired in 2001, more than 6,000 hikers from every state, every Canadian province, and at least 15 countries had stayed at the church. After retiring, Father Time helped maintain four miles of the trail and the Kay Wood Shelter, three miles south of Dalton.

Kay Wood, who died in 2010 at 91, was nearly 70 when she started an AT thru-hike at Springer in 1988, but had to quit after a bad fall in Pennsylvania. She returned to the trail in 1989 and finished it when she summited Katahdin at the age of 71.

Kay's trail name was "Grandma Kay" and she lived along the trail in Dalton, where she and her family welcomed hikers to their home. She loved to talk with hikers, including the legendary Grandma Gatewood, who stopped once for a cold drink.

Grandma Kay was an AT maintenance volunteer leader and worked on maintaining the trail from her 40s well into her 80s. She attended a volunteer recognition meeting on Mount Greylock, the highest peak in Massachusetts, 24 days before she died. Grandma Kay helped develop the shelter design used in Massachusetts and the first shelter of such design was named in her honor in 1980.

Cynthia "Screamer" Behr, who stayed at the shelter, wrote this tribute to Grandma Kay three years after her death: "When I stayed at the Kay Wood Shelter in 2013 on my section hike, I was forever impacted by Gramma Kay's story. It impressed upon me how even posthumously we could have such a profound impact that we are still affecting people and providing a place for fellow AT hikers to stay. What a legacy to leave and pass on! The true essence of paying it forward. Ms. Kay, even after your death you changed my life. You're one of my heroes. You go girl!"

62

When Cosmo Catalano Jr. isn't managing theater productions at Williams College, he's often working on the Appalachian Trail or giving rides to backpackers like me.

I meet Cosmo at the Williamstown Papa John's, where AT hikers get half off everything. Two southbounders told me about the deal a few hours ago when I was descending Mount Greylock, which I'd climbed after leaving Cheshire.

Papa John's manager, Brock Pecor, says word of the half-price food "has been spreading like wildfire," and that two weeks ago there were about 20 hikers at once sitting outside eating pizza at the restaurant, which is near the trail.

Cosmo has stopped to give two other backpackers eating here a ride in the rain to the YMCA in nearby North Adams, where Fly Away told me she planned to camp tonight, when she passed me on the 8.4-mile, 2,511-foot climb up the mountain.

Cosmo says he'll be back to give me a ride to the Williamstown Motel, about two miles west.

When he returns, Cosmo tells me he first picked up the pair where the AT crosses the highway that leads west to Williamstown and east to North Adams. They called him from the pizza place to ask for another ride after a thunderstorm hit.

I tell him I'd hoped to use the computer at the motel, but learned it's not available. So, he says he'll wait while I check into the motel and drop my stuff off in my room, and then take me to the Williams Department of Theatre, so I can use a computer there.

"You're sure a great guy," I say. "Why do you go so much out of your way for hikers?"

"Cause it will be great if someone helps me out the next time I'm on the trail," he says. "You get a little karma going. It's always a good thing."

Cosmo (photo: John Taveras)

Cosmo, 62, who doesn't have a trail name, has hiked about 600 miles of the trail in sections and hopes to hike the rest of it after he retires next year.

"I might be able to get it all done," he says, "before I get too decrepit."

Cosmo, who seems to be following in the footsteps of Grandma Kay, has been an AT volunteer since 1999 and is on the ATC Stewardship Council and the AT management committee of the Appalachian Mountain Club Berkshire chapter. He also maintains two miles of trail and works on chapter trail work projects. He and another guy were working on a project in July when they heard some kids coming up the trail.

"We think it's a family out for a day hike," he says, before they met Mama Bear, Little Butt, Strong Man and Spicy Guy, and learn they're hiking from Harpers Ferry to Katahdin. "I think it's a great idea. I like to see kids on the trail. They're the next generation of trail stewards.

"I think, if I were the parent and I were doing this, I'd be completely frazzled. Sometimes you see kids on the trail and they're kind of grumpy because their parents are making them hike. We didn't get that vibe at all. Everybody seemed to be having a great time. We thought that was pretty cool."

Cosmo, who got a master of fine arts degree from the Yale School of Drama in 1979, leaves me alone at the theater, where he's been the technical supervisor and production manager since 1983.

After using the computer, I walk back to the motel through the pretty campus of Williams, one of the country's top liberal arts colleges, and tiny, upscale Downtown Williamstown.

Earlier Monday, I'd been lucky to be on the 3,491-foot summit of Mount Greylock on a sunny afternoon, when I could see Massachusetts, Connecticut, New York, Vermont and New Hampshire.

The overlooks with the spectacular views weren't crowded, even though there's a road to the summit and the 93-foot tall Veterans War Memorial Tower, which was built from 1931 to 1932 with a globe of light on top that can be seen for up to 70 miles. Also on the summit is the historic Bascom Lodge, which was built with local stone and old-growth red spruce from 1932 to 1938, mainly by the Civilian Conservation Corps.

Historic Bascom Hall and Bascom Hill are on the University of Wisconsin campus in Madison, and I wonder if there's any connection between them and the lodge, and learn there is. Both were named after John Bascom, the first Mount Greylock State Reservation commissioner. Bascom graduated from Williams in 1849 and was a professor there both before and after he was UW president from 1874 to 1887. In addition, Bascom Lodge serves great ice cream made there and there's also great ice cream made and served on the UW campus.

On Tuesday morning, I'm packed and set to leave when I realize I don't have my hiking poles. I think they might be at Papa John's or the Williams theater department, but are most likely in Cosmo's pickup truck.

Fortunately, Cosmo gave me his card, so I call him. He says he's out in the woods working on the trail, but will call his wife, Mary Pfister, and ask her to drive to his truck, which is parked at a trailhead near North Adams, and check for the poles.

I call him again in half an hour and he tells me Mary found them and left them for me in the bed of the truck. I thank him again and then get a ride back to the trail from the father of the motel owner.

I pick up the poles and start hiking. I haven't walked far when I approach a house next to the trail and see a hose suspended from a hook on a pole in a patch of daisies. The hose has a gadget to turn the water on and off and next to it is a sign that says: "AT HIKERS PLEASE HELP YOURSELF TO THE WATER."

I drink some and have hiked a couple more miles when I see Cosmo and three others, including High Octane, the ridge runner I met at Upper Goose Pond, building a water bar.

Silvia

One of the workers is Silvia Cassano, 31, a trail management assistant in the ATC's New England Regional Office, where six days ago an employee met Finn and me at the door and said that the place isn't air conditioned and that there are no services inside for backpackers, but that we could get water and use electrical outlets outside.

I tell her the place seemed inhospitable to hikers when I was there and she tells me it wasn't set up to be a visitor center. She says the office is where it is because it's in the former summer home of Mary Margaret Cashell Kellogg, who donated the house and 140 acres to the ATC and

AMC in 2004. The AMC runs its Berkshire trails program in the building, which is called the Kellogg Conservation Center.

The house, one of the oldest in Berkshire County, was built beginning in 1744 on a farm that's listed on the National Register of Historic Places. Mary Margaret, who died at 94 in 2011, was once the dean of women at Dickinson College in Carlisle, Pennsylvania.

I suggest to Silvia that the ATC get information into the guidebook that says backpackers aren't welcome in the building and then they'll be unlikely to stop.

I watch the four work for a while, then hike a couple more miles to finish the 90.5 miles in Massachusetts and reach the Vermont border, where I meet Jenny, 32, who says she's spent much of the last year traveling and has returned home to Vermont to hike the Long Trail. Jenny takes a picture of me next to a sign that says "WELCOME TO VERMONT" and has details about the LT, and then we both hike into the Green Mountain State.

63

"We've got to stop meeting like this," Tabitha "Fly Away" Hubbard says on the fourth day she passes me in the morning.

"I think it's time you stop and tell me your story in more detail," I say on our third day in Vermont, "since we've spent so many days hiking briefly together."

So, Fly Away, 28, looks for a spot with a couple of rocks for us to sit on and then tells me how she happened to start the trail last year, when she carried 230 pounds on her 5-foot-6 frame, and about the trials she's endured to reach Vermont.

She says she heard of the trail, which is about 45 miles from her home in Mount Carmel, Tennessee, because her older cousin hiked it. She then read *A Walk in the Woods*, after her mom got it for her for Christmas. In 2009, she started reading and watching movies and YouTube videos about the trail. She also researched backpacking gear and bought some.

But in January 2011 she tore the anterior cruciate ligament and medial meniscus in her right knee while playing ultimate Frisbee at the University of Tennessee-Chattanooga. She says her weight ballooned from the 190s to 230 during the first two months she was recovering from the injury.

"You do nothing but sit around and eat all day," she says.

But she was still determined to do the trail and felt ready when she hiked the Springer approach trail on March 5, 2014, and headed north the next day.

Fly Away says she got her trail name seven days and 69.6 miles later when a hostel owner gave her and others a ride from Dicks Creek Gap to Hiawassee, Georgia. He strapped her backpack to the top of his Jeep with bungee cords. During the ride, the pack flew off the Jeep and got a few holes, but was still usable. The hostel owner said nothing like that had happened before.

She took a zero day in town and when she resumed hiking a cough she'd had for several days got worse and she even had trouble catching her breath on level ground. So, she returned to Hiawassee and saw a doctor who told her she had bronchitis and had to take a week off the trail. She then packed up and went home.

Twenty-four days later, she returned to the trail, but two days after that she had to stop hiking again because of a bad right knee. An orthopedist told her she had severe arthritis and a bone spur in her knee and needed to rest it, which she did, while working for a month in Virginia at Woods Hole Hostel, where I met Mama Bear, Little Butt and Strong Man. She then had to leave Woods Hole to care for her sick grandparents.

So, 2014 didn't go well for Fly Away on the AT, but this year has gone much better, even though she singed her hair and got blisters on three toes in a stove accident in Virginia, about five miles south of Shenandoah National Park. She's made it 995 miles from Pearisburg, despite hiking on knees that hurt every night and sometimes during the day, too.

"They get swollen pretty bad at the end of the day," she says, "and they stiffen up at night."

Nevertheless, she's hiking faster than me now and is intent on making it to Katahdin.

Fly Away, who's writing a journal about her hike, says one special moment was watching a doe give birth about 200 feet off the trail in southern Virginia. A highlight was a little after the trail's halfway point in Pennsylvania when Scott Jurek, one of the world's top ultrarunners, stopped to speak with her and three women hiking with her, and pose for pictures, even though he was racing to finish the AT in record time.

Scott was very impressed, she says, when he learned that one of the other hikers was Nan "Drag'n Fly" Reisinger, of Camp Hill, Pennsylvania, who became the oldest woman to thru-hike the trail when she finished it last year at the age of 74. Drag'n Fly broke the record of Nancy Gowler, who was 71 when she did her thru-hike in 2007.

"He said, 'You're my hero,' and made one of the guys with him take a picture of him with her because he was excited to meet her," Fly Away says.

She says Scott also took time to talk with Hendo, an Army combat veteran of Iraq and Afghanistan, about her hike with her mom to raise money for the group Stop Soldier Suicide, and was impressed with her, too.

Fly Away

Scott had left Springer on May 27 and was trying to break the record of 46 days, 11 hours and 20 minutes set by Jennifer Pharr Davis in 2011. He beat her by 3 hours and 13 minutes when he summited Katahdin on July 12 after 46 days, 8 hours and 7 minutes. He estimated that in his last four days he slept no more than four hours, during which he covered more than 200 miles. He slept one hour before his final 15 miles through Baxter State Park.

Scott got support from his friend Speedgoat, the ultrarunner I met in Pennsylvania last year, when he was trying to break the record. Speedgoat joined Scott in Pennsylvania for two weeks in June to help him push the pace.

Speedgoat quit his record attempt in Virginia with about 825 miles of trail left when he knew he wouldn't be able to beat Jennifer's time. He wrote a follower to say that he fell behind her pace because his "feet were really bothering" him and that a Virginia section "killed" him.

"I fell off the pace around the Priest in Virginia," he wrote. "I had two bad days in a row, no energy, yada, yada. I stopped because I felt the record was out of reach. I believe I needed 56 per day with 15 or so days left. It was not in the cards to attain that, so I went home, as I said I would."

Sadly, another ultrarunner I met on the trail last year, Brian "Bilbo" Clark, died at a shelter in southern Virginia, 32 miles north of Pearisburg.

I met Bilbo, who was 60 and from Sweetgum, North Carolina, on July 28 at Bearfence Mountain Hut in Shenandoah National Park. He was found dead by hikers on August 14 at War Spur Shelter, 249 miles south of where we met. Linda Clark, his wife of 38 years, says he was sitting at a picnic table and had been eating dinner.

Linda says she didn't want an autopsy and the medical examiner concluded Bilbo died from a heart attack, which she and the couple's three children found hard to believe because he seemed to be in great shape.

"He was rarely ever sick and never had heart problems," Linda says, "and before hiking the trail he had a checkup with a cardiologist to make sure he was fine."

She says that Bilbo was 35 when he quit smoking and started running, and that he loved to travel to places to run marathons and ultramarathons.

"He would get off the couch and say we're going to California, so he could run a 100-miler."

Bilbo told me that he had finished about 12 Ironman triathlons and four 100-mile trail runs, including two of the toughest, the mountainous Wasatch Front in Utah and Hardrock 100 in Colorado. He decided to thru-hike the AT after retiring from his job as a chemist.

"He dreamed of and planned to hike that trail for years," Linda says.

He decided to start at Katahdin because he wanted to get the toughest part done first and liked the idea of hiking toward home So, he and Linda made a vacation of their 10-day drive to Maine, and then he headed south.

Bilbo told me he had sprained ankles when he started, but he kept hiking because he expected them to get better. Instead, they got worse. So, after 319.4 difficult miles, he left the trail in New Hampshire's Pinkham Notch, took a bus from Gorham to Boston, and flew home. He then went to

Harpers Ferry and planned to hike to Springer, then hike from Harpers Ferry to Pinkham Notch this year.

Linda says that she and her children think that maybe a clot from his injured ankles killed him and that he was a wonderful man.

"He loved everyone. He loved meeting new people. He'd do anything for anyone anytime. He was extremely generous."

She says she'd gotten a note from a woman named Marni, who wrote: "Everyone on the trail knew your husband as Bilbo and he was well liked by the other hikers. The thing that really stood out about him during his stay with us was the way he spoke of his family. You could tell he adored you all. He was so proud!"

Phillips "Redwood" Patton, of Santa Cruz, California, a southbounder I met last year, wrote to tell me that he was at War Spur Shelter in October and that many hikers had left reminiscences about Bilbo in the register.

"Sounds like a pretty good way to go, all things considered," Redwood wrote. "I never met him, but he sounded like a cool guy."

After talking with Fly Away, I hike to the 3,936-foot summit of Stratton Mountain, where I climb a fire lookout tower and enjoy expansive views in all directions of mountains, forests and lakes. The mountain is known as the spot where Benton MacKaye, the forester, planner and conservationist who proposed the Appalachian Trail in 1921, got the idea while sitting in a tree.

At the bottom of the mountain, I reach beautiful Stratton Pond, which, like Upper Goose Pond, is the size of a small lake. In the woods, 0.4 mile from the pond at Stratton Pond Shelter, I get a kick out of Joe Nicholson, 25, a glassblower from Chester, Vermont, who's hiking the Long Trail and has spent his first three nights suffering in the cold because he decided not to bring a sleeping bag in his 41-pound pack.

His brother and hiking companion, Robert Nicholson, 28, had warned him he was making a mistake, but Joe wanted to carry 10 days worth of food, instead of his bulky bag.

"I just figured I could do the first half in 10 days," Joe says. "I just wanted to keep going so I could spend time in the woods. I brought some warm clothing and I thought it would be enough. I wasn't expecting the nights to get so cold."

So, he's called his girlfriend and she's bringing his bag from Chester, about 45 minutes away, to a side-trail trailhead, 3.6 miles from the shelter. Joe plans to hike there and back tonight with his headlamp, so he doesn't have to spend another night in the cold without a sleeping bag.

The shelter is dark and crowded, so I walk back to the pond and find a flat, grassy spot near the shore for my pad and bag and enjoy the sunset and starry night. My bag is wet with dew at dawn, but I don't mind because I get to see the pond looking sensational at sunrise, ringed by a narrow layer of fog just below the trees, reflected in the pond in the early morning light.

64

Tom "Fatman Walking" Smith follows backpackers north along the Appalachian Trail in the van he bought to give them rides from the trail to town and back.

When I meet Fatman Walking, he's herding hikers into his van at a trailhead along Vermont Highway 11-30 and is about to leave for Manchester Center, 5.4 miles west. I've just arrived at the trailhead, after hiking 10.5 miles from Stratton Pond.

"Do you want a ride to town?" he asks. "Sure," I say, because I want to buy food and spend the night at a hostel near there.

I climb in and find a van full of grateful backpackers. Fatman Walking tells me he's been giving hikers rides since mid-June and I tell him I'd like to write a story about him.

So, after he drops the hikers off, he grabs me a Coke from the van's refrigerator and we sit and talk.

He tells me he's a 49-year-old general contractor from Phoenix and got the idea to spend the summer giving hikers rides from Limping Eagle, a guy who did the same thing when Fatman Walking thru-hiked the trail in 2013, a year after getting divorced.

"I always wanted to hike it," he says. "I grew up in New Hampshire and knew about it. I've been backpacking since I was 13. My brother did the trail in 1989, but I had a family."

He says that he's 5-foot-6 and weighed 275 when he started the trail, and that his brother gave him his trail name.

"He thought it was funny. I kind of liked it."

Fatman Walking says that his hike was tough: "In the back of my mind, I thought I'm never going to make the whole thing. But somewhere along the way, even though I was miserable, I realized I wanted to make it."

Helping him and many other hikers was Limping Eagle, whom Fatman Walking met in Duncannon, Pennsylvania. He says Limping Eagle was prospecting with a metal detector and was heading to Missouri when he picked up a couple thru-hikers in Duncannon and took them to a special event where hikers were getting fed, which is called, appropriately enough, a hiker feed.

He enjoyed the hikers so much that he changed course and helped hikers with rides and food all the way to Katahdin.

"I saw him at least 50 times. He was just always there. He gave out sodas, hot dogs. Ever since I met Limping Eagle and saw what he was doing, I told myself one of these years I'm going to come back and do this."

Fatman Walking

In 2014, Fatman Walking hiked many miles of the Pacific Crest Trail, until frequent forest fires forced him to quit and hike the Oregon Coast Trail, instead. Then, he bought a bike and cycled from Portland to Minnesota, before heading by train and bus to New Hampshire to visit his family.

This year, he decided to emulate Limping Eagle and bought a 1987 Econoline 350 Trans Van, complete with a bed, stove, refrigerator, toilet and shower. Then, he headed to Harpers Ferry with Franny, his super-friendly border collie, lab, Jack Russell terrier mix.

In Harpers Ferry, he met the legendary Janet "Miss Janet" Hensley, who's been doing what he's doing since 2010. Miss Janet, who's in her early 50s, grew up listening to the stories of the many hikers her mother fed and invited into their home near the trail, just outside of Erwin, Tennessee. In 2000, she started a hostel in her Erwin home and by 2009 had hosted 10,000 hikers.

Then, with her three children grown, she decided to hit the road in a van and help hikers. She follows the hiker bubble from Springer to Katahdin from March to September or October and accepts donations for her services. On the way home, she helps southbounders.

Last year, Miss Janet was far ahead of me. This year, I'm hoping to meet her. Fatman Walking says he's seen her several times, most recently in Bennington, 40.1 trail miles south, so I know she's likely somewhere nearby.

Fatman Walking says he and Franny spend most nights at a trailhead and sometimes hike a bit up the trail before the first hikers arrive. Then, he drives them to town and returns to the trailhead for more. I'm on his third trip of the day. Many hikers have his phone number and call ahead to tell him when they'll need a lift.

Some hikers give him donations and he charges hikers for rides to distant destinations and for slackpacking, but isn't even breaking even.

"A lot of people out here don't have the money."

But he says the experience is well worth the cost and he plans to keep going until he reaches Katahdin.

"I'm loving it. I just like being around the hikers. You've got great stories constantly. I'll be back one year doing the same thing."

I think that some year when I want a break from backpacking or biking, I might do the same. But now I'm thinking mainly of food and then going to Green Mountain House Hiker Hostel, where I'm going to spend the night.

I borrowed a cell phone yesterday to call the owner, Jeff Taussig, from the top of Stratton Mountain to make a reservation. He told me the place is a couple miles outside of Manchester Center and that I should call him for a ride after I get to town and do whatever I need to do.

Jeff

After Jeff, 63, of Richfield, Ohio, picks me up, he tells me he hiked the entire trail in sections from 2001 to 2006, and did 700 miles of the PCT in 2006 and 2007.

In 2008, he retired from the family business, which sold supplies to the printing industry, and, he says, his wife, Regina Taussig, 61, who's home spending time with their two children and four grandchildren, suggested that he find something to do other than "micromanaging her life."

"My wife encouraged me to pursue my hiking passion and the hostel business was certainly something that allowed me to stay in contact with the hiker community," says Jeff, who doesn't have a trail name.

So, he and Regina looked for a town in New England that needed a hostel and found a place with two homes and a barn in the country, near Manchester Center, which seemed ideal.

"These two homes were rental units, used and abused, and the price was right," Jeff says.

He and Regina worked with a contractor to fix them both up and in July 2008 opened the hostel in the larger house, with eight beds in three rooms, a kitchen, dining room, living room and deck. The hostel is a hiker's dream, and the $35 cost includes use of a washer and dryer, eggs, pancake mix, lots of sugary cereal, soda and a pint of Ben & Jerry's ice cream. There's also a computer with Internet access, a TV with lots of movies to watch, and even a phone with free long distance for hikers like me.

The guidebook says the hostel is "not a party place, no alcohol," so it draws a quieter crowd. Jeff says the partiers get motel rooms in town, instead.

He sells a few hiking-related things, including the AT Passport Book, in which hikers can place stamps from a wide variety of people and places on the trail. The passport book was Jeff's idea and he and Regina have developed and promoted the book, which costs $7, with all profits going to the Appalachian Trail Conservancy.

Jeff says Mama Bear and the Cubs stayed at his place and that he let them stay together in a tent, at Mama Bear's insistence, even though he usually doesn't allow tenting. He says they took a zero day at the hostel and went to see a movie in town.

"I thought she was very sensitive to the needs of the kids. She was trying to make the hike enjoyable for her children. I wouldn't have sensed any feeling that the kids wanted to go home."

Another visitor, he says, was Jim "Bismarck" Hammes, 53, who spent six years mainly on or near the trail, apparently doing multiple thru-hikes, before being arrested in May at Trail Days in Damascus. Bismarck, an accountant, has been accused of embezzling $8.7 million over 11 years from Cincinnati-based G&J Pepsi-Cola Bottlers, where he was a controller.

He fled and disappeared after learning in February 2009 that he was suspected of embezzlement, grew a beard and long hair and lived openly on the trail, where he was well known, well liked and often photographed. He was caught after a 2014 thru-hiker who spent a day with him saw a clean-cut picture of him in March on the CNBC TV show *American Greed*, thought the guy was Bismarck and contacted the FBI. Like many others who met Bismarck, Jeff thought he was a nice guy.

Jeff says the hostel is open from June 1 to mid-September and that it's full most nights from mid-July to mid-August. He and his family members use it during the ski season. He says running the place is a lot of work and that he struggles to break even, but that he enjoys it, nevertheless.

"The hiking community is a friendly bunch and the hikers come from such diverse backgrounds. They have great stories to tell. It's a lot of fun, although there is a saying in the hostel-owner community that each year we can't wait for the first hiker of the season to come and the last hiker to go."

65

Maggie "Solo" Byelick, Cindy "Cindy Lou" Louderback, and Sue "WalkerBee" Rush say they'd never be hiking the Appalachian Trail without the help and inspiration of trail icon and iconoclast Warren Doyle.

I've read about Warren, who's hiked the entire trail a record 17 times and has devised a way for groups of hikers he leads to thru-hike the trail on a strict 140-day schedule with just a daypack and van support.

So, I'm excited when I learn, after taking my first zero day of the summer so that I can go for a run in the country, that Solo, Cindy Lou and WalkerBee, who are spending the night at the Green Mountain House with me, are on Warren's "2015 Expedition" and that I'll likely get to meet Warren, 65, in the morning.

Solo, 56, of Moncure, North Carolina, who runs a commercial office rental business, says the women are three of 12 hikers left from about 80 "hopefuls" who started learning from Warren 27 months ago in five sessions of classes and day hikes and 16 three-day backpacking trips. She had planned to hike with her husband, but went alone when he couldn't come.

Solo says only the most dedicated and fittest survive to do the hike with Warren, who first hiked the trail in 1973 at the age of 23, in what was then the fastest time of 66.33 days. He's completed the trail eight more times with thru-hikes and eight other times with section hikes, and is working on section hiking it a ninth time.

He founded the American Long Distance Hikers Association in 1983 and in 1989 he started the Appalachian Trail Institute, which he runs with the Appalachian Folk School out of his home, an old 19-room farmhouse with outbuildings, 12 miles from Damascus in northeastern Tennessee.

Warren holds five-day seminars on how to thru-hike the trail and about 75 percent of the people who finish the seminar succeed, three times the rate of others who try to thru-hike. He also prepares hikers for the group thru-hikes, such as the one the women are on, which is the ninth he's led. The success rate has been nearly 100 percent. The next one is scheduled for 2017.

Warren

"You have to earn what he calls 'sweat equity.' You have to prove yourself to him," says Solo, before he'll allow you to join the expedition. "A lot of people realize that it's way over my head."

"Warren doesn't let anyone step foot on the trail, if they're not prepared," adds WalkerBee, 55, a registered nurse from Greenville, South Carolina, whose trail name dates to high school.

"It's something I've wanted to do for a long time," WalkerBee says, "to see what the trail teaches me, what it has to offer and seeing the way the trail provides for you."

Cindy Lou, 61, of Birmingham, Alabama, says she'd backpacked the Smokies, but still works full time as an office manager and couldn't take six months off to backpack the trail.

"It's something I've wanted to do for 20 years. I like doing challenging things," says Cindy Lou. "If it weren't for Warren, I wouldn't be able to do it. He will do anything to help someone complete the AT. It's a passion for him. He wants them to complete the AT, rather than being the one that never reaches their goal."

Warren helps the hikers with training and encouragement, and by carrying their clothes and equipment in bins in a van. Each morning, the women and others on the hike, take what they need for the day in daypacks and hike north. Warren drives his car north to the day's destination, then hikes south to the van and drives it north to meet his hikers.

The hike's participants have known from the start of the hike on April 29 where they'll begin and end each day until they climb Katahdin on September 15.

"I think it's fabulous," says Solo. "It's a really, really great service. I wouldn't be interested in backpacking. I don't want to carry a heavy pack like that and I like having a schedule. My friends and family know where I'm going to be each night."

After talking with the women, I'm in the kitchen when I'm surprised to see Sparrow, the Pennsylvania woman I met in New York last year, talking with Jeff about getting a bed for the night. She's trying to do much of the trail with day hikes and left me a "welcome back" note at the Connecticut border, and food and drink for me and other backpackers. This weekend, she's hiking in Vermont. After I thank her for the note and the treats, we talk a bit and then she goes to sleep on the top of a bunk bed in my room. Later, I go to sleep on the bottom.

In the morning, Jeff takes me and several others, including the women hiking with Warren, back to the trailhead. I introduce myself to Warren and tell him that I'm glad to meet him and we talk briefly about his coaching Jennifer Pharr Davis when she set the AT speed record that Scott Jurek broke. In the afternoon, we meet again at a shelter and I ask why he's hiked the trail so many times and keeps hiking it.

"Why do people go to church?" he asks rhetorically. He says he loves "the freedom and the simplicity" of the trail.

Warren, who was an American studies professor and founding director of the Hemlock Overlook Center for Outdoor Education at George Mason University in Fairfax, Virginia, and taught at Lees-McRae College in Banner Elk, North Carolina, considers himself a "social-change educator."

As part of that education, he's written advice for thru-hikers that emphasizes the need for them to change and adapt to the trail. He writes that hikers can wear one T-shirt the entire trip, don't need to cook, don't need to always carry water and can survive without showers, which is the way I've approached the trail, for the most part. I do have an extra T-shirt for town and a long-sleeve one for cool weather and I do take a shower when one's available.

But Warren, who's famously frugal, has done two of his thru-hikes without taking a shower and is known for hiking in cheap sneakers, like Grandma Gatewood, not filtering or treating his water and eating lots of Little Debbies.

Warren, whose glasses are held together with duct tape, tells me he never stays at places that charge, mostly sleeps in his car on the trail and survives on Social Security. He asks for a $1,000 donation from each person on the trip for expenses of the trip and folk school.

I tell him that I know that there's been much written about him, some of which I've read, and that he's got many miles to hike. So, I say that I'll read more about him and call him after the hike, if I've got more questions.

Earlier in the day, I'd also enjoyed the view from Bromley Mountain, where I met a thru-hiker I'd read about in the *Lakeville Journal* at Maria McCabe's house in Salisbury.

Warren "Last Chance" Wolf, 66, of the tiny town of Buck in southeast Pennsylvania, says he had asked two women the best way to get from a trail detour to Falls Village, Connecticut, where he wanted to pick up a resupply box at the post office.

The women asked if he was a hiker and, when he said yes, they said they'd take him the 10 miles round trip. When they were on the way, they said there was a catch. They were reporters and their paper did a feature story on one hiker a year, and he was going to be the hiker this year. The cost of the ride was an interview for the story.

Later in the day, he decided to spend the night in Salisbury and, like me, stayed at Maria's, where he took a zero day. He "had a ball talking to her" and considers her "a real character" and, like others who wrote in her register, "a warm, wonderful person." Maria, who turned 86 on August 1, eight days ago, and still maintains her house and gardens, "let out a howl and elbowed (him) in the ribs" when she told him she's outlived two husbands and two suitors, and had just gotten her driver's license renewed for six years. I regret that I didn't get to spend much time with her because I arrived too late and left too early.

Last Chance

Last Chance says he got his trail name when his wife, Nina, said he should try the hike because "this could be his last chance" to live a dream he'd been thinking about since 1976, when he was fishing in a river near Katahdin, met a thru-hiker and learned there was a trail from Georgia to Maine.

So, he started training and buying equipment, and quit his job as volunteer coordinator at the Lancaster County Penn State Extension master gardener program. He started in Harpers Ferry on May 26 and plans to hike to Katahdin, then return to Harpers Ferry and hike to Springer.

Today is his first day on the trail in 20 days because a bug bite on his hip became badly infected and a doctor in Manchester Center told him that he had a staph infection and that he should stop hiking until the infection was under control and healing. So, Nina picked him up and brought him home and is now supporting him so that he can slackpack for a while.

That was the second time he had to leave the trail and recover at home. The first was when he slipped in the mud at a Pennsylvania shelter and dumped a pot of boiling water on his legs. Luckily, he was only half a mile from a highway, where an ambulance picked him up after other hikers helped him get there. A trauma center doctor said he had first and second-degree burns on his left leg and should take time off the trail and let the burns heal. He returned after eight days.

Last Chance says that he met Mama Bear and the Cubs shortly after entering Pennsylvania and that he and they hiked at about the same pace for about a week.

Once, he says, he was ahead of them when "here come these kids behind me and they scrambled right past me on the rocks. I was impressed that these kids were really well behaved and they really seemed to like hiking. I thought it was cool. I thought it was going to teach them some life lessons really early – how to take care of themselves and be independent, as well as rely on others. I think it's going to help them tremendously later in life."

After descending the mountain, I see some water containers next to a Forest Service road and stop for a drink. Also there is Rob "Tabasco" Hambrick, 56, a backpacker from Sentinel, Oklahoma, who carries Tabasco sauce and cayenne pepper in his backpack.

He says his pack weighed 50 pounds, without food and water, before he started hiking and he asked a friend who had hiked the AT to help him lighten it. When he dumped the contents out, there were four full five-ounce glass bottles of Tabasco sauce.

"Have you lost your mind?!" asked his friend. Tabasco says he cut back on the sauce, but adds: "I'll run out of water, but I'll still have Tabasco sauce."

We're talking when Fatman Walking shows up with more water. He says he also left water yesterday that he got at the Green Mountain House.

"Just want to make sure that hikers have water," he says, while also giving Tabasco a beer and me a Coke.

In the evening, I stop for the night at Lost Pond Shelter, where I meet Priscilla "Jersey Girl" Meyers, 66, of Milmay, New Jersey, who's hiking with new hips.

She says she had the originals when she started what was supposed to be a thru-hike in 2009, after she retired from her nursing job.

"I was very proud of it," she says, "because I turned 60 on the trail."

She became interested in backpacking in the late 1990s and started taking backpacking trips with the Appalachian Mountain Club. She started thinking of thru-hiking in 2001, when one of her daughters got married and thru-hiked the trail with her husband on their honeymoon.

But her hike didn't go as well as that of her daughter and she had to leave the trail at Clingmans Dome in the Smokies with a foot injury. Her husband, Ron, picked her up and dropped her off farther north a few weeks later, and she ended up hiking 751 miles of various trail sections. In 2010, she hiked 115 miles, then got new hips in 2011 and 2012.

In 2013, she did 276 miles, slackpacking with Ron's help, and in 2014 she mostly backpacked 188. This year, she's doing some of both, and plans to have only 442 miles left in New Hampshire and Maine to hike next year.

Jersey Girl says she worries about jarring her artificial hips into her thigh bones and that her doctor told her not to hike over boulders.

"I fall all the time," she says, "and I do boulders."

66

VICKY GUITAR DIDN'T KNOW ANYTHING about the Appalachian Trail when she opened Qu's Whistle Stop restaurant in February 2014, but by summer she knew all about the hikers who provide a big boost to her business.

"I was oblivious to the whole situation," Vicky says, even though her restaurant, in a former train station eight miles west of Rutland, Vermont, is just a half mile west of the trail. "But I learned quickly. That's the extra summer punch."

During July and August, hikers account for at least 25 percent of her business and sometimes as much as 50 percent, says Vicky, 53, of Proctor, Vermont.

"July was huge," she tells me, after I eat a huge, delicious breakfast.

That's why she's expanded her summer hours and added facilities so that hikers can camp for free and charge their equipment.

"I love the hikers because I like the stories they tell, the experiences," she says. "I think it's amazing what they do. The bond between the hikers is pretty phenomenal."

She says Mama Bear and the Cubs arrived early July 25, 17 days ago, and went to the library and Wonderfeet Kids' Museum in Rutland before returning and camping overnight.

"I thought they were great. They're all still smiling and having a great time. But I also worry. The trail's pretty dangerous in some spots."

Last summer, Bismarck, the AT hiker arrested in May in Damascus and accused of embezzling $8.7 million, and his longtime trail companion, Teri "Hopper" Hanavan, stopped. Hopper was with Bismarck when he was arrested and her reaction indicated that she didn't know he was wanted for a crime.

"They were great," Vicky says. "They were just like every other hiker. They appreciated what we were doing for them."

Vicky

In fact, she's got a postcard from the couple with a picture of them standing on top of Katahdin last year posted under glass, with similar postcards she got from other hikers.

Vicky says she's never hiked the AT, but plans to hike seven miles of it this month "just to say I did part of the trail."

After talking with Vicky, I talk a bit with Alex "Torch" West, 33, a high school science teacher from Fairfax County, Virginia, while we wait for heavy rain to stop. I met Torch, who's thru-hiking the Long Trail, at the Green Mountain House, and we've hiked at about the same pace since.

Torch, who got his name when he made a mistake with his stove that caused a small fire, knows a lot about birds and he tells me the names of some filling the forest with songs I don't recognize. They include titmice, blue-headed vireos and eastern wood peewees.

Torch tells me the restaurant's pancakes are great, crisp on the outside and soft inside, so I order a couple and give him one. I'd actually ordered three pancakes earlier, along with an omelet, toast, home fries and three pieces of French toast with Vermont maple syrup.

Torch

However, when waitress Brenda Heath brought me everything at once, I realized that I should have ordered one menu option at a time, but had let my hunger go to my head. Brenda, though, was nice enough to take the pancakes back and not charge me for them. I'm glad I'm eating one now, though, because Torch was right about them.

Torch heads back to the trail in the rain, while I wait until about 12:30, when it stops. I'm walking toward the trail when a woman in a van stops and asks me where the trailhead is. She gives me a ride and I show her.

She says that she's Gail "Gutsy" Johnson, 64, of Pickens, South Carolina, and that she thru-hiked the trail in 1996, when about 10 percent of the thru-hikers were women. She's going to wait at the trailhead for her husband of 43 years, Dan "Odometer" Johnson, 65, who's been section hiking the trail since 1995 and will finish it when he reaches the highway to Manchester Center.

Gutsy says she had a mid-life crisis at 45 and became bored after two of her sons left home and the third wasn't going to be home much longer.

"I was ironing and cleaning and I said: 'Wait a minute, there's got to be something better than this.'"

Then, Gutsy, who hadn't been a camper or backpacker, went on an AT section hike in Virginia in 1995 with members of her hiking club.

Gutsy

"After a week, the others had had enough, so I asked my husband if he thought I could do it alone and he said yes. So, I went forward on my own for another week. It was what made me decide I could thru-hike the AT."

She says she "was hooked" and started making plans to thru-hike the trail. She went solo, although Odometer, who worked in quality control at a Caterpillar small engine plant, slackpacked with her occasionally and backpacked with her through the White Mountains.

Gutsy wrote an account of her hike every night and when she was in a town mailed them to Odometer, who put them online. She's been told that she wrote the first online journal of an AT thru-hike.

Gutsy completed the trail in five months, despite taking several zero days while struggling for a month with fatigue, headaches, leg pain and a swollen ankle, all symptoms of Lyme disease, which was diagnosed at a medical center in Hanover, New Hampshire. She was prescribed doxycycline, felt better in a few days and enjoyed the rest of her hike.

After finishing, she returned to college, got bachelor's and master's degrees and taught first grade, from which she's retired. During the summer, she hiked the Pacific Crest Trail in sections from 2001 to 2006 and has finished about a third of the Continental Divide Trail.

Gutsy says that in 1998 she and Odometer helped support Earl Shaffer, the first person to thru-hike the trail in 1948, when he did his third thru-hike at the age of 79 on the 50th anniversary of his first. She says they connected with him because they'd met Earl's nephew and his wife at the church she and Odometer attended and went hiking with them.

She and Odometer hiked into the woods occasionally in Georgia and North Carolina to give Earl food, including applesauce cake baked by a niece, cook him dinner and encourage him.

"He loved seeing us, for the cake, of course. It was his favorite."

Gutsy says another of Earl's nephews invited her and Odometer to climb Katahdin with Earl. She says they started the climb at dawn and got down after dark.

After I return to the trail, I meet Odometer, who had open-heart surgery in March to get his aortic valve replaced. When he did his first AT hike of 15.4 miles in North Carolina and when he hiked with Gutsy, he had no plans to hike the whole trail. But he kept hiking and after about 10 years decided to finish it with "great support" from his wife. He got his trail name after his biggest hiking day, when he did 30 miles.

Odometer says Earl called climbing Katahdin "the most difficult part of the trip" and that he and Gutsy consider climbing it with him a highlight of their time on the trail.

Other interesting hikers I've met since I left Green Mountain House, two days ago, include Joe "Cool Breeze" Fennelly, 67, who loves the trail and has thru-hiked it three times, and Topi "Finn" Ruohisto, 27, a Finnish thru-hiker who hates the trail, but is determined to finish it once.

Cool Breeze, who lives with his 91-year-old mom and 90-year-old dad when he's not hiking, says he's worked as a proofreader in his family's typesetting business, but has dedicated most of his life to backpacking the AT and many other trails, since his first AT thru-hike in 1978.

"I decided this is what I want to do with my life. I decided I was going to have a wealth of time or a wealth of money. To spend my life in the elements seemed to be a whole lot better than being in an office."

Finn, on the other hand, a prison guard in Finland, will be glad to never see the trail again after he finishes it. But he was looking forward to the hike when he started.

Cool Breeze

"I read about this three years ago. The idea got stuck in my head, became a dream. I decided I just had to do it and here I am."

But he says he got sick of the trail in the middle of Virginia and calls the hike since then "one thousand miles of nothingness."

"I've hated it. I've become a brain-dead monkey. I watch my feet for 12 hours a day and the next 12 hours I watch the roof of the shelter. Pennsylvania fucks you in the ass. I got so miserable there with the rocks, no water and horrible heat."

"Why don't you quit then?" I ask.

"I have my pride and I told Facebook friends and work friends I'm going to do it," he says. "I just have to do it. One motivation is people told me I couldn't do it. "It's just work now. It's not torture anymore."

Finn says, though, that he's looking forward to the beauty of New Hampshire and Maine.

"It will be great in Maine," he says," when I wake up and know that I made it."

67

Bill Mercier welcomes hikers at the Mountain Meadows Lodge, even though he says they're often demanding, talk too much, and eat all of the homemade granola at the all-you-can eat breakfast.

"Hikers are a pain in the ass in this business," Bill tells me, partly tongue in cheek, after his wife, Anne, charges me the hiker rate of $59 for a room that's normally $124 and $9 for breakfast. "I don't make any money off of them and they're very needy. Some want to be chatty. If it were a full-paying guest, it would be different."

For example, he points to me asking a while ago if he had some duct tape I could use, and says that helping me took a little time from his preparing for a weekend wedding.

Many hikers stop at the rustic lodge because the trail crosses Bill's property along Kent Pond, what Bill says is the longest stretch of the trail on private land, even though it's only a few hundred yards long.

Bill, 55, says the previous owner of the lodge wasn't friendly to hikers. But that changed in 2006 when he and Anne, 56, who have been married 34 years and have two children and five grandchildren, bought the place. He says they make most of their money hosting weddings and that accommodating hikers during the week is mainly a courtesy. But he adds that he's a backpacker himself, so he actually likes hikers.

He says he's hiked many miles of the AT and lots of other trails and has recently returned from hiking with a friend the Wonderland Trail, a 93-mile-long path around Mount Rainier.

Bill says hikers can be very helpful sometimes when they agree to do a fair amount of work for a free night at the place or less work for a free tent site outside.

"It's a win-win. But there were times when kids wanted to work for stay and were lazy potheads."

Bill

That wasn't the case, though, one Sunday night last year when he was hosting a wedding reception and then he and two others faced a late night of work cleaning up to get ready for a business meeting the next day.

"Here come some hikers, very, very nice kids who asked: 'Can we tent, get something to eat?'"

"I said: 'Here's the deal. These people will be done about 7:30 to 8. I would love it if you could help clean up. Just come back when there are no cars in the lot. You get to eat everything left.'"

"Thirteen or fourteen kids eventually came up. All the furniture from three rooms had to be moved back. They moved all the furniture, mopped, swept and washed dishes. They just tore it up. It was just so fortunate because we were facing three or four hours of work. It took the kids 35 to 40 minutes. They got tenting, food and beer and I was all ready for my business meeting. We just had the best time."

I arrive at the lodge the day after eating at Qu's Whistle Stop. I'm looking forward to relaxing a bit after spending last night on the ground in a shelter that was packed with people wanting to stay out of the rain, then climbing 4.3 miles and 2,008 rugged feet toward Killington Peak, the second highest peak in Vermont at 4,229 feet. I don't take the 0.2-mile side trail to the top because the day is cloudy and foggy,so there won't be a good view.

Torch, who also spent the night at the shelter, passes me on the way up and says goodbye because the Long Trail leaves the AT at the bottom of the mountain. He says he and Jenny, the woman who took my picture when I entered Vermont, plan to spend the night at the The Inn at Long Trail, while I plan to head for the lodge.

Torch has given Jenny the trail name of "Camina" because she often talks enthusiastically about the Camino de Santiago in Spain, which she recently hiked. She says it's wonderful and encourages me to hike it, too.

Later, I talk with thru-hikers Keon "Krusty" Mostofi, 25, and Charlie "Little Be" Goudreault, 22, both from Duluth, Minnesota, the home of Grandma's Marathon, my second favorite after Boston.

The University of Minnesota Duluth graduates say that Scott Jurek, the ultrarunner who set the trail speed record, grew up in the Duluth suburb of Proctor and graduated from the College of St. Scholastica in Duluth, stopped for about 20 minutes to talk with them and a few others and get his picture taken with them, just as he did with Fly Away and her companions.

Little Be says he and Krusty were at a campsite at about the 780-mile mark of the trail in Virginia, had been following Scott on Instagram and "knew that he was going to pass us that day or the next day."

"He came up with an entourage of about six running buddies," says Little Be. "We kind of waved him down and told him we're from Duluth. He said, 'Sweet.'"

"He kind of joked around," says Krusty. "He told us we looked like a couple hippies. We told him that he needed to eat some more food. He was a skeleton."

"It seems like he was stopping a lot," says Little Be. "I think it's cool that he stopped and talked with people. I expected him to just blow by."

If I'm lucky, I also might get to meet a hiker aiming for a speed record this summer, just like I was lucky last summer to meet and interview Speedgoat.

Heather "Anish" Anderson, 34, who's also an ultrarunner, in a post July 30 on the Fastest Known Times website said that she's going to try to break the AT self-supported speed record of 58 days, 9 hours, 40 minutes set by Matt Kirk in 2013. The women's record of 80 days, 13 hours, 11 minutes, was set by Liz "Snorkel" Thomas in 2011. Anish planned to start the trail early this month, so she's probably in Maine or New Hampshire.

Anish's trail name is short for Anishinaabe, which she chose in honor of her Native American heritage. In 2013, she backpacked the Pacific Crest Trail self-supported in 60 days, 17 hours, 12 minutes, breaking the old record of 64 days, 11 hours, 19 minutes. Like Matt, she won't even take rides into towns to get food because getting a ride is considered support, but, also like Matt, she will accept food and drink from trail angels.

"I hope in my endeavor to not only bring parity to the male and female self-supported records, but if possible lower it overall," Anish wrote.

"This is my second journey through these ancient mountains," added Anish, who thru-hiked the trail in four months in 2003 after graduating from college, "and I look forward once again to the joy, struggle, challenge and beauty of a 2,000+ mile hike undertaken in pursuit of finding and expanding my personal limits."

After my night at the lodge, I get more than my money's worth for breakfast. The homemade granola is great and I eat plenty, but not all of it. In the evening, I reach The Lookout, where there's a platform with expansive views above a privately-owned, unfurnished, one-room cabin where the owners let hikers spend the night.

I'm about to climb a ladder to the platform when a woman I saw at the lodge sees my Madison Mini-Marathon T-shirt and asks if I'm from Madison. I say yes and she says she's from Madison, too.

On the platform, she tells me she's 34, worked for eight years at Epic, a medical software company in the Madison suburb of Verona, and owns a home on Madison's East Side, about three miles from mine. Last year, she quit her job as a project manager to travel and went to 31 countries before starting her AT thru-hike.

"Did you grow up in Wisconsin?" I ask.

"Yes, in Wausau," she says.

Skittles

"I've got a 34-year-old niece who went to school in Schofield (a Wausau suburb)," I say.

"So did I," she says.

"Are you Tish?" I ask, referring to the high-school friend of my niece Evonne Berry, who told me before I left that her friend was hiking the AT and that her pictures had been featured on Instagram. Evonne sent me a link to the site and I could see why the beautiful photos had attracted many thousands of followers.

"Tosha" says Tosha "Skittles" Kowalski.

I tell her how I know about her and she takes a picture of me and someone else takes a picture of the two of us with a spectacular view in the background so that she can send them to Evonne.

Skittles and several others at the cabin decide to hike 2.6 miles to the next shelter, while I linger for a while and think about staying for the night and enjoying the sunset. I decide, though, I'd rather hike to the shelter and talk a little more with Skittles and her friend Emily, who had worked a year at Epic for Skittles and also quit to travel. She was a dog sled safari guide in Finland before returning to hike the trail.

The shelter is crowded and there are lots of people tenting outside. I find a patch of grass for my pad and bag, then walk down to a stream, where I talk with Skittles and Emily.

Skittles, who has a bachelor's degree in English and journalism from the University of Wisconsin in Madison and a master's in education from the University of Wisconsin in La Crosse, says she was at the South by Southwest Festival in Austin, Texas, in March 2013 when she saw a sticker that said: "Quit your job, see the world, fall in love and find yourself."

She took that advice to heart and, with inspiration from Emily, she quit her job at the end of January 2014, worked her last day a month later, and then flew with a one-way ticket to the Finnish city of Rovaniemi, the capital of Lapland, about four miles south of the Arctic Circle. From there she headed about 35 miles north to work as a volunteer for a family who run a sled dog tourism business. She cared for 65 Siberian huskies in exchange for room and board.

After that, she traveled and did other volunteer work for room and board. She did farm work and took care of sheep, chickens, ducks and cows on a farm in Norway, did farm work and took care of animals on a horse ranch in Ireland, and did gardening and house projects for a family in Poland.

She returned home last December, flew to Finland in February to visit the family she had worked for, and then returned again to prepare to thru-hike the AT. Emily had told her half a year earlier that she was looking for someone to join her on the trail and Skittles agreed to go.

They didn't start the Springer approach trail until April 20 because Emily's job in Finland didn't end until early spring. When she returned, they had less than a week before starting their hike. The late start proved fortuitous because it was the last day of three weeks of rain on the section of trail they would have been hiking and, after that, rain was rare for them.

In June, Instagram contacted Skittles to ask if she'd agree to have her photos featured and she said OK. She's also writing a blog.

After talking with the women, I lie down and listen to the hikers talking about their exploits and laughing, as they fart around the campfire. I laugh, too, because it reminds me of the famous fart scene in Mel Brooks' *Blazing Saddles*.

In the morning, I leave before dawn, as usual. But, for the first time on the trail, many of the other hikers at the shelter leave before me. They're hoping to hike 26.3 miles today to Hanover. I plan to get there tomorrow.

68

WHEN KATHY "SPLASH" KONING asked for six months off her job to thru-hike the Appalachian Trail with her son, her employer said no. So, she quit.

"I loved my job. I didn't want to leave," says Splash, 56, a clinical social worker who helped people with brain injuries, autism and developmental disabilities at a small nonprofit.

But she'd dreamt of thru-hiking the trail since she hiked part of it in the Smokies with classmates when she was a student at Western Michigan University.

"It's been on my life list. It's been one of my dreams," says Splash, of Fishers, an Indianapolis suburb.

Then, in February, her son, Dan "Smoke" Koning, 26, also of Fishers, told her he was going to hike the trail this year after leaving the Army, where he was a satellite controller.

"I was going to do it just to take some time and reset," says Smoke, who has a degree in mechanical engineering from Purdue. "I was tired of sitting behind a desk. It was a way to get back to being in nature and all that. It was a good challenge, too."

When his mom asked by text if he'd mind if she joined him, he texted back "sounds good," and Splash, who got her trail name from falling in the water a lot in previous adventures with friends, began planning.

Splash, the only woman I've met, other than Mama Bear, thru-hiking the trail with her child, says that at first she planned to ask for six weeks leave to join Smoke at the start of his hike and another six weeks at the end. But then she thought: "That's not been my life goal."

When she asked for six months, her employer said she could have only three because it would cost too much to keep her benefits going any longer. Now, after four months on the trail, she says that quitting was the right decision.

"I'm glad I did it," says Splash, who also has two daughters, 24 and 28, and has remarried since getting divorced about five years ago. "I was ready to shake up my life. Part of my reason for coming out here was just to break out of my routine. I doubt that I'll want to work full time again."

She says she's enjoyed much of the experience, but that it's often been tough.

"It's hard work. It's hard work going up mountains. It's harder than I thought it would be. I'm really tired at night. I like to hike, but I don't like to hike all day, every day."

But, she says, "I still really love some of the things about it. I love living outdoors. I love the simplicity of it. Every day you get up and head to Katahdin. I think it's cool to have a dream, set a goal, and go for it."

I ask the two, who left Springer on April 8, how hiking together has been working out.

"He's been an awesome hiking partner," says Splash, who notes that Smoke could easily be hiking much faster and have more independence, if he were hiking alone.

Smoke, whose trail name comes from "popping smoke," a military term for laying down smoke, says that he's been happy hiking with his mom and that he's been able to hike as fast as he wants each day and meet up with her at the end of it.

"Lots of the time, she wakes up earlier, so she hits the trail, he says, adding that, like Splash he has mixed feelings about the hike: "I think it's a worthwhile thing to do. There are times I enjoy it and times I don't. It's proving to myself that I can cut ties with the standards of going through life and have that work."

I've been talking with the Konings at the home of Randy and Linda Hart in the village of West Hartford, Vermont. I'd been running down a hill into town, the day after meeting Skittles, and was on a bridge over the White River when I heard Randy ringing a big bell from his front porch, a couple hundred yards away.

A hiker ahead of me was heading over to the house, so I joined him and met Randy on the porch, where he offered me a soda from a cooler. There were a few other hikers on the porch, along with the Harts' collie and black Lab, and several more hikers in the yard, relaxing on the grass outside their tents.

Smoke and Splash

Randy tells me I'm welcome to stay, too, in the yard or in a big room above the garage where there are beds, a TV, a VCR, a radio and a fan. The Harts' place isn't listed in the guidebook and I'd been planning on hiking for a couple more hours to a shelter four miles away, but it's early evening and I've already hiked 16.4 miles, so I'm more than happy to stop.

Randy, 55, a handyman, says he his wife, Linda, 57, a postal worker, started hailing hikers in 2001 and letting them stay at their place for free because they wanted their nephew, then 19, to get to talk to hikers before his planned thru-hike in 2002, after his first year of college.

"He'd watched hikers walk by his entire life," Randy says. "He wanted to know what's so great about this trail that people would hike 2,000 miles. We wanted him to have contact with hikers."

He says the first year about 20 to 30 hikers stopped, but they welcomed many more in 2002 because they wanted to give hikers the same kind of trail magic that their nephew was getting.

"He was ready to give up the trail a couple times in Georgia and got trail magic."

The first time, Randy says, his nephew was sitting in a shelter treating his blisters when a retired Vermont teacher showed up in the rain with apple pies from McDonald's. He was the only guy in the shelter, so he got all the pies. The second time, it was also raining when two people hiked up the trail with steaks and baked potatoes for hikers.

"He told us about it. We flagged down every hiker we saw coming across the bridge and gave them a soda and told them they could camp out."

When their nephew was about to arrive, they put signs in the shelters just before and just after West Hartford telling hikers to stop for a "mini trail days." They served hamburgers, hot dogs, corn, macaroni and beer to about 100. Since then, their nephew finished his thru-hike and the Harts have continued welcoming hikers.

Flooding caused by Tropical Storm Irene in August 2011 caused serious damage to the village, including the Harts' house, but they rebuilt. In 2012, four hikers stopped for three days to help. Last year, Randy says, 1,127 hikers stopped and there have been more than 1,000 this year. There were 30 hikers here this morning enjoying pancakes, eggs and coffee.

There's a jar for donations on the kitchen counter, but no sign asking for them. Randy says that's because Linda "is afraid some people who can't donate won't eat."

""Thirty or forty young people might leave nothing and an older guy will leave twenty dollars. Donations aren't enough to cover the cost," he says, noting that a dozen eggs that were $1 are now $3."Sometimes it gets pretty scary."

Nevertheless, he says, "I love it. I love meeting all the different people and talking to them about their jobs. The best thing is seeing the smiles on their faces. It's so heartwarming."

He says the hikers have also been great for the two daughters the couple had together, now 24 and 22.

"They got to interact with people from different countries, different states, different jobs. Everyone was good with the kids. We've never had a really bad hiker in 14 years."

Randy

He says they don't have their place listed in the guidebook because "we don't want people to be expecting to get stuff here, if we're not here. We feel so guilty about that, that we try to be here all the time."

Randy says that Mama Bear and the Cubs camped here and that he approved of the 5-year-olds hiking the trail, although he had doubts at first.

"I thought it was a good thing. I was a little concerned about their welfare, being on the trail so long. But they were in great shape, happy, optimistic. They were enjoying themselves."

After we're done talking, the couple's youngest daughter, Bobbi, and her friend, Jeanna Roy-Rogers, volunteer to drive to a nearby town to get pizza for hikers who want to order some. So, we not only have a great place to stay, but we're well fed.

I sleep in the room above the garage and leave just before dawn and breakfast because I want to hike the 9.9 miles to Hanover in time to spend much of the day there. After 7.4 miles, I reach Norwich, Vermont, where several residents have left drinks, cookies and fruit in front of their homes for hikers, and I enjoy a mid-morning snack.

After mailing a few things home from the Norwich post office, including a full notebook, I finish the 150.2 miles in Vermont and cross the Connecticut River into New Hampshire and, a half mile later, Hanover. I stop first at the Dartmouth Outing Club, where hikers are allowed to use the computers. The club also has a list of area trail angels who let backpackers stay at their homes for free.

While there, I learn from a few hikers that Carol and David Jalbert have stopped letting backpackers camp in the backyard of Country Clothes in Kent because of some people who caused problems. I guess that they were most likely yellow-blazers and, whoever they were, I think it's sad that a few campers are making the hike harder for the vast majority of respectful backpackers.

After spending a little time at the outing club, I explore the quaint college town, where I've been once before. Then, I was on a camping trip with Craig and we stopped to see Dartmouth College and the town where Bill Bryson, the author of *A Walk in the Woods*, was living when he decided to hike the AT after seeing many backpackers walk by.

After parking next to the college campus, I accidentally locked the keys in the car and the friendly police opened it for free. This time, I get free food from businesses that attract hikers – a free donut at a bakery and a free slice of pizza at a pizza place. I buy and eat a lot more food before stopping in the evening at the Hanover Food Co-op at the edge of town.

While I'm there, a thunderstorm strikes, so I wait for a couple hours and read the paper. When the storm ends, the sun is setting. I walk about half a mile to where the trail leaves town and enters the woods, right next to a baseball field. Camping's not allowed, but it's getting dark; the grass is soft and nobody's around. So, I put out my tarp, pad and bag, and settle in for the night.

BAXTER PEAK
KATAHDIN
BAXTER STATE PARK
MILLINOCKET (19 MILES)
QUEBEC
100 -MILE WILDERNESS
MONSON
KENNEBEC RIVER
CARATUNK
STRATTON
AVERY PEAK
RANGELEY
SADDLEBACK MOUNTAIN
ANDOVER
BALDPATE MOUNTAIN
GRAFTON NOTCH
VERMONT
MAHOOSUC NOTCH
GORHAM
MAINE
WILDCAT MOUNTAIN
MOUNT WASHINGTON
FRANCONIA NOTCH
WHITE MOUNTAINS
LINCOLN
MOUNT MOOSILAUKE
TRAIL MAGIC!
FREE
HANOVER
NEW HAMPSHIRE

69

Bill "Ice Cream Man" Ackerly says he welcomes backpackers to his home, just as he did patients to his office when he was a clinical psychiatrist living in Cambridge, Massachusetts.

"To me, it's an extension of what I did all my life," says Ice Cream Man, 87, explaining that he made his office like a living room so that his patients would feel comfortable when they came in to talk.

He says he also tries to make backpackers comfortable at his home, 25 yards off the trail, where he gives them ice cream bars, lets them camp in his yard, and provides water, electricity, Wi-Fi, two decks and a porta potty. All he asks of hikers is that they sign his register.

"It's fun and they like me" he says of thru-hikers. "I think they're the best. They contain the ultimate of perseverance, dedication, trust, hope, humor and consistency, with or without pain. They're just an amazing group of people. I take care of them and they take care of me."

Ice Cream Man, who also advised psychiatric residents at Harvard University, says his symbiotic relationship with hikers started in 2003 when he and his wife, Frances, began giving hikers water at their weekend home in the mountains, about three miles east of Lyme, New Hampshire.

After Frances, his wife of 57 years, died in 2011, he sold his Cambridge home and now lives full time in the mountains, where he still treats four or five patients who travel to see him.

"Most of them," he says, "I don't charge anything."

He also charges nothing for the hospitality he offers the hikers he invites to his home with a colorful sign along the trail with his real name, two plastic flamingos and a painting of him holding a double-dip ice cream cone in one hand and a bottle of water in the other. The sign points to his home and says:

"His Icecream Brings All The Hikers To The Yard

His Water Tastes Better Than Yours

Damn Right, His Croquet Game Is Better Than Yours

It's all FREE Yeah There Is NO Charge!!"

The sign mentions croquet because there's been a well-manicured croquet court in the backyard for 50 years, but Ice Cream Man, who's played thousands of games of croquet with hikers, says he's not playing now: "I don't play anymore because I don't like to win."

He says he's had "only one unpleasant experience" with a hiker, and that guy was drunk: "He started becoming belligerent and I had to talk to him severely."

Ice Cream Man says he understands and admires hikers because he spent much of his life hiking and backpacking himself, often with his wife and their three sons and daughter.

"We did a lot of hiking as a family, since they were young," he says.

When two of his three sons were 15 and 17, they took a bus to Georgia and hiked most of the Appalachian Trail. He and Frances climbed Katahdin with them.

He's also climbed all of the 13 other peaks over 4,000 feet in Maine and the 48 in New Hampshire, including 6,288-foot Mount Washington, which he last climbed three years ago with one of his sons and his 6-year-old grandson. The three climbed 3,768 feet over 4.5 miles to reach the summit, which is 91.6 miles north on the AT.

He says Mama Bear and the Cubs stayed at his place and he thinks the twins are getting a great lesson in resilience and endurance. When I ask him if he thinks the twins will remember the hike, he says: "Some, not a lot. They're too young to remember much of it. I wish I'd done it with my kids. Those kids are so lucky."

Earlier in the day, on my way from Hanover I met two other trail angels after going down Moose Mountain. Marsha Barden, 69, and her boyfriend, Dennis McGonis, 62, both of Lebanon, New Hampshire, who have backpacked together in the White Mountains, were grilling hot dogs for hikers on the back of their Toyota Tacoma at a road crossing, and also had chips and soda.

They say they've been feeding hikers two or three times a week for two or three years from late June to the end of August.

"Seeing how we can't thru-hike the AT ourselves, we hike it through you guys," says Dennis.

Cary and Ice Cream Man (c.p.)

"We like to meet everyone," says Marsha. "They're from all different countries, all different states. They're all super-nice people."

On the deck outside Ice Cream Man's house, I talk with Bekah "Micro" Barnett, 26, of Indianapolis, who like Gutsy, was diagnosed with Lyme disease on the trail, which is a serious threat to thru-hikers, especially in New England.

Micro, who got her name because of her love for beer, says and she and her boyfriend, Sean "Big Foot" Eaton, 27, also of Indianapolis, had taken three days off the trail in New York City and she felt fatigued when they resumed their thru-hike.

"We started hiking and I was really, really exhausted," she says, adding that she'd also had a headache and neck ache for a week to ten days.

They'd only hiked three miles when they reached a road and saw a sign inviting hikers to breakfast at a home about 300 yards away.

"Over breakfast our host, Amy, mentioned her previous dealings with Lyme. She said, 'I know I have Lyme disease because I get constant headaches.' I was tipped off and she volunteered to take us to the local clinic."

At the clinic, Micro told the doctor that she'd been in the woods for four months, that she and Big Foot had picked deer ticks off of each other, and that she'd battled fatigue, headaches and neck and stomach pain.

The doctor, though, wasn't convinced she had Lyme because she'd never had the distinctive red bull's-eye that's a sign of the disease. The doctor said Micro's symptoms could be from carrying her backpack and excessive daily exercise. She tested her for Lyme, but wouldn't give her a prescription for doxycycline, which can cure Lyme, until she saw the test results, which would take a week.

Micro

"I pretty much begged her for a prescription," Micro says, "because I was in a town and there was a pharmacy there."

But the doctor said no, so Micro and Big Foot returned to the trail, where Micro struggled to hike 80 miles over the next week, until she got the positive test results and doxycycline.

Finn

"The headaches were gone an hour after the first pill and my mind unfogged," Micro says. "I've met many hikers that have had Lyme, since I was diagnosed."

I ask her why she, like the vast majority of hikers, is still wearing shorts, instead of pants or running tights, like me.

"Because, it's hot," says Micro, who's writing a blog about her hike.

Also camping at Ice Cream Man's place is Finn, the prison guard from Finland who hates hiking the Appalachian Trail, but is still determined to finish it. He says that he thinks many hikers feel like him, but don't want to admit it.

"People like social aspects of the trail. People like the people on the trail, not the trail itself."

He says now he's downhearted, too. He explains that he recently fell for a female backpacker, but that when the Long Trail, which she was hiking, split from the Appalachian Trail, they split, too.

He says he had "three nearo days," meaning days of few miles, because of her and also a night of bliss with her at The Inn at Long Trail, four nights ago.

"What's her name?" I ask,

"Jenny," he says.

"Jenny?!" I say. "Torch told me he and Jenny were going to share a room at the inn."

I tell him I met Jenny at the Vermont border and Torch at the Green Mountain House, where Jenny also stayed. Torch and I had stopped at a shelter so that we could go out for breakfast at Qu's Whistle Stop, but Jenny had hiked on to the next shelter, where she met Finn and spent a rainy day with him before Torch and I arrived. So, I guess flings can end, start and end quickly on the trail.

"I told her some jokes and she laughed at them," Finn says. "I liked her and for some crazy reason she liked me."

"Why didn't you stay with her?" I ask.

"I have this stupid Katahdin to hike to." And, he says, Jenny was hiking too slow for him and was going to meet an old college friend on the Long Trail.

"It was," he says, "really sad."

70

Chet West was working on his backpacking stove in 2001 when it blew up, nearly killing him and leaving him legally blind and in a wheelchair much of the time. Now, he explores the mountains he loves vicariously through the Appalachian Trail backpackers he welcomes to his home hostel in Lincoln, New Hampshire.

Chet, 44, says he used to spend lots of time hiking trails and bushwhacking in the White Mountains.

"I grew up next to the trail. One of my passions was following the mouth of a stream to the source."

Chet was a guide at Lost River Gorge, a tourist attraction managed by his father at the base of Mount Moosilauke, just off the trail, six miles west of Lincoln.

"I walked and cycled everywhere," he says. "I never had a driver's license."

I'd arrived at Chet's One Step at a Time Hiker Hostel a day after climbing Moosilauke and three days after leaving Ice Cream Man's place, and he's invited me into his home to talk.

He says he was preparing for a backpacking trip when the stove exploded.

"The last thing I remember is pressing, pumping and hearing a pop. I put my arms up in front of my face and I inhaled the fire. It fried my lungs."

He was severely burned, spent 8 1/2 months in a drug-induced coma, and was near death numerous times.

"It was completely devastating. However, I am of the belief that I don't say why me, I say why not me. We're all given trials in our lifetime and we have to choose to rise or fall."

In 2007, Chet got a settlement for his injuries. He won't reveal the type of stove that blew up or how much money he got, which I assume he's barred from disclosing by the settlement. He used some of the money to buy a house that he knew would be ideal for a hostel because the big attached garage had been converted to a shop.

"I knew this house and the lady who had it before me had a craft shop out here. I saw it and jumped on it."

Now, the former shop is a hostel and holds three bunk beds with plywood for hikers' pads, two couches and lots of mattresses scattered about on the floor. There's room for about five tents in a designated area in the backyard, and a laundry and bathroom with a shower for hikers in the basement, where there's also a room for the woman who helps Chet.

When potential guests, like me, show up at his door, West makes sure they're backpackers by asking them when they started the trail, what's the last mountain they climbed, what's the next mountain they'll climb and when they expect to finish.

If he's satisfied with the answers, he invites the hikers in and then spends much of the day listening to their stories and telling them his.

"Everyone that comes through here has their own story, and it's so amazing and such an honor to have people from all over the world, from all walks of life, come through my home."

Chet has seen the hiking community change over the years. Starting in the late 1990s, he says, many more hikers focused on the miles and getting the trail done, rather than just enjoying the journey. That's also, he adds, when hikers started to party more.

The most hikers he's had in his hostel at once was 37 in 2009, which, he says, was a very rainy year on the trail.

The hikers sign a big whiteboard and donate whatever they want in cash or by bartering, such as an artist painting a picture, a musician playing a song, or a chef cooking a meal for everyone.

"I have grandma's cookies from all over the world," Chet says. "If someone wants to give me $100 for sleeping on a plywood bunk bed, I won't deny them, but typically I get from five dollars to twenty dollars per night. The donations go back to help maintain the place."

Before climbing Moosilauke, the first of the imposing White Mountains, I'd spent the night alone in the woods and in the morning I stopped at Hikers Welcome Hostel, 0.3 mile from the base of the mountain, to pick up a pair of shoes that were shipped there.

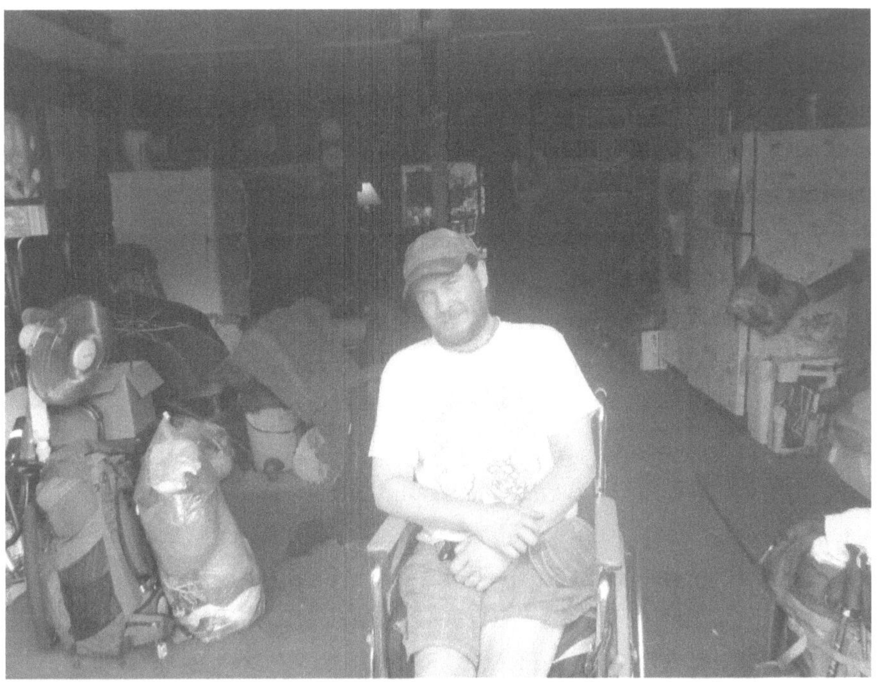

Chet

Breakfast has been served, but there's still a plate full of cold pancakes, covered with another plate to keep the many flies off. I'm hungry and stuff myself with them.

The few hikers still here say hostel employees have shuttled 16 others to the north side of the mountain so that they can slackpack 9.3 miles south and spend another night at the hostel. They say the employees told them that the mountain is difficult and dangerous to descend when headed north.

It's too late for me to get a ride and I don't want to start slackpacking, anyway, so I hike back to the mountain and start the 3,759-foot climb over 4.6 miles. After 0.9 mile, I stop at a shelter, read the register and see an entry that Warren Doyle left three days ago when he was heading south.

He wrote about hiking the Beaver Brook Trail, which is the name of the part of the AT I'll be hiking when I descend Moosilauke.

"I can't believe I have done the Beaver Brook trail 18 times. The first time (in 1973) I was just a step or two from a fall that probably would of seriously injured or killed me."

That first time he was most likely hiking north, like me. So, after hearing at the hostel that the descent is dangerous and reading Warren's note, I'm quite worried about what awaits me and, as I climb the steep, rocky trail with no switchbacks, I ask hikers slackpacking down if it'll be dangerous.

"It's technical," says one. "It's not suicidal," says another, which isn't remotely reassuring.

By the time I reach the treeless alpine terrain on top, 0.8 mile from the 4,802-foot summit, the sunny day has turned cloudy and very windy. I'm alone and walk across the rocky surface in the fog and with a sudden case of the runs.

At the start of the Beaver Brook Trail, there's a Dartmouth Outing Club sign advising inexperienced hikers to take a different trail down the mountain. It says: "THIS TRAIL IS EXTREMELY TOUGH. IF YOU LACK EXPERIENCE PLEASE USE ANOTHER TRAIL. TAKE SPECIAL CARE AT THE CASCADES TO AVOID TRAGIC RESULTS."

The 2,932-foot descent over 3.8 miles is next to the brook, full of rapids and cascades with a mist that makes the trail a little wet and slippery in spots. I head down cautiously, but as quickly as I can under the circumstances, because I have only a couple of hours of light left.

The trail is treacherous in parts, with many blocks of wood for footholds fastened to some steep, slick rock slabs, and metal rungs to grab. I'm relieved when I reach the bottom safely and find a flat spot near the brook to spend the night.

I'm exhausted and feel sick, so I go to sleep without eating. When I awake in the middle of the night and get up, I feel dizzy, and hope I can hike the half mile to the road in the morning.

After waking up, I make it to the trailhead and meet Doug "Rocket Turtle" Paradis, 64, of Richardson, Texas, who's section hiking the trail and today is slackpacking up and down Moosilauke the safer way. He says he's a retired engineer and has wanted to hike the entire AT since 1967, when he was a scout and hiked about 40 miles of the trail through Great Smoky Mountains National Park.

"It became mystical to me," he says.

He spent many years reading trail journals and in 2009 started at Springer after taking early retirement. While we're talking, it starts to rain and I warn him that the trail is treacherous and will be more so when wet. But he starts hiking, anyway.

I also meet his sister, Mary Rose Paradis, 62, of Grafton, Massachusetts, and brother, James Paradis, 56, of Bellingham, Massachusetts, who have dropped their brother off and offer me a ride to Lincoln.

They drop me off at Flapjack's Pancake House, a popular place in this resort town of about 1,000. I sit at the counter and, even though I had plenty of pancakes yesterday, I figure I should order pancakes at a restaurant known for them. So, I get the blueberry. They're great, but I can't finish them because I still feel sick.

I cross the street to the municipal building, where I sit and rest for a couple hours before walking the half mile to the hostel and meeting Chet. When I take a shower, I look at myself in the mirror and think I'm even thinner than I was last year when I decided to quit.

With no weight left to lose, some kind of illness and the toughest part of the trail ahead in New Hampshire and Maine, I think about quitting while I'm ahead and returning next year to finish. I don't know how long I'm going to be sick and I don't want to wait around Chet's and Lincoln long enough to find out. I also think it could be unsafe to keep going in my somewhat emaciated state.

Unlike last year, when I was deciding whether to give up being a thru-hiker, I don't have that concern. Now, I'm deciding whether I want to finish in two summers or three. I'm leaning toward three because then I can be in great shape when I hike the Whites and Maine and really enjoy the experience.

After talking with Chet, I walk to the library and ask the librarian how I can get from Lincoln to Wisconsin. She says there's a bus in the morning that goes to the Boston airport and Amtrak station. After thinking some more, I decide to go home and buy online a train ticket from Boston to Chicago.

I've now hiked 1,799.7 miles of the AT, including 351.4 this summer and have 389.4 to go. I plan to return next summer when I'm not sick and weigh more, and finish them.

After a restless night at Chet's, with a few quick trips walking across the yard to the basement bathroom, I walk about a mile to the convenience store/gas station to catch the Concord Coach Lines bus and head back to Madison.

When I get home, my mom and her friends tell me I look old and sick because I'm so thin. I feel lousy for a week and my weight drops from 140 to 135, the lowest I've weighed as an adult. I weigh 20 pounds less than what I used to think was my ideal running weight, so I think I made the right decision. I know I wouldn't have wanted to spend a week sick at Chet's.

I'm sure of my choice seven weeks later after I've trained for a fall marathon so that I can take advantage of my low weight and try to run a time fast enough to qualify for the Boston Marathon. I succeed for the first time in seven years. Sometimes, if there are too many qualifiers, the slowest don't get in, but I think my time will probably be fast enough. So, I'm happy because I'll most likely get to run my favorite marathon and I'll most likely be in great shape to finish the trail next summer, too.

71

FRANK SPOON HAD NEVER TAKEN a hike in his 57 years before he retired at the end of 2015. Then, boredom set in, and he decided to spend a couple nights in the woods hiking the trail up Springer Mountain.

I meet Spoon, who uses his last name as his trail name, when I'm going down North Kinsman Mountain on my second day back on the trail in August 2016. I've flown to Boston, taken a bus to Lincoln and hitchhiked back to where I left the trail last August.

Spoon says he was an associate prison warden at three federal prisons when he reached the mandatory retirement age of 57. Jan, his high school sweetheart and wife of 35 years, was still working and he got tired of just hanging around their home in the Texas city of Port Neches, about 95 miles east of Houston.

"One day you wake up and you realize you're not in charge of anything, anymore. I thought, 'I've got to get something to do.'"

So, he decided in April to visit his parents in his hometown of Alamo in central Georgia.

While there, he says, "I was thinking, 'you know what, I think I'll go and hike a little bit.' So, I called my wife and told her I was going to go hiking."

That was going to be a new experience for Spoon because, he says: "I never hiked a day in my life. Never owned a backpack."

He says his sister, who lives in Georgia, "said there's a nice place to hike in Amicalola Falls State Park. She said she'd been there once and hiked toward Springer."

"It's pretty. It's up in the mountains. You'll enjoy it," she told him.

"I thought I'd just hike for a couple days. How hard could it be to just walk in the woods? I didn't think it would be that much different from walking around town."

But, when his brother heard about his plans, he said: "If you're going to go out in the woods, you need to be prepared."

Spoon

Spoon took that advice to heart and headed to a Bass Pro Shop in Savannah, where he bought "the biggest backpack they had on the shelf," which was a 100-liter Kelty pack, nearly double the size of mine.

He also bought a sleeping bag, a two-person tent, a hammock, a double-wide blow-up air mattress, a rechargeable lamp, a solar panel to recharge it, a "huge" medical bag, a "monster raincoat, it must have weighed four pounds," waterproof boots, hiking shoes, Crocs, 14 packs of Mountain House freeze-dried food, a backpacking stove and a three-pronged chair that he strapped to his pack. He planned on using the chair to sit next to campfires.

His brother drove him about 235 miles northwest to the state park, where his pack weighed 83 pounds on the scale at the visitor center. He's 5-foot-10 and weighed 267 when he started.

Spoon put the pack on his back and started the steep climb up the 604 steps to the top of Amicalola Falls, a spot where some backpackers who'd planned to thru-hike the Appalachian Trail turn around and call it quits. He didn't know he was heading to the AT on the Springer approach trail.

"'This is going to be a long trip,'" he says he thought of the two or three days he planned to hike, "but I was determined."

After about five hours, it was getting dark and he hadn't reached the first shelter, 7.3 miles up the trail and 1.5 miles from the Springer summit and the start of the AT. So, he stopped in the woods and camped. The next morning he got up early and made it to the top, where other people who planned to thru-hike sometimes quit. There, he met a section hiker who was backpacking to the North Carolina border.

"He said, 'You know you're on the Appalachian Trail. You can make it all the way to Maine, there's no doubt. If you get tired, you can always come out."

And, he told Spoon: "'You'll find out you need to lighten that load a little bit.'"

"He actually put the idea in my head and I'm thinking: 'You know what. I think I probably could. I don't have anything else up.' I'm thinking, 'I'll call my wife and tell her I'll be out a few more days and just keep hiking.' I wanted to lose some weight, not be in front of the TV."

Spoon also met a park ranger, who asked him where he was going. "He said: 'I can see you're a beginner.'" Then, he told him he could get help lightening his load in 31.7 miles, when he reached the Mountain Crossings hostel and outing-goods store at Neel Gap.

"When you get there," the ranger told him, "they're going to look at you like a guy who just cut his neck with a knife and the sharks are circling."

After 20.8 miles, Spoon went two miles off the trail to the small town of Suches, and sent home about 25 pounds of stuff, including pots and pans, boots and one of his two types of water filtration systems.

"I thought, 'My knees are still good. My legs are good. I think I'll keep going for a few days.'"

At Neel Gap, he got rid of another 22 or 23 pounds, including his heavy raincoat, and thought he'd head to Maine.

"I've listened to all the other hikers. They're talking about the AT. That's when I called my wife and said, 'I'm going to hike the Appalachian Trail this year.' My wife didn't know what the Appalachian Trail was. She said: 'Well, you be careful and let me know when you're coming back.'"

After the call, one of their three children, said to Jan: "You know, mom, it takes five or six months to hike the Appalachian Trail."

When he spoke with her the next day, she said: "You are coming back, right, honey? That trail is five or six months long."

"Yeah, I may not go all the way, but as long as I feel OK, I'll keep walking," he answered.

By the time he reached Hot Springs, after 273.7 miles, he was hiking 12 to 13 miles a day and enjoying the adventure.

"I'm thinking I can make it to Katahdin," so he called Jan and told her he was going to try to finish the trail.

"She said, 'Well honey, you've always been real determined. If you want to do it, just be careful and call me.'"

Now, he weighs about 190, he's hiked 1,816 miles and he's enjoying the trip.

"I like the woods. I just like getting up in the morning and going. Every day, you see something different."

After meeting Spoon, I fall on my way down the mountain and bang my right arm on the rocks. I get a couple of big bruises and peel off a piece of skin about the size of a quarter.

A couple miles later, I stop to wash off the blood and get a bite to eat at Lonesome Lake Hut, the first of eight Appalachian Mountain Club hostels along the trail in New Hampshire.

The huts are large facilities with kitchens, dining rooms and rooms with bunk beds, which cost more than $100 a night for a bed, breakfast and dinner. This one has a capacity of 93. All hikers are welcome to stop for water and leftover food from breakfast for free. The huts also sell soup for lunch, as well as homemade bakery, candy bars and energy bars.

A few thru-hikers a day are also allowed to "work for stay," which means helping the staff with chores, in exchange for getting to eat leftovers and sleep on the floor in the dining room. Many thru-hikers like that option and try to arrive in the late afternoon, when they'll most likely be allowed to stay, if they're needed.

When I arrive, it's late morning and there's cold oatmeal in a bowl on a table for free; tomato-rice soup, maple cake and "grandma's pumpkin pie" for $2 each; and cornbread for $1.

I wash the blood off my arm, drink a lot of water and then eat some of everything for lunch. It's all great, even the cold oatmeal.

Russell

While I'm eating, I talk with Russell Gens, 21, of Lexington, Massachusetts, one of the "croo" of six college students who run the place.

Russell, who's majoring in computer science and environmental studies at Tufts University in the Boston suburb of Medford, says he enjoyed hiking and backpacking while growing up, and a couple of his friends who had worked at a hut convinced him to try it this summer.

He says the workers get a week of training in May, but that they mainly learn how to cook on the job. Each of the AMC huts serves the same entree each night, but employees can be creative with soup, salad, bread and dessert.

He says the recipe for the pumpkin pie came from his late grandmother Wincey. I tell him it's delicious.

Russell says he's learned a lot about cooking, guest service and time management and has had a great time at the hut, which is just above a beautiful mountain lake.

"Just being in this place," he says, "is a huge privilege."

I leave the hut and follow the AT along the lake and then down the mountain to Franconia Notch. My badly-bruised arm hurts and I feel a little twinge on the inside of my left knee, but otherwise I feel OK.

I hike about a mile on a bike path to the Franconia Notch State Park visitor center, where I call the Notch Hostel, about six miles away. An employee there says someone will pick me up.

While I'm waiting, I get some Gifford's chocolate ice cream, which is made in Skowhegan, Maine, and is almost as good as the great ice cream made on the University of Wisconsin campus. Then, I wait in the parking lot for my ride.

Serena Walsh, who owns the hostel with her husband, Justin, picks up me and another hiker and brings us back to her place. I get settled in and then talk with Spoon and other hikers, while babying my left knee when I walk up and down the hostel stairs.

I'm glad to be back on the trail and happy to have had no problem making the 1,972-foot rock scramble over 2.5 miles to the 4,358-foot summit of South Kinsman, which is considered a tough climb in the White Mountains. And I'm looking forward to many more tough miles above timberline ahead.

I'm sad, though, when I think about the death of Ice Cream Man, who was 87 when he died May 23 after choking on a piece of food while eating with friends in a Norwich restaurant.

"Bill always loved the out of doors and was always young at heart," his sister Carita Warner told *Boston Globe* reporter Bryan Marquard, "He defied all age images. I don't think he ever grew old."

"He was just getting ready for another year of sitting on the porch and talking with hikers. I really wanted him to have one more summer in the house," his son John told *Valley News* correspondent Dillon Walsh. "His body was definitely falling apart a little bit, but his mind and the spark in his eye was still totally there. He was just a great conversationalist."

72

SERENA AND JUSTIN WALSH HAD just climbed Mount Rainier and were heading home when they realized their "dream jobs" in office cubicles weren't so dreamy, after all.

After they climbed Rainier in July 2014, they were in the Seattle-Tacoma International Airport when Serena was reading *AWOL on the Appalachian Trail*, the book that David Miller, the author of the AT guidebook I'm using, wrote about his hike.

"AWOL talked about his thru-hike and all the hostels he stayed in and the idea came to me that this is what we should do. If it wasn't for AWOL's book, I wouldn't have had this idea," says Serena, 28, about the couple's decision to leave their jobs in the Boston area and open a hostel near the AT in the White Mountains, in which they'd been hiking most weekends year-round for several years.

"I turned to Justin and said: 'We should open a hostel in the White Mountains.' I realized, oh my God, there's no hostel in Lincoln. That would be an ideal place for one." (She didn't consider Chet's hostel, which isn't listed in the guidebook.)

Justin, 30, then her boyfriend, immediately checked out Zillow to see what places were available. He found an 1890 farmhouse, about two miles west of Lincoln, with 4,000 square feet that had been on the market for three years.

"It was literally the only property in the area appropriately sized and for sale," Serena says. "Nobody wanted it because it's a behemoth. This property doesn't make sense for anything but a bed and breakfast or a hostel."

Justin was then a construction field engineer and Serena did environmental health research. "We were both literally working at our dream jobs," Serena says, "and Justin was making a ton of money."

Justin and Serena

Nevertheless, she says, they asked themselves: "Why are we spending our days working in cubicles just so that we can afford to escape to the White Mountains every weekend?"

And then they decided to take a risk and pursue their dream. They checked to make sure that the property could legally be used as a hostel and then bought it three months after finding it.

"We were so obsessed with this concept," Justin says. "This is all we talked about."

He says they spent every weekend working on the place with the help of family members and friends. They painted, built showers and bunk beds, installed fire escapes and did hundreds of other projects to turn the house into a hostel that could host 30, and were ready to open by summer. But first they married and spent a two-week hiking honeymoon in the French and Swiss Alps.

Justin says the hostel opened on July 15, 2015, was full the first weekend, and has been busy since with hikers much of the year and skiers in the winter.

He says about 60 percent of the hikers in the summer are thru-hikers and that people from 30 to 40 countries have come to hike Franconia Ridge, a 1.7-mile section of the AT that's above timberline, goes over three mountains and has remarkable views. That's where he proposed to Serena in August 2014.

Justin says he and Serena "can relate to the hikers because our favorite thing to do is the same thing."

"We instantly form intense bonds," he says. "These hikers are living with you. We end up becoming best friends. Relationships with hikers are part of what makes this a fulfilling job. It's been so much more fulfilling than an office job ever could be. We work our butts off, but it's awesome."

There's heavy rain on Saturday, the day after I arrive and Franconia Ridge is just 4.7 miles north on the trail, so AT hikers decide to spend another night at the hostel. Serena decides that we should all enjoy beer and food at a new brewpub in Littleton, about 25 miles north.

So, about 20 of us crowd into vehicles and head to Littleton. We're drinking and eating around a big table when Serena says this is one of the best hostel days ever.

"This is a hamily," she says, combining hostel and family. "This is an epic day."

On Sunday, it's still cloudy and rainy, but the forecast for Monday is for sunny skies. So, I leave in the afternoon and climb 2,473 feet over 2.9 miles to the Liberty Springs campsite, where I stop for the night.

The site has wooden platforms for tents, and caretaker Quinn Nichols to collect the $10 fee and maintain the campsite and nearby trail.

Quinn, 25, of Hopkinton, New Hampshire, studies food policy and politics at The New School, a university in New York City. She says that this is her second year as a caretaker and that she works 10 days on and four days off from late May to the middle of October for the Appalachian Mountain Club.

She says her main job every day is dealing with the composting toilet by "literally stirring human poop, 70 gallons of it" with the wood chips that have been flown in by helicopter. Today, she also transplanted 50 little conifers from a spot where they were "super concentrated" to an area that had been damaged.

Quinn

Sometimes she's bored or lonely, she says, but for the most part she likes the "off-the grid, disconnected way of life."

"It seems so idealistic," she says, "sometimes to be removed," which is why she doesn't have a smart phone. When she's not working, she studies, reads and writes.

In the morning, I get up at dawn and climb 895 feet to the summit of 4,800-foot Little Haystack Mountain and the start of Franconia Ridge. I'm hoping to see stunning views, but I'm disappointed because there are no views, just clouds, fog and wind as I climb Mount Lincoln on my way to the summit of 5,263-foot Mount Lafayette and the end of the ridge.

The sky gradually clears, though, and it's sunny about two hours later when I climb 4,458-foot Mount Garfield and enjoy a magnificent 360-degree view of peaks over 4,000 feet.

I love the view, but I'm not happy because my left knee started to hurt as I climbed Garfield and gets worse as I descend and keep hiking on a very rocky, rooty, tough trail. By evening, when I stop to sleep alone in the woods, I have a tough time bending my knee at all. I struggle to set up camp and eat dinner and then take four ibuprofen, what backpackers call vitamin I. I have trouble even taking off my shoes and socks before going to sleep.

In the morning, my knee isn't much better and I don't know how I'll manage to hike the 16 miles to the next road crossing at Crawford Notch. But it's only about a mile to Galehead Hut, and I think that I'll rest my knee for a day or two there, if there's room.

About half a mile from the hut, though, I meet Claire Walden, who's hiking south. She tells me she'd spent the night at the hut and is headed to a parking lot about four miles away on the Gale River Trail, which I've just passed. She says she'll wait for me and give me a ride to Littleton, so I backtrack and then hike behind her on a trail that's not very rooty or rocky and follows the gorgeous Gale River downhill.

In Littleton, I catch a bus at a convenience store/gas station to Lincoln and the bus hasn't gone far when I realize I forgot my hiking poles outside the store. The driver calls the store for me and an employee looks for the poles, but can't find them. So, my luck runs out the third time I forget my poles on the trail.

I walk two miles back to the Notch Hostel, where I use the phone to make an appointment in the morning with Rodney Felgate, who practices family medicine and is the only doctor in Lincoln. I also do some online research and conclude that I might have sprained my medial collateral ligament.

Rodney, who has a British accent, weighs me, checks my height and checks my blood pressure himself. He graduated from medical school in London in 1962 and in 1973 moved to Lincoln, where he's raised a big family. He grabs and tests my knee, tells me that my ligaments are fine, and says that I've bruised a bone. He shows me the bruise that I hadn't seen on the inside of my knee and says that after several days of rest, I'll probably be able to hike again.

I'm leery about continuing the AT, though, especially now that it's much rockier and riskier, because I love running and I've been lucky to have run for 51 years without having any serious injury, unlike many of my running friends. I want to finish the trail, but not if it means there's much risk of a serious knee injury that could put an end to my running.

However, a friend from Madison is planning to meet me in six days and hike with me for two weeks, so I decide to take it easy, hike and run a little on fairly flat trails, and see how I feel when she arrives.

I don't want to just hang out around town, though, so I take a bus about 75 miles to Manchester and rent a car. Then, I borrow a big cooler from the Notch and become a trail angel. I buy soda, cookies and chips in Lincoln and drive to Kinsman Notch at the north base of Mount Moosilauke late each afternoon to feed hikers. I also give them rides into and out of town, like Fatman Walking did in Vermont, and enjoy being a trail angel almost as much I enjoy backpacking.

73

After Tony "Mississippi" Lang's hip and thigh bone were shattered by a bullet in Afghanistan in 2013, doctors told him that if he walked again, he'd be using a walker.

But Mississippi, 48, has no walker and is carrying a backpack when he strides from the highway into the parking lot where I'm just about finished doing trail magic on a Sunday evening.

"Are you coming from town?" I ask.

No, he says, adding that he took the wrong trail down Moosilauke and had ended up about four or five miles down the road. A driver had given him a ride back to the Appalachian Trail.

"I got on the wrong trail and realized it about halfway down. I wasn't about to turn around. I figured I'd come out somewhere."

I give him some soda, cookies and chips and he tells me his story.

Mississippi says he was working for Blackwater, a private military company, when he was shot by the Taliban. He joined the company when he was 36, after serving in the Army for 15 years, including two years in Iraq.

He ended up with an artificial hip and a titanium rod in his thigh. He says his knee on the same leg has been held together with a plate and 20 screws since he tore it up when he crashed a dirt bike years ago.

After he returned home to Tupelo, Mississippi, life was a struggle. "I got on the pain pills real bad," he says. "I got so depressed, I couldn't stand it. I had to do something totally different."

So, in 2014 Mississippi started working hard in physical therapy, swam a lot and began riding a bike. He also worked as a welder and played bluegrass on his guitar in clubs at night. In 2015, he watched a National Geographic documentary on the Appalachian Trail.

"I thought that's something I want to do. It inspired me to push myself."

Mississippi

Then, in April, he decided he was ready to try backpacking the Georgia section of the trail, and left his girlfriend of about four months.

"I gave her my car keys and told her I was going for a walk. I'm still walking."

His cousin gave him a ride to Amicalola Falls State Park, which is where he threw his pain pills in a garbage can and started hiking. The first week without the pills was tough, he says, but he made it 78.5 miles on the AT through Georgia.

"When Georgia was done with, I thought maybe I'll do another day. That day turned into a week, that week turned into a month."

Now, four months after he started, he's hiked 1,799.7 miles to the parking lot where I'm a trail angel, and he's headed to Katahdin.

"It's amazing what walking can do," he says. "It's healed me."

Mississippi does have to be more careful, though, because of his artificial hip and titanium rod. He uses a spear for a hiking pole and says that going down is harder than climbing and can be painful.

"Going down, that continuous jarring, it hurts going down. Once I sit down for a few minutes, it's all right. I carry ibuprofen. That's all I take now."

He says that after finishing the trail, he's heading to New Milford, Connecticut, where a day hiker he met offered him a job in his restaurant, Dagwoods New American Lounge. The hiker had invited him out for lunch and took him to meet his mom and dad.

I tell Mississippi I can take him into town for the night, and tell him about the Notch and Chet's place. He picks Chet's to save money.

When we get to Lincoln, he recognizes the town and says his former wife of 20 years had moved to Concord, New Hampshire, about 65 miles south, and her father had shown him around the area when he visited his two sons, now 25 and 18, about five years ago. I take him to the supermarket and then drop him off at Chet's.

Rick and Kate

Before meeting Mississippi, I'd arrived at the trailhead to find a pair of trail angels providing the best spread for hikers that I'd seen on the trail.

Rick Combs, 60, and his friend Kate, 61, both from Westminster, Massachusetts, were grilling chicken for sandwiches and also offered cold cuts, chips, carrots, fruit salad, strawberries, oranges, cookies and muffins on a table under a canopy. They also had chairs for hikers.

Rick, a systems manager, and Kate, a psychiatric nurse practitioner, say they drove about 120 miles to the trailhead because they're "looking for more remote locations where people need stuff."

Last weekend, they drove about 70 miles to a trailhead near Bennington, Vermont, where they did trail magic for the first time this year.

The pair say they've been trying to climb all of the 48 peaks over 4,000 feet in New Hampshire and decided to help thru-hikers after meeting many of them on the trail. They've fed about 30 today.

"We've spent more money and had less fun doing other things," says Kate, who backpacked the trail from Springer to Hot Springs when she was 16 and hiked through Connecticut, Massachusetts and part of New Hampshire when she was in her mid-20s.

Kate's helping care for her 6-month-old granddaughter, Layla Jean, and says the baby is the result of a romance that started on the trail in 2010 when her daughter, Jocelyn Baldor, met fellow backpacker Lucas Fykes.

Jocelyn, Lucas and Layla Jean

Jocelyn, 33, and Lucas, 32, show up and tell me they met just outside the bathroom at the shelter called the Fontana Hilton in North Carolina. Jocelyn was hiking with a female friend and Lucas was hiking with a male friend.

Jocelyn says the four hiked about 300 miles together to Damascus, when her friend left. Jocelyn, who had her "first date" with Lucas in Gatlinburg at Ripley's Aquarium of the Smokies, kept hiking with him.

"By then, everyone thought of us as a couple," she says. "We hiked out of Damascus sharing a tent and a cook pot and then hiked all the way to Massachusetts."

After they left the trail, she moved from Massachusetts to Kentucky to live with Lucas, and finished the trail in 2012. In April 2015, the couple went to North Carolina to hike for the weekend and Lucas proposed at the Fontana Hilton. They're getting married next summer.

Now, they're living in Vermont, where Lucas, who graduated from the University of Louisville Brandeis School of Law in May, is getting a master's degree in energy law at Vermont Law School in South Royalton. Jocelyn, who got a master's degree in social work from Western Kentucky University in Bowling Green in 2013, is a grant manager for the state of Vermont.

Later that evening, it's dark and raining when I stop at a grocery store in North Woodstock, a mile west of Lincoln, and see a pack outside. I figure the owner of the pack probably needs a ride somewhere, so I wait and meet Jurgen Smit, 29, of Johannesburg, South Africa, who's just bought several pounds of food.

Jurgen says he'd love a ride about five miles north to the Liberty Springs trailhead in Franconia Notch, where he's going to put up his tent for the night, before climbing to Franconia Ridge.

He says that he quit his auditing job about a year ago because he "didn't like auditing and didn't like sitting in an office all day." Then, he moved into his parents' house, lost his girlfriend and "was pretty depressed and pretty fat." That's when he went out for lunch with a friend, who told him about the AT.

"I thought this is exactly what I want to do and two hours later applied for a U.S. visa."

He says he's loved the experience, but that, if he had to do it over again, he'd skip Pennsylvania and its rocks and do Vermont twice.

When I ask Jurgen his trail name, he says that he doesn't have one.

"I don't like trail names. English people also don't like them. It's an American thing, really. Some of them are just ridiculous. Like Red Dragon because a guy wears a red beard. I feel silly calling people that, so I ask what their real names are."

I drop Jurgen at the trailhead and it's raining heavily when he walks into the woods to find a spot for his tent. I drive back to the Moosilauke trailhead so that I'm there in case any hikers want a ride in the morning. I read for a while and then push my seat back and almost flat before going to sleep.

74

WHEN MAC SMITH LEARNED the hole was nearly full in the outhouse he maintains on the Appalachian Trail in Maine, he set out to fix the problem.

I meet Mac after he'd hiked the 4.8 miles of trail he maintains to the campsite with the outhouse and was about halfway back to the trailhead. Mac, who's 69 and a bit overweight, is wearing black cords and a white T-shirt and carrying a daypack on a warm day, and is breathing heavily before he takes a break to chat.

I'm hiking to the campsite with my friend Kirsten Johnson on my first day back on the trail after taking seven days off to let my bruised knee heal. I'm still leery of my knee and Kirsten's been having a back problem. So, after I pick her up at the Concord bus station, instead of meeting her farther north, as we'd originally planned, we decide to drive to Maine and first backpack an easier section of the trail than the rugged White Mountains.

Mac, of Phillips, about 14 miles away, is a volunteer with the Maine Appalachian Trail Club, which manages and maintains 267 miles of the AT and 40 miles of side trails. He says he'd picked up a backpacker headed to nearby Rangeley on Highway 4 and, as he always does when he sees a hiker, asked him, "How's the trail?"

"He said, 'Well the outhouse is full,' and that's how I found out."

Mac had been at the outhouse about two weeks ago, in early August, and thought there was enough space in the hole to last the season. But he didn't figure on the increase in hikers this year after the release last August of the movie *A Walk in the Woods*, which is based on Bill Bryson's book about the AT.

He says the outhouse is the third at the Little Swift River Pond Campsite since 1980, when he started maintaining this section of trail, and that a new one isn't scheduled for four years. So he's got to find another way to deal with the issue now.

Mac says the latest outhouse dates to around 1993, when he and his brothers dug a hole a foot square and five feet deep. Then, they and others lugged the outhouse in pieces about a mile to the campsite after bringing it most of the way in a four-wheeler on an old logging road. After they put the pieces together, there was 18 inches more storage capacity above the hole.

But when Mac arrived today the hole was nearly full, as reported. So, he says, "I took a pole and pushed it down there to see if it was trash or shit. It was shit."

Then, he got a stick with a Y shape and moved the shit from side to side for about half an hour and ended up with storage space of about 22 inches below the toilet seat. Tomorrow, he's going to return with RID-X, a product with billions of bacteria and enzymes used to treat septic tanks. That will dissolve some of the waste and he'll also add leaves to do the same thing and reduce the odor.

"It should be fine for this year," Mac says, "and then we'll decide what we're going to do."

He says there are three options: The first is to tip the outhouse up, dig a hole about two or three feet deep nearby, and then dig the waste out and bury it. The second is to dig another deeper hole and move the outhouse. The third is to bring in a new moldering privy, in which the waste decomposes to compost, sooner than scheduled

Mac says the standard outhouses in Maine are being replaced with moldering privies over 17 years and that seven have been replaced, with 34 to go.

But, he says, dealing with the outhouse is a minor problem compared with all of the brush from the trail in the spring after blow-downs during the winter. This spring, the brush was 3-feet high across the trail and it took him many days to clear it.

He says he typically wears the black cords on the trail to keep ticks away.

"These are the pants I have. I'm used to it. I sweat a lot, anyway."

Mac grew up in Phillips and became interested in the trail in 1962 when he met his first thru-hikers while visiting his aunt and uncle, who were fire rangers on Saddleback Mountain, about eight miles north of here on the trail.

"I always said I was going to hike it."

Mac

Mac, who's gay, decided in 1982 that he better live his dream soon when his "friends were dying off left and right of AIDS." So, he thru-hiked it in 1983.

He has a degree in accounting from the University of Maine, but spent much of his life working as a meat manager in a grocery store in the Boston suburb of Waltham. On his days off, he returned to Phillips and built the house he lives in now, after retiring in 2014.

Mac says family members used to help him maintain his trail section, but now they're older and he's doing it himself.

"I'm glad I got this one because it's flat. It's an old-lady section, I call it."

That's the reason Kirsten and I decided to hike it first. But I learn that maintaining it is a lot tougher than Mac makes it sound when we reach the campsite and I read Mac's entry in the outhouse register on May 18, 2015:

"Reached the outhouse at 1:30, took me 10 days to clear from Rt 4 and I must have another week to go. Never seen such a mess in my 35 years of maintaining this section. There is still brush in the trail, but a hole is cut to Rt 4. I've had years in the past that I've cleared from Rt 4 to here in one day. Enjoy your hike. Mac Smith maintainer Rt 4 to Little Swift River Pond outhouse. Fir tree missed outhouse by 7"."

Three days later, he wrote: "I couldn't believe all the brush someone removed from the trail. Thank you. Thank you! Today I worked from the outhouse to the other side of campsite. All 7 tent sites are open and most of the tops are on the ground and cut up. I'll be back after the holidays. Mac"

I tell Kirsten, 56, who retired in June from teaching English as a second language in a Madison elementary school, about the comments, while she sets up her tent and I lay out my tarp, pad and sleeping bag.

Then, we walk down to the pond, which is really a sparkling small lake. There's a canoe with paddles on the shore, but it's sitting in muck and we decide it's not worth getting full of mud to go canoeing. So, we just enjoy the view and do some reading at the end of our first day together on the trail.

In the morning, we've got 8.4 miles to hike to Highway 17, from where we'll try to hitch a ride back to where we started. We're hiking south because there was a better parking area at the Highway 4 trailhead.

So, after nearly 1,829 miles of backpacking continuously north, I'm now not hiking the trail continuously and I'm hiking it in the opposite direction. I'm just happy, though, that my knee feels OK and that I'm back on the trail.

I've hiked a few miles when I meet a thru-hiker I'd spent a couple days with at the Notch Hostel before leaving a day ahead of him. Sponge Bob, a recently retired doctor from Hawaii, had been hiking about my pace, so I figure this is about where I'd have been, 145 miles from Franconia Notch, if I hadn't bruised my knee and hadn't had plans with Kirsten.

But now I've hiked only about 26 miles since leaving the hostel and I've got about 347 to go. I hope to do a lot of them by hiking various sections with Kirsten in the two weeks she's here in whatever direction works best.

75

Paul "One Braid" Fuller makes a mean milkshake with his vintage 1960 Hamilton Beach milkshake mixer, just one of many vintage items and antiques in his hostel in the hamlet of Caratunk, just off the Appalachian Trail in western Maine.

One Braid, 77, of Waldoboro, Maine, who's recently reopened his Caratunk House after closing for 11 years, says the place is filled with antiques because he's been an antique dealer for 40 years and promotes antique shows.

The hostel is a summer sideline that One Braid, who thru-hiked the trail northbound in 1990 and southbound in 1992, operates "to give back to the trail, to stay in touch with the hiking community."

One Braid, who wears his hair in a ponytail, tells me about the place and himself, while I enjoy the huge milkshake he's made me with whole milk and chocolate ice cream, and a homemade muffin filled with wild blueberries, and Kirsten eats a hamburger.

He says he got his trail name because he braids his hair when he hikes to keep it clean and has never heard of a hiker with the same name.

We're surprised and delighted to find One Braid and the hostel because it isn't listed in the 2016 guidebook and we thought we'd just be waiting at the trailhead for a ride back to our car, after hiking for three days and 33.4 miles. But we saw a sign at the trailhead for the hostel, about a quarter mile away.

One Braid says he isn't listed because he didn't submit his information in time. He says he's known as the "Elmer of the North" because, like Elmer Hall, who hosts hikers at the antique-filled Sunnybank Inn in Hot Springs, he's also a great cook.

In fact, he says he founded Slates, one of Maine's top restaurants, in Hallowell, just outside the capital of Augusta.

"More legislation was created in my restaurant than in the State House," he says of the place he started in 1977 and sold in 1982. He also started the annual Maine Antiques Festival, the largest in the Northeast, and sold that too.

"When something starts making money, I leave it. I like to create and make society better than when I started and don't care about the money part."

He gives money to friends and causes he believes in, such as gay rights, what he calls "human rights."

In 1990, One Braid, who's gay, organized a fundraiser for AIDS victims and raised $20,000. In the winter of early 1998, he walked 400 miles through Maine from Canada to New Hampshire in opposition to a referendum seeking to repeal a 1997 state law protecting gay rights. Voters repealed the law in February 1998 and repealed a similar law in 2000, but rejected an effort to repeal such a law in 2005.

One Braid says he tries to make just enough money running the hostel, where beds are $20 and a private room $30, to stay in business. His $7 breakfast includes French toast with syrup, loaded with wild blueberries in season, home fries, orange juice, bananas and omelets "with more color and more vegetables than seen on the entire trail."

He also shuttles hikers and has a resupply store with reasonable prices in what was a horse stall. He sleeps in a barn attached to the house.

"I don't do it for money," he says. "I do it from my heart. I make a profit to survive."

One Braid says that the house, built in 1890, was the worst in the town of about 70 and had no plumbing and no running water when he bought it in 2000. He and some friends turned it into a hostel that sleeps nine and he opened it for the 2000 hiking season. He opened it again from 2001 through 2004, but then closed it because, he says, "I had to make a living."

He reopened because he considers running the hostel to help hikers "a mission in life."

"I love it. I'm very fortunate to have the health to do it. I like to put smiles on people's faces and make their journeys memorable. When I welcome someone here, I usually say, 'This is your home as long as you're here and treat it as such.'"

One Braid says he thru-hiked the trail twice because "I didn't get enough the first time, I guess. I can't imagine hiking that trail without loving it."

He thru-hiked the Pacific Crest Trail in 1994 and then hiked it again over 2004 and 2005. In 2004, he got as far as Northern California by late June and then returned to Caratunk to run the hostel.

In 2005, he tried to thru-hike it again, but was stopped by heavy snow in the High Sierras. He left the Sierras and headed to the Canadian border, then hiked south to Northern California. He hiked through the state of Washington in the snow in June "for the challenge."

"Most of the time the snow was a couple feet deep," he says, "and at times the drifts were 20-feet deep."

The section of trail Kirsten and I had just finished wasn't nearly as challenging, but tougher than the first one we hiked. We'd driven to Monson, which is the last town before the start of the 100-Mile Wilderness, the last stretch of trail before Baxter State Park and Katahdin.

I'm looking forward later to hiking the wilderness, where there are only private logging roads and no towns to resupply. But now Kirsten and I had hiked south on an easier section of trail.

We left our car at Shaw's Hiker Hostel before getting a short ride to a trailhead at the trail's 2071.3-mile mark. The trail was mostly flat, but we had to ford two rivers and two large streams and climb two mountains, including Moxie Bald, which was full of delicious blueberries.

While we're talking with One Braid, Jarrod "Poet" Hester, who owns Shaw's with his wife, Kim "Hippie Chick" Hester, arrives to give us a ride back to our car.

Poet, 37, says he and Hippie Chick, 36, thru-hiked the trail in 2008 after quitting their jobs as teachers in Ocala, Florida. The high school where Poet taught operated on the quarter system and Poet's last day was April 1. When he told his students he was leaving to hike the Appalachian Trail, they thought it was an April Fool's joke. But it was no joke and the couple started the hike on April 7, Poet's 29th birthday.

Poet, who taught English, wrote a haiku in the register of each shelter the couple stayed at and at others that were just off the trail. He loves poetry and thought the poems would be a short, simple way to capture the moment of each day. He says he usually wrote one or two a day during the six months he and Hippie Chick were on the trail. The couple have a picture of each haiku and are thinking about publishing them in a coffee-table type book someday.

After finishing their hike, which they loved, Poet returned to his job at the high school and Hippie Chick, who'd been teaching at a middle school, got a job there teaching Spanish.

Six years later, in November 2014, Poet was still teaching and Hippie Chick was staying home to care for their daughter, Julia, now 3, when they got a chance to buy Shaw's, which started serving mainly hikers in 1977.

Hippie Chick's mother and stepfather, Jaime and Paul Renaud, who own the Appalachian Trail Lodge in Millinocket, the northernmost hostel for AT hikers, were visiting them and talking by phone on a Friday with Shaw's owner about possibly buying the place, when Hippie Chick and Poet overheard them.

The owner had offered the Renauds a lower price because, if they bought it, they'd keep it as a hiker hostel, while another potential buyer wanted to turn it into a traditional bed and breakfast. The Renauds had until Monday to decide and were leaning against it when Poet said, "Hey, why don't we buy Shaw's?"

The two were familiar with the area and the hostel business because they'd visited the Renauds in Millinocket, about 28 miles south of Baxter State Park, during many summers.

They decided over the weekend to do it and Paul then told the owner that the couple would buy it, if they could get the same price, and the deal was done. Poet quit his job and he and Hippie Chick took over for the 2015 season.

Hippie Chick says that she and Poet, who's become known for his bountiful breakfasts, like the business, which they open on Memorial Day and close on Halloween. The rest of the time they visit family in Florida and travel in their camper.

"It's great," says Hippie Chick. "It's very busy. It's a life of extremes. I like the energy and I like having all that time off."

I pay her $70 for the ride, which I consider a bargain, considering that Poet had to drive about 95 miles and two hours round trip to shuttle us. Hippie Chick says the costs of the shuttles are based on the time it takes and how rough the road is.

Kirsten

The route from Monson to Caratunk was smooth highway driving. But the couple also shuttle hikers in and out of the 100-Mile Wilderness, and also bring hikers supplies, on rough logging roads that can beat up a vehicle.

I thank Poet and Hippie Chick and then Kirsten and I look for another section of trail to hike. My knee still feels OK and so does Kirsten's back, so we decide to drive 115 miles southwest to Andover, Maine, and hike sections with tough mountains to climb.

76

HIKING THE APPALACHIAN TRAIL isn't enough for Polly "SunButter" Sullivan, her three children and their two dogs. They're including the AT in their attempt to hike the 5,400-mile-long Eastern Continental Trail from Key West, Florida, to Belle Isle, just off the coasts of Labrador and Newfoundland.

SunButter, 36, says that she; Isabella "Butterfly," 12; Elijah "Mountain Dude," 14; Gabriel "Trash Panda," 15; and their golden retriever, Charlie "Mountain Mutt" were only planning to thru-hike the AT when they started their trail adventure three years ago.

When I meet the family, they're staying in a cabin at the Covered Bridge Campground on the Ellis River, a few miles outside of Andover. Kirsten and I are spending the night in the same campground before resuming our hike tomorrow. The campground is next to the Lovejoy Bridge, which was built in 1868, is 70 feet long and is the shortest of Maine's nine covered bridges.

SunButter says that she learned about the AT in 2007, when she; her husband, Matt, whom she met in the Navy and married in 2001; and the kids were living about five miles from Harpers Ferry. She saw thru-hikers and wondered what they were doing and why they looked so dirty and worn out.

She says she learned to love hiking in the mountains when she was a 17-year-old exchange student in Switzerland and hiked in the Alps, and thought that she'd try to thru-hike the trail someday.

"I thought I'll wait until the kids grow up and then I'll hike the AT," says SunButter, who got her trail name because she likes sunflower-seed butter. "I had no intent of hiking it with the kids at that time."

But in 2010, when the family was living in Coral Springs, Florida, about 20 miles northwest of Fort Lauderdale, she decided to homeschool the children and started thinking about taking them on the trail.

She spent the next two years doing research on the trail and preparing for a hike. Then, in January 2013, she decided to do a test hike with the kids of about 150 miles from Coral Springs to Melbourne, where her father lived.

They hiked about 10 miles a day on the beach, or as close to the beach as possible. Each night, Matt would bring them home to spend the night until they got closer to Melbourne, when her father would get them at the end of each day.

"I wanted to make sure they were capable," she says. "It went well. It was a great time."

So, on March 6, 2013, the four of them and their dog went to Amicalola Falls State Park and headed north on what they planned to be a thru-hike.

"The first morning there was snow," SunButter says, "and the kids were so excited."

They had a heavy, four-season, four-person tent and heavy synthetic sleeping bags good to zero.

The children all carried backpacks, but SunButter, who weighed 245 then and weighs 145 now, carried most of the food and gear. She doesn't know how much her pack weighed.

"I refused to weigh mine. I have to do what I have to do. I won't torture myself with it," she says, reminding me of Mama Bear, who had a very heavy backpack and expressed similar sentiments when I hiked with her and her twins in Virginia

"The kids carried lunch and breakfast and snacks and I carried all the dinners," she adds. "They would eat through theirs and some of mine."

SunButter says the kids' excitement with snow wore off when it snowed often and was continually cold. Their shoes froze three times. They averaged about eight miles a day and had finished about 110 miles when a big snowstorm forced hikers off the trail, and folks from Franklin, North Carolina, came to rescue them.

"It was rough. I didn't feel safe. By the time we got to the road to Franklin, we had snowballs of ice on our shoes," SunButter says. "We got our butts handed to us. We learned a lot. I left with the intent of never coming back. I said, 'Screw this.'"

But, she says, "I was familiar with the trail community, so I missed it, and Matt encouraged me to go back out there."

So, on April 13, 2014, they headed north from Springer again. I tell her that she and the kids remind me a lot of Mama Bear, Strong Man, Little

Butt and Spicy Guy, who started the trail three weeks after her. She says they never met the four.

This time, SunButter says, they had a much better idea of what they were getting into and how to handle it.

"The kids were excited. I felt more determined and prepared."

In 2013, she says, she had been cautious, to be on the safe side, stayed with the children in the tent after hiking, and shied away from the social aspect of the trail. But in 2014 she was different.

"I turned into a hippie. I totally embraced it. I loved it. We had a great time."

But, she says, "My marriage fell apart. He suspected me of cheating. I wasn't cheating. The trail life was wonderful. The phone calls were not."

So, she and the kids left the trail again at the 631.3-mile mark in Pearisburg, where I bought Mama Bear and her twins lunch after hiking with them for a day and a half. SunButter and her kids had bypassed Great Smoky Mountains National Park, where dogs aren't allowed on the trail.

She says she and Matt are now separated and he works for the U.S. Embassy in Kabul, Afghanistan. In regard to the children, she says, "He's in full support of the way they're being raised."

This year, she and the kids decided to section hike the ECT, which starts in Key West, the southernmost point in the United States, and consists of the Florida Keys Overseas Heritage Trail, the Florida Trail, a road walk through southern Alabama, the Pinhoti National Recreation Trail, part of the Benton MacKaye Trail, the Appalachian Trail and the International Appalachian Trail. Scotty, the owner of the Vango/Abby Memorial Hostel, hiked most of it in 1999 when he hiked from Key West to the tip of the Gaspe Peninsula in Quebec.

SunButter put her home on the market and then they left on January 2 from Key West. They were joined by Gooch, Mountain Mutt's pup.

"Think of us as the crazy homeschooling family RVing across the U.S., only without the RV," she wrote on her Facebook page.

She also wrote, before leaving from Key West: "As the time gets closer to our start date, I question my sanity. When looking at the big picture, it can become overwhelming. It is one thing to talk about your dreams and another to take action. I don't fear failure, only regret."

They hiked from Key West to Key Largo, with 76 miles on the Florida Keys Overseas Heritage Trail, and 30 miles on roads, where the trail is still being built.

"We are starting to get over the initial shock of road walking," she wrote. "We were scared of crocodiles, alligators and bears. But death by a thousand skeeter bites is closer to reality, so far."

Then they hiked 890 more miles in Florida, mostly on the Florida Trail, which stretches from the Big Cypress National Preserve in southwest Florida to Gulf Islands National Seashore on the Panhandle. The first few days they walked through water up to 2-feet deep with alligators and snakes. Gooch was nearly bitten by a water moccasin that struck and missed.

One night in northern Florida, they were walking at night on a path near water when an alligator snapped at the dogs.

"I took a walking stick and kept hitting it," SunButter says. "It bit the stick."

She says that once in Florida a woman saw Butterfly in a restaurant and called the police because she suspected the girl was a child abducted from Tennessee. Police in three cars stopped them to check.

"We have had the police stop and talk to us on almost every road with traffic and we had animal control talk to us twice," she wrote. "Everyone has been professional and I greatly appreciate the concern. It's just a little stressful sometimes."

For several weeks, Mountain Dude took time off the trail and stayed with his grandmother to recover from a stress fracture in his foot. By May 13, they reached Lake City in northern Florida and decided to take a break.

Two months later, they headed to the northern end of the 100-Mile Wilderness and started hiking south on the AT on July 30, a month ago. They've hiked 231.7 miles since then and SunButter has also bought a house in Marshall, Missouri.

She says they'll probably hike until mid-September and hope to get through the White Mountains before traveling to Marshall.

"Then we'll become section hikers," she says, "and do as many miles as we can each year until we're done."

Before getting a spot in the campground, Kirsten and I had been planning to stay in Andover at Pine Ellis Lodging, but then we learned that the hostel's owner, Ilene Trainor, also owns the campground and decided to stay there, instead.

We had picked the hostel because we've decided to try slackpacking and Ilene has a shuttle driver for slackpackers and loans them daypacks. Because of its location, hikers can slackpack 33.6 miles over three days and return to the hostel or campground to spend the night. It'll be my first time slackpacking on the AT and I hadn't considered doing it until I injured my knee. It will also be easier on Kirsten's back.

Hostel manager Naomi "Muffin Angel" Learned, 65, says she and her husband moved here from Connecticut 20 years ago and, until this year, she'd been working about two hours a day making beds for Ilene, 78, who started the place 27 years ago with her husband, Paul, who died nine years ago. Muffin Angel's husband died about five years ago.

This year, Ilene asked her to start managing the hostel, which has room for 18 hikers. She's started making muffins and gives them to guests, along with coffee.

"I thought that would make hikers happy," she says, "and be a little extra special treat for staying with us."

Muffin Angel says the Hawaiian muffin, which has coconut and pineapple and a cherry on top, is very popular. She enjoys the work.

"I love it, meeting all the different people from all the different places and enjoying the friendships."

77

WHEN PETER "FLASH 52" CONTI left Springer Mountain on March 3, 2015, it was two years to the day after he shattered his left hip into 23 pieces in a motorcycle crash.

Flash 52, whose trail name comes from his old racing number, was racing his new dirt bike on an 11-mile loop track in southern New Jersey when his handlebars clipped a tree and he was flung over the bike.

Doctors, who put 15 pins and four plates in his hip, damaged a nerve in his leg while putting his femur back in the socket. That left him with chronic pain, numbness in his left leg, and a foot that doesn't function properly.

Flash 52, who'd been doing triathlons and training for his third marathon, which was two weeks away, was told he'd probably never run again. For more than a year, he mostly sat around "waiting to get better" in his home in Annapolis, Maryland, where he and his wife, Joanna, raised four children.

He also retired from Mentor Financial Group, which he owned with a partner. The two ran seminars teaching people how to buy and flip real estate without cash or credit.

While recuperating, he saw the movie *Wild*, based on Cheryl Strayed's book about hiking part of the Pacific Crest Trail, and also read *AWOL on the Appalachian Trail*, the book by trail guidebook author David Miller about his thru-hike.

Flash 52, who'd never hiked before, was inspired by the movie and the book, and thought that, if he could hike the AT, his leg and foot would get much better. He decided to take a walk and made it a mile from home before he had to call Joanna to come and get him.

Like Mississippi, he decided to work himself back into shape. He started exercising on an elliptical machine, swimming, getting physical therapy, and buying the gear he needed to hike the trail.

Flash 52 on Baldpate Mountain

When I meet him, Kirsten and I are climbing 2,167 feet over 3.1 rugged miles from Grafton Notch to the west peak of Baldpate Mountain. Flash 52 is hiking with a noticeable limp, but he has no problem keeping up with me, as he tells me his story.

He says he really struggled, though, his first season on the trail, when he managed 2.6 miles the first day, using a brace to stabilize his ankle and keep his foot up, so he doesn't trip on it. He averaged six to nine miles a day at about a mile per hour, and made it 318 miles before norovirus and complications from his injury forced him to quit.

He returned to the trail in the fall and section hiked two to four days at a time into the winter, finishing 185 miles in northern Virginia and Maryland. He also continued working out, lost 30 pounds and had more energy when he returned on Feb 5 to the spot where he quit last year.

Flash 52 had the trail mostly to himself at first, sometimes hiking through deep snow. He's using his car and shuttle drivers, as Kirsten and I are doing, as he hikes north to Katahdin, and is now hiking 10 to 12 miles per day.

Before I met Flash 52, Kirsten and I had left our car at Pine Ellis Lodging and gotten a ride to Grafton Notch in Gloria "Roadrunner" Brown's Dodge Journey. Roadrunner, 69, shuttles hikers for Ilene and Muffin Angel, her sister-in-law.

She says that she's been shuttling hikers for five years, after moving from Stafford Springs, Connecticut, to Andover, to help Muffin Angel, who's been legally blind since birth. She says she promised her brother on his death bed that she'd help care for his wife, who seems to do a pretty good job of running the hostel and caring for herself.

Roadrunner says she enjoys her job: "I love driving, seeing the scenery. I enjoy meeting people."

I was last at Grafton Notch nearly three years ago, when I was on my way to Bar Harbor, Maine, to run the Mount Desert Island Marathon in mid-October, a week after running the Green Mountain Marathon in Vermont, and stopped to hike a few miles on the trail. I met a thru-hiker who said he still hoped to hike the last 265 miles in time to climb Katahdin.

I was also here when I was 23 and was on a September camping trip. I stopped and backpacked the section that Kirsten and I are going to slackpack. So, technically, I could skip this section in my attempt to hike the whole trail, but I'd rather hike all of it since I started two years ago.

It was very windy 43 years ago when I hiked 0.9 mile in the exposed saddle from Baldpate's west peak to the east peak and I felt as if I could get blown off the mountain. The next day there was a point where the trail was flooded by what appeared to be a beaver pond. I decided to walk around the pond and locate the trail on the other side. I couldn't find it for a long time and was scared I'd be lost in the woods with nobody to help me. I saw only one other hiker during my time on the trail.

Today, there's little wind on a sunny, warm day and Flash 52, Kirsten and I enjoy marvelous views from Baldpate's two peaks before descending to a rural road, where Roadrunner picks us up after we've hiked 10.3 miles.

The next day it's rainy, so we don't hike and I'm in the library when I hear a familiar voice and then talk with Jurgen Smit, the South African hiker to whom I gave a ride nine days ago, when I was a trail angel. The following day, we get a ride from Roadrunner again and are going to hike 10.1 miles southbound, up and down two mountains.

When we get dropped off, Flash 52 gets dropped off about the same time, after getting a shuttle from The Cabin, a hostel a few miles outside of Andover. Toward evening, I see Serena, the owner of the Notch Hostel, hiking north. She says she's taking a few days off to backpack.

Flash 52 hikes much of the day with us and talks about the fabulous all-you-can-eat dinners and breakfasts at The Cabin. That sounds fine to us, so we tell Flash 52 that he might as well get a ride from Roadrunner with us back to Andover, and then we'll give him a ride to The Cabin, where we'll eat and camp that night. He says the place is owned by Bear and Honey, a couple in their 80s, and that a woman named Hopper works there and shuttles hikers.

"Hopper?!" I say. I tell him that Hopper is the trail name of the companion of Bismarck, an accountant who pleaded guilty last October to embezzling $8.7 million from the company where he was a controller, and had spent much of six years on the AT before being caught in Damascus during Trail Days in May 2015.

Four days after Bismarck was arrested, Honey's son, Karl Humbarger, who helped out at The Cabin, left a post on The Trek website that said Bismarck had worked hard at the hostel for room and board and was welcome back.

"Bismarck was by hiking standards more honest than most hikers I've encountered from my experience," Karl wrote. "He was 'work for stay' for 3 years at The Cabin in Maine in the Fall. He helped build a garage here and was as meticulous and conscientious as any experienced craftsman I've worked with. ...Bismarck if you read this, after your ordeal is over, I welcome you back with open arms at The Cabin and Thank You for your help."

Bismarck won't be able to return for quite a while, though, because in June he was sentenced to eight years in prison. When he pleaded guilty to one count of wire fraud, he agreed to repay nearly $7.7 million. He had invested and traded the money he embezzled and had paid at least $2.7 million in estimated federal income taxes on the profits, but hadn't filed income tax returns for multiple years.

At the sentencing, U.S District Judge Susan Diott told Bismarck that she'd never before seen so much "collateral damage" in a case before her and noted the impact on his daughter with his first wife and another from an extramarital affair. Bismarck said that he was "terribly sorry" and that he knew he had been selfish much of his life, but that he had changed on the AT. Hopper told the judge that Bismarck had helped guide her back into her faith, as they attended church services along the trail.

I'd seen pictures of Bismarck and Hopper, who's in her late 40s, so I recognize her when we arrive at The Cabin. I introduce myself and tell her that I'd read a long story about Bismarck on the SB Nation website. She says the story was "bullshit," which I guess is because it said some people suspected Bismarck of starting the house fire that killed his first wife, even though investigators concluded it started by accident. His second wife divorced him after he disappeared.

Hopper hadn't responded to an email from William Browning, who wrote the story, so I tell her I'd be happy to write her version, if she'd like to talk with me. She says no. When she shuttles me, Kirsten and Flash 52 in the morning, she does tell us a little of her story, but says she doesn't want me to write about it.

This time, the three of us hike a strenuous 13.2 miles over two mountains, with a steep 2,190 foot drop over the last 2.8 miles. After that, my knee, which had been fine for my and Kirsten's first seven days of hiking, hurts and is hard to bend again. So, I'm worried and wonder if I can keep hiking.

By morning, though, after ice and ibuprofen, it feels better, and the weather forecast looks ideal for at least four days. So, Kirsten and I decide to tackle the treacherous 26 miles through the Presidential Range in the White Mountains. It's considered one of the toughest sections of the trail and is known for erratic weather and snow and freezing conditions, even in the summer, and rugged hiking on boulder fields, with many miles above timberline. The trail summits Mount Washington, which has hurricane-force wind gusts an average of 110 days a year. I've been on the summit once before, when Craig and I took a road to the top.

But, before leaving, I want to learn about the history of The Cabin, where the food and hospitality have been wonderful. So, I ask Earle "Bear" Towne, if he'll talk with me and he's happy to oblige.

Bear, 89, says he grew up in Durham, New Hampshire, but moved to Chico, California, where he was a carpenter and contractor, and lived with his wife and son. He hiked sections of the Pacific Crest Trail as often as he could.

In 1993, he was living in New Hampshire again when he met Margie "Honey" on a hike organized by the Appalachian Mountain Club.

"We got along good and she liked the outdoors. She liked to hike and that was important. The fishermen would call her a keeper. She had a good disposition."

Bear got his trail name because it's "something to go with Honey." He says they have a great time together: "She's always sweet. We have fun."

The two married the next year and built the hostel. Bear says they decided to go into the hostel business "because we like to be with hikers." He says the location is great because hikers who want to slackpack usually spend three nights and also pay for shuttles.

"In business, you've got to have a catchy name," Bear says, so they called their hostel The Cabin.

"To keep the business going, either Margie or I would drive to Grafton Notch every night, so hikers would be with us for three nights and hike every day."

They were initially listed in the guidebook in 1998, which is the year that Earl Shaffer, the first person to thru-hike the trail, did his third thru-hike on the 50th anniversary of his first.

Bear says he and Honey were section hiking parts of the trail in 1998 and met Earl at a book signing in Hot Springs. Then, they helped him out when he got to Maine.

"He needed all the help we could give him," Bear says. "We would help him all we could."

Bear says Earl, then 79, stayed at The Cabin and Margie fed him hard-boiled eggs, oatmeal, Fig Newtons and dark brown sugar because "he didn't have many good teeth left."

"He hiked dawn to dusk, but he'd get turned around lots of times. He said, 'Do something with those blazes, so I know if I'm going north or south.'"

Cary and Bear (photo: Kirsten Johnson)

At night, Earl told stories about his service in the South Pacific during World War II, when he did arduous and risky duty as a forward-area radioman. Earl said after his first thru-hike that he did it to "walk the war out of my system."

"He played the guitar until everyone was asleep," Bear says. "Every now and then he did some yodeling. The dog loved to lay right there and listen to him. We all did."

Bear says he had a stroke four years ago and hasn't been able to hike since. Before that, he says, the place was so busy that he hadn't been able to hike much then, either.

"I was trying to get out of it so I could hike, but I didn't get out of it soon enough. But it's too late now. I didn't move quickly enough."

Now, he helps Hopper with the cooking and does whatever else he can to help hikers. He doesn't want to talk about Bismarck.

Honey, 84, who's cheerful and often smiling, does still hike and also shuttles hikers. Her brother Bob Cummings, who died in January at 86, was a well-known environmental reporter in Maine and his reporting led to the creation of two prominent state land preserves.

Kirsten and I say goodbye to Bear and head to Gorham, New Hampshire, where we spend part of the day and have pizza for dinner, while I watch Wisconsin play LSU at Lambeau Field in Green Bay in the college football opener.

We leave before the game ends and drive to the trailhead at the AMC Pinkham Notch Visitor Center to spend the night, and I'm excited to learn that the unranked Badgers upset the No. 5-ranked Tigers. After that, we attend an evening outdoor astronomy program before Kirsten sets up her tent at the edge of the parking lot, while I sleep in the car.

Then, we get up before dawn and start the tough 3,316-foot climb south over 7.3 miles to 5,366-foot Mount Madison.

78

Gregory "Chief" Duffy brings backpackers to Springer Mountain when they start the Appalachian Trail and picks them up at Katahdin when they finish.

Chief, 60, who retired from the Navy, tells me about his job while driving me into the 100-Mile Wilderness from the Appalachian Trail Lodge in Millinocket, the hostel closest to Baxter State Park.

I've driven to Millinocket after hiking through the Presidential Range with Kirsten, who's taking the train back to Madison. Even though I made it OK through the rugged mountains, with a bevy of boulders and beautiful views, I'm still worried about my knee. So, I've decided to hike the fairly flat 50.8 miles of trail before the Katahdin trailhead, climb the tough 5.2 miles to the summit, and then think about whether I want to risk my knees in 2017 on the 204.9 miles I'll have left to hike.

Chief says that from February through April he worked his first season for the Hiker Hostel outside Dahlonega, the hostel closest to Amicalola Falls State Park. He picked up hikers who flew to Atlanta or took the train to Gainesville, and then brought them to the hostel to spend the night before bringing them to the start of the approach trail in the park or to the Springer trailhead.

He also brought plenty of backpackers back to the hostel when they quit their planned thru-hikes, not long after starting them.

"I picked up three or four people at Springer Mountain that had gone up the approach trail and they were done," he says. "A lot of people have unrealistic expectations."

He picked up many more at the trail's 20.8-mile mark at Woody Gap and 31.7-mile mark at Neel Gap.

"Almost every night, there was someone who wanted to come off the trail at Woody Gap." At Neel Gap, he says, there were nights that there were too many quitters to handle and he only picked up those who wanted to spend a night at the hostel.

"There are at least four or five shuttle drivers in that area who stay busy all the time."

Now, he's working his second season at the lodge from May 15 to Oct 15. In late May and June, he picks up southbounders who arrive by plane or bus in Bangor, about 75 miles from Millinocket, or by bus in Medway, about 10 miles away. Then, when they're ready to hike, he takes them about 35 more miles to the Katahdin trailhead.

From August to October, he picks up hikers who have climbed Katahdin, need to wait a day to climb it because there are no spots left in the shelter or campground near the trailhead, or want to wait for better weather. He also shuttles hikers like me who want a ride into or out of the 100-Mile Wilderness. His wife, Karla, 61, also works at the hostel.

Chief, who's hiked about 1,000 miles of the trail and plans to finish it, says he and Karla, who's also a backpacker, enjoy the work.

"We just like being around the trail and the hikers. We're all just one big family when we're out here. We all take care of each other."

He says that what's "really fun" is picking up thru-hikers he dropped off when they started at Springer after they've finished by climbing Katahdin. The hikers are surprised to see him. That's happened about 12 times this season and it's still early.

He says that last year he picked up Mama Bear and the Cubs in Baxter State Park and that they spent a couple nights in the lodge.

"I was completely impressed. They were the most independent and confident children I've ever met. They were so cool."

Mama Bear told me that the rangers didn't think she was so cool in September when she asked for a permit to climb Katahdin for herself, her 5-year-old twins and her 11-year-old son. She said unfriendly Baxter State Park rangers told her that a park rule requires that children be at least 6 to climb Katahdin, so they wouldn't give her a permit for Strong Man and Little Butt.

She said that she replied: "You can't tell me that. We've come over 2,000 miles and you're not going to tell us we're not going up there."

She said they were at a standstill until the rangers relented and gave her a special permit for the twins to climb the steep, rocky, rooty 5.2-mile trail to the summit. But, when she and the children reached timberline and huge boulders with about 2.25 miles to go, the wind was ferocious and the children started crying and wanted to turn back. So, they did.

"I was kind of devastated,'" she says. "But I made the right choice. I always make the right choice for my kids."

When she reached the bottom of the mountain, the rangers, now friendlier, told her that the Abol Trail was an easier way to reach the top. They took it the next day, connected with the AT with one mile left to the summit and reached Baxter Peak. They planned to take the AT down to hike the part they missed, but the wind was howling again and other hikers advised her not to try it.

So they returned the way they came, a little disappointed, but knowing, she said: "It's the journey, not the destination."

This year, she returned to Damascus with all three children and hiked to Harpers Ferry so that Spicy Guy could hike the 551 miles he missed in 2014, when his dad picked him up for sailing camp, and she and the twins could hike the 161 miles they missed when they canoed from Waynesboro to Harpers Ferry.

Chief takes me into the wilderness on a private logging road after stopping at the entrance, where I pay $12 to use the road. Then he drops me off at the trail's 2,133.1-mile mark.

The wilderness is beautiful with lots of lakes, ponds, and streams, and I swim in one of the lakes with a great sand beach. After 19.7 miles, I climb 1,520-foot Nesuntabunt Mountain, the only mountain in this section of the wilderness, and get an incredible view of Nahmakanta Lake below and Katahdin 16 miles away, as the crow flies. The summit is 56 miles away on the trail.

After three days and 40.9 miles, I leave the wilderness and spend the night at Abol Bridge Campground, where there are campsites on the west bank of the Penobscot River and another incredible view of Katahdin.

In the morning, I get up early and hike half a mile to the entrance of Baxter State Park, which is named after Percival Baxter, the wealthy philanthropist and former Maine governor who bought the land for the park and donated it to the state. He bought and donated 201,018 acres from 1930 to 1962 and left $7 million to maintain the park. He asked that the park be kept "forever wild," which is why it has no electricity, no water service and no paved roads.

After entering the park, I hike 0.3 mile to the information board and meet Jon "Long Jon" Schmidt, the 6-foot-tall AT steward who registers backpackers, assigns them a spot in the shelter or campground, if any are available, and answers their questions before they hike the 9.1 miles to the shelter and campsites near the Katahdin trailhead.

The Birches two shelters and campsite have space for 12 AT hikers and sometimes there are more spots in Katahdin Stream Campground. Each hiker needs a spot before getting a permit to climb the mountain from the rangers in an office near the campground. If there are more hikers than overnight spots, hikers can hike into the park, take a shuttle to Millinocket, and then return in the morning to get a permit and start climbing.

Long Jon, 56, says he first got a job as a trail crew intern at the park in 2010, after retiring from the Navy.

"So, I was a 50-year-old guy working with 19- to 23-year-olds."

In 2012, he was the trail crew leader and in 2015 he got his current 16-week job working with AT hikers at the information board and along the trail from early July to late October.

He says almost all of the hikers are agreeable and easy to deal with, and he thinks problems that have been in the news about groups of thru-hikers celebrating with alcohol on Katahdin are overblown.

The issue got a lot of publicity in 2015 when ultrarunner Scott Jurek set the trail speed record. A park ranger at the summit gave him citations for hiking in a group of 16, more than the 12 allowed; for littering because he popped the cork on a bottle of champagne and sprayed some of it at the Katahdin summit; and for drinking alcohol in public, all against park rules. The ranger said the champagne on the rocks attracted bees and made the summit "smell like a redemption center."

Scott said he had only a group of 12, but that other hikers, including members of the media, had tagged along. He also said that his friend who had brought the champagne had told rangers about it and they said just don't drink it in front of children. And he said he never litters, had packed out what he'd packed in along the entire AT, and had left the summit as clean as he had found it. He got a lawyer to challenge the citations and agreed to pay a fine of $500 for drinking alcohol on the summit, with the other citations dropped.

Scott's friend Speedgoat is trying to break the record this year. I wrote about Speedgoat in 2014, after meeting him in Pennsylvania when he was also trying to break the record. He quit in Virginia with about 825 miles to go when the record was out of reach. This year, he left Katahdin on August 3 and I was hoping to see him again, but missed him.

Long Jon says hikers who want to celebrate with alcohol on the summit just need to be discreet.

"Nobody's going to give you a hard time if you crack a beer on the summit. I refuse to enforce something like that. People pee on the summit, too. The rain comes, and it dissipates and it's fine."

He says the park also has a policy against cell-phone use on the summit, which he considers "absurd." He says he empathizes with hikers who want to call and say, "Hi mom, I'm at the summit."

"Just be respectful, be discreet and put others' interests above your own."

He says he enjoys the job: "What's there not to like? I like the surroundings. I don't like black flies and mosquitoes, but that's just part of being outside. I like the quiet. I enjoy working with the hikers. I like having the answers."

After talking with Long Jon and getting a spot in the campground, I hike 9.1 miles through the park and then get a climbing permit and one of the daypacks that the rangers lend backpackers. After that, I hang out with a group of excited backpackers because they expect to complete their thru-hikes tomorrow.

I recognize the area because Craig and I parked in the lot here in 1999 when he was 17 and we got a permit to climb Katahdin. We were about halfway to the summit when it got very misty and foggy and we decided to turn back.

Sunny skies are forecast for tomorrow, so I'm also excited and looking forward to the climb. In the morning, I get up when the sky lightens, leave my backpack in the rangers' office and begin hiking. I've gone a little more than a mile and the climb is still gradual when I feel pain under my left kneecap with every step I take.

Long Jon

I'd like to keep hiking, but I know that wouldn't be smart with a climb of 3,720 feet over four miles just ahead. So, I turn around and arrive back at the campground in time to get a ride back to Millinocket with Chief, who has just arrived with a group of hikers.

At first, I'm disappointed that I failed a second time to summit Katahdin, but later I think it's a good thing because I'd rather do it at the end of my hike, if I decide to risk my knee and return in 2017 to finish the Appalachian Trail.

79

IN 1971, PAUL "OLE MAN" RENAUD stepped on a land mine in Vietnam that severely damaged his right leg and left him blind in one eye. In 1998, he walked a mile for the first time in 27 years. In 2006, he finished the Appalachian Trail.

Today, Ole Man, 66, and his wife, Jaime "NaviGator Renaud," 55, own the Appalachian Trail Lodge. I stop to talk with them after Chief gives me a ride here from Baxter State Park. I'd left my car in the parking lot of a park across the street before Chief shuttled me into the 100-Mile Wilderness.

The couple tell me about their long journey on and off the trail, while we eat delicious pizza at Angelo's, a restaurant about a block away.

Ole Man, who grew up in Fall River, Massachusetts, says that he was drafted into the Marines in 1969 and sent to Vietnam a year later. He'd been there about four months before ending up in the hospital for 14 months after the mine exploded.

Then, for more than a quarter century, he dealt with a lot of pain in his right leg and lower back, and in his left leg from compensating for his right. He couldn't walk a mile. He married in 1973 and then stayed home to care for his daughter and son.

After his wife died of cancer at 40, he was living in Ocala, Florida, in 1992, when he was fixed up with NaviGator, a registered nurse who grew up in Miami, married at 17 and had two daughters, 12 and 7.

"He called me several times. We talked a lot before we met," NaviGator says. "Twenty-four years later, here we are. We hit it off."

The pair married in 1992 and settled in Ocala. In 1998, Ole Man saw a chiropractor and, after four months of treatment, he was out of pain.

"I started walking in the morning," he says. "The first mile I walked was from my door around the block. As time went on, I felt pretty good, so I kept on walking and built up mileage over time, doing about 12 miles a day."

Ole Man and NaviGator

In 2000, he entered a March of Dimes Walkathon of about six miles and finished 48th of about 3,200.

"I was feeling really good. I was walking faster than most of the people. When I saw how good I did, I said, 'OK, if I could do that, I wonder what else I could do.'"

About the same time, he says, NaviGator's daughter, Kim, met Jarrod Hester in high school. Jarrod's parents told Ole Man about a friend of theirs who had thru-hiked the Appalachian Trail. (Kim and Jarrod are now Hippie Chick and Poet, thru-hikers and the owners of Shaw's Hiker Hostel in Monson.)

"It piqued my interest," says Ole Man, and he decided that he wanted to try it.

So, in 2001 he bought backpacking gear and trained with a 50-pound pack for about eight months. As part of the training, he headed to Amicalola Falls State Park to see what backpacking was all about. He did the approach trail to Springer Mountain and did well hiking for about a week.

In 2002, he decided to try a thru-hike and started in late March. He got his trail name a few days later, when a hiker came into a hostel looking for him and said: "Hey, has anyone seen the old guy with the gray hair and ponytail?" And then, he was dubbed "Ole Man."

He had hiked about 182 miles and was about 15 miles into Great Smoky Mountains National Park when he stumbled on a rock that then rolled and crushed his right ankle. He asked the orthopedic surgeon, who put screws in his ankle, if he could do anything to fix his foot drop, the same problem that Flash 52 deals with.

He says the doctor was amazed that he had kept his leg after the mine blew up in Vietnam.

"The doctor asked why they didn't take my leg off at the knee. He said, 'You shouldn't have this leg.' I said, 'I'm not giving up hiking. I am going to hike the Appalachian Trail.'"

In late May, he got his cast off and started training to join the trail friends he had made in March. He hiked with them through Baxter State Park and then to the Katahdin summit on August 9.

"I was pretty emotional, even though I hadn't done the whole trail. It was pretty special."

Ole Man "learned some very important lessons" from his first backpacking trip: "lighten the load, slow down and it's not about the miles, it's about the journey and the people."

He still wanted to do a thru-hike and NaviGator wanted to join him. She'd gotten her trail name when the two, who sold their Ocala home in 2003, were living out of their pickup truck for a few years and seeing the country. She says she likes maps and giving directions.

"One day, he was driving," NaviGator says, "and wanted me to look at the map. He was frustrated and said, 'You're the navigator and I'm the driver.'"

They started the trail together in 2004, but, on the fourth day, NaviGator started to feel pain on the inside of her right ankle that hurt much more as she climbed Blood Mountain and then descended to Mountain Crossings at Neel Gap at 31.7 miles.

Winton Porter, the owner then of the outing-goods store and hostel, let them stay in a cabin and that night NaviGator couldn't put any weight on her right foot and had to crawl to the bathroom. She went to a doctor, who said she had a spiral stress fracture of her right tibia and put her leg in a cast.

Ole Man and NaviGator wanted to stay in the area until they figured out what do, so they returned to the Hiker Hostel, where they had spent a few days before starting their hike. The hostel, which is where Chief worked this past spring, needed help, so they worked there, started to learn the business and decided that one day they'd own a hostel near the trail.

Ole Man says they'd made a pact before starting their hike that, if one had to stop, the other would keep going. So, after a week at the hostel, NaviGator flew to Florida to get their truck and a few days later Ole Man returned to the trail. NaviGator supported him along the way and was also a trail angel.

"She'd go to the trailhead," he says, "and make fresh, homemade lemonade for hikers."

Ole Man could have slackpacked much of the trail, but never did.

"I felt I was doing the trail with my pack," he says. "My pack was part of me."

When Ole Man reached Troutville at 729 miles, they decided to drive ahead to Harpers Ferry to save time to Katahdin and then return to do the 290 miles he skipped. He'd hiked 1,300 miles when he left the trail in Tyringham, Massachusetts, because he'd gotten very sick and lost a lot of weight and muscle mass.

In 2005, he hiked the miles he'd skipped and he finished in 2006. NaviGator hiked with him a bit and joined him as he summited Katahdin on a perfect day, but mostly continued to support him with the pickup truck.

Shortly before reaching Baxter State Park, Ole Man saw a Jif Peanut Butter jar taped to a tree with business cards for the Appalachian Trail Lodge. Then, he met NaviGator, who said: "I found a place. We need to buy it." He showed her the business card and said "Oh, you're talking about this place."

They stayed at the hostel and learned it had been for sale for 10 years and needed lots of work. It had been built in 1901 as a boarding house for workers at the Millinocket paper mill, which closed in 2008.

The couple knew a lot about the business because they'd returned to the Hiker Hostel and helped out again.

So, they understood what they'd be getting into and told the couple who owned it that they were interested in discussing a deal. Two days later, they agreed to buy the hostel and the nearby Appalachian Trail Cafe, and took over in 2007.

Since then, they've fixed up the hostel and cafe, started shuttling and opened a gear shop to help outfit southbounders who arrive in June without knowing much about what they're doing. Ole Man says when people call to say they're starting to hike south in June, he tells them that they're making a mistake.

"People call me and I try to talk them out of it. It's cold, it's wet and it's full of bugs."

Nevertheless, many still show up and he says nearly half "are unprepared and don't have a clue as to what they're doing, what they're getting into. There are so many ill-prepared people. Some people don't know what a blaze is, how to put up a tent."

Once, he says, a hiker arrived with a seven-pound lawn chair that he planned to sleep on in his tent. Many have overweight packs and many have unneeded knives that they leave behind.

"I've got machetes. I almost had a samurai sword, but the guy wouldn't give it up."

Like the folks at Mountain Crossings, he helps backpackers get rid of what they don't need and get what they need. Then, he says, they'll more likely make it through the 100-Mile Wilderness and thru-hike the trail.

He or Chief will also drop five-gallon buckets with hikers' food at the halfway point of the wilderness, where Chief dropped me off, so that hikers can carry less weight.

"This is the most important 10 days of the whole hike," Ole Man says. "If you can get through there, you can do it."

He says a few hikers quit after climbing Katahdin and more quit before entering the 100-Mile Wilderness. Many more keep hiking.

Mama Bear and the Cubs impressed him.

"She was pretty cool. Those kids were pretty well behaved. More families ought to do that. Get their kids away from the computers and out in the woods."

Ole Man says Bismarck and Hopper stayed at the hostel for three years in a row. "He was a nice enough guy. I never had any reason to distrust him. He was very friendly. He had a lot of friends."

He says he and NaviGator were at Trail Days in 2015, but he had to leave for a funeral in Florida before Bismarck was arrested.

"We shook hands and I left shortly after that. About two hours later, Jaime called me and said Bismarck was just arrested by the FBI. It was kind of a shock. It was so hard to digest that."

NaviGator, who runs the cafe, which is open during the hiking season, says it's popular with the community and with hikers, who provide 30 percent to 40 percent of the business.

She tempts hikers with the Summit Sundae Challenge. The 4 1/2 to 5-pound concoction consists of a banana; 14 heaping scoops of ice cream, one for each state the trail passes through; a Snickers bar, the favorite candy bar on the trail; a handful of M&Ms, a popular trail candy; a homemade doughnut; chocolate syrup; whipped cream; and cherries for $14.99.

Hikers who finish it and hold it down for five minutes get their name on the Pole of Fame, which holds 75 to 100 names; a bumper sticker; the big bowl it came in; and a T-shirt that says: "I conquered the Summit Sundae Challenge." Ole Man says about a quarter of hikers who start it, finish it.

NaviGator says that the cafe makes chocolate, molasses and squash doughnuts and that a Navy chef used the recipe for the squash variety to make the dessert for a special lunch at the Pentagon for a Polish general.

The chef, the son-in-law of a Millinocket family, had eaten the doughnut at the cafe and liked it so much he asked waitress Deb Valley for the recipe.

"It's top secret," Deb joked. "I have top secret clearance," the chef replied. So, Deb wrote the recipe for him on a napkin.

After the Pentagon lunch, the chef sent the cafe a napkin with a note that read, "Thank you AT Cafe." He also sent the fancy menu for the lunch in which the doughnut is called a squash beignet. The framed menu is hanging on a cafe wall.

Ole Man and NaviGator say they love the work and the hikers, who come from across the globe. They also love the off season, when they see the rest of the world. They take everything they need in their carry-on bags and stay in hostels.

"Hostels are the best way to travel because you get to meet people and mingle with other travelers," Ole Man says. "You get a lot of information. And the lighter you can travel, the better off you are."

I tell them I also like to travel light and stay at hostels. After dinner, we walk back to the lodge and I say goodbye to Ole Man and NaviGator.

In the morning, I eat breakfast at the cafe, get a few of the delicious chocolate doughnuts to go, and then leave to see a little of the Maine coast. My knee continues to act up, especially when I get out of the car and put more weight on it, so I'm more convinced I made the right call in not continuing to climb Katahdin.

After I get home, I learn that Speedgoat broke his friend Scott's Appalachian Trail speed record by 9 hours and 29 minutes when he finished on Springer Mountain on September 16 with a time of 45 days, 22 hours and 38 minutes. Speedgoat ran the last 85 miles in 23 hours without stopping to sleep and Scott ran the last 30 miles with him.

80

JEREMIAH "ISHAEL" PIMPARE DRIVES up to 110 miles in the evening to pick up Appalachian Trail hikers at three trailheads and bring them to a hostel run by the Twelve Tribes religious commune, and then drives the same distance in the morning to return them to the trail.

I meet Ishael when I'm walking along a New Hampshire highway on my second morning back on the trail in August 2017. I'm headed 3.5 miles to an Appalachian Mountain Club shuttle bus center for a ride back to the car I'd left at a trailhead yesterday morning.

The AMC operates two scheduled bus routes to various trailheads in the White Mountains and I'd gotten to Highway 302 in Crawford Notch in time to get the 8:45 bus, but missed it because I couldn't find the bus stop in time. So, I figure I'll have to wait for the 1:25 bus to leave from the Highland Center.

When Ishael sees me walking with my pack, he guesses where I'm going and stops to offer me a ride in his van. He's headed back to the hostel in Lancaster, New Hampshire, after dropping off hikers. The trailhead with my car isn't far out of his way, so I offer him the $20 I'd pay for a shuttle bus and he takes me there.

On the way, he tells me a little about the Twelve Tribes, which I've heard about on the trail because they also run hostels for AT hikers in Rutland, Vermont, and on Stoneybrook Farm, about 12 miles from Harpers Ferry.

Ishael, 71, says the Twelve Tribes originated in Chattanooga, Tennessee, in 1972 and now have communities around the world in which the members give up their money and possessions, take Hebrew names and follow the tenets of the first-century Christian church.

He says he was raised as a Catholic in rural Maine, had been a logger and welder, and had built the home near Katahdin in which he and his wife, Elizabeth, lived before moving to Exeter, Maine. They were living in Exeter in 1981 with their three daughters, 7, 5 and 2, when they decided to join the

Twelve Tribes community in Island Pond, Vermont. Ishael says they had given up on Catholicism and that the Twelve Tribes offered them the religious life they were looking for.

"They were living a life that was closer to anything we had found to the way the early church lived."

The founder of the Twelve Tribes, which is commonly considered a cult, had moved his followers to Island Pond from Chattanooga and Ishael says there are about 400 Twelve Tribes members living there.

Now, Ishael and Elizabeth, 64, live with 32 other Twelve Tribes members in two homes in Lancaster, where the commune runs a clothing and shoe store called Simon the Tanner and a hostel for hikers. One of their daughters is a member.

Commune members pick up hikers at trailheads that are far enough apart so that hikers can spend a night at the hostel and then return twice after hiking each of two other trail sections.

Ishael says the hostel lets commune members meet people from all over the world whom they'd never meet any other way, and show their lifestyle to hikers "searching earnestly in their lives for a meaningful existence."

"Our objective is to meet the lonely and the lost sheep," he says, and then give them a chance to join the community. "We freely offer it to them because it was offered to us."

Ishael says hikers get the "red carpet treatment, including a hearty breakfast that will get them to the top of Mount Washington," and are asked only for a donation. The guidebook says a $20 donation is suggested, but Ishael says most hikers donate about $4 or $5, while the actual cost for the commune is about $15 a hiker.

"Some are generous," Ishael says. "Middle-age hikers and above donate more. It's up to them. They have to live with it."

So, except for saving a soul once in a great while, the place operates at a loss.

"If we were trying to do it as a business and exist on donations, we couldn't do it," he says. "It's not a business to us. It's a service. Most of you people see us as trail angels."

Ishael drops me at the trailhead and we talk a little more before I thank him and he heads back to Lancaster.

Ishael

I walk to the car I rented two days ago in Concord after flying to Boston and taking a bus to the New Hampshire capital. I decided to backpack again because my knee has felt OK since about a month after I left the trail last September, and I'm reluctantly willing to risk injuring it again because I miss the trail and I want to backpack the 210.1 rugged miles I need to finish it.

I got the car to drive between the sections of the trail in New Hampshire and Maine that Kirsten and I hiked last year and those I hiked myself. I started hiking at dawn yesterday on the Gale River Trail, the same side trail to the AT that I limped off of with my bruised knee last August.

Since then, I was surprised when I ran into Sciencetooth, the thru-hiker from Florida I spent time with during my last weekend on the trail in 2014. Sciencetooth had told me he'd taken lots of time off the trail to be with an injured female backpacker from Madison. I told him that Madison is the best place in the country to live and that he should move to Madison to be with her after he finishes the trail.

I saw him again last fall when I was running along a Madison bike path. He was biking home from his job at REI, recognized me, and stopped to talk. He said he'd headed to Madison after finishing the trail and is living with the Madison woman he met there. Later, he showed up at my house to hang out with my roommate, Katie Shaw, a manager at REI.

After 4.6 miles of climbing, I get to the AT and I'm excited to be back on the trail again. After a little more climbing, I reach the AMC's Galehead Hut, where I stop for a bowl of delicious mushroom soup, blueberry coffee cake and a peanut butter fudge bar.

There are several thru-hikers at the hut and it's fun to be part of the hiking community again. One asks me my trail name and I say I don't have one, but I'm thinking of using "Scoop," a name a thru-hiker suggested on my next-to-last day on the trail last summer.

I tell him other suggestions I've gotten have been "Marathon Man," "Blaze Runner," "Clark Kent," and "Jimmy Olsen." He likes "Scoop" and I kind of like it, too, even though it's a trifle trite. I haven't heard of any other hikers named Scoop during my time on the trail, so, this summer I'm going to be "Scoop."

Thru-hiker Rayden "McLovin" Spano, 21, of New Britain, Connecticut, tells me that two days ago he met an 82-year-old man who's trying to become the oldest person to thru-hike the AT.

McLovin, who got his name because he looks like the character of the same name in the movie *Superbad*, says that he met Grey Beard a little north of Kinsman Mountain, which is where I fell and bruised my knee last August. He says Grey Beard started at Springer and flipped to Katahdin before hiking south.

"He was really energetic," McLovin says, "and, as he approached, he had a smile on his face and said, 'You look like a thru-hiker' and I said, 'I am.' He introduced himself as Grey Beard, potentially the oldest man to hike the AT."

He says Grey Beard was carrying a "decent-sized backpack" and seemed to be having a good time.

"He was in really good spirits. He was light on his feet. He had a lot of youth about him. He was in better spirits than most guys my age. He seemed like he was really enjoying himself compared to most guys out here."

McLovin also tells me that there's a baby on the trail with her thru-hiking parents.

I'm glad to be backpacking again and have hiked about 14 miles before it starts getting dark and I find a spot in the woods to spend the night. The sky is clear when I go to sleep, but a couple hours before dawn I wake to thunder and see lightning in the distance. I hope the storm will miss me, but when it starts sprinkling, I gather all my stuff and sit on a rock under a tarp. I've learned from the two other nights I got caught in the rain on the trail without shelter that rolling up in the tarp doesn't work and that lying under it doesn't work, either.

This time, even sitting under the tarp doesn't keep me perfectly dry. I learn that old tarps like mine can leak and I get a little wet. The storm is mainly over by dawn, so I pack up and hike 5.3 miles to the highway where I meet Ishael.

After he leaves, I drive about 20 miles to Lincoln, where a doctor diagnosed my knee injury last year. I want to buy a tarp and food, and go to the library to see what I can learn about Grey Beard and the couple with the baby.

I find a story online that says Grey Beard is Dale Sanders, of Bartlett, Tennessee, and that he's trying to break the record set in 2004 by Lee Barry, when he was 81.

The couple with the baby are Bekah and Derrick Quirin, both 25, of Roanoke, Virginia, and their daughter, Ellie, who was 12-months-old when they started their hike in March.

After leaving Lincoln, I head north to hike the 44 miles I've got left in New Hampshire, and on the way I stop at the Highland Center, where I see McLovin, who says he's waiting for a ride to the Twelve Tribes hostel in Lancaster.

He tells me that he had stayed at the commune's hostel in Rutland and had worked on the group's organic farm, about an hour's drive away.

"I did it because I wanted to give back to them and I wanted the experience," he says. "They taught us a lot about organic farming and answered questions about the Twelve Tribes. There were former thru-hikers who were part of the community. The wife of a farmer was a former thru-hiker."

I wish McLovin luck and tell him I might see him again because I'm going to hike some sections of the trail southbound, and then I drive to Pinkham Notch, where Kirsten and I started our last section hike south through the Presidential Range. I'm going to sleep in the car before hiking north through the difficult Wildcat Mountains.

81

Matthew "Odie" Norman's mission in life is helping Appalachian Trail hikers keep in touch with each other after they leave the trail.

So, he's created The Hiker Yearbook, like a high school yearbook, packed with pictures of hikers, and their trail names and email addresses.

"I saw the connections made on the trail between people who were on a spiritual journey and I knew that when they got home most of those connections would be lost forever because everyone knew each other by trail names and it's hard to look up someone by the name of Twinkle Toes," says Odie, who was inspired to create the yearbook after thru-hiking the trail in 2013.

"I got my life purpose. It was to reconnect hikers after the trail."

When I meet Odie, 34, of Huntsville, Alabama, he's heading south and I'm heading north the morning after a difficult day hiking through the Wildcat Mountains.

Odie's hiking against the bubble of thru-hikers to take pictures of as many as he can for the yearbook, which is what he's done every summer since 2013, hiking about 600 to 700 miles a year. He says his goal this year is to hike 800 miles and he encourages hikers he misses to upload their pictures to his website. He says 700 hikers uploaded pictures last year.

"I have to be on the trail hiking," he says. "That's how I meet the hikers and hear the stories."

Odie says I've qualified for the yearbook every year I've hiked because he includes hikers who have hiked about 200 miles or more.

"It's important that it's not just thru-hikers because I try to capture the hiker family."

Odie says that when he joined the family in March 2013, he had no backpacking experience and had learned about the trail just a few months before. Then, he was driving from Alabama to New York for temporary work helping an insurance adjuster check out hurricane damage from Superstorm Sandy.

Odie

"On the drive up there, I saw the Appalachian Trail four or five times. I started looking it up on the internet in New York."

Back then, he owned a lawn care company he started after spending four years in the Navy, in which he enlisted at 22.

"It was very successful, but I was unhappy. I didn't know why and that's why I hiked the Appalachian Trail. I thought that if I could simply walk away from everything, I could figure out what was worth going back to. It was wonderful. Every day was great. I was happy."

He says he loved the hiking and the physical challenge, but his "favorite part of the Appalachian Trail is the people."

He says his trail name is short for Outside Club: "I would hike with so many different groups that I didn't have one group. I knew everyone. I really learned that it was the people and the connections that mattered in life."

Odie says he had pictures of 412 hikers in his first yearbook in 2014, 1,580 in 2015 and 1,978 in 2016. He says the yearbooks, which are hardbound with full color on thick paper, sell for $59 and cost him about $36 to self-publish. He sold 42 in 2014, 520 in 2015 and 700 in 2016. He hopes to sell 900 of the 2017 edition.

He says he loses money on the books, which have no advertising, and lost about $7,000 last year because, in addition to the publishing cost, he pays a woman in Huntsville for 10 hours of work a week on the project, and has travel expenses for him and his girlfriend, Tracy Devitt.

He says the two met in March 2015 at a kickoff party for AT hikers at Amicalola Falls State Park and that Tracy, a former preschool teacher, hiked 1,700 miles of the trail that year. Since then, she's lived with Odie in the 1987 short school bus that he's converted into a camper. He gave her the trail name of Leave No Tracy and now she works at hostels and meets hikers in towns, while Odie hikes.

When he says that he hopes to start making money by selling advertising in the yearbook, I say that I doubt that companies will pay much, if anything, to advertise in a book with annual sales of less than 1,000. He says advertisers say that, too. But he then tells them that he gives the yearbooks for free to hostels on the trail, where many more hikers will see them for many years. And he hopes that will make a difference.

For now, though, Odie says he and Leave No Tracy are living on the money she makes at hostels and the small monthly pension he gets from the Navy, which considers him disabled because of an operation he had in the service when a couple of pins were used to fix a bone in his foot, which hasn't hampered his hiking.

"I call it my lucky break," he says.

Odie says that hostel owners and others with trail connections also help him and Leave No Tracy.

"The trail feeds us really well. A lot of people take us out to dinner. People think I'm crazy because I don't care about the money. I care about the mission, reconnecting hikers after the trail."

After talking with me, Odie says he needs to hike quickly to reach the first peak I climbed yesterday morning, where he's going to meet Leave

No Tracy and hike the AT down to Pinkham Notch. She plans to take a gondola from the notch to the peak, where there's an observation tower and a ski area. I tell him I sure wouldn't want to hike down that very steep trail.

When I'm making the 2,057-foot climb over 1.7 miles, I think that I would have been better off taking the gondola myself, if I hadn't wanted to hike the whole trail, because the climb is much more like rock climbing than hiking, and I often have to look for the next foothold or handhold to stay on the trail and avoid falling.

Adele and Blaze

I'm relieved to reach the top and I'm enjoying the view when I meet Ike and Adele, two hikers who summit shortly after I do. Adele, a thru-hiker, says the two met on the trail in Tennessee and have been inseparable ever since.

Adele first spotted Ike at a hostel in Erwin, but thought he was with another. Two nights later, Adele was in a shelter when Ike walked in with other hikers, but seemed unattached. Adele says the two were instantly attracted to each other, left together in the morning, and started sleeping together that night.

Daniel "Adele' Autry says other hikers, who fed Ike mashed potatoes and peanut butter, had talked about taking the stray dog to a veterinarian or Humane Society. But he decided to adopt the blue healer, instead.

"I decided that, if I couldn't find his owner, I'd take him and keep him. He had a collar on, but he didn't have any tags."

Adele says the lab mix he had for 12 years died two years ago and that for the last two weeks he'd been thinking of adopting a dog to join him on the trail.

"I'd been hiking with some friends and a dog, and I liked the dog and the idea of having a dog around. I'd actually thought about going into a town animal shelter and adopting a dog."

He posted info about Ike on Craigslist and Facebook, but nobody claimed him. The other hikers had been calling the dog Dwight, Adele says, so he decided to call him Ike, after President Dwight Eisenhower, whose nickname was Ike. Adele notes that Eisenhower's campaign slogan was "I like Ike."

Adele, 31, of Birmingham, Alabama, says he was working as part of the crew on private yachts when he decided he needed a change, and that a good change would be spending six months on the trail and seeing what happens. He had read *A Walk in the Woods* when he was 18 and after that had a goal of hiking the trail by the time he was 30. So, he missed by a year.

He got his trail name because one night on the trail he was talking in his sleep and his friends heard him say "Hello," the name of an Adele song.

Adele says the dog's trail name is Blaze "because he's white and I've been following him the whole way. He's my blaze. He smells all the hikers, so he stays on the trail. There are times when I'll hike off the trail and he'll be on the right trail waiting for me to figure it out and telling me that's the wrong way, dummy."

He says Blaze has no problems on the tough climbs: "He's like a little goat. He goes right up."

And, he says, Blaze is the faster and stronger hiker: "I slow him down. He's always ahead of me. Day after day, I'm always the one who wants to stop before him."

Adele has to carry about five pounds of dog food because Blaze got too hot and tired when he carried it himself, and he has to keep an eye on the dog's paws so they don't get cut on rocks. Some places won't let him stay with a dog, but he says that the trouble is well worth it.

"I love it. He keeps me company and keeps the animals away. When it's cold, he sleeps on top of me in the hammock and keeps me warm."

82

TWO DAYS AFTER HIGH-SCHOOL sweethearts Jonathan "Squatch" and Kristin MacFarland returned from their honeymoon, Kristin was diagnosed with a rare thyroid cancer. A little more than three years later, she died and Squatch was overcome with grief.

"After my wife died, I was adrift for a little while, then I started drinking a lot and partying. You just get pissed off and miserable and angry. That's the cycle of grief, I guess," Squatch says, while telling me his story in a shelter along the Appalachian Trail in New Hampshire, after we both spent much of a day hiking in the rain.

I'd finished my second day hiking south from Maine's Grafton Notch, the place last summer where I first slackpacked on the AT, when I was worried about reinjuring my knee and my friend Kirsten was worried about reinjuring her back. We slackpacked for three days and hiked 46.8 miles north of the notch and now I'm hiking 31.1 miles south. I'd driven to the notch after I spoke with Odie, finished a trail section at Highway 2, near Gorham, and then hitched a ride back to my car.

Squatch, 29, a bricklayer from Ephrata in southeast Pennsylvania, says he and Kristin, who were 23 when they married in 2011, had been together since they were 15. He says Kristin saw some seven doctors about her health problems, but that they were misdiagnosed.

He says doctors told her that she was suffering from hypothyroidism and that what turned out to be a 13- centimeter tumor was a goiter. By the time medullary thyroid cancer was diagnosed, chemotherapy didn't work and Kristin died in January 2015.

Squatch says the cancer was caused by a rare, inherited endocrine disorder called multiple endocrine neoplasia 2A that Kristin had had since birth. If that disorder had been diagnosed when Kristin was a child, doctors would have removed her thyroid.

"I'm a man of fairly deep faith," Squatch says. "We were praying one night, and I said, 'Lord, if you heal her, I'll serve you the rest of my life.' Two months later, she died. It's not a good way to die. At the end of the day, he did heal her because she's no longer in pain.

"A few months ago, I'd feel this feeling in my head and voice in my head: 'Hey, we had a deal. I healed your wife, so when are you going to uphold your end of the bargain?' This happened every day. It nagged at my heart and my conscience.

"One night, I was thinking, I'm going to go live in the wilderness to think. All right God, we'll see what's going on."

He says he then felt God say: "'I will restore you. I'll heal you, but you need to trust me.' I knew if I stayed where I was at, I'd end up on drugs. So, I decided to go into the wilderness for three or four months."

Squatch says he knew about the Appalachian Trail because an uncle had hiked some of it in Pennsylvania, Connecticut and New York, and he decided in May that he'd hike it, too.

"I thought I'd go on the Appalachian Trail from Maine to Georgia and hopefully by then get my heart cleared and my head cleared. Then, I'll become a missionary in America."

He chose to hike from Katahdin to Springer because: "I don't like to do it the way everybody else does it. I heard about the big bubble and I prefer the solitude."

Squatch says he'd never done any hiking or backpacking and didn't do any research on what was needed to hike the trail before heading to Wal-Mart and an Army Navy surplus store to get the equipment he thought he'd need.

He says he bought a backpack that weighed about six pounds and filled it with a heavy tent; a heavy sleeping bag good to zero; a water filter; two big tarps; 100 feet of half-inch thick rope; a travel case with toothpaste, powder and athlete's foot cream; five days worth of clothes; an eight-quart pot; a thermos; two big bags full of medical supplies; a first-aid kit; a fishing line, sinkers and hooks; two compasses; a handful of maps; four books, including a bible and guide to edible plants; a shortwave radio; a holster; two foot-long survival knives; a handgun and 50 rounds of ammunition; and a box of granola bars. He also bought hiking poles, but didn't know about the AT guidebook.

When Squatch says he brought the gun for protection from "bears, cougars and nut cases," I tell him he should probably get rid of the gun and ammo to save weight because there are no cougars, the bears almost never attack hikers, and, although there are some nut cases, they're rarely dangerous. He says he brought little food and the edible plant book because he planned to live off the land. He did no hiking to train for the trail and estimates that his pack weighed from 75 to 100 pounds. He weighed 275.

In mid-July, one of his friends drove him to Baxter State Park and they got permits to climb Katahdin. Squatch says rangers told him that he should leave his backpack at the ranger station and borrow a daypack to climb the steep trail to the summit.

"I said, 'Is this a requirement or a suggestion?' They said it's highly suggested."

He disregarded the suggestion and started the climb on a sunny, warm day with his friend, who went ahead. The two saw each other again when Squatch was still climbing and his friend had summited and was headed down. On the way up, Squatch ate ants, lightning bugs and pine needles, and reached the top after seven hours. He then camped on the mountain, which isn't allowed.

"I was the only one up there," he says. "It was beautiful."

The next day, he headed down. "I almost fell off the side because I got off the trail," he says, adding that he lost his hiking poles when he fell and then got caught in a thunderstorm. His clothes and the stuff in his pack got soaked because he had no raincoat and no pack cover.

In the early evening, he reached the bottom and started hiking south on the AT through the park, where camping isn't allowed along the trail.

"I got about one and a half miles up the trail, hiked three hundred or four hundred yards off the trail and set up camp," he says. "I was trying to sleep, but everything was wet. I was hypothermic. I'm freezing, starving, exhausted. I'm starting to get a panic attack. I'm thinking I've got to go."

He says he got out of the tent about 1 a.m.

"I calmed myself down and tried to light a fire. But everything was wet. It's just not working. I'm ripping pages from my edible plants book to get a fire going, which I did, but it wouldn't last. I got warmed up a little, but not anything significant."

Squatch

Squatch says he went back into the tent, but then got up at 4:30 a.m. and, with tears in his eyes, decided to quit. He threw his tent and sleeping bag into the woods and walked to the ranger station. He got a shuttle to Millinocket, but decided on the way that he wasn't a quitter and that he would return to the trail.

He ate at the Appalachian Trail Cafe, bought four pounds of peanut butter and three boxes of cereal, spent the night at the Appalachian Trail Lodge, and took the shuttle back to the park in the morning. He then headed back to the trail, picked up his tent and sleeping bag and headed into the 100-Mile Wilderness.

Along the way, he cut his shorts into a loincloth for hiking because his legs sweat a lot, and he wears it over boxer briefs.

"Most people look, but then look away," he says. "They assume there's nothing under there."

One couple met him and gave him his trail name of Squatch, short for Sasquatch, also known as Big Foot.

As he hiked, Squatch learned more about what he really needed on the trail and started giving stuff away or leaving it at shelters. He managed to trade his heavy sleeping bag for a lighter one and buy a big log of summer sausage and a couple Snickers bars, but still didn't have enough food.

"I was rationing my food. I was hungry."

By the time he got to Monson, his pack was falling apart. So, he bought a new one at Shaw's Hiker Hostel and also picked up a food package, with beef jerky and dried fruit, that his uncle had sent him.

When he left Monson, his pack weighed 41 pounds and he weighed 245. He still carries a gun and 10 rounds of ammo, which weighs seven pounds, and which he says he might ditch in Gorham.

"I'm getting it figured out. It's coming together," he says. "I'll get to Georgia, Lord willing, one of these days. My goal right now is to get out of New Hampshire. My first goal was to get out of Maine."

Squatch has mixed feelings about the hike: "It's all right, but it's not that great. It's fun, but it isn't like I love every minute of it. As I go along the trail, I'm not having a blast. The hardest part is I look around and don't have all the fancy gear. But it's what I have to do to become a better man."

He says the hike is serving its purpose: "I commune with God every single day. I do a lot of praying while hiking. I'll hike until I get it figured out. If I get called to that spot, then I'm done hiking."

I ask him if he ever talked to a lawyer about suing his wife's doctors for malpractice. He says he thought about it, but didn't. I tell him I've got a law degree and that, based on what he's told me, he might have a good case, but that it might be too late to sue because of the Pennsylvania statute of limitations. I suggest he call relatives when he gets to Gorham and ask them to contact a lawyer to check.

About dusk, another hiker staying at Gentian Pond Shelter comes back from the nearby pond and says there's a moose in the water. I walk over to the pond to see my first moose in Maine and while I'm standing at the edge of the water, a beaver swims just below me, looks up and sees me, then dives into the water before returning to grab a branch and swim away.

I'm a little tired after a long day that I'd started at dawn with a hike through Mahoosuc Notch, a stretch filled with huge boulders that I have to climb over, duck under and go around. It's often called the toughest mile of the trail. I go very slowly and deliberately to avoid falling and I'm relieved when I leave the notch about four hours after I enter it.

When a group of University of New Hampshire students told me yesterday that it had taken them four hours to hike through the notch, I thought it probably took them so long because they were inexperienced and had goofed around. Now, I understand.

About an hour after leaving the notch, I stop at Full Goose Shelter to read the register and enjoy seeing Adele and Blaze again. In the afternoon, I'm walking along a ridge as I climb Mount Success in a cold driving rain, when I meet three guys hiking north, anxiously looking at their smartphones.

"Have you seen any blazes lately?" one asks.

"I haven't been looking for them because it's pretty obvious we're on the trail," I answer.

They aren't so sure because they, like many AT hikers, are using the Guthook app trail guide that's supposed to tell them exactly where they are on the trail and provides lots of other information. The app indicates that they aren't on the trail and that it's off to their right. They talk it over for a bit and then decide that the trail must have been relocated and the app not updated. But the trail doesn't seem new to me.

On my way down the mountain, I see a dog and then a group of Harvard University students hiking north. Like the New Hampshire students, they're mostly incoming freshmen with older students leading them. Many universities in the Northeast take new students on similar backpacking trips before school starts.

The students ask me if the dog is mine. I say it isn't and that I thought it was theirs. The dog follows them, so maybe one of the students will end up with an unexpected pet.

Yesterday, before meeting the New Hampshire students, I meet a hiker going north and assume he's out for the day because he has what appears to be a daypack on his back.

But Tom "Daypack" Rottman tells me he's actually on his fourth AT thru-hike and that the base weight of his pack is six pounds. Rottman, 58, of Chicago, a retired real estate developer, says he doesn't cook, doesn't filter his water, and uses a tarp tent. He's got tattooed on his left arm the AT symbol and the years he's thru-hiked it: 2008, 2010 and 2016.

Daypack says he hadn't planned to thru-hike this time and that when he started at Springer, he was just planning a long hike to get in shape for hiking New Zealand's rugged Te Araroa Trail. But he won't be starting that hike until November, so, when he got as far as Damascus, he decided to keep going. He wants to keep going now, too, so, after talking with me for a bit, he takes off.

Daypack

Later yesterday, after talking with the New Hampshire students, I descend Mahoosuc Arm, the scariest and most treacherous descent I've done on any trail. I creep down 1,605 feet over 1.5 miles, much of it on sheer, slanted rock. I keep to the side of the trail and grab conifer branches to keep from falling and I'm very happy to reach the bottom in one piece. I then spend the night at a campsite near the entrance to Mahoosuc Notch.

After my night in the shelter with Squatch, I start the 5.6 miles to the highway near Gorham and, along the way, meet McLovin, the thru-hiker I met my first day back on the trail. He says he's been hiking slowly since he bruised his hip in a fall while descending the boulder field on treacherous Mount Madison. He says another guy fell and bruised his face and a woman fell and broke her nose. I tell him I felt fortunate not to fall when Kirsten and I climbed it last year.

But I do fall a few times on wet roots and wet rocks today, even though I'm trying to be very careful. I get cuts and scrapes and I'm wary and weary by evening, when I reach the trailhead. I'm also hungry because I ran out of food in the morning and, since then, have eaten only wild blueberries. I walk to White Mountains Lodge & Hostel, which is just off the trail, and ask a guy who works there if I can get a shuttle the 36 miles back to Grafton Notch.

He asks a woman named Tracy if she'd like to take me. "It'll be $75," she says. "That's fine," I say, and, after I get some water, we leave in a Ford Escape. It occurs to me that Tracy might be Odie's girlfriend, so, I ask, "Are you Leave No Tracy?" "Yes" she says, and then I say that I know about her because I interviewed Odie.

Leave No Tracy says she's 31 and is from Marion, Indiana. She says she has a degree in kinesiology from Indiana University, but was teaching preschool and had recently ended a relationship when she went to the Amicalola Falls State Park Kick-Off Weekend in early March 2016 to learn about hiking the Appalachian Trail. She met Odie, who was working at the festival, when she asked him for information.

"I didn't know what to do with my life at the time." she says. "I just wanted to put myself out there."

When I say that Odie says he met her in 2015, she says that Odie often gets stuff like that mixed up. She says she was hesitant about getting involved with him because of just getting out of a relationship, but that he was very insistent. She went back to Indiana, then returned to the park to hike the trail. She quit after 1,700 miles because she ran out of time and money.

After Leave No Tracy drops me off at Grafton Notch, I eat dinner, sleep in my car, and then drive north in the morning to hike the miles I've missed in Maine.

83

WHEN POLICE CHIEF MARK "BATMAN" LOPEZ spots Appalachian Trail hikers, he offers them cans of cold Coors Light from the cooler in his squad car, and then lets them drink the beer while he gives them a ride to town.

Batman offers me a beer after he pulls his GMC Terrain into the trailhead where I'm getting set to hike 32.2 miles south and summit four Maine mountains over 4,000 feet on the way.

"Thanks," I say, "but I'm one of the few Wisconsin guys you're going to meet who doesn't like beer."

Batman says he just heard something similar from a German backpacker to whom he gave a ride into Stratton, five miles west on Highway 27. "He said, 'I'm probably the only German guy you'll meet who doesn't drink beer.'"

He then gives me a bottle of water, which he also keeps in the cooler. He says most hikers are happy to get the beer and also happy to get a ride into or out of Stratton, and he's happy to help them, even though the town is five miles out of his Carrabassett Valley jurisdiction, which stretches east from the trailhead.

In fact, Batman keeps a list of the hikers he's helped, and I'll be number 95 this year. He helped 280 last year and 150 in 2014, two years after he became chief, following 25 years with the Maine State Patrol.

Batman, 53, says he got his trail name because he's fought crime for 25 years and he shows me the bat symbol he's got tattooed on his right calf. He says he's backpacked 74 miles of the AT from Highway 27 north to Monson and a little in West Virginia and Virginia.

He says his girlfriend, Ashley "Puddin'" Ellis, 32, a whitewater raft guide and restaurant cook, thru-hiked the trail in 2012, and that the two of them like to help as many hikers as they can to give back for the help she received.

"This is really fun. We meet some great, interesting people."

Batman

They invite some of those people to camp at sites they've cleared at their home in the woods, about 500 yards off the trail, and let them use the shower and bathroom.

He says one of those hikers in 2016 had the trail name Black Santa and, even though marijuana was then illegal in Maine, he had no qualms about telling the chief he got the name because he gave marijuana to fellow hikers.

Batman says Puddin' was hiking on the AT in Tennessee with her pit bull, Glover, when she found a pit bull and border collie mix that was scratched and beaten up. She was going to take it into town until other hikers told her it would be killed. So, she adopted it, as Adele did with Blaze in Tennessee, and called it Roan. Batman says the trail became too hard for Glover, but that Roan made it to Katahdin.

He says that last year he gave a ride to a hiker who also had a dog named Roan. "I said, 'Oh, so you rescued that dog in Tennessee.' She said, 'How could you possibly know I rescued this dog in Roan, Tennessee?' I said, 'My girlfriend did the same thing, and when I go home tonight, I'll be petting it.'"

But Batman also has more serious matters to deal with and he says one of those was yesterday afternoon, when he got a report of a hiker found dead on the trail about four miles north of here. He says a 62-year-old nurse, who was thru-hiking, found the man and reported it. He was able to get to the body in about 90 minutes by using a dirt road that took him near the trail.

In fact, he tells me I'm parked next to the car of the dead man, who was Gerald Gabon, 55, of Milton, Ontario, about 35 miles southwest of Toronto. Batman says he probably died of a heart attack, but that his family members can't believe it because he was in great shape.

Batman says George Largay, the husband of Gerry "Inchworm" Largay, a 66-year-old thru-hiker who disappeared on the trail in July 2013 and whose body was found in the woods in October 2015, was waiting in this lot for his wife when he notified Batman's office that she hadn't arrived the previous day, as planned. That led to a search that included about 130 people, dogs, horses, ATVs, planes and helicopters.

Searchers learned that Inchworm, who was a retired nurse from Brentwood, Tennessee, a Nashville suburb, was seen by hikers at the Poplar Ridge Shelter, 21.5 miles south of here, and that one took her picture when she left in the morning. She and her hiking partner, Jane Lee, who left the trail in New Hampshire, had started at Harpers Ferry and planned to hike to Katahdin, then return to Harpers Ferry and hike to Springer. George met them at trailheads with supplies and to take them places to spend the night.

A forester found Inchworm's body in her sleeping bag in a campsite she had set up to wait in the woods, while she hoped to be rescued. According to her journal, which she had sealed in a waterproof bag, she left the trail to relieve herself in the morning and couldn't find her way back in the dense woods. She tried to text George for help, but the text failed. She then climbed a couple ridges to text him again, but still couldn't reach him.

She heard aircraft during the search and tried to be seen by cutting up her Mylar emergency blanket and hanging pieces in the sun, lighting fires and waving her red fleece when planes were flying by. She survived for at least 19 days in the campsite, which was about 65 yards from open woods with good visibility where she would more likely have been seen from the air; a little less than half a mile from a well-worn path that crosses the trail and becomes a public road; and 1.75 miles from the trail.

While Batman and I are talking, a backpacker heading north walks out of the woods and Batman offers him a beer and a ride to town. He happily accepts and is enjoying the beer in the squad car when I say goodbye to Batman and start the 2,832-foot climb over 5.2 miles to the top of 4,228-foot North Crocker Mountain.

I haven't gone far when I meet ridge-runner Victoria "Bluegrass" Jofery, who says she helps care for and teach hikers to care for the section of trail I'm hiking.

Bluegrass, 25, of Sharon in northwest Pennsylvania, says she has a degree in psychology from Slippery Rock University in Slippery Rock, Pennsylvania, and was working with developmentally delayed children last year when she took a leave of absence to thru-hike the trail.

She says she had first planned to thru-hike the Pacific Crest Trail, after meeting a single woman hiking the PCT solo. Bluegrass was doing day hikes in Yosemite National Park in 2014 and had been told that she shouldn't hike alone, but the thru-hiker convinced her that taking a solo trip was feasible.

"She told me, 'if the trail calls to you, surrender to it.' The whole lifestyle called to me."

So, she saved money for two years and decided to thru-hike the AT, instead of the PCT, because she'd been to Shenandoah and Great Smoky Mountains national parks and was more familiar with the Appalachians.

Bluegrass got a leave of absence and left Katahdin on June 8 to hike south because she wanted to avoid the crowds and it fit in better with her school schedule. She says she got her name from her first "tramily," what backpackers call a group of backpackers who hike together or near each other. She says two of the hikers were Georgia musicians, and she had trained as a classical violinist and likes bluegrass.

"It was only a matter of time and several sing-along sessions that I embodied the spirit of bluegrass. A lot of bluegrass music speaks about life as a rambler, which I identified with greatly while hiking all over the country."

Bluegrass finished the trail on November 28 and returned to work, but she says: "I realized I just wanted to be back on the trail. I wanted to be back outside."

She looked for jobs that would let her work with people in the backcountry and was hired by the Maine Appalachian Trail Club for the ridge-runner job, which runs from the end of May to the end of October. She answers questions about the trail, gives group lectures, does basic trail maintenance, and provides local community outreach.

She works five days on and two days off, or 10 days on and four days off, and gets paid $15 an hour for eight hours a day. She says she hikes about 10 miles on an average day and usually camps near shelters or designated campsites, if she's not in town or at her base camp, a six-person tent under a tarp, on a platform near a shelter.

"I'm able to make it from one shelter or camp to the next, talk with hikers along the way, perform trail maintenance and remediation, and visit/teach hikers at camp around dinner."

Bluegrass says the most enjoyable and most important part of her job is explaining to hikers why the alpine areas on her section are rare and fragile and how hikers should treat them with care and not hike off the trail. She also explains the geology and biology of the area and identifies plants.

"I express my passion for how incredible the area is. A lot of hikers are receptive to hearing about it. I try to say it in a way that's exciting to learn about."

Despite her efforts, she says, some people, usually hikers out for a day or two, walk where they shouldn't, litter, cut vegetation, and leave burnt trash in fire pits.

"Overall, AT hikers have it together," she says, but adds that some camp in alpine areas on mountaintops so that they can see sunrises and sunsets and some in large groups can be too noisy.

"The AT can be a party place."

I ask Bluegrass about Inchworm and if she could understand why Inchworm couldn't find her way back to the trail.

"I can empathize and understand how one can leave the trail and have difficulty finding their way back," Bluegrass says. "The dense Maine woods can be intimidating or disorienting and even the most experienced hikers can get turned around at any point during their hike."

Bluegrass says that she's not sure how close searchers got to Inchworm's campsite, and adds that it likely would have been difficult for

Inchworm to hear them: "Given the area she was set up, there is a major river and several streams that may have masked the sounds of voices, despite how close searchers got to her."

Bluegrass says Inchworm's fate should serve to let all hikers know that they need to have the skills to leave the trail and find their way back. She says hikers need to be observant, stay calm and know what to do when they get lost.

"Her story should be a lesson all hikers learn from, that getting lost venturing off the trail is a reality we all could face, despite experience level. Being prepared for this scenario is the responsibility of each hiker."

Bluegrass says the job is the best she's had and she'll be back next season: "I love it. I've never done something more meaningful. I've never loved a job so much."

84

TOM "GREY EAGLE" YOUNG HASN'T QUIT his Appalachian Trail thru-hike, despite dealing with an ulcer, sciatica, shin splints, falls that injured his arm and put a gash in his head, and a lightning strike that knocked him off the trail and left him crying and terrified. He says he presses on because he's 75 and has a wife of 52 years who wasn't happy he started the hike and would never let him do it again.

"I can't finish next year. That's not an option. At my age and my circumstances, I can't get away to do it again," says Grey Eagle, the oldest backpacker I've met on the trail. I meet him as I climb North Crocker Mountain on the same afternoon I meet Batman and Bluegrass.

Grey Eagle, a retired Army colonel, says that he first heard of the trail in the 1970s, when he was stationed at the Pentagon, and he and his family would pass under an AT bridge over Interstate 70 in Maryland when they headed home to St. Marys, West Virginia, for holidays.

"I would see the AT sign and say, 'I'm going to do that trail someday.' "

But he had long forgotten about the trail in January 2016, when he read a story in Parade magazine about the movie *A Walk in the Woods*, and then watched the film.

"I started thinking about doing it. I was getting bored and tired and losing my physical and mental facilities by sitting around," and he says he thought about Army slogans, such as "be all you can be" and "do all you can when you can."

Grey Eagle says he retired from the Army in 1996, then worked for defense contractors until 2010, when he fully retired. He spent much of his career in the Middle East and speaks Arabic.

He says he had no hiking experience, other than what he did in the Army. "I never went to the mountains and never hiked overnight."

He didn't tell his wife, Jane, at first, about his plans and used his experience as a military intelligence officer to keep her in the dark when he did research on the equipment he'd need for the hike and then bought it. When he did tell her, she thought he was being ridiculous.

"She thought it was preposterous. She wasn't up for it, but eventually realized that's how it was going to be."

Grey Eagle says he trained three or four times a week for a year with hikes of five to eight miles around his hometown of North Myrtle Beach, South Carolina. He carried a backpack that weighed as much as 25 pounds and would climb the stairs and walk up the circular ramp at the two seven-story parking garages in town. He never left town to train on trails because that would have upset Jane even more.

"I was already on thin ice with my wife about doing this. The last thing I could do is go to the woods every weekend."

But Jane did drive him to Amicalola Falls State Park, even though she was unhappy about it, and he started the Springer approach trail on March 21 with a pack that had a base weight of 21 pounds. He's 5-foot-7, weighed 165 and was in good shape. He named himself for the eagle insignia of a colonel and grey for his age.

"Since I was old and retired, I thought I'll just be old Grey Eagle."

He says he has arthritis in his lower back and for the first couple weeks he suffered with sciatic nerve pain in his butt after a day of hiking. He alleviated the pain, as he had done for six months before he started, with ibuprofen. During his second week on the trail, he started feeling "a very dull, sharp pain in the top of my stomach."

He went to a hospital in Hiawasee, Georgia, where a doctor told him that he had the beginning of an ulcer, which, Grey Eagle says, was caused by the ibuprofen and eating improperly on the trail.

"The doctor said I shouldn't go back out on the trail, but I know you will, so I'll keep you in the hospital overnight." He then gave him medicine intravenously to treat the incipient ulcer.

Grey Eagle says the stomach pain went away and, after two or three more weeks on the trail, so did the pain in his butt. He attributes that to the hiking strengthening muscles that were flabby.

He also hiked through bad shin splints that started in Tennessee and falls in Virginia and Vermont that injured his right arm. When he was descending difficult Mount Moosilaukee in New Hampshire, he fell and injured his head.

Grey Eagle

"I was trying to catch up to another guy," he says. "I tripped, fell flat on my face and hit a rock."

He says the rock pushed his glasses into his forehead and left an inch-long gash above his right eye. His glasses were bent, but usable, and he tied a bandana around his head to stop the bleeding. Another hiker told him he thought the gash needed stitches.

He went to the Notch Hostel, where I stayed after I bruised my knee. But, unlike me, he didn't go into nearby Lincoln to see the one doctor in town because folks at the Notch didn't think it was necessary and, he says, "I just didn't want to stop."

He also hadn't felt like stopping in Massachusetts when there was thunder and lightning in the distance as he headed toward Mount Bushnell, even though he passed two shelters on the way. He says he'd been stupid and was walking on rock when "a gnarly, orange bolt of lightning three feet long came out of the rock and hit me on the bottom of my left foot."

"The force of it was like being hit by a baseball bat, as hard as you could hit someone. It knocked me into the bushes about six or seven feet off the trail. At the same time, there was the heaviest rain and hail I've ever seen. I was lying there, not knowing my condition. For about thirty seconds to a minute, I was curled up in a fetal position. I was really in bad shape. I wasn't sure I was living. As a nonbeliever, I was making proclamations to the Almighty, 'help me here.' I looked down at my legs to make sure they were still there."

He says it was still hailing dime-size hail five minutes later when he tried to get up.

"Finally, I stood up and did the dumbest thing I could imagine. I got my phone and called my wife. I was so alone in the moment. I was crying. I was hurting."

He says he thinks calling Jane was dumb because it was something she didn't need to know and it would get her needlessly worried, even though she's been supportive since they met in Harpers Ferry and she realized he was likely to make it to Katahdin.

But, he says, "She basically talked me down off that mountain. She led me to the logical conclusion that I was still alive. I came down crying the whole time. I thought, Jesus, I really escaped somehow being killed by lightning."

He hiked about three miles before he reached a highway and a store near the trailhead. When he told the owner what had happened, she closed the store and drove him about four miles to a hospital in Great Barrington, where a doctor did an EKG, found no arrhythmia (an irregular heartbeat), and said, "You're a lucky guy."

Since then, he says, the hiking's been "all downhill."

Grey Eagle says he's met Grey Beard, the 82-year-old hiker trying to become the oldest person to thru-hike the trail, once in Virginia and once in Pennsylvania, where they spent the night in the same shelter.

"He was looking for me because he'd heard about the oldest colonel on the trail. He was in pretty good shape."

Grey Eagle says Grey Beard had a truck and was using it like I'm using a car to do a variety of flip-flops.

After meeting Grey Eagle, I hike a little longer, and then find a spot in the woods to sleep because there isn't much daylight left. I've got enough water for tonight and the morning because I carried more than usual up the mountain. I knew I might not reach the next water source before dark.

In the morning, I'm looking for footholds and handholds to climb a cliff when I meet a hiker coming down.

"This isn't hiking; this is rock climbing," he says with a foreign accent.

"Where are you from?" I ask.

He says he's Philippe "Swag of Switzerland (SOS)" Schuppisser, 27, a thru-hiker from Baden, Switzerland.

"Since you're from Switzerland, you should be used to this," I say.

"Our hiking trails are smoother, with more switchbacks," he says, "and, on climbs like this, there are ropes and handles to hold on to."

I agree with SOS about the rock climbing, which is sometimes scary, and keep heading up.

85

WHEN I MEET MICHELLE "NORTHSTAR" HOLMES, I'm surprised because she's only the second Black backpacker I've seen on the Appalachian Trail and the first Black woman. I'm impressed when she tells me she's 62, is hiking with two replacement knees, and is an associate professor at Harvard Medical School.

Northstar, who's hiking the entire AT in sections, says she and her husband, Derrick Jackson, who's also Black and sometimes hikes with her, are also surprised when they see Black people on the trail.

"We rarely, but not never, see African-Americans hiking or backpacking," she says. "Each time is a cause for celebration."

She says Derrick, a freelance writer and former Boston Globe columnist and associate editor, is waiting for her at the trailhead where I met Batman yesterday. I meet her in the morning, while descending South Crocker Mountain.

"You're the Barack Obama of the Appalachian Trail," I say, then add, "I should have said Michelle."

I say I've seen only one other Black backpacker on the trail. He's Beach Bum, whom I talked with in Daleville, Virginia, during my first summer on the trail in 2014. Beach Bum told me he was ending his hike because his dog, a mostly pit-bull mutt, was tired of the trail and had often been simply sitting and refusing to walk. He planned to start hitchhiking home to Florida in the morning. So, I let him and the dog stay in my motel room and he and I went out for dinner.

Northstar says that she and Derrick, who wasn't a camper and backpacker when they met, have backpacked throughout the United States and Canada and have climbed all of the 48 New Hampshire peaks over 4,000 feet, some with their sons, Omar, 31, and Tano, 26. They live in the Boston suburb of Cambridge.

She says she'd always wanted to hike the AT and decided to do a thru-hike in 2007, when she was 52, because she was at an impasse at work, was worn out from parenting teens, and had arthritic knees that were getting worse. "It seemed like a good idea to hike while I still could."

But she quit after hiking 407 miles in six weeks because she hadn't met a compatible person or group to hike with, as she had hoped, and she was suffering from groin pain. She says that, like today, most of the thru-hikers were college age or retirement age. She says that she couldn't keep up with the young hikers and that the old ones were mostly married men whose wives questioned their reasons for hiking.

"These gentlemen were very careful about any appearance of impropriety. I remember one such man who I had met on several occasions. One evening, I and another woman set up our sleeping bags in a shelter in the pouring rain. Along came this gentlemen and he started setting up his tent in the rain a short distance away. We had to urge him strenuously to share the shelter with us. The only older women I met were already paired, either with a spouse, or sister, etcetera. I think this is changing. In recent years, I've seen more older women hiking alone," she says.

"While hiking alone, I decided that I didn't feel a need to complete the AT all in one go. Hiking it in sections had many appeals to me. The biggest was the ability to share the experiences with family and friends. Other advantages included the ability to hike sections northbound or southbound, avoid atrocious weather, pick the most beautiful season, and spread the happiness out over many years."

She named herself Northstar "because of the legend of Harriet Tubman following the North Star to lead fugitives from slavery to freedom. At the time, I was thru-hiking northbound, so it seemed appropriate."

Since 2007, she's hiked about 1,100 more miles and hopes to finish the trail by hiking about 350 miles in each of the next two years. She backpacks and slackpacks and does a variety of flip-flops, and has been mostly slackpacking since 2014, when she had both of her knees replaced at the same time because her arthritis got much worse.

"It got harder as my knees deteriorated. Once I decided to section hike after my thru-hike attempt, I have done it every which way: solo multi-day backpack, with and without friends, with and without Derrick, slackpack with Derrick's support, northbound, southbound, whichever way I like or seems easier.

Northstar, who's run the Boston and New York marathons, says her orthopedist said she could do whatever she wanted with her new knees, except long-distance running, and that her knees feel OK.

"They aren't 100 percent pain free and they're not like my native, 19-year-old knees. But they are pretty damn good and they allow me to hike and that makes me very happy. Since my knee replacements, I've been doing the trail as much as possible by slackpacking and minimal backpacking to reduce the strain on my knees."

Northstar says she grew up in the Boston suburb of West Medford in a mostly Black community where people didn't camp and hike, but that she grew to love the outdoors as a kid because her mom started sending her to sleep-away camp when she was 6. When she was in college at Radcliffe in Cambridge, a friend invited her to her family's "vacation cottage."

"The cottage was a mansion. Despite my friend's modest demeanor and ripped blue jeans, like mine, she was from old money with family Appalachian Mountain Club membership. Her father told me he could get me into the AMC. I was tempted, but declined. The invitation-only policy back then made me suspicious of being truly accepted."

But, she says, "Policies loosened and in 1984 I was given a gift membership. In the 1990s, I became far more involved and trained as a backpacking trip leader."

She also says she was on the AMC advisory board for a while, but that AMC life was not compatible with families, so she switched her volunteering to the Boy Scouts of America, where she's become a national leader and played a role in the BSA admitting LGBT members and its pending plan to admit girls.

She says she and Derrick, as scoutmasters, decided in 2003 to let girls unofficially into their troop after hearing one of their sons and his friends talking about girls in "a disrespectful and objectified way."

"I thought these boys need to know girls as companions, not the objects that the media is teaching them."

Northstar, who was a Girl Scout, says Girl Scouts don't require girls to camp and that means few girls get that experience.

"The sisters of the Boy Scouts often wanted to do what their brothers were doing, and why shouldn't they have that opportunity?"

So, girls have participated in the troop's camping trips and wilderness backpacking trips. One girl thru-hiked the AT the year after she graduated high school, the only member of the troop to do so.

Northstar says that in 1980 she and Derrick started a group called Blackpack, a group of Black people who took camping and skiing trips together. The group lasted about 20 years and ended when everybody's children became teens and had their own busy lives.

"I would say very few of the families continued or did much camping outside of the excursions with us, although some did."

A few years ago she and a Black psychologist friend tried to start a group called Terrapy, which was nature therapy for Black women.

"The idea was just to get outdoors, hike, maybe spend a night, maybe work our way up to a backpack. We couldn't get a lot of traction. I think we have to start with the young. That's why my energy is with the Scouts."

She thinks there are so few Black people backpacking because some associate it with working in the fields as slaves, some associate it with poverty, and some fear meeting hostile people in the woods where they can't get help.

When I ask her how people react when they see her on the trail, she says: "You've gotta know mostly I'm in the woods to get away from people reacting to me. It really varies. However, I would say the vast majority of the time people are polite, friendly and don't react as if I'm different from any other hiker. I've never had an incident where I felt threatened, scared or hostile intent, which is what most of my Black friends who haven't hiked are most concerned about. I do have periodic wacky, stupid, annoying incidents."

For example, she says in 2001 she and Derrick were on the AT in New Hampshire climbing 4,000-footers when they met a northbound thru-hiker who, as soon as he saw them from a distance, screamed: "'My God, I've never seen a Black couple on the AT.' As we passed him, we said, 'Yeah, well join the club, we haven't either.' We just shook our heads. Clearly, this guy had been in the woods by himself too long. He was really uninhibited."

Northstar says this summer she and Derrick were taking a rest day in the 100-Mile Wilderness and hiked three miles from a road to a pond and then back to a road. On the way, they met a middle-aged white hiker heading to the road to meet his wife.

She says that when they returned to the road, the man was waiting for his wife and said: "'Wow, that hike up must have been difficult for you.'"

"I felt really aggravated. I mean the 100-Mile Wilderness is so remote, so obscure. You have to pay the logging companies to go on the roads. No one you meet there is a casual or inexperienced hiker. Not to mention, I'm walking around with like $1,500 of expensive hiking equipment strapped to my body. Any red-blooded AT gearhead freak would recognize that. But no, he didn't see any of that, or think where we were. All he saw was an older Black woman in the woods, and I'm automatically inexperienced and out of shape."

Northstar says that when she's not in the woods she's an epidemiologist at Harvard, where she got her medical degree. She studies the connection between diet and breast cancer and lifestyle factors that affect the quality of life and survival after breast cancer.

A few hours after meeting Northstar, I see a bronze plaque in honor of the men of the Civilian Conservation Corps near the spot where they completed the AT on August 14, 1937.

A day later, I stop to read the register in the Poplar Ridge Lean-to, where Inchworm spent the night before the morning she left the trail and got lost. The last known picture of her is hanging in a frame on a wall, with a caption telling a little of what happened to her. She's smiling and standing in front of the lean-to in the morning, while carrying her backpack and wearing the red fleece she waved to try to be seen by people in the aircraft searching for her. Section hiker Dottie Rust, of Thurmont, Maryland, took the picture.

The next morning, I climb 4,120-foot Saddleback Mountain and I'm walking across the alpine terrain, with spectacular views on a sunny day, when I see a northbound hiker I met four days ago, after I took four hours to hike through dangerous, but dry, 1.1-mile-long Mahoosuc Notch.

Daniel "Noon" Lilley, 55, tells me that he hiked through the notch, filled with huge boulders, when they were wet and slippery, the day after he met me. He fell three times, once putting a large gash in his left knee. He says he'd been moving slowly on a ledge when he slipped and fell into a crevice.

Noon

Noon says he thought the gash would have needed eight to ten stitches, if he had been able to get them. Instead, he washed it with water, put Neosporin in it and wrapped it with a gauze bandage. "It continued to bleed," he says, "but by night it was pretty much done."

He continued hiking and had gone only about 100 yards when he found Marlin "Longfish" Conrad, his 65-year-old hiking partner, with a three-quarter inch gash in his head that was still bleeding: "He said he'd tried to jump between two boulders, missed, fell six feet down and hit his head. He said he was really lucky that he didn't get knocked out."

Noon says Longfish, of North Yarmouth, Maine, also cleaned out his wound and they both kept hiking. Noon took a day and a half off to rest his knee, but it still hurts and he isn't sure he'll be able to continue. He thinks Mahoosuc Notch is the toughest stretch of the trail. Many hikers agree.

"I also found the Wildcats very, very tough. That may have contributed to Mahoosuc being more difficult because I was tired out from doing the Wildcats."

Like me, he thought the steep climb from Pinkham Notch to the first Wildcat Mountain peak, which was much like rock climbing, was especially risky.

"That was the first time that I felt that, if I did the wrong thing, I could get hurt very badly."

Noon, of Rochester Hills, Michigan, about 30 miles north of Detroit, says he spent 10 years hiking nearly 1,000 miles of the trail from Springer through Shenandoah National Park and is trying to finish the last 1,200 miles this year. He's taken a leave of absence from his job as a program manager at Chrysler.

"I wanted to complete a goal that would take too long otherwise and my wife wanted me to finish it, so it wouldn't interfere with family vacations."

He's hiking to raise money for a craft-making business started by Iraqi refugees at the Evangelical Nazarene Marka Church in Amman, Jordan. The refugees fled after ISIS came into their towns and painted the Arabic letter nun (pronounced noon) on the homes of Christians, who were given 24 hours to convert to Islam, leave or die. He's raised a little over $2,000.

About five miles after meeting Noon, I finish the section and hitchhike nine miles to the small, outdoorsy town of Rangeley, where I pay Linda Dexter, 63, the owner of Ecopelagicon, a gift shop and outdoors outfitter, $30 to drive me back to my car. As we're riding, she says she thought I was only going to Stratton, not to the trailhead, which is five miles farther and costs $40. I offer to pay her the extra $10, but she says to forget it.

Dexter says she's owned the store for 24 years and has been shuttling hikers for eight or nine.

"I used to pick up hikers thumbing and I just started getting requests to shuttle hikers to nearby trailheads. So, as part of the business, I decided to come up with a fee schedule."

She mostly shuttles hikers from 20 to 30 miles, but has driven some as far as 97 miles to Monson and 79 miles to Gorham.

"A lot of people," she says, "want to go to Gorham to get the bus."

She enjoys the work.

"It's fun. You get to meet a lot of neat people. Hikers are a good bunch of people. You don't find people doing this kind of a trip who are jerks. They don't last."

86

"Rush hour, I call it," Greg Caruso says about arriving for work and finding a line of Appalachian Trail backpackers waiting for a canoe ride across Maine's Kennebec River.

Greg, 47, says he's had as many as 20 northbound hikers waiting for him when he arrives at 9 a.m. to ferry hikers across the 400-foot-wide river, just outside the tiny town of Caratunk, where he lives. He can take two hikers at a time on the minute-long ride in his 40-foot-long Old Town Tripper canoe, which has a white blaze in the center of the floor.

I'm just starting a 37-mile southbound hike to the spot where I met Batman four days ago, and stop to talk with Greg when he's free on August 25. I've left my car at the Caratunk hostel of One Braid, who made me a great milkshake and Kirsten a burger after we hiked from Monson to here last summer. This time, I buy three chocolate chip shortbread cookies, baked by Cara, for the trail. One Braid says he or his shuttle driver will come and get me after I finish the section.

The Appalachian Trail Conservancy pays Greg to provide the free service because the Kennebec is considered too dangerous to ford, unlike the many other rivers along the trail in Maine. That's because it can rise quickly and unpredictably when hydroelectric facilities release water, and because of its slippery rocks and strong current. The ATC and Maine Appalachian Trail Club started the service after a hiker drowned while trying to ford the river in 1985.

Greg says this is his second year on the job, and before this he worked for 25 years as the operations manager for Northern Outdoors, which operates a resort, campground and brewpub that's popular with hikers and is two miles down the road.

That job, he says, "had tons of moving parts," such as scheduling, hiring and training and was "organized chaos."

Greg

"I was looking for something different," he says, so he applied for the job that requires him to be a registered Maine guide. He also works as a guide for anglers, hunters, rafters and snowmobilers.

Now, he says, he likes the short hours that give him time for other things, including spending time with his wife, Elizabeth Caruso, a raft guide, and their two sons, 11 and 13. He says the pay "is good enough that it made me change careers," and he enjoys dealing with the hikers.

"I enjoy talking to the people. It's interesting where people are coming from and how they get here. You have the idea of AT hikers as smelly hippies and that's not the case at all. They're of diverse backgrounds and ages."

Greg works from 9 a.m. to 2 p.m. from July 1 to September 30 and from 9 a.m. to 11 a.m. from May 26 to June 30 and October 1 to October 9. Hikers can make reservations for rides at other times for $50 for up to two hikers, but Greg says that doesn't happen often.

He keeps track for the ATC of the number of hikers; which direction they're headed; whether they're thru-hikers, section hikers or day hikers;

and whether they're doing flip-flops. He also counts the number of groups and number of dogs.

Greg says his busiest day was the Saturday of Labor Day weekend last year when he ferried 55 hikers and that he typically ferries 20 to 30 a day during the busy season. He took 2,640 across the river in 2016, and this year, he's ferried about 1,800 as of this morning.

Hikers are required to wear life jackets, which the ATC supplies, and Greg says the couple thru-hiking with a baby contacted him ahead of time to see if he had a life jacket that would fit their child. He said they were lucky that he still had an infant life jacket that he used when his boys were babies.

He said they were southbound during June, when the black flies and mosquitoes are awful.

"It was the first time I took an infant across. It was during bug season, which to me is crazy. It's horrid. The bugs are horrible."

When I ask him what he thinks of trying to thru-hike with a baby, he says: "I think it's a little crazy, but to each his own. The infant doesn't really have a decision in it."

As we talk, I see two loons in the river and Greg says bald eagles are also common. He says that when there are no hikers to ferry, he reads and fishes for brook trout, salmon and smallmouth bass.

He says he's taken day hikes on parts of the trail and proposed to Elizabeth after they climbed Katahdin in March 2001. He says the mountain is easier to climb in the winter because the rocks and huge boulders are covered by snow.

He says they reached the sign that marks the summit at Baxter Peak on a beautiful, sunny day and he then pulled out a ring and asked Elizabeth to marry him. "She started crying," he says.

After we talk, Greg takes me across the river, and then I hike for four marvelous miles through a forest of hemlock and white cedar, while a stream full of rapids and waterfalls flows alongside the trail.

At Pierce Pond Lean-to, next to the trail, I meet a woman who introduces herself as Grace Note.

"I read your note in the log at the shelter a little south of Mahoosuc Notch, and I've been hoping to meet you, but didn't think I would," I tell her.

Grace Note (c.p.)

She'd written that she was happy to make it to Maine and that maybe Mahoosuc Notch, which was 1.6 miles ahead, would be her Katahdin because she wanted to return to Maryland to compete in the rugged Savage Man half-Ironman length triathlon in mid-September, and that she was the oldest woman to do it at 62. She also wrote that she wanted to spend more time with her husband, Steve.

Grace Note says she's Ellie Hamilton, 65, of Grantsville, Maryland, and that she decided she wanted to finish the trail that she started in 2009. Back then, she planned to thru-hike and made it to Maryland before she decided to quit, in part because she'd lost 20 pounds and had only 110 pounds left on her 5-foot-1 frame. She didn't think she could afford to lose more weight.

She says she chose the name Grace Note, which is an extra note at the end of a tune as an embellishment, to state what she hopes to bring to the trail.

"People would hike their hikes and live their lives just fine without having met me, but I hope it will be just a little nicer because of me, like a grace note."

She says she's a musician herself and plays the piano and guitar, along with singing in a community chorus.

Hiking the trail had been a dream of hers since she was 15.

"I heard about the trail from my mother when I was 15 in 1967, that there was this continuous footpath from Georgia to Maine. I felt that I was born knowing that and wanting to do that. But then there was college, marriage, babies and college again. Not until I retired did it start getting real again."

She says she attended Michigan State University without graduating, got a nursing degree at 41, worked as a registered nurse, and has three children and five grandchildren with Steve. He's going to pick her up after she takes the ferry across the river tomorrow and they're going to celebrate their 45th anniversary.

Grace Note says she's backpacked sections of the trail since 2009 and this year had about 868 miles left when she started at Culvers Gap in New Jersey on June 5. She had planned to hike for about a month and stop somewhere in Vermont, but Steve, who's following her in an RV, encouraged her to keep going.

"He really, really wanted me to make it," she says.

"I started crying when I got to New Hampshire because I didn't think it was going to happen. I thought that when I got to Maine that would be fine. But I really wanted to hear loons. I really wanted to see the 100-Mile Wilderness."

She's got mixed feelings about New Hampshire and Maine: "I'm enjoying part of it, but there are times that I feel like throwing in the towel. It's much, much harder than I expected it would be. I've read a gazillion books and I wasn't prepared for how physically difficult the northern part of the trail would be. I didn't realize how much rock climbing there would be and the rocky, steep descents scare the dickens out of me."

When she tells me that she's worried about climbing Katahdin and that it took her three hours to make it through Mahoosuc Notch, I tell her that it took me four and that I'm worried about Katahdin, too. I also say that I feel the same way about the rock climbing and the scary descents.

After I leave the shelter, I hike a few more miles before camping next to Carrying Place Stream. In the morning, I hike past pretty East Carry and West Carry ponds, both fine for swimming. For 3.3 miles, the trail coincides with the 13-mile portage between the Kennebec and Dead rivers that Col. Benedict Arnold and about 1,000 of his men took in 1775. They followed the route, called the Great Carrying Place, on their way to Quebec City during the Revolutionary War. Their attempt to capture the city from the British failed.

In the afternoon, I meet a northbound hiker with a staff in his right arm and a left arm that shakes repeatedly. He says he's Stephen "Tao" Burchett, 59, and that he thru-hiked the trail last year. He says he sometimes had trouble hiking and that after he finished he was diagnosed with Parkinson's disease. This year, he wanted to thru-hike the Pacific Crest Trail, but there was too much snow in the High Sierras, so he's thru-hiking the AT again.

Tao doesn't have much time to talk, so I tell him that I think what he's doing is incredible, and keep hiking. In the evening, I reach the Little Bigelow Lean-to and find that 10 college students have filled the shelter, which has a capacity of eight, and are cooking dinner.

Elana Desantis, 20, says she's one of two upperclassmen leading a group of eight incoming freshmen at Tufts University. She says that Tufts has been organizing such outdoor group experiences for 31 years. This year, 300 freshmen of a class of 1,300 are taking backpacking trips, canoe trips, a mix of both, or doing trail work.

Elana, who's going to be a junior, says the trips are meant to give students a chance to get to know each other and the leaders in small groups.

"Coming to college in general is pretty overwhelming and a nice thing about the trips is you get to be with a small group. It's a more manageable way to get to know people and it gives you people to know when you first get to campus. Also, the leader can be an adviser during college and a lot of people stay close to their leader."

Her group is doing 2-1/2 days of backpacking and 2-1/2 days of canoeing.

"It's a lot of people's first experience with backpacking and canoeing," says Elana, who has lots of experience herself.

Elana, right, and other Tufts University Students

She says she did lots of climbing in the Adirondacks while growing up in a suburb of Albany, New York, and has climbed 18 4,000-footers in New Hampshire.

I think Elana realizes her group shouldn't be monopolizing the shelter because she says, without me complaining, that the "shelters are for everybody." She says there are two tent platforms nearby.

I don't want to debate with her, so I don't talk about the shelter and don't tell her I don't have a tent and would want to stay in the shelter, if it rains. But I'm thinking that large groups should sleep in tents and leave the shelters for individual or small groups of backpackers.

When I talk with Elana, there are two backpackers with tents in back of the shelter and a few more arrive later and also can't use the shelter. I set up my pad and bag on a tent platform and, when the students are loud well into the night, I think that the tenters might be having a little trouble sleeping.

The next day, I summit four mountains, including 4,090-foot Avery Peak on Bigelow Mountain, which has marvelous views of woods, water and mountains. The peak is named in honor of Myron Avery, a Maine native and the man mainly responsible for making Benton MacKaye's dream of an Appalachian Trail come true.

In the evening, I reach Horns Pond, where there are two shelters, each with a capacity of eight. Each has a sign that says: "Please, do not stay in Lean-to if you are in organized group."

Horns Pond is essentially a lake and is only 5.1 miles from the next highway, so I think that backpacking groups out for just one night might use it, and that's why there are the signs and two shelters. Tonight, though, there's only me and one other backpacker.

In the morning, I hike to the highway, and start hitchhiking 18 miles to Kingfield, where I plan to call One Braid for a 44-mile ride to Caratunk. Then, a woman who's driving into the trailhead parking lot to wait for her backpacking husband says she'll take me.

She says she's Hettie F. Barnes and she's going to pick up Wes Barnes, whom I met three days ago before he got a canoe ride across the Kennebec. He told me he thru-hiked the trail southbound in 1978 from August 1 to December 17 and is now section hiking. Hettie says he called her to get him because one of his knees is acting up.

She's an insurance agent and storyteller and lives in Catawba, Virginia, which is a mile from the trail. She's spent most of her life in the Appalachians of Southwestern Virginia, Eastern Kentucky and Eastern Tennessee and tells stories of the mountains, sea and world at schools, churches and festivals. She says that she and Wes hiked to McAfee Knob, the Catawba Mountain ledge with stunning views, on their first date and that Wes, who's a carpenter, is living in New Hampshire to be near his parents and because he likes the state.

Hettie drops me off outside a convenience store, where a clerk lets me use a phone to call One Braid. He says he'll send someone to get me, and I say I'll be at the library. About two hours later, Boulder, 50, of Portland, Maine, picks me up. He says that he's been working at the hostel since June and does whatever's needed, and that he thru-hiked the trail northbound in 2006.

After I get back to my car, I drive to Shaw's Hiker Hostel in Monson. I'm going to get a shuttle into the 100-Mile Wilderness tomorrow morning, and hike 61.8 miles south, back to Monson. Then, I'll have to only summit Katahdin to finish the Appalachian Trail.

87

When northbound section hiker Kathy "Seamstress" Gentry reached the White Mountains in 2012, she decided she'd had enough of the Appalachian Trail she'd started 13 years before.

"I enjoyed the hiking until I got to the Whites," says Seamstress. "It was boulder scrambling, not hiking."

But, Seamstress, 55, of Nineveh in southern Indiana, says she had thought of returning and "my husband said I need to go back and insisted I get out here and finish it."

She says she retired from her technician job at AT&T when she was 48 and that the last five years for her and Steve Gentry, her husband of nine years, had been "a little rough." While they rehabbed and flipped two houses, her mother died and Steve had both knees replaced.

"He was the catalyst for me to come back. He wanted that for me. He wanted me to have the accomplishment of actually finishing it."

So, on July 11, she returned to New Hampshire's Franconia Notch, where she left the trail five years ago, and has hiked 305.3 miles to East Branch Lean-to in the 100-Mile Wilderness, which is where I meet her on the Tuesday before Labor Day. I'm headed south after getting a ride into the wilderness from a shuttle driver for Shaw's Hiker Hostel in Monson.

Seamstress says she was a divorced, single mom with a 14-year-old daughter when she started the trail after being inspired by Jean Deeds, who wrote *There Are Mountains to Climb*, a book about the AT hike she started in 1994.

Jean, whose book inspired many women to hike, was 51 when she quit her job as public relations director for the Children's Museum of Indianapolis and headed for Springer Mountain. She hiked about 1,900 miles in five months before breaking a leg when she slipped on a wet rock in Maine. A year later, she returned to the trail and finished it. After that, she led groups of women on hiking trips to places around the world.

Seamstress

Seamstress read stories about Jean in *The Indianapolis Star* newspaper and then bought her book. Before starting the AT she had done one short backpacking trip in the 1980s with her husband then. "That was a disaster. I said I'd never do it again."

But she changed her mind after reading Jean's book and decided to start in Virginia's Grayson Highlands. After that, she did about 100 miles one week a year while she was working and more after she retired.

"It was just something to look forward to each year. It was a cheap vacation. I enjoyed the people and the small towns, if not more than the trail."

She says she's also been inspired by Ray Jardine, who's known for his outdoor adventures, including being the first person to climb the west face of El Capitan in Yosemite National Park, and for his contributions to ultralight backpacking. His company, Ray-Way Products, sells kits for backpackers to sew their own lightweight gear.

Seamstress got lots of ideas from Ray and made her own backpack, wind suit and rain jacket to save weight. She also uses a stove she made from a soda can and has food she dehydrated herself. She carries a tarp tent that weighs about two pounds and says her pack's base weight is 11 or 12 pounds. Mine weighs about the same, but I don't have a tent or stove.

Seamstress says that in 2012 her hiking partner left at Franconia Notch and she was hesitant about going on, but she decided to keep hiking and arranged for a shuttle driver to pick her up at her motel in North Woodstock.

"I was going to continue, but the shuttle driver never showed up. All I needed was that last excuse not to continue."

So, she walked to nearby Lincoln, took a bus to Boston and flew home. I tell her that in 2015 I also took a bus from Lincoln to Boston and headed home after quitting the trail because I was sick and thought I had lost too much weight.

Now, though, we'll likely both finish in about a week. Seamstress says she thinks she'll finish the wilderness on Sunday, and that her husband will meet her before she climbs Katahdin.

"Finishing will be kind of overwhelming because I don't think it's really hit me what an accomplishment it will be; something nobody will ever be able to take away from me."

While Seamstress and I are talking, Tristan "Waffles" Register, 19, cooks and eats his dinner. He says he's getting set to hike at night and "doesn't like anything about the trail" he started to keep his dad, Perry "Snakeman" Register, who enjoyed the trail, company.

"It was his idea. He always wanted to do it. I went with him so he wouldn't be alone," says Waffles, who got his trail name because he's tried to get waffles for breakfast whenever he's in a town. "I don't like the mountains. I like the flat and the sand. I'm a Florida boy."

He also says he doesn't like the younger hikers on the trail because of their drinking and pot smoking.

"Everyone I've met under the age of 25, beer is their first thought when they get into town. I don't like anyone under 40. The older hikers respect everyone a lot more. When they get into town, they don't think the first thing to do is to get beer. You don't come out here to drink beer and smoke weed."

Waffles says he and his dad, a 50-year-old accountant in Fort Lauderdale, Florida, left Harpers Ferry on May 23 and planned to hike to Katahdin before doing the southern half of the trail. He had just finished his first year at Florida State University in Tallahassee and had never backpacked before the two started.

But he could backpack quickly and got tired of hiking behind his dad and doing only about ten miles a day.

"I can do ten miles a day before 11 in the morning. I was walking behind someone who was kind of a pain."

So, Waffles and Snakeman split up at Mount Greylock in Massachusetts and he hiked ahead of his dad. Snakeman quit the trail just before Mount Moosilauke because of foot tendon problems, bought a car in Hanover, and is supporting his son and other hikers.

Waffles plans to hike the 67.8 miles to the base of Katahdin tonight, Wednesday and Thursday and climb the mountain on Friday. Then, Snakeman will drive him to Springer and he'll hike north.

"I'm going to do at least 500 miles of the south," he says, adding that if he does the 1,022 miles to Harpers Ferry, it'll take him less than 60 days.

When I ask him why he's going to continue hiking, since he doesn't enjoy it and says he'd rather be back at school, he says: "I wouldn't think of going home. Once I start, I've got to finish. Too many people know I'm out here. They'd say, 'you didn't even get halfway.'"

Waffles reminds me of Finn, the Finnish hiker I met in 2015 who expressed similar sentiments about the trail and about finishing.

As we talk, Grey Eagle, the 75-year-old retired colonel I met eight days ago, listens. He got a shuttle into the wilderness with me this morning, got dropped off before me, and is hiking north.

Grey Eagle says that he's been mostly slackpacking since we met because of swelling in his left knee. He thinks the problem is with his anterior cruciate ligament and it hurts on the outside of his knee. But the swelling has gone down since he started slackpacking and he plans to backpack the rest of the way to Katahdin.

"It hurts," he says, "but it doesn't keep me from hiking."

Grey Eagle and I had gotten a ride from Gary Tabor, 69, of Monson, who's been driving for Shaw's for 11 years. He says that for the first six, he drove on weekends and after finishing his day job as a products scheduler at Hardwood Products in nearby Guilford. Gary, whose wife was a librarian for 40 years, enjoys the work and will get a third of the $85 I paid for my 67-mile shuttle.

"Meeting people is probably the best," says Gary, who's backpacked the trail in New Hampshire, Vermont and Maine. "Most people have stories about themselves, different places they've been and where they want to go. It's quite interesting."

The interesting people include, he says, the couple hiking the trail with a baby, who stayed at Shaw's.

"I can't imagine doing that. They had a blanket and the baby was crawling around on it."

He says the hikers have been good for Monson and notes that it's a town of only about 650, but there are four places to eat.

"Thirty years ago hikers were looked down upon as dirty and smelly. But over the years the town has realized that not only do they smell funny and look funny, they spend a lot of money. Money does talk. Actually, I think it's saved the town. In the summertime, it's really busy."

Gary says one of the biggest changes on the trail has been the use of cell phones and social media.

"When it started ten years ago, it was looked down on. It was going to ruin the trail. It wasn't going to be a wilderness experience."

But Gary thinks the phones have ended up being a plus in letting people communicate easily and has been especially good for the hostel business.

"We do a lot of food drops," he says. "Now, they can call from the mountains and say, 'We'll be there in two hours.'"

In the morning, I get up at dawn, as usual, to get an early start and see that Grey Eagle is leaving before me. I tell him that I'm almost always the first person to leave the shelters and say that maybe we'll see each other again on Katahdin. Then, I head south to hike 46.7 miles more in the 100-Mile Wilderness. I figure it'll take me about four days because there are many mountains to climb.

After three days of rugged hiking, including plenty of rock scrambling, I reach Wilson Valley Lean-to on Friday evening and find that a hiker has sent a tent up in the shelter. I'm getting my stuff set up when a woman looks out from the tent and says, "Hi Scoop. It's me, Grace Note."

Gary

We talk for a while about our hikes and she says that she thinks she was probably too negative a week ago when she told me how difficult she believes the trail has been in New Hampshire and Maine. I tell her I didn't think she was too negative and that I still agree with her. But the trail tomorrow, at least, looks fairly easy, with not much climbing in the 10.4 miles I've got left to hike in the wilderness and 3.3 miles after that.

On Saturday, I finish the wilderness and I'm excited when I return to Shaw's, knowing that I've only got to climb Katahdin to finish the trail. In the morning, I go the Appalachian Trail Visitor Center in Monson to see if I can get a permit to make the climb. The weather looks good for Monday, but that's Labor Day and there are no permits available for hikers who drive into Baxter State Park. And rain is forecast for the rest of the week.

But I know that hikers who get a shuttle into the park from the Appalachian Trail Lodge in Millinocket can get a permit, so I ask Hippie Chick at Shaw's to call her stepfather, Ole Man, at the lodge to see if there's room for me in the shuttle on Monday. He says there is, so I drive to

Millinocket, where it rains Sunday night and is still cloudy in the morning when Ole Man drives a group of hikers, including me and Seamstress, into the park to climb Katahdin.

He drops us off at the rangers' cabin, where I got my permit last summer after hiking into the park. Then, I started climbing Katahdin, but quit after a little more than a mile because my bruised left knee started hurting and I didn't think it was wise to continue such a steep climb with an injured knee. This morning, my knee feels fine, but the ranger tells us that the forecast has changed, and now there's a good chance of thunderstorms this morning, and possible clearing in the afternoon.

That sure doesn't sound ideal, but it's not raining now, so I start hiking the trail, which gains 4,179 feet in the 5.2 miles to Baxter Peak. As I climb the wet, rocky trail, with streams of water sometimes running down it, the sky becomes misty, the wind picks up and it starts getting cold. The mist reminds me of the misty, foggy day when Craig and I tried to climb Katahdin, but then it was warm.

Several day hikers ahead of me turn back, telling me that the hike seemed too risky to them after they reached timberline and a trail over huge, wet boulders. I keep going, like the AT hikers ahead of me. But, after nearly three miles I also reach timberline and the boulders. The mist has turned to drizzle and it's much colder in the strong wind blowing over the exposed alpine terrain.

I know I'll have to scramble over the boulders for nearly three-quarters of a mile and, like the day hikers, I also decide it's too risky to continue, even though I've got more experience with boulder scrambling than they do. But my experience also makes me well aware of the risk, especially when the boulders are wet, and I decide I'd rather return on a sunny day when I'm less likely to get injured and can enjoy the hike and the beautiful views from the summit. I'm disappointed, but I know I'll most likely be able to try again.

When I'm on my way down, a thru-hiker in his 20s who reached the summit passes me and says he thinks I made the right decision, even though he succeeded. Andy says his trail name is Orphan Andy because, like Waffles, he started the thru-hike with his father, then kept going when his dad quit.

By the time I reach the ranger cabin, the sky is clearing. As I wait for Ole Man to get here to give hikers a ride back to Millinocket, some of the hikers I rode with this morning return from the summit.

One of them is Seamstress and, when I ask her how she felt summiting Katahdin, she says, "I was too cold to process anything."

She still needs to hike 9.4 miles through Baxter State Park and half a mile more to Abol Bridge to finish the trail, which she plans to do tomorrow. Steve plans to meet her at the bridge so they can share the moment she finishes. She decided to climb Katahdin today because tomorrow's forecast includes thunderstorms.

Another person who rode with Ole Man is thru-hiker Jesus "Gaucho" Meza, 60, of Santa Rosa, California, who says the conditions above timberline were horrendous in the cold with "hard drizzle," and "winds at least 50 mph."

"It was brutal up there. It felt like a blizzard with the wind. Everyone got drenched. It was so cold up there my hands were numb."

When I ask him why he kept going, despite the conditions, he says: "It was my only chance to make it. I'm not going back without making it. That was my chance to summit right there. I was thinking a nice hot cup of coffee would be so good. I·wanted a snack, but I just didn't want to stop."

He says he slipped and fell twice on the boulders on the way down, but didn't get hurt when he landed on his butt and his elbow.

Gaucho, a UPS driver, says he thru-hiked the Pacific Crest Trail last year and that the AT "is the toughest of the two absolutely" because of its roots and rocks. He says that in a couple years he plans to hike the Continental Divide Trail because he's grown to love long-distance backpacking.

"It's addictive. I love this lifestyle: freedom, space, being with nature."

Also having finished this summer is Deacon, the section hiker I met at Springer my first morning on the trail when I was planning to thru-hike, and last saw in Damascus when he was headed home after hiking about 468 miles. He hiked the trail in four sections and started his last one on June 22 where the Long Trail and Appalachian Trail split in Vermont. He finished on August 7, after hiking the last 489 miles.

In his online journal, he wrote about himself and his hiking partner summiting Katahdin: "The climb is the most difficult we've experienced on the entire trail. We pull ourselves up shear rock face by grabbing rebar set into stone."

After reaching the top, he wrote: "I am overwhelmed as I grab the wood Katahdin sign, and the entirety of the last four years passes through my mind. There is tremendous ambivalent feelings, even tears to think that it's all over, yet overjoyed that I've stuck with this task that I almost quit many times. This was the most difficult thing I've done in my entire life. I shall rejoice in it always."

Meanwhile, I've still got to finish the last 2.25 miles of the trail. I could try again soon, but I've already bought a plane ticket for Wednesday. I could change it, but the forecast is still for rain the rest of the week.

So, I decide I'd rather return in 2018, pick a sunny day to summit Katahdin and then, after succeeding, go to the Gaspe Peninsula in Quebec and hike some of the International Appalachian Trail.

88

NEARLY 18 YEARS AFTER a "scared" Gary "Darth Vader" Keckley started the Appalachian Trail on Springer Mountain, he finishes it "bawling" on Katahdin. His son, Adam "Dog Whisperer" Keckley, who has hiked most of the trail with him, summits Katahdin, too.

I've summited shortly before the two on September 4, 2018, the day after Labor Day. The sky is sunny and the temperature is in the 60s with light winds. It's a great day for climbing what I consider the toughest mountain on the trail and the views are magnificent.

So, I'm glad I stopped 2.25 miles short of the summit in miserable weather on Labor Day last year, and have driven from Madison to Maine to finish the trail four years, three months, and two weeks after I started what I thought would be a thru-hike in 2014.

Darth Vader, 66, of Franklin, Tennessee, says he was frightened and had no thoughts of finishing the trail when he started it on October 8, 2000. "I was just scared shitless," he says. But he got over his fears and hiked 70 miles before returning home.

Dog Whisperer, 32, of Nashville, who was 15 when he joined his dad on his return to the trail for 2-1/2 days in February 2001, didn't think about finishing, either. In fact, says Dog Whisperer, the two didn't really think seriously of hiking the entire trail until they reached Harpers Ferry in 2012.

So, Darth Vader is understandably overcome with emotion as he comes close to the summit, and he collapses in tears about 200 feet from the top. Dog Whisperer, who has already summited, walks down to his dad, puts his arm around him, and helps him to the sign marking Katahdin's Baxter Peak and the "NORTHERN TERMINUS OF THE APPALACHIAN TRAIL." Darth Vader kisses the sign and cries again. He's hiked 2,203.4 miles in 33 sections over 195 days.

"All these years, there's always been the next section to do, the next climb to get over. There's always something around the corner that was the next big challenge and you had to save your mental energy for that. All that saving of energy just released from me. I lost it," he says about how he felt when he stopped just short of the summit.

"I couldn't move. My body just stopped moving. It wouldn't go. It's like it's saying, 'no, I don't want to finish.' Adam came down, put his arm around me. I started bawling. I started crying like a baby. We struggled up it, got to the sign and I couldn't believe it."

Darth Vader says he's happy that his two daughters trained to climb Katahdin and have made it to the top with him and his son. A son-in-law also joins them.

Dog Whisperer, who has 344 miles of the trail left to hike, says the two overcame several challenges over the years, so he understands why finishing the hike is hard to believe. He says that for him even starting the trail was a big challenge.

"For me, that was a lot. I was not an athletic kid. I was introverted and liked being inside. Camping didn't appeal to me. The idea of hiking never entered my brain."

But his dad's stories about his first time on the trail and "the freedom of getting on the trail and going from A to Z" appealed to him, so he decided to try backpacking, too. He says his dad took him camping for the first time on a short hike before they returned to the trail together.

By the next year, they'd reached the trail's 166-mile mark at Fontana Dam, just before Great Smoky Mountains National Park. But, before they could return to the trail, Darth Vader, an architect, severely broke his right leg in a construction accident. Dog Whisperer, who does drafting and marketing for his dad, says they were working on an addition to Darth Vader's home and were 15 feet above the ground on scaffolding his dad had built when it collapsed.

They both fell, with Dog Whisperer escaping serious injury when he landed on grass, but his dad landed on concrete, "obliterating his ankle," says Dog Whisperer.

Darth Vader says one of the doctors who treated him was his friend and told him in his hospital room, "'If you do everything we tell you to do, you might be able to walk again.' That to me was the end of the Appalachian Trail."

But, he says, "I went through therapy and got back to walking and then got back to hiking and a year and a half later we summited Clingmans Dome," which is in Great Smoky Mountains National Park at 199.1 miles and is the highest point on the trail at 6,643 feet.

Dog Whisperer was 20 in October 2006 when the two reached the trail's 377.5-mile mark in a blizzard on a bitter cold day that they were unprepared for. He says that he had no hat or warm jacket and that he and his dad hitched a ride off the trail in Carvers Gap.

"That was my personal breaking point," says Dog Whisperer, who decided then to quit the trail, but changed his mind two years later and started hiking with his dad again at the trail's 724-mile mark in Daleville. He says he was motivated by the fact that his dad had kept hiking.

He says the two first thought they could actually make it to Katahdin after reaching Harpers Ferry.

"When we were in Tennessee, I had just thought of it as a hobby, never thinking we were going to finish." But, he says, "Every time we'd go out, we'd come across thru-hikers. They would encourage us. When we got to Harpers Ferry, we decided we were going to do more miles and take the whole thing more seriously."

They persevered, even though Dog Whisperer injured his knee when he twisted it while hiking on jagged rocks in Pennsylvania. He says that he thought he injured his anterior cruciate ligament, and that the injury was painful, but he remembered leaving the trail in Carvers Gap and knew that if he left it again, he might not return. So, he hobbled along with a brace on his knee, which, he says, didn't feel 100 percent until a few years later.

He got his trail name in Pennsylvania when he took care of another hiker's dog for four hours when she went into town, and took it for a walk on the trail. "The dog instantly warmed up to me," he says.

Darth Vader got his name off the trail at a construction site in Georgia when he got upset with workers who were behind schedule. He pretended to be Darth Vader and that's what the crew started calling him.

Dog Whisperer did have to leave the trail again in Massachusetts and fly home after getting very sick with what he thought was norovirus. He says his dad got walking pneumonia and had to leave the trail after a couple days in Tennessee.

Probation Termination **(c.p.)**

Dog Whisperer says it was difficult each time the two started another section. "Every time we got back, the first three days would just suck. You'd feel like you never hiked before. After that, it felt normal."

This summer, they decided to make a determined effort to finish, hiking 152.7 miles from Grafton Notch to Monson in June and July, when they struggled with mud, mosquitoes, black flies and heat. He says they wore head nets and walked quickly. The conditions were better in August and September, when they hiked the last 114.5 miles.

Dog Whisperer says that he hiked the first 70 miles of the trail in 2016 and plans to finish the trail in April by hiking from Carvers Gap to Daleville. He says he liked the challenge of the trail and the camaraderie of being with other hikers. And he says that hiking with his dad for 18 years "was a blessing."

"I kind of grew up on the trail. It's basically priceless from where I started to how much time I got to spend with my dad for 18 years."

He says he might do another long-distance hike. "I wouldn't mind doing the Continental Divide Trail."

Darth Vader says that hiking one long-distance trail is enough.

"Hiking the Appalachian Trail just is the most demanding spiritually, emotionally, physically, mentally thing I've ever done."

Also on the summit is thru-hiker Randy "Probation Termination" Forrest, who left Springer on February 13 and endured freezing cold, snow and/or rain every day for the first two months, hiking through waist-deep snow, tendinitis and a fractured ankle to reach Katahdin.

Probation Termination, 58, of Titusville, Florida, says finishing the hike is "the greatest feeling in the world" and "the greatest accomplishment of my life." He says he's proud to have "accomplished something that very few people have even thought about doing."

In fact, says Probation Termination, he hadn't even thought about doing it himself until about a year before he started, which is when he and his wife, Hadassah Forrest, 46, who's retired from the Navy, were looking for something to see on Netflix and then watched a National Geographic documentary on the AT.

"I knew what it was, but had never looked into it. I knew it ended in Maine, but didn't know it started in Georgia."

He did, though, remember his dad talking about hiking the trail: "It was a dream of his, but he never got around to doing it."

And he and Hadassah had owned property 30 miles from Springer for 10 years and had grown to love the mountains.

So, Probation Termination, who retired in July 2017 from a 34-year career as a probation and parole officer for the state of Florida, decided he was going to accomplish his dad's dream.

He says he'd taken a few camping trips by car, but had never done any backpacking, so he decided to learn about it by watching YouTube videos of people hiking the trail. He says about 25 people a year start posting videos of a planned thru-hike and about five finish the trail.

He decided he was going to also post videos, and has about 2,400 followers on his YouTube channel. Some emailed him tips, he says, such as putting his puffy at the end of his sleeping bag to keep his feet warm on cold nights, and making oatmeal by putting hot water in the plastic oatmeal bag to avoid having to clean a bowl.

He says the daily videos he's filmed with his phone also let his family and friends follow him and will help him remember the trip.

"I enjoy doing it and I know I'm going to have that for life. I can go back and look at it, remember it and share it with friends."

He says that, after doing his research, he decided to leave in mid-February for several reasons, with the most important being to lower his chances of getting bit by deer ticks and contracting Lyme disease.

"That scared me the most. Lyme disease is a lifelong deal if you don't get it in time."

He says he also started early because he wanted to avoid the crowds leaving in March and April. He says he's had norovirus and wanted to avoid the greater threat of getting it in crowded shelters. He also thought the chance of getting Giardia would be less with fewer hikers to contaminate the water and he wanted to avoid the heat.

He says his strategy was successful because he never saw a tick and didn't get Lyme disease, norovirus or Giardia.

He researched equipment and settled on an ultra-light backpack and tent made from Cuben Fiber, also called Dyneema Composite Fabric, just like Deacon. He said he was happy with his Arc Blast backpack and loves his Duplex tent, which, he says he'll "use until the day I die." He also loves his Vertice rain jacket, which he also uses as a windbreaker. He says the jacket is "the best piece of equipment he has." He bought the pack, tent and jacket from Zpacks.

After he got his gear, he and Hadassah, who hiked about 400 miles with him on sections of the trail, including his Katahdin summit, took short backpacking trips on and off the trail. They learned a little of what to expect when they hiked the 8.8-mile approach trail from Amicalola Falls State Park to Springer.

"It took us four to five hours and opened our eyes. We were wiped out."

Probation Termination says he also knew he might have issues with his body because he'd been a competitive racquetball player and suffered injuries that led to two surgeries on his right knee and surgery on his right shoulder. He'd also broken his left ankle after college and sprained it several times since. "It wasn't 100 percent from the get-go," he says.

But he was excited to start and was happy on the trail, despite lousy weather for two months when there were several days of snow and several days when the high was below freezing and the low overnight was in the teens. "It was better than being at work," he says. The nights were long, but, he says, he didn't mind spending many dark hours in shelters.

"I found out I could sleep for ten, twelve, fourteen hours and be fresh the next day."

He says that, despite the bad weather, he never went a day without seeing another hiker, including thru-hikers, section hikers and day hikers.

He took three days off in Erwin, Tennessee, because of tendinitis, but his knees and shoulder held up OK. He was in New Hampshire, before the White Mountains and about five miles from Hanover, on a trail full of roots and rocks when he slipped on a root and rolled his left ankle.

He says he was lucky to have been only about 50 steps from a dirt road and was on the road for only a couple minutes when a couple in a truck stopped for him. The couple were exploring and cut their trip short to take him on about a 45-minute ride to an emergency room in Hanover.

The doctor who treated him was a hiker and told him he'd fractured his ankle and would have to take a minimum of a week off the trail. So, he flew home, where he got to see his son, Ben, 26, before he left for the Air Force.

Probation Termination says he returned to the trail 24 days later and felt as if he was starting over when he was out of breath and had to hike slowly. He says his ankle was tender and he did about 1 1/2 miles an hour at most.

But he and Hadassah were hiking quickly when they climbed Katahdin and passed me just after I'd reached timberline, where I turned back last September, and started struggling to climb huge boulders. They were out of sight when I did something dumb.

I couldn't see how to get over a gap from one boulder to another, so I decided to leap. I didn't make it and fell about three feet to the ground. Luckily, I landed on my butt and suffered only cuts on my arms and elbows.

After putting bandages on the cuts, I took more time and found a safe way to bridge the gap. I told myself that, since I didn't get seriously injured and could keep hiking, the experience was valuable because I learned never to do something so stupid again.

I was careful the rest of the way and I was happy when I finished the boulders and had only 1.6 miles of fairly easy hiking to reach the top. Unlike Darth Vader, I neither cried, nor kissed the sign. And, unlike Probation Termination, I don't think finishing the hike is the greatest accomplishment of my life. That's been raising Craig.

But I am excited and elated to finish the trail, and I smile as I enjoy the experience and the wonderful views with the other hikers happy to reach the summit.

Acknowledgements

When I decided after a few days on the Appalachian Trail that I wanted to write a book about people I met while hiking it, I didn't know how many hikers and others with trail connections would take the time to talk with me and let me write about them.

I told people I wanted to write about that I was a former newspaper reporter writing a book about people along the trail and asked if I could interview them and write their stories. Nearly everyone I asked said yes and I want to thank all of them for taking time to talk with me and making this book possible.

After writing the stories, I emailed them to the people I wrote about, others I met along the trail who wanted to read them, relatives, friends and acquaintances. Many of them responded with questions, comments, suggestions and encouragement that I really appreciated. They inspired me to keep writing and helped me ask better questions and write better stories.

My many stories, though, wouldn't have become a book without the encouragement and excellent editing of my Madison friend Terry Shelton, who was the city editor at the *Wisconsin State Journal* in Madison during some of the time I was a reporter there and edits books. Terry also wrote the description of the book on the back cover.

The book was designed and produced by my perspicacious publisher, Kevin Revolinski, who's written many books and newspaper articles and owns Back Burner Books.

Terry, who was familiar with my efforts to make my newspaper stories accurate and as good and complete as possible, while I pushed deadlines at the *State Journal*, sometimes to his chagrin, and Kevin were patient with me as I proofread draft copies of the book several times and made lots of changes.

Many of those changes were suggested by my friends Samara Kalk, a reporter at the *State Journal*, and Andriette Wickstrom, a teacher in Storm Lake, Iowa, and by Charli "Sturdy Peasant" Fulton, a retired lawyer who thru-hiked the AT with Warren Doyle's 2017 Expedition and lives in

Madison. They carefully proofread a draft copy of the book, found many mistakes and suggested other ways I could improve my stories.

The book's illuminating illustrated maps were drawn by my ingenious illustrator, Haley Schulz, who lives in Madrid, Spain, and, like Terry and Kevin, patiently made the many changes that I requested.

Terry "Birdman" Martin, of Berea, Ohio, and Maury "Deacon" Hall, of Port Clinton, Ohio, both of whom I hiked with on the trail and wrote about, let me publish great pictures they took along the trail, which they completed with section hikes. Many other hikers I wrote about sent me pictures of themselves on the trail for me to use in the book.

Warren Doyle wrote a fine poetic foreword, while Cosmo Catalano Jr., Deacon, Joanna "Seeker" Ezinga, Jeffrey "Baby Steps" Johnson, Andy "Captain Blue" Niekamp, Angela "Walkie" Shirley and Pete "NoBigDeal" Smith wrote great descriptive blurbs.

About the Author

Cary Segall learned to love journalism and telling stories when he was growing up in Green Bay, Wisconsin, where he delivered the newspaper of Packers coach Vince Lombardi, was sports editor of the East High School newspaper and covered high school sports on weekends for the Green Bay Press-Gazette. He worked on the sports desk of the *Wisconsin State Journal* while attending the University of Wisconsin in Madison and took his first backpacking trip on the Appalachian Trail with the UW Hoofers Outing Club. Cary graduated with a bachelor's degree in wildlife ecology and spent three years as a ranger-naturalist in the National Park Service before returning to the UW and getting a law degree. He was a public-interest environmental lawyer before quitting, mainly to care for his newborn son, Craig, for six years. He also got a master's degree in journalism from the UW before becoming a reporter for fourteen years and a copy editor for seven at the *State Journal*. He also continued backpacking and hiking on the AT and in U.S. and Canadian national parks with, and without, Craig. After retiring from the *State Journal*, Cary decided to pursue his longtime goal of thru-hiking the AT. He hadn't planned to write about his hike, but he quickly found that the trail is full of interesting tales and, being a reporter at heart, he wanted to tell them. So, he interviewed hundreds of backpackers and others with connections to the trail and wrote their stories.